Themes *in* Southwest Prehistory

The publication of the Advanced Seminar Series
is made possible by generous support
from The Brown Foundation, Inc.,
Houston, Texas

School of American Research
Advanced Seminar Series
Douglas W. Schwartz, General Editor

Themes in Southwest Prehistory
Contributors

E. Charles Adams
Arizona State Museum
University of Arizona

Linda S. Cordell
University Museum
University of Colorado

Patricia L. Crown
Department of Anthropology
University of New Mexico

Jeffrey S. Dean
Laboratory of Anthropology
University of Arizona

William H. Doelle
Desert Archaeology, Inc.
Tucson, Arizona

David Doyel
Estrella Cultural Research
Scottsdale, Arizona

Paul R. Fish
Arizona State Museum
University of Arizona

Suzanne K. Fish
Arizona State Museum
University of Arizona

Murray Gell-Mann
Santa Fe Institute
Santa Fe, New Mexico

George J. Gumerman
Santa Fe Institute
Santa Fe, New Mexico

Jonathan Haas
Collections and Research
Field Museum of Natural History

Bruce Huckell
Arizona State Museum
University of Arizona

Keith W. Kintigh
Department of Anthropology
Arizona State University

Debra L. Martin
School of Natural Science
Hampshire College

Randall H. McGuire
Department of Anthropology
State University of New York - Binghampton

Ben A. Nelson
Department of Anthropology
State University of New York - Buffalo

Janet D. Orcutt
National Park Service
Santa Fe, New Mexico

Fred Plog
Department of Anthropology
New Mexico State University

Stephen Plog
Department of Anthropology
University of Virginia

J. Jefferson Reid
Department of Anthropology
University of Arizona

Katherine Spielmann
Department of Anthropology
Arizona State University

Joseph A. Tainter
U.S. Forest Service
Albuquerque, New Mexico

Steadman Upham
Dean, Graduate School
University of Oregon

David R. Wilcox
Museum of Northern Arizona
Flagstaff, Arizona

W. H. Wills
Department of Anthropology
University of New Mexico

Themes *in* Southwest Prehistory

Edited by
George J. Gumerman

SCHOOL OF AMERICAN RESEARCH PRESS
SANTA FE, NEW MEXICO

SCHOOL OF AMERICAN RESEARCH PRESS
Post Office Box 2188
Santa Fe, New Mexico 87504-2188

Director of Publications: Joan K. O'Donnell
Editor: J. K. O'Donnell
Designer: Deborah Flynn Post
Indexer: Andrew L. Christenson
Typographer: Tseng Information Systems, Inc.
Printer: Edwards Brothers, Inc.

Distributed by the University of Washington Press

Library of Congress Cataloging-in-Publication Data:

Themes in Southwest prehistory / edited by George J. Gumerman.
        p.   cm. — (School of American Research Advanced Seminar series)
    Includes bibliographical references and index.
    ISBN 0-933452-84-5 (paper) : $22.50
    1. Indians of North America—Southwest, New—History—Congresses.
2. Indians of North America—Southwest, New—Social life and customs—
Congresses.   I. Gumerman, George J.   II. Series.
E78.S7T487 1993
979'.00497—dc20   93-20323
                                                                 CIP

Cover: Detail of a masonry wall at Chetro Ketl, Chaco Canyon, New Mexico.
Courtesy Museum of New Mexico, neg. no. 67061.

Dedicated to the memory of Fred Plog

(1944–1992)

who contributed so much to Southwestern archaeology

in so short a time.

Contents

List of Illustrations ✦ *xi*

List of Tables ✦ *xii*

Preface ✦ *xiii*

1
Patterns and Perturbations in Southwest Prehistory ✦ 3
GEORGE J. GUMERMAN

2
Cultural Evolution in the Prehistoric Southwest ✦ *11*
GEORGE J. GUMERMAN AND MURRAY GELL-MANN

3
Economic Implications of Changing Land-Use Patterns in
the Late Archaic ✦ 33
W. H. WILLS AND BRUCE HUCKELL

4
Adaptive Stress
Environment and Demography ✦ 53
JEFFREY S. DEAN, WILLIAM H. DOELLE, AND JANET D. ORCUTT

5
Patterns of Health and Disease
Stress Profiles for the Prehistoric Southwest ✦ 87
DEBRA L. MARTIN

6
Processes of Aggregation in the Prehistoric Southwest + 109
LINDA S. CORDELL, DAVID E. DOYEL, AND KEITH W. KINTIGH

7
Toward an Explanation for Southwestern "Abandonments" + 135
PAUL R. FISH, SUZANNE K. FISH, GEORGE J. GUMERMAN,
AND J. JEFFERSON REID

8
Structure and Patterning
The Formation of Puebloan Archaeology + 165
JOSEPH A. TAINTER AND FRED PLOG

9
Alliance Formation and Cultural Identity in the American
Southwest + 183
STEADMAN UPHAM, PATRICIA L. CROWN, AND STEPHEN PLOG

10
The Scream of the Butterfly
Competition and Conflict in the Prehistoric Southwest + 211
DAVID R. WILCOX AND JONATHAN HAAS

11
Drawing the Southwest to Scale
Perspectives on Macroregional Relations + 239
RANDALL H. MCGUIRE, E. CHARLES ADAMS, BEN A. NELSON,
AND KATHERINE SPIELMANN

References + 267

Index + 325

Illustrations and Tables

Figures

3.1. Proportional changes in C3, CAM, and C4 Southwestern plants by elevation • *38*

4.1. Population: southeastern Utah–southwestern Colorado area • *59*

4.2. Population: Kayenta area • *61*

4.3. Population: Virgin Branch area • *62*

4.4. Relative population: Grand Canyon area • *63*

4.5. Population: Little Colorado area • *64*

4.6. Population: San Juan Basin and Chaco Canyon areas • *65*

4.7. Population: Cebolleta Mesa area • *66*

4.8. Population: Mimbres area • *67*

4.9. Population: Northern Rio Grande area • *69*

4.10. Population: Mogollon Highlands area • *70*

4.11. Population: Hohokam area • *71*

4.12. Regional population trends, AD 1–1600 • *74*

4.13. Regional population distribution at AD 400 • *78*

4.14. Regional population distribution at AD 800 • *79*

4.15. Regional population distribution at AD 1100 • *80*

4.16. Regional population distribution at AD 1200 • *81*

4.17. Regional population distribution at AD 1300 • *82*

4.18. Regional population distribution at AD 1500 • *83*

5.1. Model for analysis of skeletal remains • *91*

6.1. Reconstructed precipitation plotted as decade departures in tree-ring widths, AD 1000–1600 • *118*

7.1. Distribution of Southwestern agricultural peoples, AD 1275–1300 • *139*

7.2. Distribution of Southwestern agricultural peoples, AD 1400–1425 • *140*

7.3. Distribution of gravity irrigation in the Southwest prior to AD 1900 • *141*

7.4. Distribution of agricultural settlements in the Western Anasazi case study area, AD 1175–1275 • *146*

7.5. Environmental variability and population curves for the Western Anasazi • *147*

7.6. Distribution of agricultural settlements in the Western Anasazi case study area, AD 1425–1450 • *149*

7.7.   Distribution of early and late Classic period settlements in the northern Tucson Basin • *152*
7.8.   Distribution of early and late Classic period platform mound sites in southern Arizona • *155*
7.9.   Distribution of Southwestern agricultural peoples, AD 1600–1700 • *156*
8.1.   The Chacoan regional system, AD 1050–1175 • *171*
10.1. Map of the Indian Peak Fort site, west-central Arizona • *220*
10.2. Distribution of known late prehistoric platform mound sites in Arizona • *232*
11.1. Map of the Southwest and Mesoamerica • *245*
11.2. A Jeddito Black-on-yellow bowl from Homol'ovi II • *255*

Tables

3.1.   Radiocarbon assays on Late Archaic cultigens from Southwest desert-grasslands • *41*
3.2.   Radiocarbon assays on Late Archaic cultigens from the Colorado Plateaus • *43*
3.3.   Radiocarbon assays on Late Archaic cultigens from the Mogollon Highlands • *47*
5.1.   Skeletal and dental indicators of stress • *94*
6.1.   Hohokam settlement data in numbers of components • *122*
6.2.   Mimbres area site size and distribution of houses or rooms by period and site size class • *127*
8.1.   Elements of strong and weak patterning • *169*
9.1.   Language diversity and intelligibility in the Southwest • *187*

Preface

THE HISTORY OF OUR UNDERSTANDING of the prehistoric peoples of the American Southwest is chronicled in the region's archaeological conferences. Beginning with the Pecos Conference in 1927, periodic meetings have brought scholars and their knowledge together to offer syntheses that have been used to construct new theories of Southwestern prehistory and to set agendas for future research.

The papers in this volume result from an advanced seminar entitled "The Organization and Evolution of Prehistoric Southwestern Society," which was held in September 1989 at the School of American Research in Santa Fe. It is the second of three advanced seminars which treat the Southwest as a single entity while recognizing the great diversity within the region. The first volume published (Cordell and Gumerman 1989) resulted from a School of American Research advanced seminar chaired by Douglas Schwartz in 1983. Its goal was to synthesize the current state of knowledge of Southwestern prehistory, with a focus on subregions of the Southwest such as Mesa Verde and the Rio Grande valley. Introductory and concluding chapters provided thematic continuity.

By the mid-1980s it had become apparent to a number of archaeologists that the time was propitious to advance our understanding of the prehistoric Southwest by using the power of modern multidisciplinary techniques, the existence of large new data sets, and the willingness to conceptualize on a pan-Southwestern scale. Two conferences were proposed, the School of American Research advanced seminar which resulted in the present volume, to be followed by a larger multidisciplinary workshop at the Santa Fe Institute.

Unlike the 1983 seminar and its resulting book, the second seminar was organized topically with data drawn from the entire region. The primary goal was to view the entire American Southwest as a single, but very culturally and environmentally diverse entity, structuring our analysis around the themes that constitute the chapters of this volume. We feel that these themes—including aggregation, abandonment, warfare, health, and demography—are closely related to stability and change.

The seminar's primary emphasis was on behavioral topics rather than on subregions within the Southwest. Because no single individual is knowledgeable about a subject for all the prehistoric Southwestern traditions, an informal organizing committee selected a coordinator for each topic (the senior author of each paper in this volume), and other individuals were chosen to complement the co-ordinators' knowledge and interests. For logistical reasons, only the coordinator of each topic could participate in the seminar, but each coordinator was expected to represent the views of his or her co-authors. Through our discussions at the seminar itself, we hoped to increase our understanding of the relationships be-tween these various topics and cultural transformations.

The multidisciplinary Santa Fe Institute workshop was held in October 1990 with twenty-nine participants, half of whom were archaeologists. The others were cultural anthropologists, demographers, physicists, physical anthropologists, evo-lutionary biologists, cultural systems theorists, philosophers of science, and ex-perts in artificial life.

The two host institutions in this effort have unique missions which provided effective stimuli for these meetings. The School of American Research, a center for advanced studies in anthropology, needs no introduction to anthropologists. The Santa Fe Institute is another matter. Founded in 1984 as a private, independent, multidisciplinary research center, the Institute's goal is to understand complex adaptive systems and the relationships of their simpler constituents. Workshops and seminars are conducted by the Institute's "external faculty" and invited re-searchers whose interests span traditional disciplinary boundaries. The mission of the Institute is to address the most intractable problems in biological evolution, pre-biotic chemical evolution, cultural evolution, and individual learning and thinking. The volume that results from the Santa Fe Institute workshop will focus on the concept of the prehistoric Southwest as a complex adaptive system, utiliz-ing many of the ideas developed by nonarchaeologists who work at the Institute.

The concept for these two meetings and much of the format was formulated by Murray Gell-Mann, one of the founders of the Santa Fe Institute and a man with a deep interest in Southwestern archaeology. With the support of Robert McC. Adams and Douglas Schwartz, both of whom were on the Institute's Sci-ence Board, Murray worked with Jonathan Haas, then of the School of American Research, and with me in planning this long-term effort. With the advice of many archaeologists, we gradually evolved a structure and a list of participants that re-sulted in the two events and the publications.

The Santa Fe Institute and the School of American Research provided the con-siderable financial support for these efforts, and that support is greatly appreciated by the participants. All participants benefited from the marvelous support staff of both institutions. Every reasonable request was met with efficiency, enthusiasm, and courtesy.

I express my appreciation to Murray Gell-Mann, Douglas Schwartz, Jonathan Haas, Linda Cordell, Randy McGuire, and Joe Tainter for their advice along the long and twisted path that lead to this volume. I am also grateful to Wolf Gumer-man, Lynne Sebastian, and especially to Bob Preucel for commenting on manu-scripts in this volume.

George J. Gumerman

Themes *in* Southwest Prehistory

Patterns and Perturbations in Southwestern Prehistory

GEORGE J. GUMERMAN

As an academic I've become so accomplished at both seeing similarity and noting difference that I no longer understand the significance of either. Yet that seems the whole point of analysis: of seeing the world as a place in which everything is unique and yet in which there is nothing new under the sun.

—Wayne Fields, *What the River Knows: An Angler in Midstream*

 THE MOST PERVASIVE QUESTIONS IN ARCHAEOLOGY revolve around the nature of the evolution of culture. What changes and what doesn't and why? What are the principles of culture change, and how are they shaped by historical accident? In some situations archaeologists have been able to demonstrate causal linkages between variables such as environment and technology for explaining patterns and perturbations of culture change. They have, however, been largely unsuccessful at developing a coherent model, sufficiently general to explain change across cultures and yet detailed enough to account for individual variation.

The failure to develop and test a satisfactory overarching theory is the result of many factors, including data limitations, methodological problems, and the possibility that there *are* no significant cross-cultural principles of culture change. Some researchers believe that culture as a nonlinear dynamic system exhibits so great a sensitivity to initial conditions that deterministic probability is impossible; that is, that exceedingly minor differences in the formative natural and cultural conditions normally lead to major unpredictable qualitative change (Schaffer 1986). As a result, cross-cultural regularities are highly unlikely to occur.

Other scholars believe that there *are* cross-cultural regularities but that they are not derived from any causal laws that govern the organization of cultural systems. Instead, they derive from genetically determined human physiological limitations and historical contingencies; in other words, human biology or accident (Braun 1991). The opposing argument has also been made: that cultural systems are open and therefore susceptible to historical accident, making divergence, rather than convergence, almost inevitable (McGuire 1992; Saitta and Keene 1990). According to this view, cross-cultural regularities are unlikely to occur because of the almost infinite number of impinging unique conditions, events, and processes that shape so many of the fundamental aspects of a culture.

The theoretical prism through which cultural evolution is viewed also in some measure determines the predilection for acknowledging and therefore observing whether or not there are cross-cultural regularities in the evolution of culture. Diagnosticians of contemporary archaeological modes of explanation have stressed that archaeologists participate in different interpretive communities colored by their own varying social and intellectual heritages and that those differences influence the kinds of questions that are asked or ignored and the assumptions that are made (Patterson 1986). This concept—that different philosophical frameworks provide varying interpretations of past behavior—is a tenet of "post-processualist" archaeology (Shanks and Tilley 1987). Advocates of different explanatory philosophies often frame their positions in order to accentuate differences rather than similarities, and as a result, explanations are so polarized that they often seem more divergent than they really are. In the most general terms, philosophical frameworks for explaining culture change take either a functionalist-adaptionist approach or argue for change that is generated internally from interaction between individuals or different social segments within the society. Some researchers have tried to reconcile these different theoretical stances, but their attempts have concentrated on philosophical issues and have not, as yet, resulted in empirical tests (Earle and Preucel 1987; Preucel 1991; Trigger 1991).

The advanced seminar at the School of American Research and this resulting volume were based on the premise that there are general principles of cultural evolution and that there are also unique conditions, events, and processes. The skirmishes over whether or not it is possible to generalize about culture change are futile. There is no doubt that to generalize about the evolution of culture is possible; there are too many cross-cultural regularities to deny the possibility. The question is, Are the principles of cultural evolution so general that they are trivial and therefore cannot be used as effective heuristic tools?

Although the question cannot, as yet, be answered, the regular and patterned rhythms of change across the variety of environments and traditions of the prehistoric Southwest had their genesis, as in many areas of the world, with three interrelated trends: (1) an increase in food production, (2) a greater degree of sedentism, and (3) dramatically increasing population. Along with these three conditions, which occurred in the centuries before AD 1, there were related developments such as changes in technology, increased storage capability, and the predictability of subsistence resources (Wills and Huckell, this volume). Many of the changes in the complexity of Southwestern society centuries later can be attributed to these initial conditions.

The initial conditions of both technology and production, as well as social and demographic forces, were deeply imbedded and autocatalytic, in that they contained the necessary features that centuries later facilitated increases in complexity. This is not to suggest that Southwestern society was a closed system, immune from external influences. Certainly, changing relationships with more complex societies to the south and less complex entities in other directions also played a role in changes in the evolution of Southwestern society (McGuire et al., this volume). It is, however, the early technological and resulting social innovations that facilitated the large-scale change in later centuries. Given the appropriate environmental and cultural conditions in the Southwest during the period of experimentation with domesticated plants derived from Mexico and the autocatalytic, self-extending nature of the cultural trajectory, the general trend toward increasing complexity was predictable. In large part, the changes in complexity were due to organizational changes that were necessary to accommodate new forms of resource ownership, territoriality, division of labor, productive specialization, and supporting belief systems (Plog 1990a).

Despite the occurrence of patterned regularities in the Southwest, there are many pitfalls in considering a broad evolutionary scheme of cultural complexity. Although there was an overall increase in complexity through time, there was not a uniform temporal progression; instead, there were "hinge points" (Cordell and Gumerman 1989), or phase transitions, when critical thresholds were reached. There were also local system collapses and times and places where decreases in complexity were common (Gumerman and Gell-Mann, this volume). Furthermore, the changes in different parts of the system were probably not always contemporaneous, as might be expected in a loosely integrated open system. Changes in resource distribution, for example, may have preceded modification of kinship systems that would have facilitated economic shifts, or moiety formation may have preceded population aggregation. Nor can it be assumed that all cultural features were closely interrelated. Some parts of the system may not have been highly articulated with other parts, and linkages between some cultural and environmental aspects of the system were probably often weak and sometimes nonexistent (Trigger 1984). Finally, it must be remembered that stasis and change were probably not always adaptive, and may even have been maladaptive, since individuals and groups were at times poor interpreters of cultural and environmental situations. Change may have been ill timed, and behavioral patterns inappropriate. Culture is not an efficient, all-knowing machine.

A QUESTION OF SCALE

In constructing a framework of cultural development for a large area, there is a danger of asking questions so general that they cannot be adequately addressed with the data at hand. Is there a scale at which generalizations are meaningful for understanding culture change, rather than for just describing it? Generalizing on a grand scale is not difficult and provides a useful function. Storytelling, as John

Terrell (1990) calls the generalizing practice in archaeology, paints the larger picture, enhances cross-cultural understanding, and offers hypotheses for more particularizing studies to test. Even though the best archaeological storytelling offers great insights into the past (e.g., Willey 1991), the result is usually a description of a phenomenon rather than an understanding of the how and why of change.

One of the great questions in archaeology that has not been adequately addressed is, Where is the point along the scale from specific detail to generalization that permits understanding as well as description? Description results from staying at the extreme ends of a continuum that ranges from historical particularism to broad generalization. It is difficult to reach an understanding of evolutionary mechanisms and processes if one is so engrossed in detail that the bigger picture is not visible or, on the other hand, if one deals with theory so abstract and removed from data that the questions asked are unanswerable. Success in the understanding of cultural evolution requires an interplay between synthesizing detail and exploring generalizing principles. Traditionally, archaeologists have been more at ease with generalizing in offering explanations for the evolution of culture, often in large part because more fine-grained studies provide exceptions to every generalization.

The recent large increases in data and the finer resolution of that data, however, have permitted a dramatic reduction in the scale that archaeologists have typically used for understanding the dynamics of culture change. Over the years, we have narrowed the scope of our investigations from a "type site" that represented an entire "culture" for a specified period to the role of classes, factions, gender, age groups, families, and even individuals. Data and methodology in the past were such that a single site such as Snaketown could be treated as representative of the Hohokam (Haury 1976a). Now, it is possible to determine changing nuclear household composition over time (Wilcox, McGuire, and Sternberg 1981) and the development of classes such as Hohokam craft specialists (Neitzel 1991). These possibilities have made our task as archaeologists more difficult, but they have also made our models more realistically approximate the ways in which humans behave. An analysis of the various social segments and their interaction, even in egalitarian societies, provides a more dynamic perspective of change than does a more normative or homogeneous analysis. In taking the narrower perspective, however, we must remain cognizant of the fact that one of archaeology's primary goals is to understand the evolution of culture in the broadest sense.

CAUSES AND CONSEQUENCES

In the most general terms, causality studies may be considered either unicausal or multicausal. In reality, however, few archaeologists today search for "prime movers"; rather, we have designated certain variables such as population or climate as major conditions that are responsible for change, while recognizing that those conditions are shaped by other cultural, historical, and environmental factors. In the Southwest a limited number of cultural and physical variables have commonly been the focus of the study of change. But some of these variables are not causal, and others might be considered. The following themes were selected for detailed consideration in the advanced seminar that generated this volume: environment and demography, health and nutrition, abandonment, aggregation, external inter-action, hierarchy and political centralization, social integration and alliance, com-petition and conflict, and historic-prehistoric analogs. Our major objective is to examine in detail these various topics as they pertain to the entire Southwest.

Demography and, especially, environment have always been major factors in attempts to explain the character of (and changes in) Southwestern society. Although scientists in many disciplines have been increasingly successful in retro-dicting environments, this has not been true in the case of demography. Research-ers have made considerable progress in refining the theoretical implications of demographic change (Netting 1990) but have had much greater difficulty address-ing the empirical aspects of calculating demographic figures. Dean, Doelle, and Orcutt (this volume) have demonstrated that archaeologists are making progress in understanding population trends and in estimating actual figures. The top-ics of health and nutrition are largely correlates of demography. New analytical techniques have vastly increased our ability to evaluate the health of extinct popu-lations (Martin, this volume), but it is still difficult to articulate health profiles within the broader theoretical topic of culture change.

The twin themes of abandonment and aggregation are perennial topics in Southwestern prehistory (Cordell, Doyel, and Kintigh, this volume; Fish et al., this volume), and the two terms are usually used as rubrics to categorize many differ-ent forms of settlement behavior. The phenomena of abandonment and aggrega-tion are often reflections of other changes in the social and natural environment, although they in turn may initiate further change. The intertwined developments of social hierarchy and political centralization—that is, the increase in the de-gree of structure in a society—are similar to changes in population distribution, in that they not only reflect change in other parts of the social system but them-selves cause change in that system. The degree of social integration in a society is also closely correlated with the development of hierarchy, as is increased social complexity with the formation of formal alliances (Upham, Crown, and Plog, this volume). Competition and conflict, only recently revived as major topics of inter-est in Southwestern archaeology, are the reciprocals of alliance formation (Wilcox and Haas, this volume). The adaptive advantage of competition therefore has to be modeled with some form of cooperation and alliance.

It cannot be assumed that the germs of culture change are embedded in the themes discussed here; often, these topics may be simply a measure (rather than a cause) of change in a broader systemic perspective. Nor are we presently in the position to identify all causal variables or to assign relative weight to them and their contributions to observable change. As formidable as it is to control the data of each variable in sufficient detail to understand the phenomenon, it is even more difficult to characterize the relationships between variables with sufficient precision to identify causation. A step toward understanding change is to try to understand in as much detail as possible those variables that are most amenable to archaeological investigation, such as the nature of the natural environment, and then to examine each in relation to others. Since culture is a complex adaptive system, however, it cannot be successfully analyzed by studying the individual components of the system and combining them. Instead, it is necessary to understand the properties of the entire system as well as the detail of its components. As an example of both the difficulties and the possibilities that are afforded through the examination of individual variables and the necessity to examine detail within a larger context, it is worthwhile to look briefly at the example of the increasing density of population.

POPULATION AGGREGATION AS A
WORLDWIDE PHENOMENON

As numerous commentators have noted, since the end of the Pleistocene and the adoption of intensive food production many populations have tended not only to increase but also to group themselves on the landscape in ever denser numbers (Binford 1968; Cohen 1977; Rindos 1984). This observation is simply a description of the phenomenon and obscures the numerous ways in which the more densely packed populations formed, interacted, fissioned, and regrouped. Furthermore, it is a statement about locational arrangements and does not address the dynamics of human behavior.

Clearly, there must be numerous advantages to a society as a whole (or at least to certain segments of the society) in forming larger population centers under certain natural and cultural conditions. The decisions leading to aggregation, however, and the local expressions of the larger communities, hamlets, villages, towns, and cities, have been shaped by such diverse factors as technology, environment, social and political structure, ideology, tradition, economics, demographics, health and disease, and the impact of other cultures. Not all these variables are inextricably linked in a feedback loop. The degree of integration and the relative importance of the different variables will vary among groups, times, and places. Nevertheless, the large number of cultural and natural conditions that may impinge on decisions to aggregate means that attempts to understand the phenomenon without taking those factors into account will provide partial explanations, at best.

The large number of factors affecting aggregation allows for the possibility of an even greater diversity of community organizational forms. As a community increases in size and in number of interacting individuals, there is an exponential increase in the kinds of social forms that can be produced. The wide range of architectural forms in aggregated communities even within similar traditions (Cordell, Doyel, and Kintigh, this volume) hints at the great variation in social order that existed; but even when the architectural form is quite similar, the social arrangements may have been very different. Dean's (1970) classic study of the development of the two Kayenta Anasazi cliff dwellings of Betatakin and Kiet Siel shows that the social histories of those largely contemporaneous, superficially similar communities were quite different.

The advantages of a more closely packed population to the community as a corporate body are indicated by the worldwide distribution of this social form. But the question remains: To whom are these benefits conveyed? There are certainly disadvantages to some segments within the society, as individual, family, occupational, class, and other subgroup needs may be sublimated for the perceived greater good of the whole. Health will be adversely affected in more compact communities because of the more benevolent environment for infectious pathogens. Social arrangements have to be modified or developed to accommodate the increased interaction of larger numbers of people, or decision making will degenerate (Johnson 1982). Also, there is an increased likelihood that there will be greater discrimination in access to information and resources. Unless the many constituent elements of communities are considered, attempts at understanding the benefits and costs of denser populations will not be adequately understood.

It is necessary to narrow the focus of observation and consider the diverse elements that comprise individual communities, but it is also essential to broaden the focus and consider entire social landscapes: that is, the various groups of different levels of complexity with which the community interacts. Archaeologists have rarely considered the role that less complex groups play in relation to aggregated populations (Adams 1965). There are often hunters and gatherers, peoples dependent on less intensive forms of agriculture than those in the larger settlements, and—in areas other than the Southwest—pastoralists, whose economic and social lives are intertwined with those in larger, more permanent settlements. These archaeologically less visible groups can have a profound effect on the form and structure of aggregated communities. For example, hostilities between the groups may require more compact or defensively situated settlements, or economic diversification may enhance interdependence between the larger settlements and less complex groups. Only recently has the mutualism between the bison hunters of the Plains and the Puebloan farmers been explored in detail (Spielman 1982, 1986), and the existence of such interaction among groups of different levels of complexity within the borders has only been hinted at (Di Peso 1953).

Finally, it must be noted that more densely packed populations may be maladaptive at times, or may become so. The fact that large communities collapse and that their populations disperse, at least temporarily, suggests in virtually every instance that their structures are highly unstable (Tainter 1988).

In sum, there is a tendency in many regions for people to arrange themselves into ever larger groups. At the same time, there are many cultural, demographic, historic, and environmental conditions that affect the nature of the spatial distribution of populations, making each situation unique. Many of these conditions may not be easily recognizable in the archaeological record. The archaeologist's goal is to understand the specific situations and to attempt to place them in a broader context of overall culture change.

THE LARGER PICTURE

A great deal has been written lately about the inadequacy of traditional attempts to understand processes of change based on adaptation. The fundamental argument is that the process of adaptation does not answer the question of what generates variation in human behavior and does not explain the differential transmission of that behavior (Braun 1990, 1991; Leonard and Jones 1987; O'Brien and Holland 1990). Although these might be the most essential questions in biological evolution, it is more appropriate to reverse the question when investigating cultural evolution. Human behavior is largely learned, not genetically determined. Behavioral variation is therefore to be expected and is constantly occurring. As a consequence, it is more profitable to ask what causes patterned behavior rather than what causes variations: in other words, what is the cultural equivalent of DNA? After this question has been answered, we can address the reasons for the differential transmission of the many variations of those patterns.

There are certain periods in the history of any region when social, environmental, and demographic conditions are such that behavioral experimentation is facilitated and the survival rate for change is high. In the American Southwest these periods often occurred under especially benevolent environmental regimes, and the result has been likened to the "Cambrian explosion," when many new life-forms appeared on earth (Gumerman and Gell-Mann, this volume). Even relatively inefficient social arrangements could have been maintained under these conditions. But the pace of culture change also increased under conditions of social and environmental stress, when existing behavior was perceived as inadequate and attempts were made to cope with the new situations. Under these conditions, new cultural arrangements were introduced, but there were fewer of them—presumably because options were narrowed and fewer kinds of arrangements could be successfully maintained. It is within the overall context of changing natural and cultural conditions that the variables addressed in this volume need to be explored in detail, that we may better understand the forces of culture change.

Cultural Evolution
in the Prehistoric Southwest

GEORGE J. GUMERMAN AND
MURRAY GELL-MANN

 IN 1540, WHEN FRANCISCO VÁSQUEZ DE CORONADO and his party
slogged their way into what is now called the Southwest, they initiated
profound changes in the lives of the inhabitants, changes that would
have ramifications down through the centuries. Though most people
might consider that event the major turning point in Southwestern Native American
culture history, it was only one of a two-millennia-long series of far-reaching
changes. Interaction with other groups, population shifts, environmental perturbations, subsistence changes, social and technological innovations, and a host of
other factors resulted in both slowly evolving cultural transformations and rapid
dramatic change.

Cultural evolution is a fact that does not need to be demonstrated here.
Archaeological data from all parts of the world document change from simple
small-scale societies with foraging economies to complex polities with many specialized economic and social institutions. Even though the transformation from
simple to complex forms is so widespread, the process is not without hesitations
and reversals, and the nature of the factors that facilitate or constrain the transformations is in great dispute.

The Southwest is an ideal laboratory in which to examine the processes of cultural evolution, from Archaic lifeways based on foraging to that stage based upon
primary dependence on cultivated crops, known variously as neolithic, tribal
society, or settled village life, and then to a stage exhibiting early manifestations of
cultural complexity. The Southwest extends over three major climatic and topographic zones, encompassing a number of what archaeologists have called cultures, traditions, style zones, regional systems, and behavioral patterns. The region
therefore provides a variety of environments and cultural traditions through which
to trace and compare the transitions of its inhabitants from incipient agriculturalists to large-town dwellers. The temporal and material culture data available for the

exploration of such changes, though variable in quality and quantity through both time and space, are almost overwhelming in amount and precision compared with those from most other areas of the world. The challenge is to formulate generalizations about Southwestern culture change without allowing the multiplicity of detail to obscure regularities or provide crippling exceptions to every generalization.

All sciences have two traditions of inquiry. One is dominated by synthesizers, those who desire to find underlying unifying principles by searching for hidden symmetries. The other consists of diversifiers, those who search for heterogeneity, seeking to explore the richness and diversity of the universe and to break the symmetry sought by the synthesizers. Southwestern archaeology has cycled through both traditions.

The early archaeologists were, for the most part, of the synthesizing tradition. Investigators like Jesse Walter Fewkes and A. V. Kidder wove complex patterns out of oral tradition, existing Native American practices, and the skimpy detail of the material culture from only a few surveys and excavations. Synthesizing is easiest when the data base is small because the range of diversity is poorly represented. Some early scholars such as Harold Colton and Lyndon Hargrave did pursue the diversifying tradition, and that unusual archaeologist Harold S. Gladwin constructed grand schemes while at the same time documenting the great variety in the archaeological record.

The 1950s and early 1960s saw a reaction to the overenthusiastic synthesis and generalization of an earlier generation of archaeologists. The result was the ascendency of the diversifying tradition. Great effort was spent in trying to reconstruct the culture histories of small regions, without attempting to place those local sequences within the larger picture of Southwestern prehistory or within a general theory of cultural evolution. More recently, in the late 1970s and 1980s, there has again arisen a trend toward synthesis and generalization; at the same time, huge amounts of new data have become available, largely through massive efforts in contract archaeology. The time, therefore, is opportune for archaeologists to combine the best of the diversifying and synthesizing traditions and to offer new insights into the nature of Southwestern cultural transformations and their relationship to ideas about cultural evolution—or even ideas about the evolution of complex adaptive systems in general.

It is the tension between generalization and detail that permits plausible general explanations for stability and change to go beyond particularistic description. The broad geographic and temporal scope of knowledge about past cultural and natural realms in the Southwest encourages generalizations about the evolution of culture that may be applicable to other areas of the world as well. The wealth of available detail, however, accentuates the enormous variety in the past human and natural record, discourages facile generalizations, and makes it clear that a "normative" perspective of the past is simplistic.

THE NATURE OF THE PREHISTORIC SOUTHWEST

In order to understand change and stability in the prehistoric Southwest, it is necessary to consider the question of scale. At one extreme is the view of the Southwest as a single social entity; at the other is the concentration on the individual decision maker. How do we characterize the nature of social relationships throughout the region (Levy 1989; Tainter and Plog, this volume; Cordell, Doyel, and Kintigh, this volume)? Is the Southwest a bounded social entity (McGuire et al., this volume)? How does it change through time? How do internal relationships change (Upham, Crown, and Plog, this volume)? How does the classic division of the Southwest into Hohokam, Anasazi, and Mogollon traditions relate to cultural behavior or to entities that archaeologists call cultures (Tainter and Plog, this volume; Upham, Crown, and Plog, this volume)? What kinds of cultural behavior are represented by the many local traditions that make up the larger traditions? These kinds of questions, which deal with scale, greatly affect our thoughts about the role of social relationships in influencing cultural transformations. One of the most dramatic changes in recent Southwestern archaeology is the realization that there were many more forms of local cultural behavior than anyone previously imagined. It is the understanding of small-scale social relationships and how they change that sharpens our knowledge about the larger-scale processes of culture change.

The Southwest has traditionally been defined by the presence of certain material culture traits—particularly pottery, maize agriculture, and village architecture—the limits of which bound it on all sides except the south, where those traits extend into Mesoamerica. The anthropological definition has typically been inexact, often focusing on the Pueblos and ignoring the peoples and places that do not fit into some restrictive scheme. Depending on how tightly the cultural criteria are drawn, the culture area known as the Southwest expands or contracts. Early attempts to define the area were made primarily for the purposes of classification (Goddard 1913; Wissler 1917). Kroeber (1939) and then Kirchoff (1954) refined these definitions and attempted to account for the differences within the Southwest while recognizing the similarities that combine the diverse ways of life into a single culture area.

Archaeologists have had similar problems of definition, dealing first with the Anasazi as the model for the Southwest (Kidder 1924) and later adding the Hohokam (Gladwin and Gladwin 1935) and the Mogollon (Haury 1936). For years archaeologists debated the definitions and boundaries of those "cultural" entities (McGuire et al., this volume). By the late 1960s, however, scholars were less interested in classification than in the nature of past behavior and how it changed. Most archaeologists, especially those working on the Colorado Plateaus, with their excellent record of past environments, opted for ecological explanations of culture change and stability (Euler et al. 1979). The major explanations for change in the low deserts of Arizona were either (1) the social and political innovations necessary for the design, construction, and maintenance of public works, or else (2) the interaction with Mexican peoples. Boundaries were supposedly no longer of much interest, but since most of the ecologically oriented archaeologists also used the concept of culture as a highly integrated system, boundaries were implied, if seldom mentioned.

The question of cultural boundaries could no longer be ignored by the 1980s. By then, the tremendous diversity of cultural behavior was readily apparent in the data, which demonstrated the variety of different social forms previously included under a single rubric such as Anasazi or even, say, the more narrowly defined Kayenta Anasazi. For certain periods, the concepts of Hohokam, Mogollon, and Anasazi have lost much of their utility, except for the purpose of stylistic or technological classification (Speth 1988). Not only are the boundaries between entities often indistinct and variable through time (McGuire et al., this volume; Tainter and Plog, this volume), but the meanings of the boundaries are unknown: they may be ethnic, linguistic, stylistic, economic, ideological, social, or combinations of these. Furthermore, boundaries of various types may have existed that have not been detected in the archaeological record (Upham, Crown, and Plog, this volume). At present, archaeologists disagree about the nature of many of the boundaries that have been detected. It is most likely that there were many different kinds of boundaries reflecting different sorts of relationships and that those relationships were in various states of flux.

THE EVOLUTION TOWARD INCREASING COMPLEXITY

Complexity is not easy to define. In order to capture the intuitive ideas that most of us have of what complexity means, several different quantities would probably have to be introduced. It turns out, however, that in most scientific usage and in much ordinary discourse what is meant by the complexity of a system being observed is, more or less, the length of the description given by the observer of the regularities of the system (Gell-Mann 1992). This is obviously a subjective or context-dependent—even a behavioral—definition, but no comparable objective definition has ever been found. Probably there is none. Granted the subjectivity of the definition, it is still necessary to provide a number of comments and qualifications before the concept can be used.

For one thing, the length of an ostensive description is no good; it is just as easy to point to a complicated system as to a simple one. Likewise, since a short nickname could be given to any system, the description should be in a language previously agreed upon with a correspondent (and a distant correspondent at that, to eliminate the possibility of pointing!).

Not only the language, but also the knowledge and understanding of the world that are shared by the observer and the correspondent may significantly affect the length of message required for the description. Just as important is the level of detail achieved in the description—what is known in physical science as the "coarse graining."

Given the coarse graining, the language, and the assumed level of knowledge and understanding, the description should be as concise as possible. The length could, of course, be artificially inflated by the use of unnecessary verbiage or just by repeating things that could be said only once.

So far, then, we are discussing a definition of complexity based on (1) the length of a concise description, (2) to a distant correspondent, (3) using language previously agreed upon, (4) of the regularities of an observed system, (5) given the coarse graining that is applied, and (6) the knowledge and understanding of the world shared by the observer and the correspondent. But this definition still leaves the notion of regularities to be examined. What does it mean to separate regularities from random details?

For a finite stream of data, there is no rigorous way to distinguish a system's regular features from those that are attributed to chance. For an infinite stream, the situation is more hopeful. If possible, we should therefore be dealing with a very large body of data. As the amount of coarse-grained information increases, so does the meaningfulness of extracting regularities, since a regular pattern will be more likely to recur frequently enough to set it off from incidental features.

We can see how the foregoing observations apply in the description of a prehistoric society, with emphasis on its social structure. Evidently, complexity does not depend on the length of a message that merely designates sites or names a branch or phase of a particular ruin. We also see that the concentration on social complexity means that the coarse graining will ignore features of the remains that do not appear to bear importantly on social structure. The language for discussing that structure is fairly standard these days and is heavily influenced by certain theories, of various degrees of plausibility and usefulness, of what is considered to be a typical sequence of stages of societal development. The regularities that are actually identified are similarly constrained by the limitations of current theories. Finally, it is clear that the likelihood of recognizing patterns of social structure is increased if there is an abundance of material.

In the light of these rather obvious general remarks, we can see that the social complexity assigned by an archaeologist to a prehistoric culture really does typically relate to the length of the concise description of regularities—the various social roles, the patterns of residence, the distribution and architecture of public buildings, the arts and crafts, the technology, the utilization of plant and animal species, the relations with other cultures, and so forth—as well as to the "variety of mechanisms for organizing these into a coherent, functioning whole" (Tainter 1988:23).

Sometimes, societies are described as more or less complex merely according to how they are thought to fit into a particular presumed sequence of evolutionary stages. Such an interpretation of the meaning of complexity is really justified only to the extent that it agrees with the more general interpretation given here. Fortunately, it often does agree, and the concept of complexity as a measure of the evolutionary status of a society continues to have heuristic potential despite recent criticism (Plog 1989).

There is no question that after the adoption of agriculture, societies tend to evolve into more complex entities. The intertwined relationships among agricultural intensification, population growth, political integration, and social role diversity are major aspects of the processes of cultural evolution. Usually those changes are associated with an increase in social inequality, and it is an interesting question whether that effect was less blatant in parts of the Southwest than in societies at comparable stages of evolution elsewhere in the world, as has sometimes been claimed.

This general view of social complexity does not imply a universal and consistent trend toward increased complexity, or that all interacting groups share a similar level of complexity. Southwestern culture history is characterized by periods of both rapid and slow change. In a few cases, such as with the Cerbat people of west and north-central Arizona, there was very little change from the 1300s until the first United States military intervention in the 1800s (Euler 1981; Schwartz 1989). Apparently, those ancestors of the contemporary Pai developed an adaptive system that efficiently fitted their environments. There are numerous examples of the local development of complexity followed by a collapse and a reversion to more simple forms. Often other locales then take a leading role in the trend toward complexity. Areas of the Southwest that were in the vanguard of increasing social complexity did not usually retain that position for more than a few centuries, after which there was stagnation or collapse. The categorization of a society in terms of complexity does not, of course, indicate how the society reached that stage; it is simply a descriptive measure.

Although there are variations from locale to locale in the dynamics of culture change through time, there are a number of time periods that characterize certain stages in Southwestern culture history. In some ways the time periods are arbitrary and simply reflect convenient points from which to discuss the state of the Southwest. Generally, however, the dates do seem to delineate periods of widespread rapid change, either toward greater complexity or toward more simple social forms. Traditionally in the Southwest, as in most areas of the world, the past has been divided into a series of named or numbered stages. However, with the refinement of chronologies and the accumulation of vast amounts of data demonstrating great local variation, a simplistic concept like Pueblo I is no longer adequate. An attempt was made in a recent seminar to address that problem by identifying and naming "hinge points"—time intervals that seemed to characterize periods of rapid change throughout much of the Southwest (Cordell and Gumerman 1989). The unnamed periods used in this paper are a further refinement of the hinge point concept, underscoring dating imprecision and the fact that, in some cases, different social processes were taking place in various parts of the Southwest at the same time. Finally, it must be noted that any culture-historical overview will focus on the development and fate of strong patterns—those that tend toward greater complexity because they are the part of the archaeological record that is most apparent and has attracted most scholarly attention (Tainter and Plog, this volume). Weak patterns are more difficult to detect archaeologically and therefore are underrepresented in culture-historical overviews.

SOME KEY PERIODS OF BEHAVIORAL CHANGE
IN THE SOUTHWEST

CIRCA 1500 TO 900 BC

The domestication of maize, which began at about this time, produced trans-formations that laid the foundation for the next two and one-half millennia of Southwestern culture history (Wills and Huckell, this volume). It would be some time before there was a dependence on cultivated crops throughout the South-west, but maize was already producing profound economic and social changes. In both the low and high deserts of the Southwest there is evidence of more per-manent house structures and storage facilities. Deep midden deposits indicate long-term or frequent, repeated occupations. Clearly, the organization of labor was being transformed from a system that emphasized mobility and dispersion of the population to one more geographically anchored, with attention to control of geographic zones. Domesticated plants and long-term storage provided greater predictability about the future. Only in the mountain zone, the area later occupied by the Mogollon, is there little evidence of permanent village occupation at this time (Hard 1990). The greatest concentration of population was in the Rio Grande valley just north of the Jornada del Muerto and in the southern Arizona desert.

Evidence for the degree of interaction between groups during this early period is conflicting. Most lithic material derives from local sources, but the style of arti-facts extended from the Pacific to central Texas and from the Columbia Plateau to somewhere in northwestern Mexico (McGuire et al., this volume). Shell from the Gulf of California is found over much of this area. In short, there was a great deal of interaction and exchange over much of this huge region, but local groups seem nevertheless to have been tethered to local resources. The cultural area later known as the Southwest did not really exist at this time.

AD 200 TO 500

The development of the classic three major Southwestern traditions, the Hohokam, Mogollon, and Anasazi, occurs at this time. Although the cultural meaning and structural distinctiveness of those traditions have been questioned (Tainter and Plog, this volume), they serve as convenient rubrics for the discussion of the ma-terial culture of large areas. The traditions have been defined on the basis of artifact types, architectural style, and, to some degree, settlement pattern and geographi-cal location. Because of the wide range of behavior that has been documented within each of the major traditions, however, the terms have greater utility as labels for material culture than they do for distinctive social and political structures.

Greater investment in agriculture provided a more reliable food source, result-ing in the reduction in mobility that is probably largely responsible for the features that distinguish the Southwest from the adjacent areas with less sedentary popu-lations, such as the Plains and the Great Basin (Wills and Huckell, this volume).

Population increases dramatically in these early centuries of the millennium, except in northern Sonora. Villages are common in most major areas including that of the mountain Mogollon, although many of those villages may not have been occupied throughout the year (Gilman 1987). There are Pioneer period Hohokam settlements in the Lower Sonoran desert of Arizona, Adamana settlements in the north-central region of Arizona, and Basketmaker II communities scattered across the southern Colorado Plateaus. The villages usually consist of pithouses and underground storage facilities, often showing a considerable investment in construction labor and indicating a change in mobility patterns and increasing reliance on agriculture. The pithouse is, in fact, the typical early form of dwelling throughout much of the world during early neolithic times (Gilman 1987).

Major technological innovations during this period enhanced efficiency in the growing, hunting, and processing of food. The bow and arrow replaced the atlatl; the more efficient two-handed mano and trough metate came into common use; ceramics for the storage, serving, and cooking of food appeared throughout the Southwest; and the irrigation of crops was practiced in the Arizona desert. The earliest ceramics are all gray or brown, and most of the forms are quite simple, although technically sophisticated. Hohokam and Mogollon ceramics are very similar, suggesting common origins (Haury 1962a; LeBlanc 1982), and Anasazi ceramics have a uniformity throughout the Colorado Plateaus. There was increased domestication of turkeys, which were probably more important for feathers than for food. The technological changes, the increased dependency on domesticated crops, the reduction in mobility, and the concomitant changes in social organization are all interrelated and responsible for the character of what we now call the Hohokam, Anasazi, and Mogollon.

Health during these early centuries was generally good. Although there was widespread but low-level infection in the general population, the people were typically in better health then they were in later periods, a pattern consistent with worldwide evolutionary trajectories (Martin, this volume). A more varied diet and a less dense population than later in prehistory may account for the people's relatively good health. The number of ritually mutilated burials in the Anasazi area and the various established cases of slaughter among the Basketmakers suggest the prevalence of violence, head hunting, and witchcraft (Turner 1983; Wilcox and Haas, this volume). However, there is no clear evidence for organized warfare involving the control of resources.

There is also no strong indication of what is usually called social complexity; these people are presumed to have been simple hamlet farmers who supplemented their diet by hunting and collecting plant foods. The communities, however, were not parochial: they developed and maintained extensive and intensive exchange networks, as evidenced by the large amounts of marine shell found in even the smallest communities.

While the people of the Southwest were living a relatively simple life, societies to the south were evolving civilizations. After major remodeling circa AD 300, the city of Teotihuacán in the Valley of Mexico reached its height during this period.

Closer to the Southwest, the large central site of La Quemada was founded some-time before AD 400. The nature of the relationship of those southern polities to the Southwest remains conjectural (McGuire et al., this volume). The fact that Mesoamerica was the location of one of the world's great "pristine civilizations," however, does not mean that the transmission of technological innovations and other traits was all in a northward direction. The bow and arrow in use during this period in the northern Southwest (Geib and Bungart 1989) did not reach central Mexico until the Postclassic, about AD 900 (Hassig 1988). Likewise, the species of turkey that was domesticated both in the Southwest and in Mexico has the south-ern part of the southwestern United States and extreme northwestern Mexico as the limit of its natural range and was apparently first domesticated there (Breitburg 1988). (In fact, the relevant subspecies is confined to that area in the wild state.)

AD 600 TO 850

It is during this period that the concepts of Hohokam, Mogollon, and Anasazi seem most appropriate in terms of cultural traditions in the classic sense for which they were intended. Artifacts and facilities took on stylistic characteristics that closely identify them with one of the three named traditions. Artifact style often had a flamboyant and exuberant flair.

Population continued to increase and expand into areas previously little used for habitation, especially the uplands, although there were some local abandon-ments. The people experienced greater nutritional stress and more infections than in the earlier periods, but those conditions were still not severe. By this time, beans were grown throughout the region, providing amino acids, protein, and fat not available in maize or squash. Beans were an important subsistence item, but unlike maize they needed constant tending throughout the growing season and therefore may have encouraged increased sedentism.

Irrigation systems, ballcourts, and, somewhat later, platform mounds become more numerous and extensive in the Hohokam area. Such public structures may indicate that although Hohokam communities tended to be dispersed over the landscape, they were highly integrated into intercommunity networks. Among the Mogollon and Anasazi, a manifestation of large community or even intercommu-nity integration, the great kiva, became more prevalent and formalized, suggest-ing that ideology was an important integrating factor for much of the Southwest. The Mogollon continued to live in pithouses, as did some of the Anasazi. Anasazi dwellings and storage facilities, however, were often constructed above ground, resulting in pueblos. In some areas, such as large portions of the Colorado Pla-teaus, the Mimbres Valley and other Mogollon areas, parts of the Hohokam region, and northern Mexico, there was clustering of populations into larger communi-ties. The larger villages, however, did not grow at the expense of the hinterlands, as was common in later periods when there were wide areas devoid of perma-nently settled populations (Fish et al., this volume).

There was in many places a striking standardization of Anasazi architecture,

which, along with ceramic design styles of the White Mound and Kana-a traditions, indicates real social connectivity, with village networks and information
sharing. Larger villages in the north often consisted of modular clusters of rooms,
suggesting that communities were made up of smaller social elements. Since the
components of the larger sites are similar in size and morphology, they may represent a common social order for much of the northern region. There is no evidence
to suggest, however, that this similarity is the result of a unified social or political entity. Violence between communities was apparently quite common (Wilcox
and Haas, this volume).

In the south, the platform mounds and ballcourts, as well as the importation
of rubber balls (Haury 1937), signal an increase in interaction with Mesoamerican
societies. It was a period of decentralization in Mesoamerica, with the collapse of
the great urban state of Teotihuacán and a roughly simultaneous expansion of the
northern Mesoamerican frontier. Relatively large-scale polities, such as those of La
Quemada and Alta Vista, flourished north of the Lerma and Santiago rivers, which,
before the founding of La Quemada in the previous period, had been the northern boundary of Mesoamerica. Some researchers have argued that the new polities
were founded as outposts of central Mexican empires, and others interpret them
as relatively independent social and political entities (McGuire et al., this volume).

AD 950 TO 1100

The years 950 to 1100 witnessed great population increase and regional expansion. For the first time, there was a great deal of divergence in social forms between
localities. Some of those forms took on a considerable complexity, while others
remained more simply organized. In Tainter and Plog's terms (this volume), there
were both strong patterns—often produced by societies tending toward complexity, probably with elements of hierarchy, and belonging to regional systems—
and weak patterns—likely to be the products of simpler, probably more egalitarian societies interacting on a local scale.

Small drainages in the Hohokam country, the mountainous central zone of the
Southwest, and the western part of the Colorado Plateaus were characterized by
ceramics with local design styles and often by unique architectural features. The
development of local styles is so prevalent that early archaeologists named entire
new traditions in some areas, such as the Winslow and Virgin branches of the
Western Anasazi. The situation was different from that prevailing in earlier periods, when there had been widespread social interaction, apparently organized on
a simple level, as seen in the modularity of architecture in the north and the great
geographic extent of ceramic design styles such as Lino and Kana-a.

In other areas, there was a florescence based on earlier traditions. The Mimbres people, predominantly of central and southwestern New Mexico, aggregated
in large aboveground villages for the first time and greatly elaborated their ceramic
tradition (Anyon, Collins, and Bennett 1983)—changes concurrent with the beginnings of agricultural intensification and a climate unusually favorable for agri-

culture (Minnis 1985b). The Mimbres culture provides an example of a strong pattern not clearly associated with much social complexity.

Agricultural intensification is also evident in other places where population density increased, such as the Hohokam core area, where canal systems were extended and improved, and Chaco Canyon, where smaller but very sophisticated irrigation works were constructed. In fact, these two areas were the loci of important developments that took place concurrently with the establishment elsewhere of some local patterns and the florescence of others. Two large regional systems were initiated: the Chacoan system and that of the Salt-Gila Colonial and Sedentary period Hohokam. Both systems had considerable impact on large sections of the Southwest, but apparently little influence on each other (Crown and Judge 1991). The two large regional systems were organized differently and probably developed for different reasons. The Chacoan system evolved out of a need to manage the scarce resources of the San Juan Basin and incorporate communities in the surrounding areas, while the Hohokam system served to manage the abundance of the Lower Sonoran desert.

On the Colorado Plateaus and over much of the Mogollon area conditions were favorable to village agriculturalists: increased groundwater supplies, declining erosion, and increased precipitation. The improved climatic regime has often been viewed as contributing to the development of new traditions and the florescence of already established ones, the increase in population, the growth of large regional systems, and the establishment of permanent villages in areas that were previously used only seasonally.

The social orders that characterized the large regional systems and the more localized, simpler traditions are difficult to assess and have been a subject of great controversy (Tainter and Plog, this volume). The geographic extent of the large systems and of their exchange networks—and in the case of Chaco the obvious central planning of large towns—indicates a level of information sharing that required a high degree of coordination. The extensive regional systems were not simply aggregations of smaller local traditions but were qualitatively different in organization. Throughout the extent of each regional system a degree of peace must have prevailed, suggesting political ties as well as ideological and economic unification in these areas.

Some polities of Mesoamerica, such as Tula, were in an expansionist mode, and there was a vigorous northern Mexican frontier where, as in the Southwest, there was expansion into many areas that were unoccupied earlier (Phillips 1989). The groups along the west side of the Sierra Madre Occidental had numerous Mesoamerican characteristics, progressively weaker with the increase of distance from central Mexico. The Hohokam may be regarded as the farthest north, with the least Mesoamerican cast, of these many groups. Pyrites, mosaic mirrors, copper bells, and scarlet macaws provide firm evidence of Mesoamerican contact with the Hohokam at this time. Macaw remains are scarce, however, compared with those in Anasazi country, and the style of bell differs greatly between the two regions, suggesting different pathways of Mesoamerican contact (Nelson 1986).

The half-century from AD 1000 to 1050 has been called the Differentiation period because of the contemporaneous existence of many different sociocultural forms (Cordell and Gumerman 1989:10–11). Not all changes, however, involved increased variation. For example, much of what was called Mogollon had now lost a great deal of its distinctiveness, and some scholars refer to it as Anasazi. (In the Cíbola area a fusion of those two traditions took place, leading to widespread patterns that seem to exhibit fairly continuous evolution until the fifteenth century, and, in the case of Zuni, until the historic period.) Nevertheless, it is the range of complexity from simple organizational forms in some areas to much more complex ones in others that is striking.

AD 1140 TO 1200

This period coincides in the upland areas of the Southwest with a time of secondary environmental stress. Water tables declined slightly, and precipitation decreased rather uniformly over the Colorado Plateaus. There was a reorganization of population centers: striking abandonments (such as the Virgin Branch area and northeastern Black Mesa), cultural retrenchments (as in the case of Mimbres), the collapse of the Chacoan system, the transformation of the Hohokam system, and the appearance of new areas of florescence such as Mesa Verde and parts of the Rio Grande valley. Sites throughout the Southwest were now more clustered, as the previous period of expansion and growth in complexity gave way to one of considerable territorial reduction and, in places, a marked decrease in organizational complexity. The manner in which the Chacoan system collapsed suggests that the system was never highly integrated throughout its extent even at the height of its florescence. Whereas the system collapsed around 1140, Chaco Canyon itself was not abandoned, and there was new construction, albeit in a different form, with affinities to Mesa Verde. Furthermore, the Chacoan outliers at the extreme peripheries of the system continued to function as Chacoan-style communities for some time after 1140. Indeed, in the very remote communities, even at the height of the Chaco phenomenon, there was little evidence of sustained contact with Chaco Canyon (Lekson et al. 1988).

The Salt-Gila Hohokam network also declined. There was a contraction of the northern extent of the Hohokam and the completion of the abandonment of much of the Phoenix Basin nonriverine areas, which had begun a half-century earlier. The Tucson Basin Hohokam regional system began to develop, and elements of the Salado pattern began to appear in the core Hohokam area. Ballcourts were no longer constructed, and Hohokam platform mounds took on residential functions for the elites. Some of the hallmarks of earlier Hohokam, such as palettes, censers, and carved bowls, were no longer made, and many of the crafts took on a more uniform, mass-produced character. Far to the south, Tula collapsed, but the concurrent development of many large polities in western Mexico may have had a major effect on the Southwest (McGuire et al., this volume).

The Mesa Verde region underwent a major population expansion during this

period, a dramatic increase in construction, and an increase in interaction with other areas (Cordell, Doyel, and Kintigh, this volume; Rohn 1989). There was also major building activity in the Sinagua area near Flagstaff (Plog 1989).

Many of the Western Anasazi localities were abandoned, especially in the uplands (Fish et al., this volume), and there appears to have been a great deal of population movement and social experimentation. In some places, for example around the Grand Canyon, large areas were abandoned; in other places, like northeastern Black Mesa (Gumerman and Dean 1989), much smaller areas were depopulated. Some Pueblo groups moved farther out onto the Plains than they had before (McGuire et al., this volume).

The 1140-to-1200 period seems to be one in which, for reasons both environmental and cultural, there was a series of failures of existing lifeways and experimentation with new ones. Warfare became more prevalent and intensified in the early 1200s (Wilcox and Haas, this volume), and there were also more active cases of nutritional stress and trauma (Martin, this volume).

AD 1250 TO 1300

This was a period of dramatic change, with an acceleration of the tendency toward aggregation and agricultural intensification that began in the earlier period. During the last quarter of the thirteenth century, however, there was also severe environmental stress on the Colorado Plateaus, including the "Great Drought" and perhaps even a lowering of temperatures, which would have shortened the already marginal growing season.

Throughout the Southwest there were major relocations of population into much larger sites, resulting in a frenzy of construction (Cordell, Doyel, and Kintigh, this volume). Across a northern belt that includes the northern Kayenta Anasazi and the San Juan areas, such construction in both cliff shelters and open areas began before 1250 and terminated with large-scale abandonments at the end of the century. Across a long and broad central swatch of the Southwest, stretching from the Verde Valley to the Rio Grande basin, the tempo of construction seems to have started a few decades later than in the north. In the extreme south, for example at Casas Grandes in Chihuahua and the Trincheras of Sonora, the acceleration in construction seems to have occurred even later, about 1300.

Even while this period of construction was still underway in most of the Southwest, there was large-scale regional abandonment (Fish et al., this volume). Mesa Verde collapsed, and the San Juan Basin and much of the northwestern Anasazi area were abandoned, as was the Sinagua region around Flagstaff. Even in the Hohokam region, areas that emphasized upland agriculture were no longer used for year-round occupation. Parts of the central belt—namely the northern Rio Grande, Cíbola, the Hopi Mesas, the central Little Colorado River valley, and the White Mountain areas—had clusters of large sites. The Salado pattern, which occurred with the Classic Hohokam pattern in central Arizona, developed into a widespread phenomenon that would have an increasingly great impact over the southern belt, involving the clustering of large sites and the production of distinctive ceramics that would be widely traded and copied.

This is a period of strong patterns, which would continue in some areas until the 1450s and in others until much later. Many of the numerous cultural systems of this period exhibit strong internal cohesion. For example, there are highly patterned relationships within communities, as indicated by such things as architectural arrangements (Cordell, Doyel, and Kintigh, this volume) and by design styles on artifacts. This does not mean, of course, that all communities grew and were organized in the same way.

As well as strong internal cohesion within communities, there was intense interaction between communities. Often there were central sites that served as social, economic, and religious centers for nearby settlements. On a wider geographic scale, pan-Southwestern interaction intensified despite the greater distance between communities that resulted from aggregation and regional abandonment. Design style similarities and exchange items indicate sustained and intensive contact (Upham, Crown, and Plog, this volume). Many of the exchange networks centered on items with high symbolic content, such as design styles associated with the katsina cult of the Anasazi, which became widespread about this time. The scarlet macaw and its artistic representation became even more important than in earlier periods. Sites were spaced at regular intervals that seem to relate to communication and travel time (Jewett 1989).

These long-distance relationships undoubtedly involved instances of competition and conflict as well as cooperation and alliance. Casas Grandes in Chihuahua and Gallina in northeastern New Mexico were the locations of two widely separated groups that were both in a state of warfare with their neighbors (Wilcox and Haas, this volume). Skeletal remains also indicate a major increase in multiple pathologies and dental disease (Martin, this volume). The turkey, which had long been an important aspect of prehistoric Southwestern life, reached the apex of production at this time.

Direct Mesoamerican contact seems greatest during this period, even though Mesoamerica appears to have become decentralized in the wake of the Toltec collapse. The nature of the interaction with the south, however, is still a matter of great dispute (McGuire et al., this volume). The Hohokam continued to exhibit many Mesoamerican traits, and the katsina cult complex of the Anasazi has many southern characteristics, some of them perhaps already traceable in Mimbres ceramics. Copper bells from Mexico were now much more uniform in style across the Southwest than in earlier periods, suggesting a common source (Nelson 1986:161). Hohokam contact was intense with groups along the Lower Colorado River (the so-called Yuman area), and there was much trade in shell coming by a northern route from California to the Anasazi.

The issue of the existence of hierarchical social forms continues unresolved (Tainter and Plog, this volume; Upham, Crown, and Plog, this volume). The arguments for and against egalitarian or hierarchical types of sociopolitical organization have foundered on the use of categorical classifications such as tribe, chiefdom, or big-man forms of organization, and such categorization has proved of little help in understanding the development and organization of the variety of economic, social, and ideological systems in the Southwest (Tainter and Plog, this volume). What is apparent to all scholars is that there were various groups in the Southwest that differed in complexity and that their societies underwent processes of development and collapse in various places at various times. The argument should center around questions of how (and, if possible, why) the forms evolved when and where they did, something of the character of their organization (which might or might not fit into the usual categories), and the processes by which some of them collapsed.

It is during this period that the question of the relationship of prehistoric behavior to historic and ethnographic descriptions becomes of great concern, especially in the north. The kinds of inferences that can be made about the past, given the rich descriptions of living peoples whose cultures have been greatly transformed but still have obviously close ties to the past, have been hotly debated (Levy 1989, 1990). Following an era in which too much trust was placed in using ethnography, early history, and tradition to interpret the archaeological record, it is unfortunate that there was a reaction that went too far in the opposite direction. It would be useful to return, with caution, to the use of such materials. A simple example is provided by the techniques suggested by Murdock (1949) for the reconstruction of prehistoric social organization in ways that present some analogy with linguistic reconstruction (Levy 1990). These considerations apply even more to the succeeding period.

AD 1425 TO 1450

This was a period of very rapid change. Because it is closest to the historic period, it should have the most detailed data; ironically, however, it is replete with contradictions and unanswered questions (Kintigh 1990a). Huge areas were abandoned around this time: the Verde Valley, the central Little Colorado region, the White Mountains, the Salt-Gila Basin, and the Casas Grandes region, as well as a wide stretch of territory between the last two areas. If we were to adopt a broader definition of the Southwest, like the "Greater Southwest" of Carroll L. Riley (1987), we would also include among the casualties of the fifteenth century the Trincheras culture of the Altar and Concepción valleys of Sonora and the pueblos along the Rio Grande below the Jornada del Muerto and above the region of the junction with the Conchos River ("La Junta"). Note that with that inclusion the areas of abandonment and cultural retrenchment remain contiguous. We would also count among the survivors some villages of La Junta, as well as Riley's "Serrana Province," which covers Ures and part of the Sonora River valley.

The fact that all these areas are contiguous suggests the abandonments were related, but imprecise dating and the lack of evidence for causes inhibit our understanding of the population dynamics of the late prehistoric period. Because of the lack of accurate dates, even gross population figures are difficult to estimate

(Dean, Doelle, and Orcutt, this volume). Some of the abandonments might have occurred as early as 1375 or as late as 1520.

It is not possible to understand to what extent the profound changes that took place in or just after the fifteenth century were the result of internally generated factors or of factors impinging from outside the Southwest. The Athabascan intrusion cannot be completely excluded as a cause of abandonments, nor can a precocious Spanish impact through the spread of exotic diseases. The majority view seems to be that the major changes took place before the possible arrival of Spanish diseases and before the appearance of the Athabascans, although there is no conclusive evidence on which to base an opinion.

The environment in the north continued to be difficult for agriculturalists. Water tables were low, arroyo cutting persisted, and at the beginning of the period precipitation was below normal. Hopi, Zuni, Acoma, and the Rio Grande region were the only areas that remained occupied in the north.

The process of aggregation continued throughout the Southwest (Cordell, Doyel, and Kintigh, this volume), and communities became even larger. Also, there was a decline in the tendency toward local abandonments, accompanied by the building of new settlements, that had characterized the previous period (see Kintigh 1990a for the situation at Zuni). Episodes of flooding in the Salt-Gila drainage, which may have destroyed irrigation networks, have been postulated to explain the changes that are observed in Hohokam country. The Salt-Gila Basin was depopulated, but the Tucson area apparently retained much of its population (Doelle and Wallace 1991), albeit with altered cultural patterns. The Salado and Classic Hohokam cultural patterns disappeared, and Casas Grandes collapsed (Dean and Ravesloot 1988). Warfare apparently played a part in the Hohokam abandonment.

The large areas between the clusters of pueblos in the north may have been "no-man's land" or, as Dean has quipped, "every-man's land"—a type of commons for the use of natural resources. This was a period of major competition among the eastern Pueblos for trade with the Plains groups, although there is also evidence for the existence of "alliances," perhaps corresponding to the "provinces" identified by the conquistadores.

The connectivity between clusters of sites in the late prehistoric era, which is evident in exchange patterns, artifact distribution patterns, and design motifs, has been attributed to a variety of factors, including interaction between elite groups (Lightfoot 1984; Upham 1982), economic and social alliances (Upham, Crown, and Plog, this volume), religious cults (Adams 1991; McGuire 1986), and social, ideological, and economic control from the south (Di Peso 1974a; LeBlanc 1986). In any case, the later fifteenth century was an era of few—but intensified—social, economic, and religious networks.

ELEMENTS OF STABILITY AND CHANGE

Throughout the world there tends to be a correlation among the following elements: growing population, intensification of food production, sedentism, in-

creased diversity of social roles, and the institutionalization of long-distance economic and social relationships (Johnson and Earle 1987). The detailed reasons for
the connections among these phenomena are not altogether clear, however.

In a very general way, the similarities that have been observed in the evolution
of Southwestern societies can be attributed to some combination of three kinds of
factors: universal processes, which can be expected to take place anywhere under
similar natural and cultural conditions; the diffusion of behavioral patterns from
one region to another; and local historical accident. It is likely that all three types
of factors reflect the reality of Southwestern prehistory.

There are, of course, those scholars who do not recognize broad patterns of
similarity in Southwestern prehistory but concentrate instead on the evidence for
idiosyncratic behavior. It is certainly true that the degree of variation across the
Southwest fluctuated dramatically, and it is those very perturbations that provide
some insight into the processes of cultural transformation.

The general consistency of the earliest definable Southwestern patterns, recognizable in the first centuries AD, has often been noted (Haury 1962a; LeBlanc
1982; Martin and Plog 1973). These early parallels might be a result less of interactions throughout the region than of the generalized and informal nature of the
artifacts and structures and the requirements imposed by the environment and
the state of technology. House forms are simple and similar, but that is common
in many parts of the world shortly after a reliance on agriculture begins (Gilman
1987), with increasing residential stability stemming from greater predictability
of subsistence resources. Pottery is technologically well made, but forms and decorations are simple, often with designs obviously derived from basketry patterns.
The colors are gray to reddish brown, again a worldwide phenomenon. In short,
a simple technology (e.g., unslipped ceramics and elementary, partially subsurface dwellings with brush and dirt superstructures) limits material expression,
and artifacts and structures will take on an appearance of similarity that may not
be the result of diffusion—although the large amount of marine shell, especially
from the Sea of Cortés, does indicate widespread interaction.

In the centuries leading up to the end of the first millennium, there was a slow
development in all the major Southwestern environments, from the high and low
deserts to the central mountain zone. The century and a half from AD 1000 to 1150
saw a tremendous increase in social differentiation throughout the entire Southwest and the establishment of the first very large polities. But how do we account
for the great diversity of social organizational forms?

The increase in variety of social conventions is in many ways analogous to
the "Cambrian explosion" in biological evolution, a time when large numbers and
many kinds of multicellular organisms evolved. This is in striking contrast to the
preceding period, when there were many fewer life forms, with a much greater
degree of similarity. The sudden appearance and diversity of life forms in the
Cambrian has been attributed to the occupation of a "vacant ecology," an environment that was largely unoccupied and receptive to evolutionary experimentation
(Morris 1989). In a somewhat analogous process, there was such a great increase

in population and range expansion across the Southwest that almost every niche was filled by AD 1100 (Fish et al., this volume). Furthermore, numerous types of social organization were experimented with and succeeded for at least a short time. As has been said for the Anasazi, given the open spaces and the ameliorating environment of the period, any of a number of adaptive strategies would have worked—and did (Plog et al. 1988).

As examples of the diverse types of social—and probably political and ideological—organizations that could be accommodated under the general rubric of Anasazi during a time of benevolent environmental conditions, we may consider those of the Chacoan system, northeastern Black Mesa, and the Hopi Buttes.

The Chaco Canyon tradition in the arid and environmentally homogeneous San Juan Basin is epitomized by nine elaborately designed massive multistoried pueblos, numerous great kivas, and a network of "roadways" extending far into the countryside (Vivian 1990). The Chacoans reached a level of complexity unknown in other parts of the Anasazi world until centuries later. Certain roadways link Chaco Canyon to some of the large sites, called outliers, which had structures related to the great houses in or near Chaco Canyon. What is known as the Chacoan regional system apparently impacted a huge area of the northern Southwest and, at least in the San Juan Basin and its periphery, involved coordination in the social, economic, and presumably religious spheres (with a significant emphasis on astronomy). The variation in the Chacoan sites in the hinterlands suggests that they maintained different kinds of relationships with the center in Chaco Canyon itself.

The Anasazi of northern Black Mesa responded to the improving environment after AD 1000 in a very different way from the Chacoans (Nichols and Smiley 1985). Instead of constructing a central hub, they filled nearly every small mesa, sage flat, and valley with five- to fifteen-room farming communities. Most of the villages had their own kivas or were located near sites with kivas, and there were no great kivas or other indications of a pan-community ideological system.

The Hopi Buttes area, immediately to the south of Black Mesa, was also characterized by a dispersed settlement system. Sites were small, each consisting of several pithouses, occasional surface rooms, and, in a few cases, kivas (Gumerman 1988b). Unlike Black Mesa's relatively independent communities, however, the farmsteads of the Hopi Buttes were apparently integrated by a regional ideological system. A single large site served as a focal point for religious and probably economic activities. The site has an unusually high ratio of ceremonial rooms to dwellings and a large public plaza, serving the ceremonial and economic needs of the many scattered farmsteads.

In sum, these three traditions, all called Anasazi, took very different paths and each developed a distinctive character. Each path was successful for some period of time. But the three areas reacted differently and at somewhat different times to the increasing environmental stress after about AD 1140. The sociopolitical, economic, and ideological organizational forms they had developed under more benevolent environmental regimes conditioned their responses to periods of stress.

After the fifteenth century, with the consolidation of the Southwestern population into comparatively few "provinces," there was a reduced variety of social forms. This is not to say that there was uniformity in material culture, but that there were a few large polities, each of which practiced a degree of cooperation and coordination over a large area. The demise of many of the earlier types of sociopolitical organization tried out in the 1000-to-1150 period parallels the wave of biological extinctions at the end of the Cambrian era, which resulted in reduced morphological diversity.

There is a recognized, although poorly understood, relationship among the smaller numbers of social forms, the larger and more densely packed population centers, the presumably coordinated decision making, and the geographically extensive networks of cooperation and competition that linked the surviving polities. The polities, for the most part more complex and formally organized than many of the earlier ones, interacted with one another through an intertwining of religion, economy, and social organization. These relationships were not always stable; in some areas, such as the eastern frontier of the Southwest, some shifting of alliances and competition seems to have occurred.

CONCLUSION

About two thousand years ago, the Southwest was populated with scattered semi-mobile bands dabbling with the domestication of plants. Around four hundred years ago, the Spaniards found large sedentary communities, some with hints of statelike features, as well as unoccupied areas with the ruins of large public works. This is an overgeneralization, of course, which glosses over the remarkable variation from place to place in the evolving patterns of simplicity and complexity. The question is, How can the idiosyncratic pulse of change in each small locality be harmonized with the grander social transformations throughout the Southwest?

Proponents of synthesizing schemes prefer to focus on general trends: increasing population, population aggregation, an increasing number of adaptive strategies and then a reduction in their number, agricultural intensification, similar responses to environmental change, and the synchronous development or breakdown of regional systems. Those researchers who focus on the variety in the archaeological record recognize that imprecision in dating sometimes makes conditions seem more nearly synchronous than they are. They can point to different responses to similar environmental conditions, the role of historical accident, and the simultaneous existence of numerous cultural patterns throughout the Southwest. The two perspectives are, of course, not mutually exclusive.

In cultural as well as biological evolution, the scale of one's perspective determines the kinds of questions that can be successfully addressed. The premise of this volume is that it is worthwhile to take a broad perspective and consider the Southwest as whole—as a single but heterogeneous social entity. One can then study the evolution of culture from a hunting and gathering stage to that of ranked societies in these contiguous semiarid lands on the northern frontier of Mexico—lands inhabited by peoples with similar domesticates, roughly similar technologies, and apparent synchronisms in settlement behavior and social trans-formations. The roles played by universal processes, diffusion, and local historical accident may become clearer as a result of such a unified approach.

Numerous agents of change have been postulated for Southwestern prehis-tory, including the natural environment, technological innovation, demographic factors, interaction with neighbors and invaders, and internal social conditions. Undoubtedly, all these factors—and combinations of them—have had a role in shaping the culture history of the region.

Traditionally, environmental conditions have been the most common explana-tion for cultural stability and change in the prehistoric Southwest. There can be no question that perturbations in the environment affected the cultural history of both small drainages and large provinces. The close correlation of only a few variables (such as the numbers, density, and distribution of population) with environmental conditions underscores the important role of environment in most schemes of cul-ture change (Dean, Doelle, and Orcutt, this volume). Random historical accident, however, and the existing social, economic, and ideological conditions must also be taken into account in understanding the responses to changing environmental conditions, as the examples of Chaco, Black Mesa, and the Hopi Buttes indicate.

The conventional wisdom in our age of extremely rapid social change is that technological innovation drives social transformation. Leslie White (1959) pro-vided a formal gauge for measuring the stage of cultural complexity on the basis of the capture of energy, and more recently, Wendel Oswalt (1976) has tried to quantify the rank order of complexity on the basis of "techno-units." There is no question that the consequences of the initiation of food production in the South-west are reflected in the forms of societal metamorphosis that took place through-out the remainder of prehistory. The incorporation of domesticates from the south into the subsistence economy was the agent that made possible similar trajectories of change in different parts of the region.

Still, extractive technology changed very little in the prehistoric Southwest. It is true that the bow and arrow replaced the atlatl, permitting more efficient hunt-ing from ambush; ceramics became widespread, allowing greater variety in cook-ing and food-storage techniques and enhancing nutrition; simple water control systems were introduced, permitting new areas to come under cultivation; and the two-handed mano and trough metate made the production of large amounts of cornmeal more efficient (Morris 1990). But these innovations occurred early in the first centuries AD, and their impact on Southwestern society could not by itself account for the many centuries of subsequent social change. Later, there were technological improvements, such as the use of mealing bins to increase the effi-ciency of food preparation, the expansion and refinement of irrigation networks, and the development of building techniques that permitted the construction of multistoried structures. There is no evidence, however, of the introduction of dra-matically new technologies.

The trend toward increasing complexity in the Southwest was a result not only of technological innovation but of changes in the organization and management of social relationships. Increasing populations (Dean, Doelle, and Orcutt, this volume), increasing dependence on domesticated plants, and concomitant changes in settlement and storage behavior (Wills and Huckell, this volume) required fundamental social changes. In later centuries, extensive and sophisticated irrigation systems, road construction and maintenance, the planning and building of massive structures and elaborate public architecture, the increasing scale of cooperation and of conflict or competition, and the concentration of the increasing population into larger communities demanded ever more complex and specialized forms of social relationships (Neitzel 1991).

Such changes must have involved increasing power differences. The management of large numbers of people to develop and maintain the complex systems required specialization in knowledge and skills. The existence of great kivas and of platform mounds and compounds, as well as the spread of the katsina cult, suggests that the organization of the increasingly diverse social roles in Southwestern society was accomplished largely through ideological means. The symbolic ordering of world view is sufficiently apparent in many architectural features (Fritz 1978; Sofaer, Marshall, and Sinclair 1989) to indicate that the pervasive ideological ordering of daily life in contemporary Pueblo society (Ortiz 1962) had its origins in prehistoric times.

As is indicated by numerous papers in this volume, there are disadvantages to individuals in the trend toward cultural complexity. The incidence of infectious disease increases, as does trauma. Access to information and other resources becomes more unequal. Individual or small-group autonomy is often sacrificed for benefits accruing to much larger groups. Nevertheless, the inequitable distribution of power, information, and other resources is embedded in a social system that serves the needs of the large number of individuals who constitute the society. Changes in complexity within different localities in the Southwest region indicate that some strategies were successful for some places at some times under certain environmental conditions. None was successful consistently.

In the future, explanations for trends in cultural evolution will, we believe, require a more balanced approach than has typically been the case in the past. Narrow ruling hypotheses must be replaced by ones that consider a wide range of cultural and natural variables and various combinations of them. We would like to see a concern for the straightforward description of what appears to have happened in prehistory, coupled with a willingness to explore a variety of forms of explanation. In addition, new analytical techniques, as well as the rehabilitation of old ones (as suggested by Levy 1989), can help to provide more realistic interpretations of culture change in the past.

——— *Acknowledgments* ———

We gratefully acknowledge Robert Euler, Ben Nelson, Rolf Sinclair, and David Wilcox for their helpful comments on this paper.

3

Economic Implications of Changing Land-Use Patterns in the Late Archaic

W. H. WILLS AND BRUCE B. HUCKELL

IN THIS CHAPTER WE ARGUE that the introduction of domesticated plants to the American Southwest between approximately 1500 and 1000 BC was followed by changes in land-use patterns that suggest important economic reorganization. We interpret current archaeological information as reflecting little direct intensification of agricultural production, which may help account for previous arguments that early agricultural investment by Southwestern peoples had only minor social or economic impact (see Haury 1962a; Woodbury and Zubrow 1979; Ford 1981; Minnis 1985a). We argue instead that following the adoption of domesticates, a complex mutualism evolved between cultivation and foraging in which agricultural production enhanced foraging efficiency. The economic role of agriculture probably did not shift toward increased yields and surplus production until after the introduction of ceramics around AD 200 and the subsequent emergence of sedentary communities.

Our discussion is primarily addressed to the "Late Archaic" period, from approximately 1500 BC to AD 200, and the conditions that may have promoted continued involvement with food production, rather than the period preceding the initial acquisition of domesticates. There is an increasingly large body of data for the temporal and spatial patterning of early cultigens, much of which contradicts adoption models based on more limited evidence (see Simmons 1986; Long et al. 1986; Huckell 1988, 1990; Wills 1988a; Roth 1989). These patterns have important implications for the conditions favoring the initial adoption of domesticates, but our emphasis is the effect of plant cultivation on Southwestern economic systems rather than the changes in hunter-gatherer adaptations that promoted acquisition.

Nonetheless, it is necessary to begin with an overview of some of the socioeconomic developments during the Late Archaic that contrast with earlier archaeological indications of economic organization. For example, in the Late Archaic there was a dramatic increase and elaboration of pithouse architecture from previous time periods. Although archaeologists frequently dicker over whether semisubterranean Archaic structures are houses, huts, shelters, or some other typological creature, it remains clear that architectural structures increased in number and formality after the introduction of agriculture (e.g., Schiffer 1972; Martin and Plog 1973; Plog 1974; Gilman 1987). Intensive excavation studies in many areas of the Southwest have revealed large numbers of architectural structures dating to the Late Archaic in places where surface indications had not suggested such features (e.g., Huckell and Huckell 1984; Nichols and Smiley 1985; O'Leary and Biella 1987; Roth 1989; Mabry 1990).

The appearance of numerous dwelling structures in the Late Archaic parallels an elaboration of mortuary practices that resulted in interment. Only a very few burials from the Southwest can be assigned positively to sites earlier than the Late Archaic (e.g., Sayles and Antevs 1941:13, 65; Waters 1986:52–58), and most Late Archaic burials are associated with sites that have pit structures (Huckell 1988). In some areas, pit structures may have been constructed for storage rather than occupation and used secondarily as burial pits (e.g., Kidder and Guernsey 1919). But pits and bags and baskets that were most likely used for storage increase markedly during the Late Archaic as well, and they are frequently found in association with larger pit structures (see Sayles 1983; Eddy and Cooley 1983; Nichols and Smiley 1985; Smiley, Parry, and Gumerman 1986; Wills 1988a). Finally, many Late Archaic pit structure sites have thick and extensive midden deposits that seem to indicate either prolonged or very repetitive settlement use (Huckell 1988; see also Agogino and Hibben 1958).

Most of these Late Archaic patterns—pit structures, storage features, and midden accretion—are found in preagricultural sites, albeit in varying degree in different regions, but not until the Late Archaic do they occur in large numbers and high local densities. Together they indicate an increase in residential stability, with greater investment in facilities at particular settlements and apparently more regular and/or long-term use of those sites. Environmental data for the period between 1500 and 1000 BC indicate generally wetter, cooler climates than today and probably higher carrying capacity for hunter-gatherers than would be possible under current conditions (see Freeman 1972; Dering 1979; Fredlund 1984; Hall 1985; K. L. Peterson 1988).

IDENTIFYING ECONOMIC CHANGE
IN THE LATE ARCHAIC

Archaeologists have often measured the value of agriculture in terms of surplus production; higher yields per unit of land than can be obtained from natural resource availability is a commonly accepted explanation for agricultural origins (e.g., Cohen 1977; Rindos 1984; Pryor 1986; Redding 1988). Yield is partially a function of labor investment, and since plants are immobile resources, increases in sedentism associated with agriculture are generally taken to indicate intensification of agricultural production (e.g., Nichols 1987).

Sedentism obviously occurs in the absence of food production (e.g., Flannery 1972b, 1973), however, and consequently the inferred causal effect of cultivation on mobility patterns ought to be demonstrated independently of the evidence employed to identify increases in sedentism. In other words, it is unreasonable to presume that plant cultivation resulted in greater residential stability when there are factors other than cultivation that may support increased group sedentism. While the earliest dated cultigens occur in contexts of intensive site use, clearly indicating linkage, data directly tied to agricultural production during the Late Archaic after the first incorporation of cultigens do not appear to reflect intensification of agricultural production. By intensification we mean increased dependence on food production at the expense of other economic tactics. In the following section we outline the justification for this conclusion.

Domesticatory Processes in Cultigens

Radiocarbon assays confirm that a suite of three cultigens—maize (*Zea mays*), bean (*Phaseolus vulgaris*), and squash (*Cucurbita pepo*)—was introduced to the Southwest between at least 1200 and 1000 BC and possibly as early as 1500 BC. Dates for the earliest maize and squash overlap statistically, but the oldest dates for beans are not reliably coeval. Bottle gourd (*Lagenaria siceraria*), identified by Ford (1981, 1985) as a Late Archaic cultigen, has not yet been directly dated to this period. These domesticated plants are tropical in origin and poorly adapted to the dryness and short growing seasons of the Southwest (Kaplan 1981; Galinat 1985; Benz 1986); thus, their survival was entirely dependent upon human cultivation.

The domesticatory dependency on maize was partially offset by the plant's exceptional phenotypic plasticity. Through isolation and manipulation (selection) of maize, humans can induce a tremendous amount of phenotypic variation in very short periods of time, often on the order of only a few years (Iltis 1983:893). The extraordinary number of maize races in the Americas is the result of human efforts to adapt maize to varying edaphic, climatic, and topographic settings (Benz 1986:22, 381; see also Johannessen 1982). An example of maize plasticity is found in the prehistoric eastern United States, where the introduction of maize around AD 200 was followed by rapid evolution of the plant (King 1987:12).

There is currently no similar pattern of rapid morphological change in maize following its first appearance in the Southwest. Nearly all early maize identified in the region to date is a many-rowed flint or popcorn, often compared to the modern race Chapalote (see Mangelsdorf 1974; Ford 1981, 1985; Donaldson 1984; Galinat 1985, 1988; Fish et al. 1986; Long et al. 1986; Smiley, Parry, and Gumerman 1986; Huckell and Huckell 1988). Since morphological changes may reflect not genetic change but environmental effects, the consistency among early maize specimens is all the more surprising (see Iltis 1983). The best evidence for diversification within Southwestern maize, probably from the existing genetic pool without new introductions from Mesoamerica (see Ford 1981; Galinat 1988), is not seen until the ceramic period, after about AD 200 (Minnis 1985a:331; Ford 1985:351).

Barring the discovery of more evolved maize varieties from Late Archaic sites, it appears that for at least a thousand years, and perhaps up to 1,500 years in some places, the plasticity found in maize was little exploited by Southwestern cultivators. This assessment does not require that prehistoric farmers were cognizant of plant genetics or even reproductive processes. Johannessen (1982:86–87) found that modern Indians in Guatemala who have no scientific understanding of genetic relationships nevertheless make decisions about selection for maize varieties that produce directional trends in maize physiology. In selecting seeds for planting, the farmers studied by Johannessen were most concerned about the length and diameter of the cob that produced the seed, as well as the color of the seeds; they were much less concerned with the size of individual seeds (Johannessen 1982:86). The lack of evidence for selection in ear characteristics for over a thousand years during the Late Archaic at least suggests that the *potential* for manipulation of maize varieties was not well exploited. However, it is possible that within this basic stock there was selection for performance in particular environmental settings, but that these adaptations (e.g., rapid maturation or drought resistance) did not result in morphological differences.

Two other explanations might account for the lack of variation in early maize morphology. First, maize may have had a fairly stable role within Late Archaic economies, such that it was not subjected to selective pressures to increase productivity through phenotypic change. Second, human population mobility might have been relatively high, making effective isolation of maize varieties difficult. In the latter case, population movement could have inhibited the development of varieties adapted to particular habitats and provoked a continual exchange of crop seed that swamped any incipient evolutionary changes.

There are also few data supporting genetic manipulation of beans or squash. Admittedly, information on these cultigens is much sparser than for maize, but several botanical reviews document surprisingly little evidence for change. Kaplan (1981:245), for example, writes in a study on the origin of domesticated beans that there is no prehistoric evidence for any increase in the size of beans through time in either North or South America. Similarly, botanists have noted a relative lack of diversity in Southwestern cucurbits (Cutler and Whitaker 1961:478). In fact, the differences between *Curcurbita pepo* and its probable ancestor, *Cucurbita texana,* are most evident only at the level of enzyme systems (Decker 1988). So again, the Late Archaic does not seem to have been a period during which much human effort was directed toward intensification of cultigen productivity through phenotypic selection.

DIETARY AND NUTRITIONAL INDICES OF ECONOMIC CHANGE

Dietary studies are probably the most direct approach to assessing the role of agriculture in prehistoric societies. Southwestern researchers have used studies of human bone chemistry and coprolite (feces) content to reconstruct ancient diets, and although these studies have suggested high levels of cultigen intake during the ceramic period (after AD 200), data available for the interpretation of Late Archaic diets are limited.

Stable isotope ratios in human bone collagen are increasingly utilized to measure proportional dietary contributions from different types of plants and animals (e.g., van der Merwe 1982; DeNiro 1987; Price 1989). New World researchers have focused particularly on maize, because it is a C4 plant introduced from Latin America to regions such as the eastern United States where C4 plants are uncommon (Buikstra et al. 1987). In such areas, a high degree of dietary input from maize should be reflected in the ratio of 13C/12C in collagen.

In practice, the estimation of dietary contributions from C4 plants in environments characterized by C3 plants is complicated by a range of factors that are poorly understood (Sillen, Sealy, and van der Merwe 1989). Parkington (1987), for example, argued that scientists do not yet know very well the combination of factors that produce 13C/12C ratios thought to indicate high C4 plant consumption; local dietary factors must be precisely specified before ratios are interpreted. As an illustration, chemists now know that high levels of protein consumption can change isotopic values to look more like C4 intake than was actually the case (Sillen, Sealy, and van der Merwe 1989:505). Elevated protein ingestion among human groups might have been a common seasonal pattern in portions of the prehistoric Southwest (Speth 1983) and must be considered in stable isotope studies.

A more immediate issue for Late Archaic agriculture is the fact that indigenous C4 plants are common in the Southwest, and many major economic plants fall in this group. Among the most common economic plants recovered from preagricultural sites, particularly in human coprolites, are amaranth and chenopodium (Fry 1976; Reinhard, Ambler, and McGuffie 1985). Amaranth is C4, as are many chenopodium species. Other C4 species documented prehistorically and historically in the Southwest and Great Basin include mesquite and several grass species (Stewart 1940; Doebley 1984; Fish et al. 1985; see Downton 1975; Edwards and Walker 1983; Jones 1985). CAM plants (primarily lower-elevation vegetation), including agave and cacti, may shift photosynthetic pathways, assuming characteristics of either C3 or C4 plants depending on local environmental conditions. Archaeological plant remains from Late Archaic contexts attest to the common occurrence of C4 and CAM plants, even in association with features containing cultigen macrofossils (e.g., Ford 1984). Moreover, the spatial distribution of C4, C3, and CAM plants in the Southwest varies by temperature and moisture gradients, leading to complex geographical patterns wherein the relative importance of different plants to human foragers would have varied with patterns of mobility (fig. 3.1).

Matson and Chisholm (1991) argued that 13C/12C ratios in human bone dated to about 2000 BP in the Colorado Plateaus indicated almost complete reliance on a diet of C4 plants and inferred heavy dependence on maize. The ratios

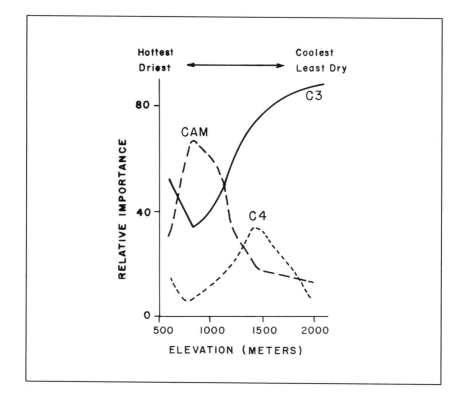

Figure 3.1. Proportional changes in C3, CAM, and C4 Southwestern plants by elevation in the Sacramento Mountains, southern New Mexico.

obtained in their study are among the lowest obtained from any archaeological sample worldwide (see van der Merwe 1982; DeNiro 1987) and clearly reflect massive C4 input. Coprolite analysis from the same contexts indicates that maize was a major contributor to the diet at these particular sites. Whether these collagen values mean that maize was a *dominant* dietary item or that the economic systems were reliant on food production does not seem as clear, however, given the presence of other C4 plants, elevational variation in plant groups, and the difficulties in interpreting 13C/12C values for individual dietary items.

Nonetheless, the indication of a high degree of dietary input from C4 plants and/or animals that consume large quantities of C4 plants does indicate a fairly intensive focus on certain types of plants and animals. Even with a high potential input from maize, the levels observed by Matson and Chisholm could point to a focus on grasses and lower elevation vegetation (CAMs) and on animals like rabbits and small mammals that feed extensively on C4 plants (large game such as deer and antelope are browsers that feed mostly on C3 shrubs and forbs). In general, the data reported by Matson and Chisholm can be interpreted as reflecting high dietary input from relatively low-return resources (cf. Hard and Mauldin 1989; Schoeninger 1990).

AGRICULTURAL TECHNOLOGY

A common indication of agricultural intensification is technological development to increase productivity. Technological indicators in the Southwest might range from digging implements (hoes, dibble sticks) to water control devices (dams, walls, canals) to field systems to processing tools (grinding stones). Little evidence now exists that documents investment in agricultural technology during the Late Archaic.

Numerous studies have suggested changes in grinding stone technology that parallel increased reliance on maize in the prehistoric Southwest (e.g., Lancaster 1983; LeBlanc 1982; Hard 1985; Hard and Mauldin 1989; Morris 1990). In general, as the amount of time spent processing maize increases, the surface area of grinding stones increases in an apparent attempt to raise processing efficiency. In southern Arizona, Late Archaic manos are larger, on average, than older manos (Huckell 1990), but increases in grinding area are most noticeable after about AD 200. Late Archaic grinding stones seem to exhibit strong continuity with grinding stones found throughout the Southwest in preagricultural settings (LeBlanc 1982).

Archaeologists have also not yet been able to document water control systems or agricultural fields that date to the Late Archaic. According to Ford (1981, 1985), small gardens requiring minimal preparation and maintenance, rather than large fields, were probably the primary cultivation practice during the Late Archaic. The lack of bordered plots, terracing, or other surface modification is consistent with the inference that cultivation areas were probably small and dispersed.

REGIONAL ECONOMIC VARIABILITY IN THE LATE ARCHAIC

Despite the lack of direct evidence in the Late Archaic for agricultural intensification, we know that important changes in settlement organization and mobility occurred at about the time of the initial adoption of domesticates; therefore, we need to consider the nature of those organizational changes more closely. In order to compare archaeological patterns during the Late Archaic related to economic change, we have divided the Southwest into three areas that correspond to major physiographic regions. They are (1) the northern Sonoran and Chihuahuan Basin and Range, which includes deserts, grasslands, and woodlands; (2) the mesa and canyon piñon-juniper grasslands of the Colorado Plateaus; and (3) the montane mixed conifer and grasslands of the Mogollon Highlands. These three "regions" are broadly drawn and conflate a considerable amount of environmental diversity, but the early agricultural data from each region come from a limited number of sites that are located in distinct ecological habitats, and thus the comparisons are clearer than our divisions indicate.

SONORAN AND CHIHUAHUAN BASIN AND RANGE

A remarkable amount of new information on early Southwestern agriculture has come from the arid desert margins and semiarid grasslands of southeastern Arizona and south-central New Mexico. These data derive primarily from radiocarbon assays on maize, especially accelerator dates (Long et al. 1986; Upham et al. 1987). Maize dates range up to 3125 BP (uncorrected), which makes agriculture in these areas as old as in any other portion of the Southwest (table 3.1). New dates contradict previous assumptions that domesticated plants were introduced to the Southwest through highland mountain ranges (Huckell 1987, 1988; Huckell and Huckell 1988; Wills 1988a; see Haury 1962a; Ford 1981). But much more important, Late Archaic agriculture in desert margins and grasslands occurs in site contexts that indicate intensive settlement occupation.

The best evidence for such Late Archaic sites comes from southeastern Arizona, and the eastern Tucson Basin in particular. Huckell (1987, 1988; Huckell and Huckell 1988) described a series of alluvial sites in the Santa Cruz, Cienega, San Pedro, and Sulphur Spring valleys that have thick deposits of cultural midden (0.30–0.75 m) over extensive areas (50–150 m). Many of these localities have pithouses, burials, hearths, apparent storage pits, and high densities of artifacts. Several sites produced macrofossil evidence for maize, with direct radiocarbon dates on maize specimens ranging between 2800 and 1600 BP. Some of these site locations and associated features were described by Sayles and Antevs (1941; Sayles 1983) and Eddy (Eddy 1958; Eddy and Cooley 1983), but only recently have they been confirmed as agricultural sites, including the Fairbank site, Benson 5:16, and the Charleston site (Huckell 1990).

In the Santa Cruz, Cienega, and San Pedro drainages, three deeply buried alluvial sites in riverine settings are found with structures interpreted as dwellings. These pithouses are round to oval in shape and range in diameter from 2.5 m to 4.5 m and in depth from 0.25 m to 0.50 m. The Donaldson site (AZ EE:2:30) on Cienega Creek is illustrative, with two dwelling structures and numerous extramural bell-shaped pits, hearths, and small pit features (Eddy 1958; Huckell 1988). Recent radiocarbon dates from the Donaldson site include wood charcoal assays at 2400±90 BP (A-4200) and 2380±90 BP (A-4201). The total areal extent of the Donaldson site midden exposed by arroyo cutting is at least 120 m in length and 0.40 m in thickness. Huckell (1988:64) argues that the Donaldson site and others known in the same area (Pantano site, Los Ojitos) reflect intensive settlement occupations, possibly by large groups and perhaps for relatively long periods of time. Evidence for domesticated plants has been recovered from each of the riverine sites above, including maize cob fragments, occasional kernels, and maize pollen. Probable domestic beans were found at Los Ojitos (Huckell 1988:64).

In addition to buried alluvial sites, important Late Archaic agricultural sites are found on terraces and lower piedmont slopes of the eastern Tucson Basin. The Milagro site on Tanque Verde Creek has been extensively tested, revealing a midden deposit at least 40 m long and 0.3 m thick (Huckell and Huckell 1984;

TABLE 3.1.

Selected radiocarbon assays on Late Archaic cultigens from Southwest desert-grasslands

Site	Sample	Material	Date	Calibrated Date[a]
Tornillo Rockshelter	GX-12720	8 maize cob fragments	3225 ± 240 BP	BC 1807–1195
Milagro Site	AA-1074	Maize cupule	2780 ± 90 BP	BC 1074–830
Tumamoc Hill	A-3750	Maize cupule	2470 ± 270 BP	BC 898–212
Los Ojitas	A-3501	Maize cupule	2270 ± 200 BP	BC 757–90

[a]Calibration using procedures in Stuiver and Reimer 1986. Date range is one sigma.

Huckell 1990). Three pit structures, seven extramural bell-shaped pits, and several smaller features were excavated; interior bell-shaped pits were found in all three structures, and two had hearths. A radiocarbon assay of 2780±90 BP (A-1074) is one of the earliest direct dates for maize in southern Arizona and is supported by a wood charcoal assay of 2800±90 BP (A-4062) from the same feature (Huckell 1988:61). Besides the Milagro site, recent investigations at the Cortaro Fan site on the Santa Cruz River also provided indications of Late Archaic agricultural production (Roth 1989). In addition, some Late Archaic structures appear to be present at the Valencia site, also on the Santa Cruz River, although the extensive reoccupation of the site in later time periods makes accurate identification difficult (Doelle 1985; Huckell 1988).

According to Huckell (1988:74), the Tucson Basin data indicate a "substantially different socioeconomic system from that of the preceding Middle Archaic period." The basis of this conclusion is a distinct change in the archaeological record, with no evidence in the preagricultural period for the co-association of structures, storage features, and dense midden deposits found in many early agricultural sites. As cultivation should have been most productive in the soil conditions found in or near riverine zones, the development of relatively stable site occupation patterns in these areas following the adoption of domesticates might be explicable in terms of an economic commitment to food production. The tremendous floral diversity associated with elevational changes in nearby mountains would have provided early desert farmers with access to a wide variety of habitats within relatively short distances (see Bowers and McLaughlin 1980). Consequently, agricultural sites were probably only a day's walk from most resource zones.

The numerous burials found in some early agricultural sites support interpretations of residential stability and may symbolize increasingly formal notions of land tenure. Ownership of land is an expectable pattern in agricultural economies, and inheritance of land is often validated through the association of the dead with property. However, complex mortuary behavior is also common among hunter-gatherers with territorial systems of land use (see Binford 1972; O'Shea and Zvelebil 1984), and therefore interments should probably be treated generally as an indication of ownership rather than food production. Late Archaic burials in agricultural sites in southeastern Arizona strongly imply that incipient food production was associated with some degree of long-term affiliation between specific groups and particular settlements.

There may be evidence for recurrent site use prior to the appearance of agriculture in the lower reaches of the Rio Grande valley. The earliest date for domesticates in this region is 3125±240 BP (GX-12720) on a sample of maize cobs from Tornillo Rockshelter near Las Cruces, New Mexico (Upham et al. 1987). At the Keystone Dam site, just east of El Paso, Texas, and 50 km south of Tornillo Rockshelter, O'Laughlin (1980) found at least 23 shallow pit structures, of which five produced radiocarbon assays between 4100 and 3300 BP. These structures were 2.0 m to 3.0 m in diameter, 0.15 m to 0.25 m deep, and probably had earth-covered, brush dome superstructures; at least one feature associated with these Archaic structures was interpreted as a storage pit. Artifact density at the Keystone Dam site was lower than reported for Late Archaic sites in southern Arizona, and the span of occupation (c. 800 years) appears to have been longer than found in the Late Archaic sites investigated by Huckell (1990). None of the Keystone Dam Archaic period structures produced evidence for cultigens, but the settlement locality was used repeatedly over an extended period before and after agriculture was introduced to the region (see Upham et al. 1987; MacNeish 1991).

These data from the southern Basin and Range province indicate that low elevation drainages were locations associated with early agriculture. Statistically, radiocarbon dates on maize from the Las Cruces area and the Tucson Basin overlap at one standard deviation, although the oldest calibrated date is from Tornillo Rockshelter. In southern Arizona, a marked change in site features occurs between the preagricultural and agricultural portions of the Archaic, which is interpreted as evidence for greater residential stability.

COLORADO PLATEAUS

Radiocarbon assays place the earliest cultigens in the northern basin and plateau region of the Southwest between about 1000 and 800 BC (Simmons 1986; Long et al. 1986; Smiley, Parry, and Gumerman 1986). Smiley and Parry (1990) report a maize date of 1600 BC from Three Fir Shelter, but the reliability of this extreme outlier has yet to be confirmed. The oldest specimens were recovered from sites that appear to have been campsites without indications of architectural structures (Simmons 1986; Ford 1981). Dwelling structures and storage facilities appear widely over the Colorado Plateaus between 200 BC and AD 200, frequently associated with maize. Most of these early architectural settlements seem to have been located within piñon-juniper woodlands, and the material patterns are used to define the preceramic Basketmaker II period (Plog 1974; Cordell 1984; Nichols and Smiley 1985).

An excellent set of cultigen radiocarbon assays has been obtained from the Black Mesa region of northeastern Arizona (Smiley 1985; Smiley, Parry, and

TABLE 3.2.
Selected radiocarbon assays on Late Archaic cultigens from the Colorado Plateaus

Site	Sample	Material	Date	Calibrated Date[a]
Sheep Camp Shelter	A-3388	Squash seed	2900 ± 230 BP	BC 1430–830
LA 18901	UGa-4179	Maize cob	2720 ± 265 BP	BC 1288–448
Jemez Cave	M-466	Maize cob	2440 ± 250 BP	BC 830–210
Jemez Cave	A-3359	Maize (cupule?)	2410 ± 360 BP	BC 968–72
Cave 1	Beta-12609	Maize kernels	2470 ± 95 BP	BC 791–406
Cave 2	Beta-12608	Maize kernels	2500 ± 90 BP	BC 796–412
White Dog Cave	Beta-12610	Maize kernels	2330 ± 90 BP	BC 507–263
White Dog Cave	Beta-12612	Maize kernels	2160 ± 90 BP	BC 378–94
White Dog Cave	Beta-12611	Maize kernels	2140 ± 85 BP	BC 358–73
BMAP D:11:3133	Beta-10078	Maize cupule	1940 ± 130 BP	BC 90–AD 226
BMAP D:11:449	Beta-10079	Maize kernels	1910 ± 90 BP	BC 87–AD 218
Three Fir Shelter	Beta-15940	Juniper bark	2590 ± 60 BP	BC 814–663
Three Fir Shelter	Beta-15939	Yucca root	2260 ± 70 BP	BC 399–210
Three Fir Shelter	Beta-15938	Juniper wood	2150 ± 90 BP	BC 363–73

[a]Calibration using procedures in Stuiver and Reimer 1986. Date range is one sigma.

Gumerman 1986). Black Mesa chronometrics indicate a range between approximately 600 BC and AD 200, with most dates concentrated between AD 1 and 200 (table 3.2). Cultigen dates tend to occur after 500 BC. This date furnishes a conservative estimate of agricultural antiquity in northern Arizona, unless the outlier date reported by Smiley and Parry (1990) is correct, which would push the period of incipient food production back to about 1600 BC.

Intensive archaeological investigations of the Basketmaker II period on Black Mesa (Lolomai phase, c. 600 BC–AD 200) have generated important insights into settlement patterning associated with early agricultural adaptations. Over one hundred Basketmaker II sites are known on the Peabody Coal lease area of Black Mesa (256 sq km), of which 35 have been studied by excavation. A suite of 140 radiocarbon determinations from 29 sites indicates that most occupation occurred between AD 50 and 250 (Smiley 1985).

Basketmaker II sites on Black Mesa consist of open-air localities and rockshelters, with the former divided into several categories based on differing associations of features. Primary distinctions include (1) lithic scatters lacking structures and interpreted as specialized resource extraction camps, (2) sites with one to two shallow structures interpreted as short-term camps occupied during warm months, and (3) sites with two to 12 deep pithouses, numerous storage pits, and dense midden deposits interpreted as winter settlements (Mauldin 1983; Nichols and Smiley 1985; Gilman 1987).

Maize macrofossils have been recovered from all site types, although not all excavated Lolomai phase sites produced maize. This means that evidence for maize is not limited to sites with greater indications of intensive occupation, such as pit structures and bell-shaped storage pits. Some large Lolomai phase sites actually had no botanical evidence for cultigens, while one site consisting only of small hearths (D:11:2045) produced about 25 percent of all maize macrofossils recovered from Black Mesa Basketmaker II sites (Wagner et al. 1984). Another Lolomai phase site, D:11:449, also represented about 25 percent of all documented maize from the Basketmaker II period, but this site had three structures and numerous bell-shaped pits (Leonard et al. 1985). Site D:11:3133 had nine pit structures excavated into bedrock but no apparent storage pits and only 12 occurrences of maize. Some of this tremendous variation must be due to sampling differences and/or preservation conditions, but it reflects a lack of clear correspondence between site type and the presence of maize.

Recent excavations at Three Fir Shelter, a Basketmaker rockshelter on the northern rim of Black Mesa, provided important complementary data for the open-air sites investigated in the lease area (Smiley, Parry, and Gumerman 1986). Three Fir Shelter was occupied repeatedly during the Basketmaker II period, resulting in a wide array of storage pits, slab-lined cists, roasting features, and hearths that were often superimposed on other features. In addition, a lens of clay may indicate a shallow structure (feature 116). Radiocarbon dates suggest use between 800 BC (possibly 1600 BC) and AD 140 and interpretations of the site emphasize intensive use that included cultigen storage, since some pits contained cached maize.

As an adjunct to the Black Mesa studies of Basketmaker II adaptations, several samples of maize from excavated rockshelters in the nearby Marsh Pass area were radiocarbon dated (Smiley, Parry, and Gumerman 1986; see Kidder and Guernsey 1919; Guernsey and Kidder 1921). Dates obtained from caves 1 and 2 in Kin Biko Canyon are statistically the same as the earliest dates on noncultigen material from Three Fir Shelter, while assays from White Dog Cave overlap with early dates from Three Fir Shelter (see table 3.2). All radiocarbon dates from the Marsh Pass area are earlier than dated cultigens from open-air sites on Black Mesa (see table 3.2). Smiley, Parry, and Gumerman (1986) argued that the use of rockshelters as intensive occupation and storage locations preceded the development of open-air habitation and storage settlements in the Black Mesa area. The temporal distribution of radiocarbon dates from open-air and rockshelter sites indicates that rockshelter use was also contemporaneous with the open-air habitations.

The Black Mesa and Marsh Pass chronometric data from Basketmaker II sites point to an extremely complex land-use pattern. On one hand, rockshelters were definitely being utilized as places for storage and domestic activities by 500 BC in a mixed foraging-agricultural economic strategy. In Marsh Pass, many of the slab-lined storage features found in rockshelters were also used for burials (Kidder and Guernsey 1919; Guernsey and Kidder 1921). On the other hand, Smiley's (1985) study of radiocarbon dates from open-air habitation sites strongly argues for their occupation during a 200-year period beginning after AD 1, with a mean at about AD 200. There appears to have been long-term stability in the role of rockshelters within northern Arizona Basketmaker II economies, perhaps largely involving storage functions, but a more concentrated time frame for open-air habitation and storage sites.

The preagricultural occupation on Black Mesa shows none of the storage indicators or evidence for architectural investment found during the Lolomai phase. The Hisatsinom phase is the preceding Archaic period of occupation, lasting from c. 1340 to 940 BC and represented by only four sites. The roughly 350 years between the Hisatsinom and Lolomai phases appear to have been a hiatus in human use of the Black Mesa lease area, as no sites are known to date to this period (Nichols and Smiley 1985). Ford (1984) is likely correct in his argument that the Lolomai agricultural utilization of Black Mesa was an increase in the intensity of land use from earlier periods. Whether a similar change took place in the Marsh Pass area is impossible to specify due to a lack of archaeological investigation.

There are, however, good Basketmaker II settlement data from Cedar Mesa in southeast Utah, about 75 km north of Black Mesa, that offer a comparison of early agricultural land use. According to Matson, Lipe, and Haase (1988), Basketmaker II occupation on Cedar Mesa (Grand Gulch phase) lasted from AD 200 to 400. A quadrat survey within an 800-square-kilometer area discovered 130 sites with Basketmaker II components (Matson, Lipe, and Haase 1988:248).

Like Black Mesa, the vegetation on Cedar Mesa is a mix of piñon-juniper woodland and shrub grassland, and like the distribution of Basketmaker II sites on Black Mesa, the location of sites on Cedar Mesa showed no strong correlations with drainages expected to have been most suitable for cultivation (Matson, Lipe, and Haase 1988:249; see Nichols and Smiley 1985). There is a significant association of Cedar Mesa Basketmaker II components with dense piñon-juniper woodlands, apparently similar to Black Mesa site patterns. Matson, Lipe, and Haase (1988:249) take dense piñon-juniper stands to be proxies for attractive agricultural soils (deep and well watered) and therefore see the correlation of Basketmaker sites with this particular habitat as evidence that agriculture was the prime determinant of site location. Smiley (1985:274) also noted a correspondence between deep soils, piñon woodlands, and Basketmaker II sites, but suggested that such sediments were highly suitable for constructing pit structures and storage pits. Both speculations are probably relevant, as is the possibility that Basketmaker sites were situated in piñon-juniper zones because of even more directly apparent factors such as natural resource availability.

Matson and Chisholm (1986) reported two Late Archaic radiocarbon dates on maize from Turkey Pen cave, a site within the Cedar Mesa survey area (1800 ± 80 BP [WSU-3513] and 1700 ± 60 BP [WSU-3512]). A total of 25 coprolites associated with Basketmaker deposits produced maize, accounting for 50 to 100 percent of total macrofossil weight in 17 specimens (Matson and Chisholm 1991:449). Piñon seed hulls were the second most abundant macrofossil remains, and Indian rice grass seeds constituted 93 percent and 99 percent of macrofossil weight in two specimens. Chenopodium and amaranth were found in ten coprolites, with

squash seeds in three specimens and cactus seeds in two. These data testify to
the importance of both cultivated and wild plant foods in the Cedar Mesa Basketmaker diet, although, as noted earlier in this chapter, it is difficult to make reliable
estimates of proportional dietary contributions from such a small sample.

Another parallel between Black Mesa and Cedar Mesa is the episodic use of
these local areas during the Basketmaker II period. Open-air sites on Black Mesa
are believed to date mostly to a 150-year period, those on Cedar Mesa to a 200-
year period. This means that during the Basketmaker II period, when agriculture
was initially adopted in the Colorado Plateaus, we find some areas utilized intensively for periods of several generations, followed by land-use systems of much
less intensity, or perhaps no land use at all. It is a pattern that seems similar to
later ceramic periods when episodes of regional "abandonment" left some areas
relatively uninhabited (see Cordell 1984).

From these data on Basketmaker II sites in various parts of the Colorado Plateaus, we draw the general conclusion that the early agricultural period manifests
a high degree of investment in food storage together with extreme population mobility. A striking degree of similarity among Basketmaker II sites over wide areas
suggests a great deal of interaction within Colorado Plateaus populations, and the
episodic occupation of local areas indicates actual population movement. In fact,
there is extremely little variation in material culture or architecture throughout
the Southwest during the Late Archaic. It is doubtful, for example, that any significant morphological differences exist between Late Archaic pithouses or projectile
points between the Tucson Basin and Black Mesa (see Berry 1982; Huckell 1984;
Wills 1988a).

Even with the mobility constraints implied by storage facilities and settlement
architecture, most authorities are convinced that Basketmaker II pithouse sites
reflect seasonal occupations, usually in the winter. Mortuary patterns appear to
indicate stewardship of particular sites and perhaps land tenure. This is probably
an indication of what Graham and Roberts (1986) term "constrained mobility," a
system in which people move frequently but have relatively stable locations within
a region for resource storage. Whatever their exact mobility strategies, preagricultural people in the Colorado Plateaus left no storage facilities comparable to those
of the early agricultural period.

MOGOLLON HIGHLANDS

The upland areas of west-central New Mexico and east-central Arizona are associated with the "classic" early Southwestern agricultural sites such as Bat Cave,
Tularosa Cave, and the Cienega Creek site. Although this area was once seen as
thousands of years ahead of the remainder of the Southwest in agricultural involvement, based on radiocarbon dates from Bat Cave, recent studies have shown
that highland domesticates are coeval with the earliest specimens in other areas
(table 3.3). The number of cultigen specimens from highland rockshelter sites
vastly exceeds remains recovered from sites in other regions, however. Coupled

TABLE 3.3.

Selected radiocarbon assays on Late Archaic cultigens from the Mogollon Highlands

Site	Sample	Material	Date	Calibrated Date[a]
Bat Cave	A-4188	Maize cupule	3120 ± 70 BP	BC 1491–1320
Bat Cave	A-4189	Maize cupule	3060 ± 110 BP	BC 1450–1115
Bat Cave	A-4167	Maize cupule	3010 ± 150 BP	BC 1440–1015
Bat Cave	A-4186	Squash seed	2980 ± 120 BP	BC 1410–1015
Bat Cave	A-4166	Maize cupule	2780 ± 90 BP	BC 1074–830
Bat Cave	A-4185	Maize cupule	2690 ± 90 BP	BC 970–796
Bat Cave	A-4184	Bean	2140 ± 110 BP	BC 380–4
Tularosa Cave	A-4179	Bean	2470 ± 250 BP	BC 893–233
Tularosa Cave	A-4181	Maize cupule	1940 ± 90 BP	BC 90–AD 132

[a]Calibration using procedures in Stuiver and Reimer 1986. Date range is one sigma.

with this fact is the intriguing observation that there is currently no evidence for the kinds of open-air pithouse sites that characterize the *earliest* agricultural sites in the desert grasslands and the Colorado Plateaus.

Martin and Rinaldo (1950) reported a shallow pit structure at Wet Leggett Pueblo as an Archaic house, but it was discovered during the excavations of a ceramic period site and has not been dated. Recent investigations at the SU site, an early ceramic period pithouse site with tree-ring dates in the AD 400s, have found aceramic features with Late Archaic radiocarbon determinations (Wills 1989). A radiocarbon date of 2110±210 BP (Beta-36719; C-13/C-14 adjusted age) was obtained on a maize specimen from the SU site.

But the archaeological record of early agriculture in the central highlands does offer evidence for dramatic changes in site use that seem related to plant cultivation. At Bat Cave and Tularosa Cave there is a distinct shift in site use with the introduction of agriculture to the region. At Bat Cave, for example, there are only limited preagricultural remains in the shelter complex, composed mostly of broken projectile points, some flaked stone tools, and perhaps a few small hearths. In contrast, the earliest maize, beans, and squash from Bat Cave are found with dense deposits of cultural debris, thick hearths, and deep storage pits (Wills 1988a). At Tularosa Cave there were no obvious preagricultural sediments, but the earliest maize was found in storage pits in the bedrock floor of the rockshelter, associated with a vast array of material culture (Wills 1988a; see Hough 1914; Martin et al. 1952). For the most part, it appears that the earliest domesticated plants at both sites occur in contexts of increased site use involving food storage, processing, and other domestic activities.

At the Cienega Creek site in the White Mountains of eastern Arizona, Haury (1957) found a series of features in an alluvial setting dating to the Middle and Late Archaic (see also Berry 1982; Wills 1988a). Hearths and piles of fire-cracked rock were found on superimposed geomorphic surfaces, indicating repeated occupation through time. Radiocarbon dates ranged between about 2800 BP and 1900 BP. Among the features were at least 47 cremation burials, 40 in a single pit (pit 3), that appear to date between 2100 BP and 1900 BP and therefore represent a Late Archaic pattern. As in southeastern Arizona and the Colorado Plateaus, Late Archaic burials at Cienega Creek surely indicate a symbolic tie between a particular social group and a specific locality.

Although pit structures seem to be absent in the higher elevations around Bat Cave and Tularosa Cave until the end of the Late Archaic, there are reports of aceramic pithouse sites on the lower San Francisco and Gila rivers that drain south out of the Mogollon Mountains. Chapman (1985) recorded 17 archaeological sites in the Gila River drainage that had surface indications of pit structures but no associated ceramics. Seven sites had four to twelve structures, three had two structures, and seven contained a single structure. A radiocarbon date reported as 350±170 BC (N-1555) is reported from the Winn Canyon site near Cliff, New Mexico, and 310 BC from the Eaton site near Gila, New Mexico, but it is unclear whether these correctly reflect the temporal occupation of the associated shallow pit structures (see LeBlanc and Whalen 1980:514; Fitting 1973).

Wills (1988a, 1988b) interpreted the appearance of agriculture in the Mogollon Highlands as an indication of changes in the mobility patterns of human groups utilizing this region. Prior to the appearance of domesticated plants in upland areas, hunter-gatherers probably only foraged there during late summer and fall months. The highlands are extraordinarily bountiful in wild food resources at this period but are notably lacking in economic food sources at other times, since most biomass is in trees and shrubs (Hevly 1983). Resource diminution is exacerbated during winter months by extreme cold, which stresses human metabolic processes. An expectable adaptation for foragers whose mobility was unconstrained would be to move seasonally between lower, warmer elevations and the uplands (see also Hunter-Anderson 1986). Winter and spring occupation would be in desert-grasslands, probably in proximity to riverine habitats, and foraging activities would concentrate on plants such as cactus, agave, and mesquite, as well as small game. The cultivation of maize, beans, and squash in highland locations necessarily modified this pattern because planting occurred in spring or early summer, a time when the best place for hunter-gatherers was at lower elevations.

Two relationships might account for spring cultivation in highland areas. First, portions of the regional population may have begun to establish a year-round occupation of the mountains, although such a system is not evident archaeologically prior to the agricultural period (Wills 1988a). Second, some groups may have begun moving into the highlands in the spring while still moving back to lower elevations for the winter. In this latter case, a possible motive for the shift in mobility might have been to monitor patterns of fall resource availability in advance. Either type of change (or a combination of both) strongly suggests increasing competition for highland resources.

Whatever the actual motivation, the presence of agriculture in the highlands formed part of a more intensive utilization of this area. Archaeological data reflect an emphasis on storage and resource concentration in particular localities, but in contrast to the Sonoran and Chihuahuan Basin and Range province and the Colorado Plateaus, the earliest agriculture was not associated with dwelling structures. Not until almost the ceramic period do we see burials (so far, only at Cienega Creek) and residential structures. In other words, there is a long period when the use of cultigens in the highlands appears to have been part of a stable land-use system (no evidence of episodic occupation such as that at Black Mesa or Cedar Mesa) without much investment in residential stability. One interpretation is that incipient farmers in the highlands continued to move to lower elevations for winter encampments.

If this was the case, it may indicate a larger regional relationship among early farmers. Lower elevation deserts and grassland could have been components of a complementary seasonal procurement system for foragers that utilized highland areas as well. The seasonal movement just described takes advantage of differential patterns of resource availability between the two broad habitats. The Colorado Plateaus have less geographical contiguity with the southern Basin and Range deserts than the Mogollon region, and consequently there is less opportunity for hunter-gatherers to move seasonally to lower elevations. Foragers based in the Colorado Plateaus are restricted to areas of less vertical relief and habitat diversity than those in the southern portions of the Southwest. Moreover, during the fall months the Colorado Plateaus exhibit the same patterns of resource availability (mostly within piñon-juniper associations) that characterize the southern highlands. From a hunter-gatherer perspective there is seasonal resource complementarity between the southern Basin and Range and the Mogollon Highlands, but resource redundancy between the Mogollon Highlands and the Colorado Plateaus (see Shackley 1990).

These ecological contrasts might provide some understanding of why there seems to have been long-term stability in land-use patterns following the introduction of agriculture to the southern Basin and Range and the Mogollon Highlands, because if upland and lowland regions were integrated within mixed economies, then cultivation simply enhanced resource productivity in each. The episodic local occupations of the Basketmaker II period, however, may reflect a need to move populations around within regions of less seasonal resource complementarity. Given less habitat diversity with which to work, Late Archaic people in the Colorado Plateaus may have periodically exhausted local resources and simply moved into new areas where they continued relatively intensive procurement tactics.

LATE ARCHAIC FOOD PRODUCTION

In all areas of the Southwest, the shift to food production was part of a pattern of increasing residential intensity. Nevertheless, the patterns that reflect greater site use intensity do not necessarily imply an agricultural economy. Late Archaic pithouse settlements are extremely similar to those of historic hunter-gatherers in the Great Basin and considerably less substantial than those of some prehistoric forager societies (see Flannery 1972a; Price and Brown 1985). Sedentism only requires resource productivity adequate to sustain extended site occupation. In our view, the adoption and maintenance of cultigens during the Late Archaic was part of an overall intensification of economic systems, but plant cultivation itself may not initially have been the focus of intensification efforts.

We oppose the view, however, that Late Archaic plant cultivation was only practiced in a "casual" manner, or that the role of food production was simply to supplement wild food resources or provide extra dietary input on an irregular basis. Such views are based on the perceived continuity in material culture and settlement systems during the adoption period and therefore an assumed lack of impact by plant cultivation on indigenous economic systems (Wills 1990). We think that arguments about the impact of early plant cultivation in the Southwest have often placed too much emphasis on a single attribute of maize—its presumed high yield relative to wild plants—and not enough on the role of cultigens within the overall economic systems characteristic of the Late Archaic.

The overwhelming need for careful tending of maize crops in order to insure successful harvests has at least two important implications for the role of Late Archaic agriculture. First, if the goal of food production was large surpluses, then there had to have been a large labor pool for cultivation and probably a large seed crop, since some overplanting would need to take place to compensate for loss from climatic factors, predation, disease, and differential seed viability. In other words, a surplus probably has to begin with a substantial surplus from previous years or a calculated accumulation of seed over several years. Second, small plots are easier to monitor and require less labor and therefore may actually have fairly high probabilities of success if labor can be allocated for the entire growing season. The product of a small plot system, of course, is limited surplus.

The productivity (yield per unit of land) from maize cultivation might be relatively high when labor can be given over to fairly intensive attention to plants. With limited labor but constant attention, maize productivity would be lower but perhaps more consistently predictable. If Late Archaic populations were organized in small, mobile groups—as the archaeological record seems to indicate—it appears very unlikely that the labor pool existed that could have supported intensive agricultural production. The lack of evidence for water control systems or formal fields is consistent with this view.

Flannery (1973) and Binford (1980) point out that any effort to concentrate resources in one place through storage will decrease the cost of those resources but may increase the costs of obtaining other important resources, especially if local natural productivity is not high or continuous (see also O'Shea 1981; S. Plog 1990a). Since cultivation depends on being able to remain in one locale long enough to insure plant survival, the capacity of local noncultigen resource productivity to support extended settlement occupation partially or completely during the growing season is critical to the success of food production.

Consequently, we expect the integration of agriculture into forager systems to occur first in places where natural productivity underwrites labor allocation to food production. At the same time, one benefit of storable crops is that they can extend site use through periods of resource lows, such as "overwintering," and probably reduce to some degree the necessity of wild resource procurement during lean periods. In the seasonal environment of the Southwest, cultigen planting must occur at locations where cultivators anticipate they will be settled during the late summer and fall when harvest takes place. Fall is typically a period of natural food abundance, particularly in the intermediate elevation piñon-juniper woodlands (see Hevly 1983). Thus, planting should generally occur in areas close enough to fall foraging ranges to minimize scheduling conflicts during harvesting.

Fall resources may be difficult to predict spatially at a local level, however. For example, while the knowledge that piñon nut masts will occur annually in certain areas (such as a mountain range) is quite good, within that area there may be far less certainly about food availability. Plant cultivation increases the predictability of resources within an area but may not correspond to local patterns of food availability. Agriculture is therefore a compromise tactic involving increased residential stability with respect to known resource distributions, and planting therefore should occur in places from which foraging would still be efficient (cf. Binford 1982:9). In that sense, agriculture becomes a useful tool within a basically hunter-gatherer economy by providing a predictable food source that reduces the uncertainty of finding resources in an area and thus allows more extensive or prolonged searches. Mobile hunter-gatherers may be unable to summon up the labor or social mechanisms needed to exploit local resource abundances fully when they occur, and the productive potential of natural resources is therefore often underrealized (Sahlins 1972). The increased spatial and temporal predictability afforded by stored cultigens in the Southwest may have helped make wild resource procurement more effective by allowing more "complete" harvesting of foods having limited periods of availability (cf. O'Shea 1981).

A variety of recent ethnographic studies of tropical forest hunter-gatherers supports the contention that within mixed economies, cultivation may facilitate foraging tactics rather than having simply a backup or "buffering" role. Bailey and colleagues (1989), Headland (1987), and Hutterer (1991) have argued that sustained occupation of tropical forests is possible only given carbohydrates furnished by domesticated plants. Bailey and colleagues (1989:73) suggest that humans must find ways to alter the density and distribution of edible resources in order to maintain a protracted presence in tropical environments. These arguments are buttressed by the lack of archaeological evidence demonstrating the presence of hunter-gatherers in tropical forests without some contact with agriculturalists. Data that point to a necessary relationship between hunter-gatherers and agriculture for extended occupation of tropical rain forests are the product of a more general research perspective that recognizes wide-ranging economic networks as a fundamental adaptation among foraging societies (e.g., Wiessner 1982; Denbow 1984; Spielmann 1986; Headland and Reid 1989).

Certainly, we are not suggesting a homology between the Southwest and the world's rain forests. Instead, we point to the illustration that agriculture need not be simply a replacement for diminishing wild food sources but can be a tactic enhancing hunting and gathering productivity. In other words, cultivation in certain areas makes it possible for natural resources to be utilized more intensively by allowing longer occupation and more effective foraging tactics. In short, the introduction of one subsistence tactic (agriculture) into a new niche allows another set of procurement tactics (foraging) to be reorganized for greater efficiency.

We think the Late Archaic was a period during which particular tactics within economic systems were rearranged in order to gain better predictability and control over the future. Cultigens contributed to this process both by providing a new food resource and by aiding the intensification of foraging activities. The rapid adoption of domesticates throughout the Southwest suggests that these new resources immediately helped buffer seasonal and annual variation in food availability (Huckell 1990) and/or that land-use patterns involving intensive use of particular foraging locales may have already been in place (Wills 1988a).

From an evolutionary perspective, the conditions favoring the perpetuation of increasingly structured foraging almost certainly involved resource competition, whether generated by cultural, demographic, or environmental factors. The increasing economic complexity represented by an expanding niche width through cultivation is consistent with Earle's (1980) argument that the initial value in domesticates is created by declining returns from foraging. But the archaeological pattern of cultigen incorporation indicates that the role of food production was much more complicated than simply adding a new set of food resources to an economy. Instead, these new resources may have had a catalytic effect on existing economic strategies that created new possibilities for foraging organization.

──────── *Acknowledgments* ────────

We are grateful to the School of American Research and the seminar participants and co-authors for the opportunity to contribute to this volume. We especially thank F. E. Smiley of Northern Arizona University, who co-authored the first draft of this paper with us. His contributions to understanding early food production in the northern Colorado Plateaus represent landmark studies in Southwestern archaeology. Each of us has had tremendous help over the years from advisors, colleagues, and students, and though we cannot thank all of them here, we trust that they realize our deep appreciation. Our special thanks go to Emil Haury, Vance Haynes, Richard I. Ford, John D. Speth, and Austin Long. Finally, readers familiar with early agriculture in the Southwest may find some key references missing from this chapter, which was written in 1989. Publication schedules made it difficult to revise our original paper, and we apologize for the obvious omission of many books and papers published since then that are relevant to the problem of agricultural origins in the Southwest.

4

Adaptive Stress,
Environment, and Demography

JEFFREY S. DEAN, WILLIAM H. DOELLE,
AND JANET D. ORCUTT

 A MAJOR STIMULUS OF ADAPTIVE CHANGE in sociocultural systems is subsistence stress caused by the interaction of environmental, demographic, and behavioral variables (Cordell and Plog 1979; Dean 1988a; Dean et al. 1985; Plog et al. 1988). Systemic stress develops when the subsistence technology available to a group is unable to extract enough food from the physical environment to support the existing population. Most cultural systems are able to handle short-term production shortfalls through buffering mechanisms (Clarke 1978; Jorde 1977) such as storage, "banking," adjustments in subsistence practices, exchange, and predation. Permanent or long-term shortfalls caused by fundamental changes in the balance between population size and productivity, however, must be accommodated in different, more profound ways. Such adjustments often produce qualitatively different adaptive systems that are likely to persist until sociocultural factors, technological advances, or new population-resource disjunctions trigger behavioral responses that create new adaptive configurations.

Because structured behavior is humankind's primary mode of adaptation, environmental and demographic factors usually are treated as independent variables whose interactions act on and transform the behavioral component of adaptive systems. Thus, systemic change occurs when population exceeds the "carrying capacity" of a particular adaptive configuration or when environmental degradation lowers the carrying capacity below the level of the existing population. Either eventuality requires social or technological responses that allow the population to survive within the newly established systemic boundaries. In any given case, however, components of the three classes of variables can act independently to alter the limiting conditions that define an adaptive system. With this caveat, we examine environmental and demographic variability as potential causes of stress on Southwestern behavioral adaptive systems and identify time periods when such stresses are likely to have been severe enough to have stimulated permanent adaptive change.

ENVIRONMENTAL VARIABILITY

The environment of the Southwest can be characterized in terms of three overlapping classes of variability (Dean 1984, 1988a, 1988b; Dean et al. 1985; Plog et al. 1988): stable, low frequency process, and high frequency process. "Stable" factors vary in space but have remained essentially constant during the study period (the last 2,000 years), and their current states accurately reflect past conditions. The three general habitats (desert, mountain, and plateau), the climate type, bedrock geology, gross topography, and the elevational zonation of climate and vegetation communities are "stable" attributes of the Southwestern environment during the last two millennia.

Low frequency process (LFP) environmental variability is controlled by natural processes with regular or irregular periodicities equal to or greater than 25 years. Important LFP variables include long-term climate trends, alluvial groundwater fluctuations, aggradation and degradation of alluvial floodplains, deposition and erosion on slopes, and changes in the composition and elevational boundaries of vegetation zones. Although the processes that drive LFP variability have long cycles, specific changes due to these mechanisms can occur over short intervals.

High frequency process (HFP) environmental variability is controlled by natural processes with periodicities of less than 25 years. Crucial HFP variables include seasonal, annual, and multiyear fluctuations in various climatic parameters (precipitation, temperature, frost-free period, drought), streamflow, vegetative production, and the temporal and spatial aspects of these factors.

Because LFP and HFP factors exhibit periodicities shorter than the length of the study period, the present states of these variables do not necessarily reflect earlier conditions. Therefore, past variability in these factors must be reconstructed by a variety of paleoenvironmental techniques. Many such analyses underlie the following characterization of past environmental variability in the three major habitats of the Southwest.

THE COLORADO PLATEAU

The Colorado Plateau is a high steppe region consisting of a vast series of sedimentary rock formations whose prevailing horizontal aspect is deformed by folding, fracturing, and faulting. Igneous flows and intrusions create localized uplands, and deep canyons are incised into the landscape. The province is characterized by relatively low rainfall, warm temperatures, short growing seasons, and comparatively mild winters. To the east, the plateau gives way to the volcanic mountain ranges and wide valleys of the Rio Grande valley.

The resources of the plateau vary with the weather, geology, and topography. Running water is concentrated in a few large, through-flowing rivers (Colorado,

Rio Grande, San Juan), a number of medium-sized streams, and reaches of many minor drainages that flow in response to upland runoff or seepage. Most watercourses, however, flow only intermittently in response to summer or winter rainstorms or snowmelt. Vegetation varies with elevation and topography, ranging from desert scrub through grasslands and piñon-juniper woodlands to coniferous forests and alpine communities. Deer, pronghorn, and mountain sheep constitute the principal big game, and rabbits, hares, prairie dogs, and other rodents constitute small game.

Agriculture is possible where water (in the form of rainfall, runoff, and groundwater), a sufficiently long growing season, and suitable land coexist. Generally, these conditions are concentrated on floodplains at intermediate elevations where surface water is adequate and the growing season is long enough to produce one crop. Higher elevations where water is abundant are too cool, and lower, warmer elevations lack reliable water supplies.

Local topography creates many exceptions to these generalizations. In canyons, groundwater is concentrated and heat conserved by the confining rock walls of the defiles. Conversely, cold air drainage from uplands can inhibit crop production. Subsistence technology expands the localities that can be farmed. Irrigation allowed farming in low areas where water could be diverted from flowing streams, as in the Rio Grande valley, or where surface runoff could be captured and channeled, as in Chaco Canyon.

LFP environmental variability in floodplain processes (Dean et al. 1985:541, fig. 1a; Plog et al. 1988:235, fig. 8.1a) is a major limiting factor in subsistence systems of the plateau. Fluvial conditions unfavorable for agriculture and natural plant and animal resource productivity exist when alluvial water tables are depressed and erosion prevails. Major fluvial degradation occurred during the years AD 250–350, 750–925, 1275–1450, and 1880–present. Periods of secondary floodplain degradation are centered on AD 600, 1150, and 1700.

Rising and high groundwater levels and alluviation favor floodplain farming. Especially beneficial floodplain conditions are indicated for the AD 100–200, 400–750, 1000–1275, and 1500–1880 intervals. LFP variability in effective moisture as reconstructed from palynological studies (Dean et al. 1985:541, fig. 1b; Plog et al. 1988:235, fig. 8.1b) parallels the alluvial record and would have reinforced the effects (favorable or unfavorable) of the fluvial fluctuations.

HFP dendroclimatic variability has three important aspects: amplitude variation, and temporal and spatial structure. Significant negative amplitude departures (Dean et al. 1985:541, fig. 1c; Dean and Robinson 1977; Plog et al. 1988:235, fig. 8.1c) specify precipitation deficiencies that directly impact crop production and exacerbate poor LFP fluvial conditions. Significant positive departures generally indicate favorable HFP conditions that can ameliorate poor floodplain states. Excessive rainfall, however, sometimes reduces production by damaging crops or eroding fields. High temporal variability (Dean et al. 1985:541, fig. 1c; Plog et al. 1988:235, fig. 8.1c), which favors the accumulation of food reserves to offset production shortfalls, prevailed during the 300–350, 750–1000, 1350–1550, and 1730–1800 intervals. High spatial variability (Dean et al. 1985:541, fig. 1d; Plog et al. 1988:235, fig. 8.1d) creates interlocality production differentials that foster interareal exchange (Plog 1983b) or plunder as mechanisms for leveling out the variability. Conversely, spatial uniformity inhibits interaction by reducing interareal production differentials. The 1000–1150, 1300–1600, and 1900–1970 periods exhibited high spatial variability, while the intervening intervals were characterized by spatial uniformity.

THE MOGOLLON HIGHLANDS

The mountains exhibit less environmental variability than does the plateau. Orographic effects make this the wettest region in the Southwest, but much of it is too cool for dependable farming. Arable land is limited in this area of narrow valleys incised into large mountain massifs. Natural plant and animal resources are much more abundant than those of the plateau, though not more varied.

The meager information available on LFP environmental variability in the mountains suggests that variability in floodplain processes (Agenbroad 1982) and effective moisture (Hevly 1988) paralleled those on the plateau. HFP variability in climate amplitude (Dean and Robinson 1982:57, fig. 8.6), drought conditions (Reid and Graybill 1984), and temporal and spatial structure was similar to that of the Colorado Plateau.

THE SONORAN DESERT

Although the desert is relatively uniform in geology and hydrology, elevational differences impart a wide range of variability to other aspects of the environment. Irrigation from the through-flowing rivers (Salt, Gila, Verde, Santa Cruz, San Pedro) provided the water necessary for intensive agriculture in the broad alluvial valleys. Nonriverine areas were used for dry and floodwater farming (Fish and Nabhan 1991). Natural plant resources are especially abundant and varied in response to local elevational, topographic, hydrologic, and edaphic conditions. In contrast, wild animal resources generally are inferior to those of the mountains and plateau.

Although paleoenvironmental reconstructions in the desert are limited, geomorphic studies indicate that LFP variations in fluvial conditions and streamflow in the San Pedro and Santa Cruz drainages (Waters 1983, 1987, 1989) during the last two millennia are broadly similar to those of the plateau (Dean 1987). Michael Waters shows how desert agricultural strategies would have had to adapt to geohydrologic changes such as downcutting and deposition and clarifies the agricultural potential of habitats such as *bajadas* that to the untrained eye appear to have limited agricultural potential.

Graybill's (1989:figs. 3.3, 3.4) dendrohydrologic reconstruction of streamflow for the Salt River from 740 to 1370 is the only measure of HFP environmental variability in the desert. Although the Salt retrodiction represents streamflow in the

Hohokam "core" area, it does not hold for rivers such as the Santa Cruz and San Pedro that do not originate in the Mogollon Highlands. The years between 900 and 1051 were "characterized by few high-magnitude annual flows and low variability" (Nials, Gregory, and Graybill 1989:66). The period from 1052 to 1196 also was favorable, although the "incidence of high-magnitude flows and the variation in flow increased" (Nials, Gregory, and Graybill 1989:67). Nials, Gregory, and Graybill argue that catastrophic floods would have destroyed canal intakes and headgates and probably silted the headward portions of canals. The use of headgates, however, has not been demonstrated (Nials, Gregory, and Graybill 1989:51, 53), and intakes were simple pole-and-brush weirs that could have been easily rebuilt. Even if flood-induced silting was serious enough to disrupt entire irrigation seasons, farming on inundated floodplains may have offset productivity lost to this factor.

Nials, Gregory, and Graybill (1989) discount double cropping as a means of countering seasonal flood damage to irrigation systems. Nabhan (1983:78) notes, however, that even in the Sells area, which is higher than the Salt River valley, some crops could be successfully planted as late as the end of August. Thus, even if Hohokam farmers missed a "primary" irrigation season in late April or early May due to flood damage (Nials, Gregory, and Graybill 1989), they likely could have exploited the secondary runoff peak that generally comes in August. Furthermore, the possibility of regular double cropping of at least some of the more resilient crops appears to have been a reasonable option.

Although Nials, Gregory, and Graybill (1989) downplay the negative effects of low runoff, deficient streamflow would have seriously threatened the subsistence and social systems. The benefits of cooperation in clearing silted canals would have been so obvious that simple self-interest would have motivated communal repairs. In times of low flow, however, self-interest could easily have led to the diversion of limited water resources by the most powerful (or the most devious) persons or groups, leading to potential conflicts.

DEMOGRAPHIC VARIABILITY

A crucial problem in assessing the adaptive impact of demographic variability is how to measure prehistoric population sizes (Powell 1988). Archaeologists have become more sophisticated in this matter, having progressed from counting sites to counting rooms or totaling floor areas to adjusting room counts (or floor areas) according to models of structure use-life and remodeling frequency. The trend is toward more realistic estimates of momentary population; that is, of the number of residents in an area at any given time. However calculated, population estimates must take three factors into account. The effects of differences in *site function* are controlled by distinguishing habitation from nonhabitation sites and identifying different types of the former. Clearly, pueblos, *rancherías,* pithouse villages, and dispersed homesteads must be treated differently in estimating population numbers. Differences in *room function* confuse the estimation of population through either room counts or floor area. Among the confounding variables are the distribution of activities between pithouses and surface rooms (Gilman 1987; Wills and Windes 1989), the ratio of habitation to storage rooms (Plog 1974), and the simultaneous use of both pit structures and surface rooms as habitations (Lekson 1988). *Chronology* may be the most important and most difficult variable to control in estimating population. High-resolution dating is crucial to establishing site contemporaneity, structure use-life, and remodeling rates; to relating demographic changes to critical environmental factors; and to determining the synchroneity and duration of the units of estimation.

The population reconstructions presented below were abstracted from the literature with little modification, and they suffer from deficiencies in all the factors listed above. Structure use-life and remodeling rates rarely were used to adjust population estimates. Nor are most of the estimates standardized for different time period lengths. When possible, we attempted to correct for these factors, but sufficient data to make such adjustments often were not available. Because most of the reconstructions are phase based, the curves represent long-term population trends rather than high-frequency demographic variations. In the accompanying figures, population is plotted on the midpoint of each estimation period.

SOUTHWESTERN COLORADO AND SOUTHEASTERN UTAH

The southwestern Colorado–southeastern Utah population curve (fig. 4.1) synthesizes data from many archaeological projects (Brew 1946; DeBloois 1975; Fuller 1984, 1987, 1988; Hayes 1964; Honeycutt and Fetterman 1985; Matson, Lipe, and Haase 1988; Neily 1983; Rohn 1977; and Schlanger 1988). The primary conclusion one draws from various locality studies and from plotting population data for many small cultural resource management (CRM) surveys is that population movement was common. Various authors have attempted to explain these demographic patterns using the environmental models presented by Euler and colleagues (1979) or Kenneth L. Petersen (1988).

Schlanger's (1988) Dolores-area population predictions, which were based on changes in climate and the elevational limits of the farmbelt, were confirmed through circa 880, after which population increased in lower areas, where farming was vulnerable to droughts, instead of in higher areas, where the agricultural risk lay in short growing seasons. Fuller (1987) notes a similar trajectory along the Dove Creek Canal system, with settlement locations corresponding to predictions based on climatic models through the 900s. Between 1000 and 1200, populations were not concentrated in high-elevation areas as predicted. Like Schlanger, Fuller (1987:123) suggests that the existing subsistence technology may have been better able to handle drought than short growing seasons.

Cedar Mesa (Matson, Lipe, and Haase 1988) experienced three occupations: the first (200–400) in a period of high winter-spring precipitation; the second (650–725) during a period of high annual precipitation, increasing summer rainfall, and above-average temperatures; the third (1060–1270) during an interval

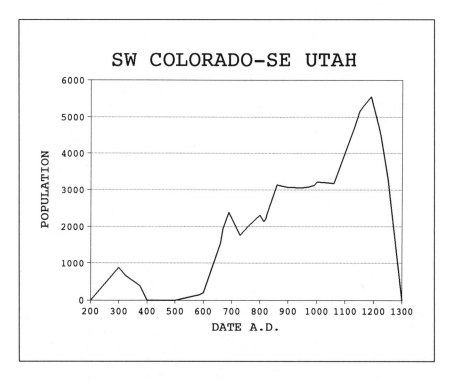

Figure 4.1. Population: southeastern Utah–southwestern Colorado area.

when moisture declined. A possible break in the last occupation coincided with a brief shift to low moisture in the middle 1100s. On the higher Elk Ridge, population increased under favorable LFP and HFP conditions before 750, declined during the 750–925 interval of alluvial degradation, and increased again during optimal LFP and HFP conditions between 925 and approximately 1130 (DeBloois 1975; Euler 1988:184, fig. 7.1). This trajectory is the inverse of Cedar Mesa's, which suggests that people moved among different elevational zones in response to varying environmental conditions.

Across the whole area, population leveled off from 800 through the mid-1000s. Growing population on Mesa Verde contributed to a large increase in the 1100s that bridged a period of favorable LFP conditions and a secondary LFP reversal at approximately 1150. LFP conditions were good from the late 1100s until the late 1200s, possibly indicating that a wider range of environments could be successfully farmed. The abandonment of the area coincided with severe LFP and HFP degradations.

KAYENTA AREA

The Kayenta branch population curve (fig. 4.2) applies to the area south of the San Juan River, west of the Chuska-Lukachukai-Carrizo ranges, east of the Colorado River, and north of a line running westward from the head of Chinle Wash. Within this area, survey-based population estimates are possible only for Canyon de Chelly (McDonald 1976), Monument Valley (Neely and Olson 1977), the Kayenta Valley (Haas and Creamer 1985), Long House Valley (Dean, Lindsay, and Robinson 1978; Effland 1979), Tsegi Canyon (Beals, Brainerd, and Smith 1945), northern Black Mesa (Plog 1986a), upper Klethla Valley (Haas and Creamer 1985), Paiute Mesa (Ambler, Fairley, and Geib 1983), the Rainbow Plateau (Ambler, Fairley, and Geib 1983), and Navajo Canyon (Miller and Breternitz 1958a, 1958b). As a result of this spotty coverage, the population numbers are low by at least a third. The shape of the curve, however, probably accurately portrays the trajectory of population variability.

The fairly static portion of the curve before 550 represents a relatively stable Basketmaker II population that occupied rockshelters and open pithouse villages (Smiley 1985). The major increase between 550 and 600 reflects rapid population growth after the adoption of the more sedentary Basketmaker III lifeway. This increase is underestimated because many Basketmaker III sites recently recorded in the Chinle Valley (Miranda Warburton, personal communication 1990) and Canyon del Muerto (Scott Travis, personal communication 1991) have not been factored into the estimate. The major jump between 800 and 850 occurred at the transition to the Pueblo I period. This apparent increase could be a result more of population movements than of growth, especially if the number of Basketmaker III people is increased. From 850 to 1250, population exhibited a fairly steady increase modulated between 950 and 1250 by fluctuations revealed by high-resolution estimates for northern Black Mesa (Plog 1986a) and Long House Valley (Dean, Lindsay, and Robinson 1978). The decline after 1225 reflects population decrements in the Monument Valley and Navajo Mountain subareas. The precipitous drop after 1290 indicates the general abandonment of the Kayenta area, while the later tail represents light Pueblo IV use of Canyon de Chelly and Long House Valley.

The general population trend correlates with paleoenvironmental variability in three ways. First, the population growth of 950 to 1100 coincides with a long interval of favorable LFP and HFP environmental conditions that were especially conducive to floodplain agriculture and upland dry farming. Second, the decline between 1100 and 1200 correlates with a secondary LFP fluvial degradation and a severe HFP drought. Finally, the abandonment of the area occurred during an interval of primary fluvial degradation and a brief but severe drought.

The area-scale population curve masks local fluctuations that appear to be related to environmental variability. For example, the settlement history of Long House Valley can be understood primarily in terms of LFP fluvial variations that affected the agricultural potential of various localities in the valley (Dean, Lindsay,

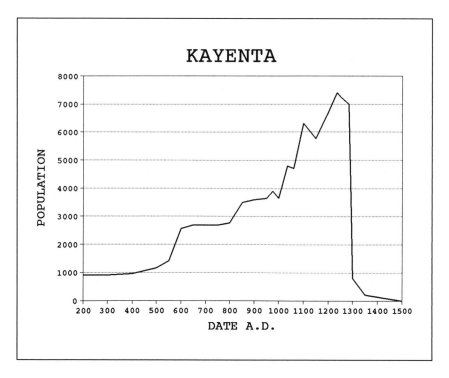

Figure 4.2. Population: Kayenta area.

and Robinson 1978; Effland 1979). Similar population-environment relationships characterized the adjacent Tsegi Canyon and Kayenta Valley areas (Dean 1969). In addition, the withdrawal from numerous peripheral areas and the abandonment of upland localities in the middle twelfth century coincided with depressed LFP and HFP conditions. On the eastern fringe of the Kayenta area, demographic variability in Canyon de Chelly and the surrounding uplands (McDonald 1976) co-varies with some fluvial changes and climatic fluctuations (Euler et al. 1979:205, fig. 5). Thus, although area scale population trends were relatively immune to environmental fluctuations, local demographic and settlement dynamics were more closely attuned to environmental variability.

Virgin Branch

Larson and Michaelsen (1990:238–39, 241) relate the demographic history of the Virgin Branch (fig. 4.3) to a dendrohydrologic reconstruction of Virgin River streamflow. The combination of reduced environmental capacity and growing population during the 966–1020 interval of low runoff probably accelerated competition for resources among mobile hunting-and-gathering groups and curtailed settlement mobility. As a result, people began to rely more on agriculture and

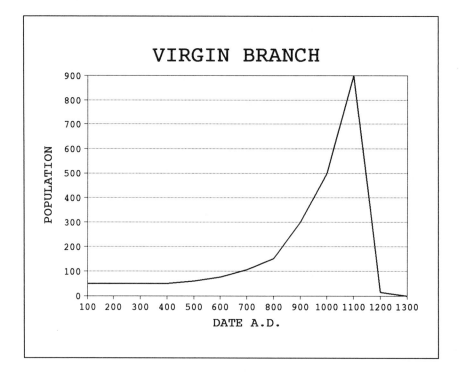

Figure 4.3. Population: Virgin Branch area.

tended to settle along reaches of the Virgin and Muddy rivers that were suitable for irrigation or water diversion. As a result of continued population growth during a period of high streamflow between 1020 and 1120, agriculture was intensified and settlement aggregated along the rivers. Between 1120 and 1180, population declined rapidly toward abandonment during an interval of low runoff, drought, and a second-order fluvial degradation. Whereas farming had allowed the population to survive lower streamflow between 1000 and 1015, by 1120 the populace had grown so large and so dependent on agriculture that it could not cope with several consecutive years of deficient runoff (Larson and Michaelsen 1990:242–43).

GRAND CANYON

Both Kayenta and Cohonina populations (Euler 1988:194, fig. 7.1) in the Grand Canyon (fig. 4.4) exhibited steady growth from around 500 to a peak at 1100, followed by abrupt depopulation by 1200. These trends bear no evident relationship to environmental variability, although local population dynamics within the canyon, as at Unkar Delta (Schwartz, Chapman, and Kepp 1980), appear to correlate with HFP climatic fluctuations. Widespread depopulation of the canyon and surrounding highlands around 1150 corresponds with the abandonment of

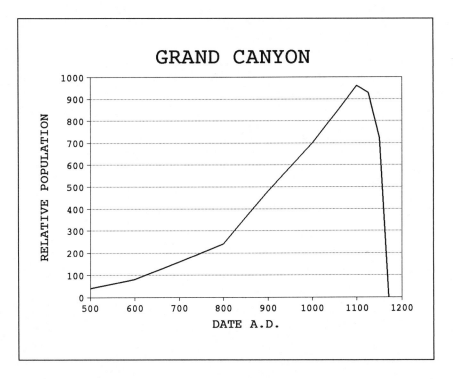

Figure 4.4. Relative population: Grand Canyon area.

many upland areas throughout the plateau and coincides with a secondary alluvial degradation and an intense HFP drought.

LITTLE COLORADO

The Little Colorado area population curve (fig. 4.5) encompasses the Hopi Buttes
(Gumerman 1988b), Wupatki (Downum and Sullivan 1990), Chevelon (Slatter
1979), Hay Hollow Valley (Lightfoot 1984; S. Plog 1986a), Snowflake (Lightfoot
1984), Pinedale (Lightfoot 1984), and Zuni (Kintigh 1985) subareas. Most of the
post-1350 fluctuations apply to the Zuni area. The other areas experienced major
growth during the eleventh, twelfth, and late thirteenth centuries. In the Chevelon
area, people moved between lower and higher localities in response to droughts.
Although Lightfoot (1984) attributes culture change in the Pinedale, Snowflake,
and Hay Hollow Valley subareas to sociopolitical factors, there are some relationships with environmental variations. Major population increases in the Pinedale
and Snowflake areas occurred during a period of favorable LFP conditions in the
1000s to 1100s; the population decreases that led to abandonment in the 1300s occurred during a period of LFP and HFP deterioration. Hay Hollow Valley population began to grow during an erosional interval in the 800s to 900s and expanded

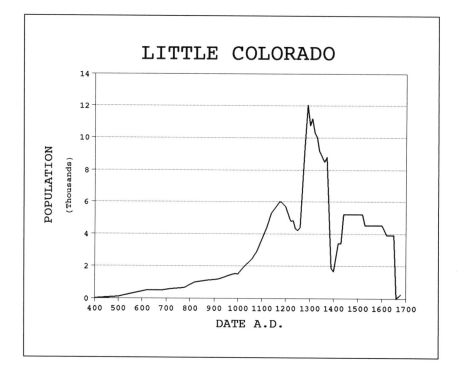

Figure 4.5. Population: Little Colorado area.

through the subsequent aggradational period. As with Pinedale and Snowflake, however, Hay Hollow Valley began to lose population during the next period of poor LFP conditions and eventually was abandoned.

Population in the Zuni area, which increased as other areas were abandoned, peaked in the late 1200s during an interval of falling water tables and active arroyo cutting. At this time, population was located in higher elevations. During the ensuing period of low water tables and entrenched channels, the declining population moved down in elevation and then back up. After 1400, population increased again and became fairly stable, and people settled at the lowest mean elevation of the entire time span. Population remained fairly stable and concentrated at low elevations (Kintigh 1985:95) during the 1500–1590 interval of floodplain aggradation. Demographic fluctuations appear to correlate better with hydrology earlier in the sequence because of reliance on floodwater farming, but "the experimentation with riverine irrigation that may have started . . . around 1300 eventually culminated in the settlement pattern shift to the locations of the protohistoric towns and in a near complete reliance on riverine and spring irrigation" (Kintigh 1985:108).

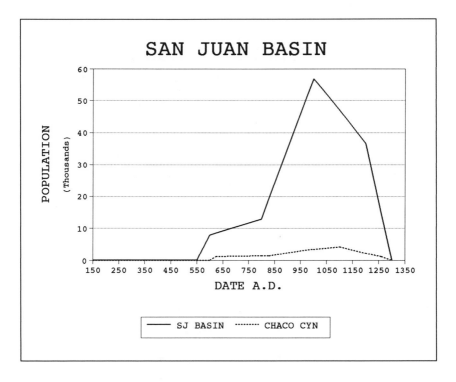

Figure 4.6. Population: San Juan Basin and Chaco Canyon areas.

SAN JUAN BASIN

There is considerable disagreement over how to measure population in Chaco Canyon and its environs (Judge 1989; Vivian 1991:64–67), but relative population curves do not differ significantly from method to method. The problem centers on how to estimate population at the large "towns," especially given speculation that most of their rooms were not used for habitation (Lekson 1988; Windes 1984). Our Chaco curve uses Hayes's (1981) estimates from room counts for all periods except 1050–1175, for which Lekson's (1988:125) estimate is used.

However measured, the Chaco Canyon population was small in the context of the San Juan Basin as a whole (fig. 4.6). San Juan Basin population (Eddy 1966; Judge 1989) grew during a period of poor LFP conditions and peaked during improving conditions. Chaco Canyon population grew at the same time but peaked later. In the 900s, construction at the towns occurred during episodes of decreased productive potential and ceased during periods of high productive potential (Sebastian 1991:128). During the 1040–1100 period of fluctuating conditions, construction at the towns increased or continued regardless of productive

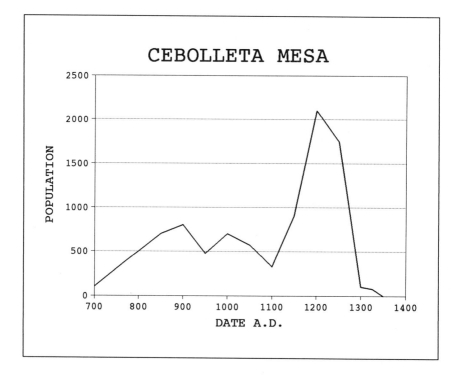

Figure 4.7. Population: Cebolleta Mesa area.

potential. The extremely favorable 1100–1140 period was characterized by little construction at the towns; instead, the "McElmo structures" were the focus of activity (Sebastian 1991:129). After about 1130, drought led to large-scale abandonments throughout the San Juan Basin.

CEBOLLETA MESA

Between 1100 and 1200, population in the Cebolleta Mesa area (fig. 4.7) (Dittert 1959:75) grew at a rate that could only have been caused by massive immigration, perhaps as a consequence of the depopulation of the Chacoan "core area" to the north. Late in the thirteenth century, population declined precipitously, a decrease that, in the absence of evidence for massive in situ mortality, must have been due to emigration. Subsequent but undocumented population increase was responsible for the large number of people encountered at Acoma by the Spaniards.

    Population trends in this area exhibit minimal correlation with LFP environmental variability, with both maxima and minima falling during intervals of aggradation and degradation. Maximum growth between 1100 and 1200 did coincide with aggradation and high groundwater levels, but population began to decline

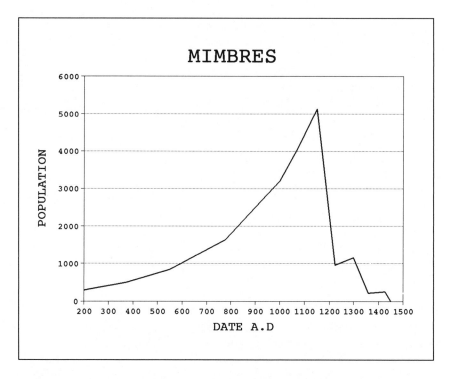

Figure 4.8. Population: Mimbres area.

before these favorable hydrologic conditions were terminated by channel incision in the late 1200s, perhaps because population approached carrying capacity.

MIMBRES

The general trends in Mimbres population (Blake, LeBlanc, and Minnis 1986; LeBlanc 1989b) are applicable outside the Mimbres Valley only through 1300 (fig. 4.8). Subsequent trends in the Mimbres Valley (Cliff phase) do not represent the Cliff-Gila area, where population "exceeded that of the Classic Mimbres period" (Blake, LeBlanc, and Minnis 1986:463).

Mimbres population growth before 1150 was accompanied by numerous settlement changes. Early Pithouse period (200–550) settlements are located in defensive situations near good agricultural land (Blake, LeBlanc, and Minnis 1986:fig. 5; LeBlanc 1989b:180). During the Late Pithouse period (550–1000), the predominant location was the Mimbres Valley bottom, but people also began to occupy the "wide-bottom side-drainages" (Blake, LeBlanc, and Minnis 1986:fig. 5). During the Classic Mimbres period (1000–1150), valley bottom population increased to the limits of floodplain agriculture (Minnis 1985b:124), and population in the tributaries grew dramatically. Initially, this growth coincided with favorable conditions characterized by relatively high and predictable precipitation and few episodes of food stress (Minnis 1985b:135; figs. 26, 28). Later, from 1090 to 1149, lower and less predictable precipitation prevailed, and numerous episodes of food stress occurred (Minnis 1985b:figs. 26, 28).

The effects of these conditions would have been most dramatic in the tributaries, where people relied primarily on dry farming, but also would have been felt in the valley bottom, where farming was being pushed to its limits. In addition, other resources (such as fuel, wild plants, and animals) had been severely depleted. The drastic decline in population in the 1100s appears, therefore, to be related to environmental reversals that were too great to be overcome by a large population. The reduced Postclassic population, which may have come from somewhere else, lived mostly in the valley bottom (Blake, LeBlanc, and Minnis 1986:fig. 5; LeBlanc 1989b:196–97). Why the area was abandoned around 1450 is not clear (LeBlanc 1989b:199–200), but this event occurred during a period of poor LFP conditions when erosion reduced crop production in the valley bottom.

NORTHERN RIO GRANDE

The northern Rio Grande (fig. 4.9) is characterized by a relatively late population increase that occurred after many areas to the west had been depopulated or abandoned. The most substantial increase in the area began during the 1100s and continued through the late 1200s, especially in the Gallina, Pajarito Plateau, and Santa Fe subareas. The Pajarito Plateau and Gallina populations peaked in the late 1200s and then declined—rapidly in the Gallina, less rapidly on the Pajarito. Population in the other areas continued to grow (Crown, Orcutt, and Kohler 1990). In the Chama, Taos, and Jemez areas, major population increases were a post-1300 phenomenon. In the Chama, population grew at a rate suggesting immigration, and evidence that aggregation occurred immediately in planned villages suggests that people may have arrived in groups (Crown, Orcutt, and Kohler 1990).

The Anasazi occupied the higher elevations of the Pajarito Plateau (Orcutt 1991) during a period of favorable LFP conditions and variable rainfall that followed the mid-1100s. The major population increase probably occurred around 1275–1325, just before or soon after LFP conditions began to deteriorate; it was accompanied by aggregation into large plaza pueblos. The population remained in the higher elevations, probably because dry farming was easier there during this comparatively dry interval (Rose, Robinson, and Dean 1982). In the 1300s, population shifted down in elevation and never moved back up, at least not permanently. This change occurred during a period of poor LFP conditions when a mild drought from 1338 to 1352 probably favored floodwater farming. Population decreased during this period and continued to do so. In the Santa Fe subarea, however, population continued to increase (Dickson 1979) as the Pajarito population declined. At one community, Arroyo Hondo Pueblo, population covaried with high frequency variations in rainfall (Rose, Dean, and Robinson 1981; Schwartz 1981:xiv).

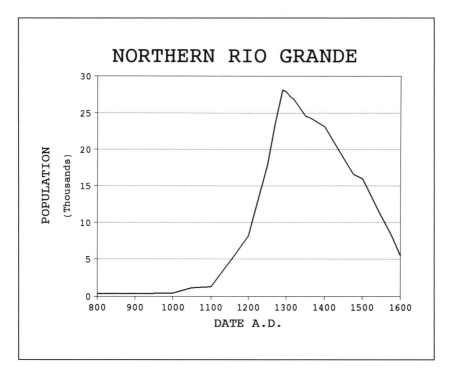

Figure 4.9. Population: Northern Rio Grande area.

MOGOLLON HIGHLANDS

Whether the first two maxima and minima in the Mogollon population curve
(fig. 4.10) (Bluhm 1960; Danson 1957; Haury 1985; Martin and Rinaldo 1950;
Reid, Tuggle, and Klie 1982; Rice 1975) are "real" is difficult to determine because
of the residential mobility that characterized this period (Reid 1989; Rice 1980).
More permanent settlements appeared in the eleventh to thirteenth centuries in
the Forestdale Valley and at Point of Pines, probably in relation to locally abundant resources (Reid 1989:75). In the Grasshopper and Q Ranch areas, however,
population increase and settlement aggregation occurred in the late 1200s to early
1300s (Reid 1989:77).

Some of the population increase of the late 1200s to early 1300s is attributed
to immigration from the Colorado Plateau (Haury 1958; Reid 1989:80), where
large populations had been dislodged by severe LFP and HFP environmental deterioration (Dean et al. 1985; Dean and Robinson 1982:57; Plog et al. 1988). The
diminished impact of drought in the comparatively wet mountains (Dean and
Robinson 1982:57–58), coupled with the diverse subsistence economies of the
Mogollon groups (Reid 1989; Rice 1980), probably made it possible to increase
agricultural production to accommodate the immigrants, at least for a time.

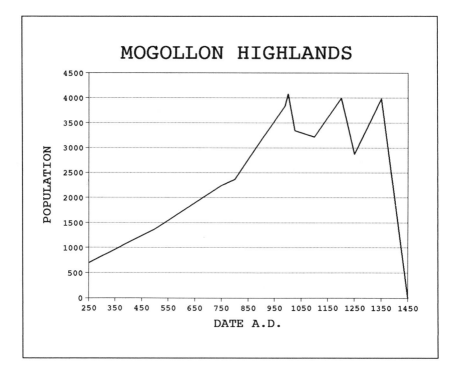

Figure 4.10. Population: Mogollon Highlands area.

In some localities, a return to a more dispersed, mobile settlement pattern preceded the post-1350 population decline that terminated the occupation of the area a century later (Reid 1989:85). These events overlap a period of below-average precipitation (1325–1350) and coincide with a major episode of fluvial degradation.

Hohokam Area

The Hohokam area (fig. 4.11) is characterized by greater residential stability than other parts of the Southwest. In contrast to the settlement volatility in the mountains and on the plateau, Hohokam sites commonly were occupied for centuries. Most Hohokam site abandonments and settlement shifts represent minor movements within proscribed localities rather than the abandonment of particular areas. This residential stability and the nature of Hohokam sites make population estimation even more difficult in the desert than it is elsewhere. In addition to spanning long time periods, sites characteristically are dispersed over large areas, not a few exceeding a square mile in extent. Furthermore, many sites are partially or wholly buried in alluvium. Finally, Hohokam pithouses and adobe structures are difficult to perceive from the ground surface. These factors render the temporal and spatial discrimination of site components extremely difficult without

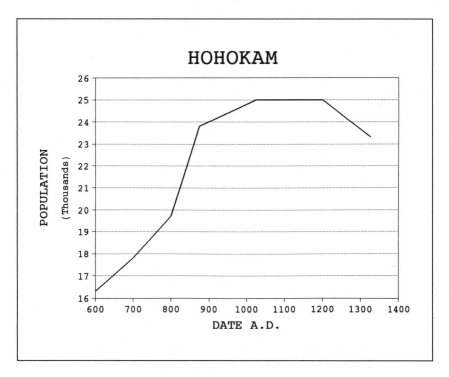

Figure 4.11. Population: Hohokam area.

extensive excavation. Therefore, Hohokam population reconstructions have primarily involved extrapolations from excavated sites or calculations based on the extent and capacity of canal systems.

The Hohokam population curve applies to the areas in which irrigation from major rivers was practiced. Included are the middle and lower Santa Cruz and San Pedro drainages, the Hohokam "core" area in the middle Gila and lower Salt valleys, and the lower Verde Valley. Due to insufficient data, the Papaguería is omitted from these estimates. Population numbers for the 800 through 1325 period are based on the aggregated number of village segments per phase (Doelle 1990) and are plotted at the approximate midpoints of the phases from Gila Butte through Civano. The figures for earlier phases are more subjective projections of the data.

Three major "transitions" characterized Hohokam prehistory. The first occurred around 800 in the Gila Butte phase, when the indigenous social system that characterized the preceding Pioneer period was reconfigured into the Hohokam regional system with ballcourts, red-on-buff pottery, distinctive mortuary practices, and other features. The second was the transition from the Sedentary to the Classic period. The last was the so-called collapse of the Hohokam at the end of the Civano phase sometime after 1350. The first transition initiated a period of population growth, the second marked a stabilization of population size coupled with major social change, and the third denoted apparently dramatic population decline and the end of the Hohokam as an archaeologically distinguishable entity.

Lacking concrete evidence, the "best guess" is that there was a gradual upward trend in regional population from the inception of agricultural reliance around 800 BC to AD 600. The Snaketown phase (c. 700–750) appears to represent a major shift in social organization (Doyel 1991; Masse 1980). In the ensuing Gila Butte phase, ballcourt construction was initiated and spread rapidly. After the initial spread of ballcourts, new varieties of maize were introduced (Cutler and Blake 1976), and population grew rapidly. Thus, the new social arrangements implied by the ballcourts seem to have preceded the initiation of population growth.

The "Preclassic to Classic" transition (Sedentary period) was an interval when population growth yielded to stability or minor fluctuation. Recent research indicates that many of the social changes evident in the Phoenix Basin Sacaton phase occurred at roughly the same time in the Early and Middle Rincon phases in the Tucson Basin.

Many scholars argue that population growth and agricultural intensification caused the maximum expansion of the canal systems and the development of hierarchical social systems in the lower Salt River valley during the Classic period. Howard (1991) argues, however, that much of the canal building occurred in the Sedentary, with expansion of some of the northern and westernmost canals continuing in the Classic. Several canals were abandoned during the Sedentary-to-Classic transition, and a significant portion of the total capacity of the system and a large area of irrigable land were relinquished.

Much lower estimates of the total acreage under irrigation led Nials, Gregory, and Graybill (1989:74) to conclude that "explanations of Hohokam culture change in which population pressure is an important variable should be reassessed." It does not necessarily follow, however, that because some population reconstructions were based on inflated estimates of potentially irrigable land, population levels could not have approached the productive limits of the agricultural system. In fact, the empirical data on canal construction (Howard 1991) suggest that unless population declined in the Salt River area during the Classic, significant population pressures may have developed.

Graybill's (1989) streamflow reconstruction indicates particularly favorable conditions for irrigation during most of the Sacaton phase and does not identify unfavorable conditions that could account for the substantial reorganization of the Hohokam system at the end of the phase. Conditions other than streamflow may have changed, however. Population growth stimulated by the favorable conditions of the Early Sacaton phase may have eventually stressed the system. Changes in more localized conditions may have forced peripheral populations back into the "core" area; for example, abandonment of the New River area by the end of the Sacaton phase may have increased population pressures on the lower Salt River agricultural systems. Finally, changing regional social systems, both Hohokam and others, may have helped stabilize Classic period populations.

Nials, Gregory, and Graybill (1989) propose that a major flood in 1358 following a series of dry years may have incised river channels, destroyed canal intakes, and thereby triggered the Hohokam "collapse" in the Phoenix Basin, a hypothesis that is supported by Piman legends (Teague 1989). Waters (1989) suggests that a major downcutting of the Santa Cruz River at the end of the Classic may account for the demise of the Tucson-area Hohokam. Doelle and Wallace (1991) see the collapse as affecting primarily the Phoenix Basin. In the Tucson area, less dependence on irrigation and more flexible social and subsistence systems allowed recovery even from the hydrologic problems cited by Waters. Unfortunately, too few data are available to provide much support for any of the current hypotheses as to the demise of the Hohokam.

ENVIRONMENTAL AND DEMOGRAPHIC SYNTHESIS

Figure 4.12 summarizes Southwestern population history insofar as it can be synthesized from the foregoing extrapolations of a fragmentary and poorly sampled archaeological record. Because the procedures used by different scholars to estimate population vary so greatly, we have little faith in the absolute accuracy of the estimated number of people. On the other hand, we are confident that, with two exceptions, the general trends are reasonably representative of the demographic history of the region.

The first anomaly is the magnitude of the population increase between 550 and 600, which is primarily a function of the initial appearance of Hohokam population estimates at 600. Projecting the slope of the Hohokam curve (see fig. 4.11) inside 600 would produce a more gradual increase in regional population that would probably more accurately portray the true situation. The second anomaly—the precipitous drop-off after 1200—is an undoubted artifact of the archaeological coverage of the region. Investigation of many areas that were densely occupied after 1300 has been limited. As a result, no estimates are as yet available for post-1300 population centers such as the Roosevelt Basin, the Hopi Mesas, the Acoma-Laguna area, and parts of the Rio Grande drainage. Although population may have dropped after 1300, the major decline undoubtedly occurred after 1500 as a result of the introduction of European diseases and European colonists.

The Southwestern population trajectory exhibits a fairly simple, unimodal configuration that would be somewhat less extreme if the anomalies noted above could be corrected. Nevertheless, it seems clear that regional population grew steadily from around AD 1, reached its maximum at about 1000, fluctuated slightly for 200 years, then dropped precipitously after 1200. By the time of Spanish colonization, population had declined to levels far below what the region had supported only 300 years earlier. Regional population appears to have peaked at approximately 100,000 people around AD 1000. Given the patchy archaeological coverage of the region, this figure undoubtedly underestimates the true number of people, perhaps by as much as half. Thus, population probably peaked at between 130,000 and 150,000 individuals in the eleventh through thirteenth centuries.

The configuration of the regional population curve is determined in no small

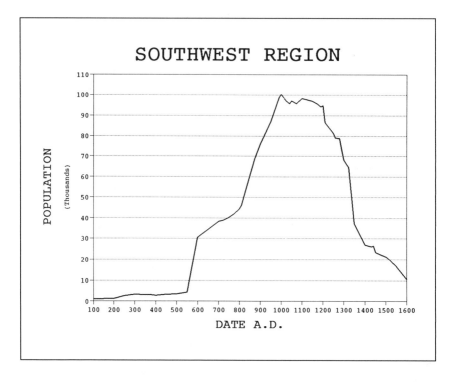

Figure 4.12. Regional population trends, AD 1 to 1600.

part by demographic developments in the desert. Hohokam population (see fig. 4.11) reached high levels fairly early and remained comparatively stable thereafter, providing a consistent floor for regional population numbers. The large number of people and low variability probably are due to a secure subsistence base provided by the natural richness of the desert biota and irrigation agriculture. Other areas lacked the cushion provided by long-term subsistence stability and were more susceptible to environmental and sociocultural perturbations. Consequently, most of the fluctuations in regional population are due to the higher demographic variability that prevailed outside the Hohokam area.

The curve has several interesting variations that probably reflect demographic reality. Although the abrupt jump between 500 and 600 is partly method induced, it probably also reflects settlement stabilization and consequent population growth on the Colorado Plateau caused by the spread of the more sedentary Basketmaker III lifeway. Continued growth between 600 and 800 probably indicates demographic changes resulting from widespread commitment to farming during this period. The accelerated rate of growth and major increase in regional population between 800 and 1000 probably are due to a combination of three factors outside the desert: first, reliance on fairly simple lowland and upland agriculture increased; second, environmental conditions especially favorable for this subsistence strategy prevailed throughout the region (Dean et al. 1985; Euler et al. 1979; Plog et al. 1988); and third, abundant underexploited space existed to absorb expanding populations. Thus, population grew rapidly during a period when environmental conditions favored farming in a variety of habitats and geographic expansion was possible.

The abrupt cessation of growth around 1000 may indicate that population had reached or—given the apparent decline immediately thereafter—even exceeded a regional carrying capacity boundary. Population apparently peaked *during* a period of propitious LFP and HFP environmental conditions that lasted from the early 900s to about 1130. If genuine, this circumstance suggests that, on a regional scale, population growth rather than environmental degradation breached a systemic threshold. Consideration of the individual population trajectories (see figs. 4.1–4.11), however, reveals that this peak is due to a major decline after 1000 in the San Juan Basin (see fig. 4.6). That this attribute of the regional curve is due to the transgression of a more localized threshold is indicated by the fact that population continued to grow after 1000 in most other areas, including Chaco Canyon, which lies within the San Juan Basin. The fact that regional population did not decrease proportionately to the decline in the San Juan Basin suggests that most displaced groups were absorbed into other areas. Nevertheless, it appears that as early as 1000, some local populations were crowding the maximum numbers that could be supported by existing technologies even under exceptionally favorable environmental conditions. This local setback was a harbinger of future larger-scale developments, particularly in that salubrious environmental conditions could not last forever.

The termination of population growth was followed by two centuries of small fluctuations around a level slightly below the maximum. These variations resemble those inferred by Stephen Plog (1986a:243–50) to represent a deviation amplifying response to a local transgression of systemic limits on Black Mesa. The similarity suggests that this process operated on a regional as well as local scale after 1000. The variations in the Southwestern curve during this interval may reflect (1) a large-scale reaction to the forcing of a regional boundary, (2) a series of local transgressions, or (3) an integration of the two in which a regional-scale phenomenon is uniquely expressed in different localities.

It is important to remember that whatever processes are embedded in these fluctuations, they are evident only outside the desert where either population numbers were fairly stable or the method of estimation is insensitive to high-frequency variations. If the former alternative reflects reality, population stability was maintained by a comparatively secure subsistence base founded on irrigation agriculture, and the number of people did not crowd carrying capacity. If, on the other hand, the estimation method masks high-frequency variability, nothing can be said about demographic responses to the breaching of systemic thresholds in the desert.

A long period of moderate environment ended around 1130, when conditions worsened in all three major habitat zones. On the plateau and in the mountains, a secondary dip in alluvial groundwater levels and minor floodplain erosion were accompanied by a severe drought. In the desert, the climatic downturn was reflected in reduced streamflow in the Salt and Verde rivers. These factors lowered carrying capacity thresholds in numerous localities, thereby decreasing the regional average carrying capacity. The depression of systemic boundaries would have had major negative impacts in areas where population was crowding these limits. The local effects of these environmental changes are evident in the demographic curves of many areas. Several localities were abandoned at this time, while others were loci of major settlement dislocations. The beginning of a permanent downward trend in Southwestern population in the twelfth century (see fig. 4.12) may be a regional expression of several local population adjustments to the environmental deterioration of the middle twelfth century.

The major regional population drop-off after 1200, though not as steep as shown in figure 4.12, integrates numerous local demographic and settlement responses to the widespread environmental degradations that occurred after 1270. Again, these demographic changes occurred mainly outside the desert, where Hohokam population still maintained a stable profile. Large tracts such as the San Juan drainage were vacated, and population concentrated in a few smaller areas in the Little Colorado drainage, the Mogollon Highlands, the Rio Grande drainage, and below the Mogollon Rim. Major population buildups in the Roosevelt Basin–Casas Grandes axis are not well reflected in the regional curve. These demographic changes represent, at least in part, the sum of many local adjustments to a primary depression of alluvial water tables, severe and prolonged downcutting of floodplain sediments, and a severe drought in the late thirteenth century. The significant declines in desert and mountain populations after 1400 are not obviously related to major environmental shifts. Furthermore, Southwestern population levels did not rebound with the reestablishment of favorable fluvial conditions throughout the region after that date. European disease vectors and, later, the presence of Europeans themselves probably account for the failure of native populations to grow appreciably until the introduction of modern health care practices in the late nineteenth century.

Apart from the correspondences noted above, Southwestern population variability does not correlate well with paleoenvironmental variability. Given the assumption of independent demographic and environmental processes, it would be naive to attribute regional demographic trends solely to environmental variability. In general, population numbers are culturally buffered from the immediate effects of environmental change except for natural catastrophes of the direst sort; therefore, population size acts as an independent variable in most adaptive situations (Dean 1988a; Dean et al. 1985; Plog 1986a).

Why, then, is the literature replete with successful attempts to relate numbers of people to environmental variability? And why are there so many evident correlations between LFP and HFP environmental fluctuations and the subregional demographic variability evident in figures 4.1 through 4.11? Two factors are responsible for the observed correspondences. First, it seems clear that demographic responses to environmental factors take place primarily on the local rather than regional level. Averaging highly variable, environmentally responsive local population fluctuations produces a smoothed regional trajectory that masks local correspondences with environmental variations. Second, the congruences probably reflect nondemographic behavioral factors embedded in the population reconstructions. Environmentally induced behavioral responses—such as increased or decreased mobility, aggregation or dispersion, settlement system adjustments, and local abandonments—would impact archaeological demographic calculations to the extent that the curves reflect both behavioral variables and numbers of people. Thus, many of the environmental correspondences apparent in local population curves may be due to behavioral adaptations rather than to environmentally induced changes in the numbers of people.

Geographical patterning of population variability through time is summarized here in a series of maps (figs. 4.13–4.18). Each map characterizes population distributions during one of the periods identified by Cordell and Gumerman (1989:5–13). The maps are purely subjective renderings of data that are themselves highly subjective and severely biased. The population numbers are extracted from the areal analyses presented above (see figs. 4.1–4.11). The contours smooth the sometimes sharp disjunctions between these areas by incorporating qualitative information on the occupations of intervening areas that lack quantitative population estimates. In addition, contours are used to indicate known variations within the areas for which estimates are available. The high relief of the demographic landscape renders strict contouring impractical; therefore, the contour lines are individually labeled. The "0" contour delimits the total area for which population data are available and is not meant to imply that no one lived outside this boundary. The resulting representations are highly impressionistic, fuzzy "snapshots" of conditions at different times. The details are questionable; the general patterns, however, are probably reasonably accurate.

Figure 4.13 represents the demographic situation at the beginning of the Initiation period around AD 400. Except in the Hohokam area, where favorable agricultural conditions supported large numbers of people, population was low throughout the region. Archaeological focus on Basketmaker II and early Mogollon sites produces population concentrations on the plateau and in the Mogollon Highlands that may be functions of the paucity of published data on intervening areas, such as the Little Colorado drainage. The "hole" in Anasazi population at the Four Corners is real, however. Fairly dense Basketmaker II populations surrounded an area that appears to have been virtually devoid of people until Basketmaker III.

Figure 4.14 depicts conditions around 800: the beginning of the Expansion period, when regional population had grown substantially. Two centers of especially rapid growth are evident. The major upsurge in Four Corners' population was fueled primarily by the Basketmaker III and Pueblo I commitment to agriculture in this area, particularly in the San Juan Basin. The less spectacular but

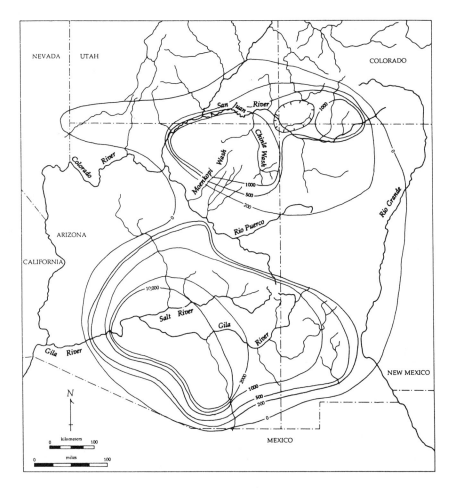

Figure 4.13. Regional population distribution at AD 400 (Initiation period).

nonetheless substantial growth in the desert was supported by the expansion of large-scale irrigation systems. Although population numbers in the Little Colorado drainage may be underestimated, the "trough" between northern and southern high-density zones that developed by this time was a persistent feature of Southwestern demographics.

By about 1100, during the Differentiation period (fig. 4.15), regional population had increased substantially. The pattern of plateau and desert population centers separated by a trough had intensified. The apparent broadening of the trough to include both the Little Colorado Valley and the Mogollon Highlands reflects the fact that population in the former area had grown to equal that in the latter. Furthermore, the "floor" of the trough had risen considerably. The wide-

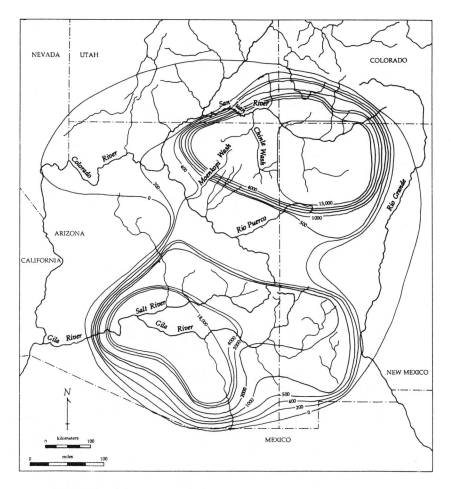

Figure 4.14. Regional population distribution at AD *800 (Expansion period).*

spread dispersal of Mesa Verde and Kayenta Anasazi settlements and the rapid growth of the Chacoan regional system are reflected in elevated values throughout the plateau, and the Sedentary period growth of the Hohokam regional system is evident in the desert.

Population distribution at 1200 (fig. 4.16) characterizes the Reorganization period. Although population numbers had stabilized, the greater complexity of the contours reflects the substantial settlement shifts that took place in the late 1100s. The northern and southern population centers remained, but the former was much more complex than the latter, and more complex than it itself had been previously. The central trough remained, but was displaced southward into the mountains as major settlement shifts doubled the population of the Little Colorado

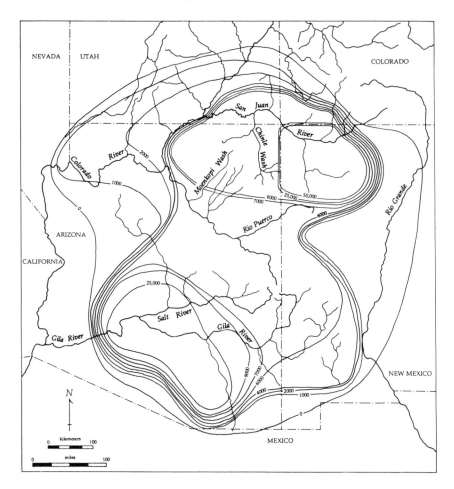

Figure 4.15. Regional population distribution at AD 1100 (Differentiation period).

Valley. Decreased population in the San Juan Basin coupled with higher numbers in both the Cebolleta and northern Rio Grande areas may reflect the breakup or reorientation of the Chacoan regional system. Reduced numbers on the north-western margins of the plateau represent the Anasazi evacuation of these areas or the adoption of different lifeways by groups that remained in place. The "hollow" in northeastern Arizona denotes the abandonment of northern Black Mesa after 1150. Entering the Classic period, Hohokam population had stabilized at a level that persisted until the "crash" at the end of the period.

Figure 4.17 reflects the major population dislocations that disrupted the Southwest at the end of the thirteenth century and initiated the Aggregation period. The spatial complexity evident in the preceding period appears to have

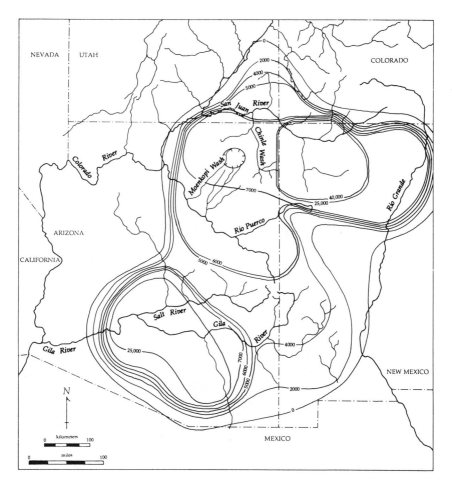

Figure 4.16. Regional population distribution at AD 1200 (Reorganization period).

intensified as populations coalesced into a limited number of loci. Hohokam population dropped slightly but remained fairly stable along the rivers of southern Arizona. Except for sporadic use by transient Puebloan groups, the San Juan drainage was vacated as people moved south and east to augment populations along the southern and eastern margins of the plateau. Immigration into the Rio Grande area added a third population nucleus to the extant southern (Hohokam) and northern (Anasazi) centers, while movement out of the San Juan drainage shifted the northern center southward into the Little Colorado Valley.

Despite these redistributions, the trough between the northern and southern population concentrations persisted in the mountain zone. By this time, however, it was augmented by a low-density arm running north-south between the

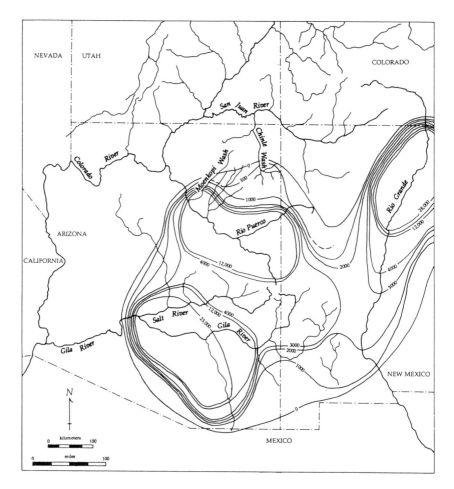

Figure 4.17. Regional population distribution at AD *1300 (Aggregation period).*

Rio Grande and Little Colorado centers. Small numbers of hunters and gather-ers undoubtedly occupied the vast territory abandoned by the Anasazi: Cerbat groups (Pai?) in the Grand Canyon area and Numic speakers (Paiute) in the north. These groups, along with the Yumans along the lower Colorado River, have a low archaeological visibility, and too little information is available for satisfac-tory demographic estimates. The growing population center at Casas Grandes in northern Chihuahua, which had important connections with the people of south-ern Arizona and southwestern New Mexico by 1300, is not shown on the map.

On the eve of European contact, population numbers probably remained fairly high, but people had redistributed themselves across the landscape (fig. 4.18). Pueblo groups continued their eastward drift, leaving tenuous connections from

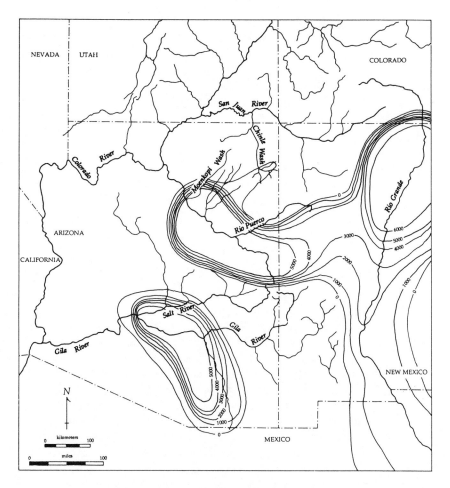

Figure 4.18. Regional population distribution at AD 1500.

the Hopis in the west through the Zunis and Keresan groups to the center on the Rio Grande. The mountains were vacated by sedentary peoples. Hohokam population apparently had crashed by this time, although evidence is increasing for the persistence of Postclassic groups after 1500. The vigor of the Casas Grandes center had waned, its population dispersed, and its influence on the Southwest diminished. As in the previous period, groups of low archaeological visibility undoubtedly inhabited the areas vacated by the sedentary populations. Yuman, Pai, and Numic groups occupied the western and northern peripheries of the region, and Athapaskans may have infiltrated the northern margin.

By 1700, the massive population reductions and relocations occasioned by the Spanish entry into the region had taken full effect. Puebloan populations were reduced to discontinuous pockets at Hopi, Zuni, Acoma-Laguna, Pecos, and the communities along the Rio Grande. Other agricultural groups occupied southern Arizona: Yumans along the lower Colorado, Pimans on the Gila, and Papagos in the southwestern deserts. Nomadic groups inhabited the peripheries and the interstices among sedentary groups: Pai, Paiutes, Utes, and Plains tribes around the margins, Apaches and Navajos in the areas between agricultural groups. This distribution was fixed by European encroachment into the region and persists to the present.

CONCLUSIONS

The basic purpose of this review of prehistoric environmental and population dynamics has been to document the physical and demographic components of the adaptive situations that structured sociocultural stability and change in the Southwest. Comparison of these reconstructions should allow the identification of periods when population and environmental oscillations converged to either stress the subsistence systems that supported Southwestern societies or release these systems from external constraint. The data allow the interaction of environmental, demographic, and behavioral variables to be examined on both local and regional scales. Local implications are addressed in the sections on specific areas. Some of the regional implications of the analysis are examined here.

Regional behavioral adjustments should be expected when major LFP environmental deterioration coincided with HFP declines and high population densities. Primary LFP degradations occurred in the early third, middle eighth, late thirteenth, and late nineteenth centuries, the last two accompanied by significant HFP droughts. Due to high population levels, the thirteenth- and nineteenth-century episodes should have had the greatest impact. The steep decline in regional population after 1250 undoubtedly is a manifestation of the widespread behavioral adaptations to the former episode. These adjustments involved extensive population redistributions, settlement shifts, and major socioreligious transformations. The nineteenth-century environmental degradation also had important behavioral consequences (major adjustments in subsistence, commercial operations, water management, and settlement), but none of these appreciably affected population, which was sustained by participation in the national economy of the United States.

None of the secondary LFP degradations appears to have visible regional demographic repercussions. The one at 1150, which was accompanied by a severe drought and high population densities, appears to have triggered widespread population redistributions and behavioral adjustments that are evident in many areas; these show up, if at all, only as a slight steepening of the downward trend in the regional population curve. Extended periods of regional drought unaccompanied by LFP degradations apparently had primarily local consequences.

Transitions from unfavorable to favorable conditions would have relaxed environmental constraints on populations and sociocultural systems. LFP transformations of this sort occurred around 400, 950, and 1475, with the period from about

925 to 1150 being particularly auspicious due to the combination of favorable LFP and HFP conditions. The first of these transitions may have in some sense initiated significant population increase throughout the region by promoting agriculture. As suggested above, the favorable conditions of the tenth century may have fostered, or at least allowed, an accelerated rate of growth. The transition to favorable LFP conditions around 1475 had no detectable positive effect on regional population, perhaps because prolonged HFP drought in the sixteenth century and, later, European contact inhibited a demographic response to this environmental release. Particularly good HFP conditions in the first and tenth centuries AD and in the early 1300s, 1600s, and 1900s had no discernable impact on regional population.

Any congruences between past environmental variability and regional demographic trends likely reflect behavioral responses embedded in the population curve (see fig. 4.12). Nevertheless, it probably is not entirely coincidental that regional population grew rapidly during an environmentally favorable interval (900–1000) and stabilized or declined during less salubrious periods (1130–1180, post-1250). On the other hand, regional population often behaved independently of environmental variability as in the post-1000 downturn during a favorable interval. On balance, however, environmental fluctuations, transmitted through and modified by various sociocultural "filters," appear to have affected human demography throughout the last two millennia. This influence probably was manifested primarily through the accretion of behavioral responses to local environmental circumstances rather than through regional adaptations to large-scale environmental fluctuations—a result that supports the conclusion (Plog et al. 1988) that the locality is more appropriate than the region for examining the effects of population-environment interactions on human adaptive systems.

It appears to be more fruitful to view the correspondences between numerical and distributional trends in population on the one hand and environmental variability on the other as quasi-independent convergences that had important adaptive consequences for Southwestern societies (Plog et al. 1988). Figure 4.12 suggests that prior to about 1000, populations were low enough to have allowed fairly simple behavioral responses to environmental variability. Except in areas of high population density, such as the desert and Chaco Canyon, these responses appear to have primarily involved settlement mobility. Small groups responded to local environmental stresses simply by moving into nearby areas that were less affected by environmental degradation and human occupation. This circumstance is reflected in the power of paleoenvironmental information as a predictor of site location shifts before 1000 in many places. The obverse of this situation is the diminished utility of environmental variability as a predictor of site locations after 1000, when growing populations filled habitable areas and curtailed settlement mobility as an adaptive response. After 1000 in most areas, other behavioral adjustments were made, involving subsistence intensification, increased intergroup interaction, and increased sociocultural complexity.

The preceding section, along with the more intensive analyses of the earlier SAR advanced seminar on the dynamics of Southwestern prehistory (Cordell and

Gumerman 1989), elucidates the degree to which sociocultural changes in the Southwest conform to the expectations generated from environment-population models of human adaptive behavior. Many congruences establish the importance of demographic and environmental variables as integral factors in sociocultural stability, variability, and change in this harsh and variable region. On the other hand, many failures of the archaeological record to fulfill the expectations of the models indicate that the effects of population and environmental fluctuations were mediated and transformed by sociocultural factors. As a result, we conclude that the relative contributions of the three types of factor—environmental, demographic, and behavioral—vary situationally. The potential roles of all three classes therefore must be assessed empirically in each analytical case, whether regional or local in scope. Such assessment depends on our ability to carefully and accurately measure variability in all the relevant factors. Before knowledge of the complex relationships among the environment, human demography, and behavior can be materially advanced from its present inadequate state, scientists must devise more sophisticated and more quantitative theories of systemic sociocultural change and develop better techniques for quantifying, measuring, and analyzing variables relevant to the task of evaluating these theories.

——— *Acknowledgments* ———
The authors wish to thank Eric Blinman and Alison E. Dean for invaluable contributions to the production of the graphs and maps that accompany this paper.

5

Patterns of Diet and Disease
Health Profiles for the Prehistoric Southwest

DEBRA L. MARTIN

THE DATA IN THIS CHAPTER are derived from the analysis of human biological remains retrieved from the American Southwest before such investigations were contested by the American Indian community (Deloria 1989). The passage of legislation in 1990 (Public Law 101–601, "Native American Graves Protection and Repatriation Act") ensures that American Indians will have final say about the nature of all future studies that rely on prehistoric human remains. Biological anthropologists, specifically skeletal biologists and paleopathologists, can no longer assume access to either the remains or the information gleaned from them (Masayesva 1991). Already, the repatriation effort has redefined the direction of studies that involve human remains (Jenkins 1991).

BIOARCHAEOLOGY IN THE AMERICAN SOUTHWEST

In reconstructing health profiles for early indigenous populations living in the American Southwest, it is clear that many of the health problems facing people worldwide today were endemic and vexing difficulties for prehistoric groups such as the Anasazi, Mogollon, and Hohokam. For example, a bladder stone from a Classic Hohokam individual has been found (Fink and Merbs 1991); iron deficiency anemia was ubiquitous among children and adults throughout the occupation of the Southwest (Walker 1985); and congenital defects such as vertebral fusion have been documented for Kayenta Anasazi (Merbs and Euler 1985). Mogollon and Anasazi children experienced disruptions in growth at many sites (Martin et al. 1991), and helminthic parasites such as pinworm and hookworm are found in Anasazi desiccated feces (Reinhard 1988, 1990). Baker and Armelagos (1988) reviewed the evidence for nonvenereal endemic syphilis (treponematosis) with cases from Tuzigoot (AD 1000–1350) and Pecos (AD 1250–1350), among others. Tuberculosis has been demonstrated to exist in a number of Southwestern skeletal series such as San Cristobal (Stodder 1990) and Pueblo Bonito (Palkovich 1984a).

These examples represent only a minuscule fraction of the kinds of health data currently available for the American Southwest, and this review is not an exhaustive survey of that literature. Starting with the earliest analyses conducted by Hrdlicka from a variety of sites (1908) and Hooton from Pecos (1930), there is an enormous and rapidly growing literature on health for Southwestern skeletal series.

Biological remains represent a data base with the potential to bring important new research programs to both biological anthropology and archaeology. It is unfortunate that the historical development of archaeology and biological anthropology was such that methods and theories developed along separate and largely noninteractive trajectories (Blakely 1977; Buikstra 1977). Although human remains are found in the same archaeological contexts as pottery and other artifacts, they have traditionally been under the sole purview of biological anthropologists, with archaeologists the random consumers of the resulting analyses. In an attempt to rectify certain misunderstandings on both sides of the potential of biological data, some archaeologists have encouraged bioarchaeology as a field of study, but usually in the mechanical sense that biological anthropologists are invited to work alongside archaeologists in the field. Unfortunately, bioarchaeological research has not come to mean that archaeologists work to understand the analytical procedures and potential of the human remains once they are in the laboratory or that biological anthropologists work closely with archaeologists in interpreting demographic, health, and genetic information within the larger archaeological context. This problem has most likely been exacerbated in the Southwest by the very low number (from the 1970s onward) of paleopathologists and skeletal biologists focusing on population-level analyses of Southwestern collections (Stodder 1989b).

The isolation of human remains from both the archaeological context and the ongoing intellectual debates in archaeology is pronounced in Southwest prehistory. Although Cordell's (1984) text, *Prehistory of the Southwest,* is an often-cited review of the archaeological data base, it contains very few references to associated human remains, suggesting that the human remains are not considered an important or accessible part of the Southwest data base.

Although an impressive wealth of data exists for many questions about human adaptation in the prehistoric Southwest, this voluminous literature lacks any systematic or regional synthesis of the biological data for diet and disease, or of how health contributed to or compromised community existence. This deficiency is at odds with the fact that since the late 1800s archaeological recovery has produced a substantial amount of human remains from the Southwest. For the Albuquerque district alone (comprising southern Colorado, New Mexico, and western Texas), Stodder (1988) estimates that from 506 excavated sites, at least 6,535 skeletal remains were recovered, but never fully analyzed.

The de facto elimination of skeletal biology, and, to a lesser degree, mortuary analyses, from archaeological synthesis and interpretation in the past is ironic because many of the current debates in archaeology revolve around issues of subsistence, diet, demography, and biological adaptation. In *Social Adaptation to Food Stress: A Prehistoric Southwestern Example,* Paul E. Minnis (1985b) presents a model that attempts to demonstrate the kinds of behavioral responses prehistoric communities make when experiencing food stress. Using archaeological data from the Mimbres region of New Mexico, Minnis reconstructs population size, storage facilities, and climate. From these and other lines of evidence, he infers a directional and hierarchical set of responses that Mimbres people made in order to survive food stress. Ironically, the model fails to take into consideration a number of important variables, the most important being how food stress affects humans physiologically in terms of morbidity and mortality, and how this in turn may affect behavior. Biology is dismissed altogether, and all individuals are assumed to have equal chances of being affected by food stress. Furthermore, the concept of food stress itself is so imprecisely defined that it is unclear how one is to use the model to assess the response. In the total absence of biological analyses, any discussion of prehistoric dietary adequacy and malnutrition for individuals within a community is extremely problematic. It should be noted that human remains from the Mimbres region do exist. Bradfield (1931:54–59) reports on the excavation of 475 burials from Cameron Creek, and Shafer, Marek, and Reinhard (1989) report on remains from the NAN Ranch Ruin. Stodder's (1988:158) research summarizing the availability of skeletal specimens for study in New Mexico demonstrates that 1,255 Mimbres Mogollon human remains exist from 79 sites.

Any model dealing with a topic as broad as food stress needs to incorporate environmental, biological, and cultural factors or risk being at best superficial and at worst misleading. Many models currently proposed for understanding human adaptation in the Southwest incorporate in-depth discussions of such issues as population size, fertility, demographic changes, subsistence regimes, the relative contributions of maize and wild resources, climatic fluctuations, and population movements. Yet, with few exceptions, these topics are discussed in the absence of any empirical evidence from the biological remains. There is ample evidence from other geographical regions of how the addition of empirical health data can aid our understanding of adaptation. A particularly striking set of examples can be found in the edited volume *Paleopathology at the Origins of Agriculture,* which focuses on changes in health related to shifts in subsistence economy in many different parts of the world (Cohen and Armelagos 1984). By integrating archaeological context and health data, anthropologists have come to understand how changes over time in environment, political and economic influences, subsistence and diet, and settlement patterns can and do have profound effects on population structure and rates of morbidity and mortality.

Through archaeological reconstruction, we can infer many aspects of subsistence, diet, and even health. Studies in ethnobiology—which encompasses analyses of pollen and of macrofloral and faunal remains—have been extremely useful (Minnis 1989b; Bruder 1991) and present new possibilities for collaboration with paleopathologists. Coprolite analysis for both dietary remains and parasitic infestation has likewise emerged as an invaluable data base from which to infer diet and disease (Stiger 1979; Scott 1979; Shafer, Marek, and Reinhard 1989; Reinhard 1988, 1990; Reinhard and Hevly 1991). Only by adding the data from the human remains to these analyses can researchers empirically resolve issues of disease load and nutritional adequacy, the impact of diet on population health and longevity, trends in fertility and mortality, and the effects of status and differential access to resources. The skeletal material from the Southwest is not without problems (see Martin et al. 1991:3–11), but a close reading of the published literature reveals a substantial and well-established data base. The remainder of this review outlines the general biological effects of disease and dietary stress in the prehistoric Southwest and briefly summarizes emergent regional and temporal trends in health for Southwestern series. The profiles focus on paleopathology data and are not inclusive of all other kinds of available studies (such as genetic biodistance data, paleodemography, or isotopic analyses).

DIET, DISEASE, AND DEATH: TRACKING THE BIOLOGICAL EFFECTS OF STRESS

Colton (1936) and others (Kunitz 1970; Kunitz and Euler 1972) have argued that disease may have played a major role in the rise and fall of populations in different parts of the Southwest at different times in prehistory. Few current models of culture change in the region rely on disease as a primary causal factor, but empirical demographic and disease data analyzed on population and regional levels may help to recommend the relative contributions of poor health, dietary inadequacies, or increased mortality during periods of environmental or cultural instability.

Stress in prehistorical analyses is defined as any insult that can cause physiological disruption (Goodman, Thomas, et al. 1988:177). Tracking biological response to stress and the causes of poor health and early death is complex and analytically challenging, but in recent years a model that systematically considers potential stressors affecting health has been successfully applied to a number of archaeological populations (Goodman, Lallo, et al. 1984:278; Goodman and Armelagos 1989:226; Martin et al. 1991:24).

In this model (fig. 5.1), the environment is viewed as the source of potential resources. In many areas of the Southwest, environmental constraints limit potential resources. Naturally occurring edible wild plants are generally low in density, widely scattered, unreliable as a dietary staple, and unpredictable in caloric contribution. Reconstruction of wild plant use for the Anasazi (Ford 1984; Wetterstrom 1986), the Mogollon (Minnis 1985b), and the Hohokam (Gasser and Kwiatkowski 1991) demonstrates much variation in the availability and use of wild plants across time and space. Wild grasses and plants could provide a range of essential nutrients, minerals, and vitamins, but they do not store well. Fresh leaves and shoots consumed daily from locally available plants may have been used in the spring, and the seeds of older plants could be harvested in the summer.

Cultigens (primarily maize, gourds, and beans for the Anasazi, maize and agave for the Hohokam) are aggregated, nonrandom in distribution, and predict-

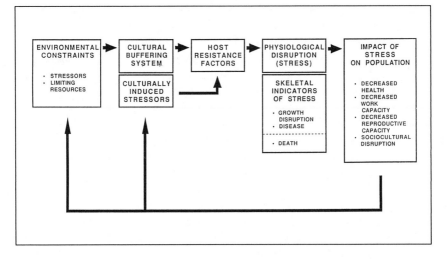

Figure 5.1. Generalized model for analysis of skeletal remains.

able in location, yield, and caloric content. Maize, beans, and squash offer a highly balanced meal, but vagaries inherent in the growing season may have greatly limited supplies in some years. An analysis of the maize species (which is a non-hybrid) used throughout the Southwest shows that it was quite low in protein and available iron (El-Najjar and Robertson 1976).

Land cleared for agricultural use can attract a variety of edible "pioneer annuals," which may have contributed to the dietary base (Ford 1984). These plants, which include *Chenopodium, Portulaca,* and *Amaranthus,* are particularly attracted to newly cleared and planted land. Older, abandoned fields attract Indian rice grass and cactus. Grain amaranths thrive in the desert and are extremely good sources of dietary protein (Sokolov 1986); the total protein intake from combined maize and amaranth diets is superior to the lipid and protein content of maize alone (Morales, Lembcke, and Graham 1988). In reconstructing the ethnobotanical remains from Arroyo Hondo Pueblo, Wetterstrom (1986) demonstrated that high-quality protein and amino acids can be found in chenopodium and amaranth seeds, and that during poor harvest years these plants could have provided a beneficial dietary supplement, especially to growing children.

The amount of meat available in the prehistoric Southwestern diet varied from site to site and across time, but there is ample evidence that many agriculturalists continued to supplement their diet with small game and, in some places, with larger mammals (Szuter 1991). Semé (1984) showed that gardening creates new niches which attract certain animals (primarily rodents and rabbits) into an area in greater quantities. Although these animals (especially rodents) may not ordinarily be hunted as a food source, their high numbers in cultivated fields may have contributed a predictable protein source to prehistoric farmers in the Southwest.

Many researchers have focused their attention on subsistence stress as a major source of poor health, but it does not seem to have been the case that diet per se was the problem. El-Najjar and colleagues (1976) interpreted a higher rate of iron deficiency anemia in canyon-bottom Anasazi (versus the sage-plain dwellers) to mean that the canyon dwellers had less meat in their diet. Reinhard (1988), however, provided an important corrective to this interpretation. Analyzing coprolites from the same sample, Reinhard found more animal bone in the canyon-bottom feces, suggesting that iron deficiency anemia could be a problem even with sufficient meat in the diet. Stodder (1989b) suggests that iron deficiency anemia in the canyon-bottom population resulted from greater rates of infection from parasites and poor sanitation, not from an increased reliance on maize. Iron deficiency anemia in the Southwest, Stodder cautions, cannot be used as an index of maize consumption.

Changes in the degree of mobility among the Anasazi and a trend toward increased sedentism circa AD 1050 were accompanied by an increase in population size. More areas were being farmed, and many of the new farming areas were marginal for agriculture. Changes in settlement location and site-size variability could buffer the people from some stressors, but they also may have provided additional stressors to be coped with.

Jorde (1977) and others (Euler et al 1979; Dean et al. 1985) have emphasized dendrochronological and palynological data in reconstructing the desert Southwest. Drought, shortened growing seasons, climatic perturbations, and the resulting unpredictable agricultural yields have been correlated with changes in settlement patterns, food storage techniques, irrigation, and population movement (Euler et al. 1979), and subsistence stress has figured significantly in many explanations of culture change and population aggregation and decline across regions and through time in the Southwest (e.g., Minnis 1985b; Dean 1988a; Judge 1989). Stodder (1989b:145), however, provides another cautionary tale. It is often assumed that environmental perturbations affecting poor agricultural yield result in subsistence stress and increased health problems. In testing this hypothesis with temporal health data from Mesa Verde, Stodder was able to show that increases in disease were more immediately attributable to sedentism and population aggregation (one response to climatic disturbance) than to the effects of poor agricultural yield and subsistence stress. Stodder rightly points out that diet and subsistence stress are only two of several factors that directly affect morbidity and mortality. Cultural processes such as political organization, settlement pattern, food processing and storing techniques, trade relations, and a host of other culturally influenced behaviors can mediate the negative effects of subsistence stress through technological, social, and ideological systems.

Though culture can buffer individuals from stress, there are numerous examples of culturally produced stressors. Densely settled villages are prime targets for easily transmissible infections like staph and strep (Armelagos and Dewey 1978), and domestication of animals can link humans to certain diseases, such as tuberculosis. In the prehistoric Southwest, the turkey (domesticated by at least AD 200 during Basketmaker II at Canyon de Chelly) may have been a source of ornithoses, shigella, and salmonella (Kunitz and Euler 1972). When the Hoho-kam populations of Pueblo Grande built a 20-mile-long canal to bring water from the river to the village, they created the potential to contaminate the community water supply (Fish 1989). Humans and animals many miles away could contami-nate the water with parasites, bacteria, amoebae, and other infectious agents, and disease could be passed on quite efficiently via the canal.

Anasazi groups to the north, living in densely populated cliff shelters at Mesa Verde, created an environment highly conducive to the spread of contagious dis-eases such as respiratory illness and dysentery (Kunitz 1970). Sedentism asso-ciated with agriculture also brings populations in close contact with human waste, and disposal of excrement in or near the source of potable water increases the potential for contamination. Studies of coprolites from Anasazi settlements reveal at least eight species of helminthic parasites (Reinhard 1988). Woodbury (1965) suggests that dogs, rabbits, and coyotes at Glen Canyon carried tick-borne fevers, Q fever, rabies, tularemia, giardia, and sylvatic plague. Van Blerkom (1985) pro-vides an inclusive list of viruses thought to have been present in the prehistoric Southwest; these include staphylococcal and streptococcal viruses, some forms of herpes and hepatitis, poliomyelitis, pertussis, and rhinoviruses.

Certain segments within a population—infants, weaning-aged children, preg-nant or lactating women, the frail elderly, and individuals with infirmity—are more at risk for severe physiological disruption. These subgroups lack "host resis-tance" (see fig. 5.1) at critical points in their life histories, and they become more vulnerable to stressful events. Many factors can make individuals more suscep-tible to becoming ill; these include blood loss, extremes in heat or cold, injuries, parasitization, and protein-energy malnutrition.

Physiological disruption cannot be directly measured in skeletal and dental remains, but stress does leave indicators. These fall into three major categories: (1) indicators of general and cumulative stress, such as effects on growth, develop-ment, and maintenance of tissue; (2) indicators of stress associated with specific diseases; and (3) age at death. Analysis of these indicators allows for an examina-tion of the impact of stress on the population in terms of morbidity and mortality, the potential effects on adult work capacity and fertility, and finally, the sociocul-tural disruption that may result when many individuals are in poor health.

Pathological alterations on bone are assessed primarily thorough the system-atic description of lesions (table 5.1). Patterns of bone growth and development also provide information on stress. Demographically, a great majority of the human remains recovered in the Southwest are under the age of 18. The growth and development of these individuals can be documented using both dental and skeletal tissue at critical growth stages; this is compared with known values for well-nourished and healthy groups, as well as with modern groups living in simi-larly marginal areas. Identifiable age-specific growth disruptions yield important information on patterns of childhood developmental disturbances and physiologi-cal disruptions.

The distribution and frequency of specific diseases (nutritional, infectious, or

TABLE 5.1.

Summary of skeletal and dental indicators of stress

Indicator	Requirements	At Risk	Severity and Timing	General Comments
Adult stature	Adult long bones	Subadults	Summation of pre-adult factors	Short stature may be response to undernutrition
Subadult size	Subadults with dental age and long bones	Subadults	Summation of factors affecting growing child	Can indicate timing of greatest stress
Sexual dimorphism	Adult male and female pelvis and long bones	Subadult	Summation of pre-adult factors	Dimorphism decreases with increased stress
Enamel defects	Any teeth	0.5 in utero to age 7	Acute stress and/or chronic undernutrition	Associated with non-specific physiological disruption
Dental asymmetry	Dentition	In utero	Early and severe	Measures developmental stress
Dental crowding	Maxilla and mandible with teeth in situ	Subadults	Chronic; severe	Can be nutritional; need to know genetic background
Dental caries	Any teeth	All	Chronic; low	Indication of refined carbohydrate diet; can lead to infection, tooth loss
Dental abscessing	Maxilla and mandible	All	Chronic and severe	Infection can become systemic and life-threatening
Osteoarthritis	Vertebrae and joints	Adults	Chronic	Indication of biomechanical stress

TABLE 5.1.
Continued

Indicator	Requirements	At Risk	Severity and Timing	General Comments
Osteophytosis	Vertebrae and joints	Adults	Chronic wear-and-tear	Indication of biomechanical stress
Osteoporosis	Femur and rib cross sections	Subadults, females, elderly	Acute to severe, pregnancy/ lactation, chronic	Related to calcium loss and malnutrition
Trauma	All bones	All	Acute	Accidents and violence
Periosteal reaction	Long bones	All	Chronic	Some systemic infections appear on bone
Porotic hyperostosis	Cranium	Subadults, females	Acute to severe	Related to iron deficiency anemia
Life tables	Well-represented skeletal population	All	Chronic, severe	Best indicator of overall adaptation

degenerative) is also an essential part of osteological analysis. Patterning and frequencies of nutritional diseases such as iron deficiency anemia are documented for many prehistoric populations and have obvious implications for understanding the adequacy of prehistoric diets. Infectious diseases, also well documented for many skeletal series, provide an indicator of demographic patterning, population density, and degree of sedentism.

In summary, agriculturalists experience a distinctly different disease ecology than that of nomadic hunter-gatherers. Sedentism, increases in population size and density, erosion of land and over-use of resources, and domestication of animals could all increase disease load. But the disease ecology of agriculturalists presents a paradox in the Southwest. On the one hand, agriculturalists tended to be more sedentary, to live in close proximity to each other—and therefore to bacteria and parasites. Yet there were dramatic increases in population growth among Southwestern agriculturalists.

How can there be concomitant increases in subsistence stress and population growth? One explanation is that subsistence stress and endemic disease would have primarily affected the very young and the very old—consumers rather than producers in the group. Death within these groups would have less impact than would widespread morbidity within the producing segments of the population (those aged 20–40). Furthermore, those children who survived would have acquired immunity to the common diseases to which they had been exposed. Surviving children might be weaned earlier, reducing birth spacing and increasing the total number of children born.

Although cultural and behavioral responses may have buffered inhabitants during some environmental perturbations, it could be argued that the Southwest was marginal enough to produce stressors of a magnitude that could not be effectively buffered. Intensifying agriculture at the expense of collecting wild resources could make it difficult to meet dietary requirements should crops fail several years in a row. This problem would be compounded if group size was growing and if there was an investment in a rigid set of subsistence strategies. At the same time, increases in sharing, storage capacity, trading, and redistribution of limited resources—along with a diversification in resource procurement—could offset the stress produced by overreliance on maize.

HEALTH PROFILES

Summarizing the paleopathological data for the American Southwest is a challenging task because few studies contain directly comparable kinds of data. Four different types of studies are typically conducted:

1. Studies of changes in health status over time, which present data on a cluster of health indicators in an attempt to document diachronic trends from Basketmaker II/Pueblo I to Pueblo III/IV. Good examples are Stodder's (1989b) study of health changes at Mesa Verde (AD 600–1300) and the analyses of Kayenta Anasazi remains spanning the years AD 800 to 1150 (Wade 1970; Martin et al. 1991).
2. Studies that compare health across different sites throughout the Southwest, which use single or multiple indicators of stress. An excellent example is Stodder's (1990) use of multiple confirmations of stress and comparison of health at the protohistoric sites of Hawikku and San Cristobal. El-Najjar and colleagues (1976) have looked at frequencies of porotic hyperostosis based on 539 crania from Arizona and New Mexico spanning the prehistoric to historic periods; dental pathology has been compared across sites by Berry (1985).
3. Studies that look for status differences among subgroups within the same site complex system in order to examine trends in differential disease loads. The most notable study of this kind comes from an analysis of Chaco Canyon remains (Palkovich 1984a; Akins 1986).
4. Studies that provide singular and particularistic descriptive accounts of unusual and usually isolated cases of pathology—the great majority of paleopathological studies (e.g., Bennett 1975; Miles 1975; El-Najjar 1979).

To summarize these diverse data sets in a coherent review, it has been necessary to focus on selected population-level accounts that utilize standardized
temporal assignments and age, sex, and health indicators. A series of preliminary
health profiles is presented here, using the temporal markers of culture change
outlined in this volume by Gumerman and Gell-Mann. These profiles are by no
means inclusive of all the research conducted on human skeletal remains; the goal
is to present a framework that others working on prehistoric health in the Southwest can refine and continue to build on in the future.

1000 BC

Although maize was introduced into the Southwest by 1000 BC, Wills (1989)
suggests that for a period of approximately 2,000 years crop cultivation was
supplemental to foraging. Widespread sedentism (as a part of increasing economic
investment in agricultural productivity) did not occur until much later (c. AD
1000). This presents an interesting anomaly in prehistoric North America, where
the transition from hunting and gathering to agriculture was usually marked by
a clear transitional period that led to a full-blown agricultural economy (Buikstra
1984; Goodman, Lallo, et al. 1984).

Human remains from the earliest horticultural foragers in the Southwest represent a unique data base but are few in number and so far mostly unanalyzed.
Stodder (1989b:156) states that "remains from the Archaic and from peoples with
Archaic-type adaptation are not abundant . . . but these constitute slowly accu-
mulating collections which should be systematically analyzed." She estimates that
approximately 70 individuals exist for study and will contribute a great deal to
our understanding of this formative period in Southwestern prehistory. It is not
yet known what the parasite load for individuals was at the 1000 BC juncture, but
Reinhard (1988) found no evidence of helminth infections in an analysis of coprolites from Dust Devil Cave (c. 5000 BC).

AD 200 TO 500

Relatively few human remains are associated with sites beginning with the first
century AD. Euler and colleagues (1979) suggest that people from this time period,
referred to as Basketmaker II populations, formed the basis for subsequent cultural developments in the Kayenta, Mesa Verde, and Chaco regions. These semi-
sedentary hunting-and-gathering groups practiced agriculture, but they clearly
continued to forage and hunt. More than any other period, this most likely represents a transition to more intensive utilization of domesticates. It therefore represents an important temporal marker for assessing health prior to more intensified
reliance on maize.

Current models for understanding health in the prehistoric past emphasize the
benefits of nonsedentary, non-dense populations with mixed subsistence strategies (Cohen and Armelagos 1984). Because so many studies have documented

the decrease in health with the adoption of agricultural and sedentary living, it is generally assumed that a pattern of robust living and good health is related to a hunting-and-gathering lifestyle. This notion has been challenged by some researchers (Rose et al. 1984; Larsen 1984), who show that complexities in environmental and cultural configurations in different areas can produce different patterns of health and disease. The Southwest then presents a rather unique situation with no clear transition from one subsistence economy to another. The major difference between Basketmaker II subsistence and that of the early Pueblo period is one of degree—of subtle differences in the amounts of time dedicated to different food resources. Stiger (1975), analyzing coprolites from Basketmaker sites at Glen Canyon (AD 300), found remnants of squash, beeweed, and prickly pear. Basketmaker coprolites recovered from Mesa Verde demonstrated the presence of maize, beans, squash, amaranth, and prickly pear (Stiger 1979).

Descriptive analyses of naturally mummified Basketmaker remains from cave sites in Utah and Arizona provide data on the physical appearance and other biological aspects of the population (Cummings 1953; Guernsey and Kidder 1921; Morris 1980; El-Najjar and Mulinski 1980), but information on health and disease has not been forthcoming and an understanding of health during this period is sketchy, at best.

Basketmaker II/III remains from Black Mesa, Canyon de Chelly, and the Prayer Rock district do not support a disease-free health profile. Dietary inadequacies, infections, and childhood illness are all documented for this period. Martin and colleagues (1991:243–49) conducted a detailed analysis for health indicators from seven Basketmaker II remains from Black Mesa, Arizona. Their analysis suggests that health problems were similar to those found for later Pueblo remains. The four adults, for example, all showed enamel defects interpreted as childhood stress occurring during the weaning period (between ages 1 and 4). Iron deficiency anemia, although slight and showing signs of healing, is present in both of the children and in one young adult female from the sample. The older adults show signs of degenerative wear-and-tear on their joints, and one severe case of osteomyelitis (infection) was found on the young adult female.

El-Najjar and colleagues (1976) presented data on the frequency of porotic hyperostosis for the Basketmaker II/III series ($n = 136$) from Canyon de Chelly which showed a very high prevalence of iron deficiency anemia. Among children aged 10 and under, 72 percent show lesions; among adults, 36 percent have signs of anemia. More females (42.3%) than males (26.5%) have the lesions. These rates are comparable to rates reported for later Pueblo groups.

In her report on Basketmaker burials from the Prayer Rock district, Morris (1980) noted that several burials have traumatic injuries. Although focusing on mortuary practice and not health, the study does report one male who may have died from a blow to the head and another individual with both a completely healed traumatic injury to the head and an active case of infection.

Although the reported cases of infection and anemia are not as severe as those for later groups, it is important to note the presence of these pathologies on the small number of individuals recovered from this time period. The small sampling of Basketmaker II/III remains shows evidence of dietary inadequacy, degenerative disease, childhood illness, infection, and trauma. The overall trend seems to indicate a continuity with later Pueblo health data.

AD 800 TO 850 AND 950 TO 1100

The time periods delineated by Gumerman and Gell-Mann (this volume) as having distinctive behavioral correlates (800–850 and 950–1100) are difficult to utilize in the construction of health profiles. Most studies reporting population-level data on health in the Southwest group individuals into much longer time spans, such as Pueblo I through Pueblo III (c. AD 700–1300) (Stodder 1989b). Compounding this problem, Pueblo I is sometimes united for analytical purposes with Basketmaker II and at other times with Pueblo II/III.

By AD 800 to 850, larger groups began aggregating in the Southwest, and archaeological interpretations suggest that the most intensive growth occurred in the Hohokam culture. In the Kayenta Anasazi region, health chronologies suggest an existence plagued by nutritional stress and other nonspecific physiological disruptions. Black Mesa, Arizona, provides an interesting comparative set of paleopathological data, since the remains are from small, seasonally occupied, open-air sites. The Black Mesa sample (175 individuals) fills an important gap in the archaeological record. Many of the burials are associated with the earlier Pueblo period (AD 800–1050), a temporal and cultural horizon in the Southwest that has attracted much less scholarly interest than those occurring several hundred years later. Remains also represent a later phase (AD 1050–1150), when some parts of Black Mesa had been abandoned. No statistically significant trends exist that would show a decline in health between the earlier and later individuals (Martin et al. 1991).

For Black Mesa Anasazi, the paleopathology data suggest a group that had generally poor health, but there is evidence that the diseases suffered were largely mild to moderate in severity. Iron deficiency anemia is present in 87.7 percent of the Black Mesa individuals, but only 10.3 percent show severe manifestations; 64.3 percent of the cases are mild in expression or healed, and 25.2 percent are moderate. These data suggest that iron deficiency anemia on Black Mesa was most likely episodic or seasonal in nature and widespread across the population, although infants under the age of 2 had the most severe and active cases of the nutritional disease.

Infection is quite high in infants under a year old (approximately 50%), and iron deficiency anemia and infection tend to co-occur (61.9%). The frequency of nonspecific infectious disease for adults is 24 percent. Growth disruption as measured by enamel defects is very high; 85 percent of the individuals from Black Mesa show defects, with the peak occurrence at ages 2 to 4.

The single health chronology summarized here, representing the periods AD 800 to 850 and 950 to 1100, demonstrates that nutritional stress was a problem for

Anasazi children throughout the occupation. The health data do not imply severe malnutrition, but rather endemic, mild-to-moderate nutritional stress that had an impact on all segments of the population. The mild nature of the iron deficiency anemia, the pervasiveness of childhood growth disruption, and the clustering of pathologies around infancy and weaning suggest a population that faced substantial health-related challenges but was not in serious health decline.

Health data from the Pueblo I/II sites at Chaco Canyon (El-Najjar et al. 1976), Navajo Reservoir (Berry 1983), and Dolores (Stodder 1989b) demonstrate similar involvement with iron deficiency anemia, growth disruption, and nonspecific infection. These pathologies are present in sufficient frequencies to lead us to conclude that at no time in the prehistoric Southwest were groups free from illness related to diet and infection. Certain case studies, discussed in the following temporal categories, suggest that these basic health problems increased in severity and frequency in some areas as groups became more invested in maize agriculture, more densely aggregated, and more sedentary.

AD 1150 TO 1200

Around the time AD 1150 to 1200, several developments in the Southwest signaled major changes in both political structuring and population aggregation. Dendrochronological and palynological data indicate climatic fluctuations that necessitated a more creative use of cultural buffers against lower agricultural yields. There are abundant human skeletal remains from sites during this time, and subtle but important shifts are noted in the paleoepidemiological patterns. At Black Mesa, for example, the frequency of traumatic lesions (related to localized infections from wounds or blows to the body) is approximately 5 percent, but at Mesa Verde it reaches 13 percent and at Chaco Canyon, 17 percent (Stodder 1989b). Although highly speculative and in need of more information from early Pueblo sites, these data suggest that there may have been an increase in interpersonal strife.

Nutritional anemia seems almost to peak during this time, with Canyon de Chelly remains (PII/III) showing 88 percent involvement. The underlying cause of nutritional anemia is not attributed solely to the consumption of iron-poor maize. Walker (1985) has elegantly argued that iron deficiency anemia is the end result of a complex interaction between factors such as food intake, metabolism, malnutrition, and infectious disease. Thus, these lesions signal problems with the consumption and/or utilization of certain nutrients but do not provide information directly about the source of the problem. By AD 1150, the highest nutritional anemia rates are in the two cliff-dwelling samples (Canyon de Chelly and Mesa Verde). Stodder (1989b) has noted that there are more active lesions (versus healed lesions) in the later Mesa Verde sample.

Mesa Verde, located in the northern San Juan region of southwestern Colorado and southeastern Utah, has yielded about 500 skeletal remains from numerous excavated sites spanning approximately 650 years (AD 600–1300). The majority of the remains are from the later time periods (AD 1000–1300) and have been examined by several researchers, the earliest report being Reed's (1965) analysis of 18 Pueblo III burials. Reed cites arthritis and dental pathologies combined with a low life expectancy as indications of a stressed population. A number of unpublished site reports from excavations in the northern San Juan region are similar to Reed's report: site-specific studies of a handful of burials which document pathologies, metric observations, and age at death information (e.g., Swedlund 1965; Nickens 1975a).

Though of limited value, these burial reports help establish an archaeological context for analysis and also provide baseline data on age, sex, stature, metrics, and pathologies. Stodder (1989b) was among the first to attempt a regional synthesis of the paleopathology of the Mesa Verde remains. Representing 466 burials from a Basketmaker III–Pueblo II phase (AD 600–975) and a later Pueblo II–Pueblo III phase (AD 975–1275) of occupation in the Mesa Verde region, these remains collectively represent individuals who lived during the periods of growth and decline in the northern San Juan region.

Stodder (1989b) presents the archaeological context as reconstructed for ecological and subsistence factors, and then provides a demographic study of patterns of mortality, growth disruption, nutritional problems, and other indicators of morbidity. Using paleoepidemiological methods, she documents a trend toward increasing morbidity and higher mortality in younger ages. Tying this in to climatic, ecological, nutritional, and political changes occurring at the end of the later period, Stodder suggests that community health became increasingly compromised.

Stodder presents compelling evidence that health declined from the early to the late periods. Subadults from the early sample exhibit a gradual increase in (1) the probability of dying before reaching adulthood, (2) the prevalence of nutritional anemia (69%), and (3) the frequency of developmental defects from birth to age 5. Peaks in childhood morbidity at ages 2 to 3 suggest weaning stress. In the later sample, the probability of dying is highest at the age of one year, and peaks in childhood morbidity occur later (at ages 4 to 5), suggesting either delayed weaning or increased birth spacing. Nutritional anemia and developmental defects are more prevalent in this group, as well. Stodder also shows that late Pueblo adult females have more indicators of stress than early Pueblo females.

Stodder's work emphasizes the importance of population analyses that take many factors into consideration in the interpretation of community health. Her study contrasts with one undertaken by Miles (1975), a clinical orthopedist who examined 179 burials from Wetherill Mesa, part of the Mesa Verde complex of sites. Though he noted the occurrence of arthritis, infections, trauma, and other ailments, Miles concluded that the Mesa Verde Anasazi were "a surprisingly healthy population" that "was capable of great physical independence" (Miles 1975:35). There is some truth to both Stodder's and Miles's interpretations, a careful reading of which suggests the existence of a robust population that showed resilience and vitality in the face of population growth, strain on resources, increased exposure to communicable diseases, and a narrowing food base. The Mesa Verdeans were survivors who showed endurance (the conclusion reached by Miles), but they definitely suffered from a variety of subsistence- and settlement-related illnesses (Stodder's interpretation).

The Chaco basin was probably the largest Anasazi community in the Southwest, with sites scattered up and down the canyon's length. Sites represent Basketmaker III (600 BC) to Pueblo III (AD 1150) occupations. Although Chaco Canyon probably supported thousands of individuals, only several hundred burials have been excavated. Akins (1986) has conducted an analysis of paleopathology for the Chaco Canyon Anasazi. Her analysis of 132 burials divided the sample into burials from the largest Chaco Canyon site (Pueblo Bonito) and from smaller sites throughout the canyon. Unlike Stodder, who was concerned with temporal trends in health, Akins was more interested in delineating differences in health between high-status (Pueblo Bonito) and low-status (small site) individuals. Her study was not diachronic, but used only later burials representing Pueblo II and Pueblo III occupations.

According to Akins, Chaco Canyon Anasazi suffered from what she terms "subsistence stress"—a condition indicated by growth disruption (88% of the sample shows at least one dental defect), high rates of nutritional anemia (84%), and degenerative diseases (Akins 1986:135). In her analysis of pathologies, Akins suggests that "authority-holding elites" (the Pueblo Bonito sample) had greater access to nutritional resources and enjoyed better health than small-site residents (Akins 1986:137–40). Palkovich (1984a, 1984b) analyzed a subsample of the burials from Pueblo Bonito and reported a frequency for iron deficiency anemia for subadults (up to 10 years old) of 25 percent (relatively low compared with other Southwest series). One Pueblo Bonito child exhibits lesions that appear to be skeletal tuberculosis (Palkovich 1984b). As mentioned previously, the stature of Pueblo Bonito individuals was also significantly greater than that of smaller-site residents at Chaco, as well as many other Southwest sites. The low frequency of iron deficiency anemia combined with greater adult stature suggest a group that was enjoying a better diet and better health than its small-site counterparts.

Human skeletal remains from the Kayenta region have also been analyzed. The area has provided thousands of excavated sites, but only a modest number of burials. Wade (1970) examined 165 burials with the primary goal of providing a diachronic analysis spanning the time period AD 750 to 1250. He suggests that health in general was poor, with a slight trend toward increased stress in the later time period. He also provides a comparison of Puerco Valley mortality profiles with those from two other regional site complexes (Pecos Pueblo Anasazi and Point of Pines Mogollon). In general, the data sets are comparable, and little distinguishing difference among the sites could be found.

Ryan (1977) combined Wade's Puerco Valley sample with burials from several other Kayenta Anasazi sites (AD 750–1300), to achieve a sample consisting of 353 burials representing Pueblo II through Pueblo IV occupations. His analysis of demographic trends, growth disruption, trauma, infection, and anemia parallels Wade's study. Based on the analysis of frequencies by time period, Ryan suggests that health decreased dramatically during the final stages of occupation. He places community health within an ecological framework, weaving together health variables with potentiating ecological factors such as drought and unstable crop production.

These studies for the Kayenta region Anasazi are but a few of the many reports available (among them, Bernor, Ponnech, and Miller 1972; Berry 1983; Merbs and Euler 1985; Martin et al. 1991). Even with overlapping samples, however, it is rare for researchers to use other previously published osteological health data. Ryan employs some of the same burials analyzed by Wade (1970), but he does not cite Wade's data on pathologies since Wade's "data presentation format makes them unsuitable for use here" (Ryan 1977:9). While preparing our analysis of Kayenta Anasazi from Black Mesa, we too were unable to use Ryan's data (Martin et al. 1991). This problem in paleopathological analyses is not confined to Southwestern studies, but it has significantly hampered comparative, cross-regional analysis.

AD 1275 TO 1300

Within a period of little more than one hundred years (AD 1275–1300), dramatic changes came about in the environment and in the relocation of groups across the landscape of the Southwest. As discussed elsewhere in this volume, fairly severe environmental stress occurred in the northern sections of the Southwest, along with a possible reduction in population size. Where populations were aggregating, patterns of hierarchy and strong regional trade systems can be discerned.

Remains from the Hohokam Classic period (AD 1000–1450) which have recently become available represent a very important part of the growing data base on health in the Southwest. Reinhard and Hevly (1991) analyzed the coprolite remains from a partially mummified child from Ventana Cave and found no helminthic infections, in contrast to the multitudes of parasites revealed from similar analyses from Antelope House at Canyon de Chelly (AD 500–1250) (Reinhard 1988).

Hohokam skeletal remains from the Classic period (1100–1450) show that enamel defects were present and seemed to peak between the ages of 2.5 and 4 (Fink and Merbs 1991). Iron deficiency anemia was present in approximately 50 percent of the individuals, and there were two cases of childhood rickets. Fink and Merbs (1991) have some difficulty reconciling what they perceive to be a contradiction between the ethnobiological reconstruction of Hohokam diet and the paleopathology data. The Hohokam diet has been shown to be quite diverse and varied, yet there is evidence in the skeletal remains of growth disruption and nutritional anemia. In this case, the human remains have provided an important corrective to the interpretation that Hohokam diet was adequate for all members during the Classic period.

It is difficult to isolate the Anasazi and Mogollon health data in order to ascertain the level of stress occurring at this time. The published data from sites such as Turkey Creek (1000–1275), Puerco (1150–1250), and Grasshopper (1000–1400), however, show multiple pathologies in frequencies that suggest a continuation of the trends in poor health noted previously. Anemia and infection continue to be endemic at this time. Skeletal remains from the Gallinas sites (PI–III) show the highest published rate of traumatic lesions (41%) (Stodder 1989b).

Perhaps the highest frequency of dental disease (carious lesions) for the Southwest is reported by Bernor, Ponnech, and Miller (1972), who found that 85 percent of the individuals from Rainbow Bridge (AD 1200–1275) had one or more carious lesion. The frequency for dental disease at Grasshopper approaches 50 percent (Stodder 1989b). These percentages are clear increases from the frequencies reported at earlier sites such as Black Mesa (26%), Navajo Reservoir (15%), and Salmon Ruin (20%). One interpretation of this data set—in light of environmental stress and population movement—is that an increased reliance on maize to the exclusion of wild resources resulted in greater frequencies of dental disease.

Akin's (1986) study does not address health at Chaco Canyon over time, but Brock and Ruff's (1988) analysis of Chacoan and other remains does begin to address temporal trends for that region. These researchers used burials from several Southwestern sites in the Chaco region (Chaco Canyon, Mimbres, Gallina, and others) and divided them temporally into Early Villages (AD 900–1150), Abandonments (AD 1150–1300), and Late Prehistoric Aggregated Villages (AD 1300–1540). The health data consisted solely of detailed analyses of the size, shape, density and geometric constitution of the femora (thigh bones) from individual burials.

Brock and Ruff propose that for males and females, bone density is the lowest during the Abandonment phase and probably reflects overall poorer nutritional quality at that time. Early Village and Late Prehistoric Aggregated Village phases show similarly higher bone densities. Although bone density is only one indicator of biological well-being, it has been shown to be very sensitive to nutritional inadequacies. This study indicates in a general way some possible problems with dietary consumption and health preceding or during the abandonment of the Chaco region.

Analyses of other Southwestern skeletal series include a study by Palkovich (1980), who analyzed 120 burials from Arroyo Hondo Pueblo, located in central New Mexico in the Rio Grande area. This enormous site was occupied during two separate periods referred to as Component I (AD 1300–1330) and Component II (AD 1370–1420). Each occupation shows growth, prosperity, and then sudden decline. Palkovich focused her analysis on nutrition- and disease-related pathologies, and did not report trauma and degenerative conditions. Few trends in health status differentiated Component I from Component II, but the Arroyo Hondo Pueblo Indians in general experienced nutritional problems, and children in particular suffered from a variety of ailments.

Palkovich paints a harsh picture for the Arroyo Hondo Anasazi. Most individuals were afflicted with some pathology, and infant mortality was very high. Of the 54 subadults aged to 10 years, she further documented a very high rate of active infections and anemia in infants under the age of one (Palkovich 1987). Normally, infants receive automatic protection from these problems from the mother (if she herself is healthy). Palkovich speculates that Arroyo Hondo infants had immediately acquired infections from their mothers, implying that maternal health was greatly compromised during pregnancy. Palkovich's study of the skeletal remains, together with Wetterstrom's (1986) ethnobotanical reconstruction of Arroyo Hondo's food and diet, strongly suggest that there was endemic malnutrition.

AD 1425 TO 1450

Human skeletal remains representing the period prior to Spanish contact come from large sites such as San Cristobal, Hawikku, Gran Quivira, and Pecos. Merbs (1989), Stodder (1990), and Stodder and Martin (1991) have summarized the health data from these protohistoric sites, and several distinguishable trends have emerged. In general, this time period is characterized by increasing endemic health problems relating to dietary inadequacies and infectious diseases. There is also evidence that densely populated settlements contributed greatly to the more severe expression of infectious diseases, and to the appearance of tuberculosis and treponematoses (Stodder 1990). There also appears to be an increase in traumatic lesions.

Heavy reliance on maize is indicated by bone strontium data from the Pecos (Pueblo IV–historic) remains (Schoeninger 1989); Spielmann (1989) suggests that as much as 20 percent of the dietary protein at Pecos and Gran Quivira was provided by meat obtained through trade with the Plains Indians. A detailed bone chemistry analysis of Pecos remains, however, suggests that bison did not replace mule deer over time, and it is possible that in the historic period the use of both meat and maize decreased and use of wild plant resources increased (Spielmann, Schoeninger, and Moore 1990).

The San Cristobal and Hawikku skeletal samples, which date from the late prehistoric through the protohistoric period, exhibit high rates of iron deficiency anemia (74% to 87%) and of dental pathology (53%) (Stodder 1990). Infectious disease affected approximately one-third of all individuals at these sites. It has been suggested that because only 16 percent of the cases of anemia at San Cristobal co-occur with infectious disease, malnutrition may have been a major concern (Stodder and Martin 1991). These frontier settlements demonstrate significantly more disease than do other Pueblo IV sites such as Pa'ako and Tijeras Pueblo (Ferguson 1980)

Merbs (1989) has summarized the incidence of tuberculosis in the Southwest and suggests that the disease began to play a greater role during these later time periods. Although a few cases of tuberculosis have been reported for Pueblo II/III sites (Chavez Pass, Pueblo Bonito, Point of Pines), the majority of the cases come from later sites such as Gran Quivira, San Cristobal, Hawikku, and Pecos (totaling at least 10 cases) (Stodder 1990). Stodder (1990) suggests that there may have been an epidemic wave of tuberculosis in the San Cristobal population, exhibited in a cluster of several adult cases. Tuberculosis can be considered an index of population density and lowered immune resistance (Hrdlicka 1908). Because only a small proportion (less than 10%) of individuals with tuberculosis ever have symptoms, the presence of several cases suggests that a much higher frequency of individuals carried the disease (Ortner and Putschar 1981).

Treponemal infections (probably due to endemic nonvenereal strains of syphilis) also are found in greater frequency in these later protohistoric sites, although a few cases occur as early as Basketmaker II (Baker and Armelagos 1988). From Tijeras, Pecos, San Cristobal, and Hawikku, a total of 8 cases exist (Stodder and Martin 1991).

Trauma increases during this time period as well. Frequencies of traumatic injury had been relatively low during the Pueblo I/II phases (5% at Black Mesa, 17% at Chaco Canyon) compared with Pueblo IV sites such as San Cristobal (23%). Cranial trauma alone ranges from 2 percent at Tijeras Pueblo to 17.5 percent at Hawikku and 20 percent at San Cristobal (Stodder 1990).

Protohistoric populations from the Southwest demonstrate higher frequencies and more severe manifestations than do their counterparts in prehistory of all the skeletal forms of infection due to common causes such as staph and strep. In addition, the prevalence of tuberculosis and treponematosis also increased from earlier periods. It is possible that infectious diseases in the Southwest that were generally mild and endemic in form became epidemic with the increasing physiological disruption brought on by malnutrition and famine, social disruption, and demographic instability (Stodder 1990).

CONCLUSION

The inventory of diseases suffered by prehistoric Southwest peoples is relatively long but very incomplete. Published data support the ubiquity of infections, anemia, dental disease, developmental problems, and trauma, but paleopathologists cannot provide a detailed scenario of how these diseases actually played out at the group level. The various indicators of stress most certainly have overlapping etiologies, but the pattern of these morphological changes confirms that stress in the Southwest was primarily chronic: it affected infants and children to a degree not seen in adults, and most likely contributed significantly to morbidity if not mortality.

Paleoepidemiology is an attempt at tracking biocultural evolution. The paleopathology profiles suggest a regularity and patterning that are consistent with, and predicted by, environmental instability and increased population. There is, of course, much local variability throughout prehistory, but even so the protohistoric period represents an increase in some pathologies. In a response to the debate concerning the role of epidemics in the depopulation of the Southwest in historic times, Kunitz and Euler (1972:40) state: "One does not need to invoke large-scale, dramatic epidemics; prosaic entities like malnutrition and infectious diarrhea are more than sufficient to do the job." They emphasize the underlying endemic conditions found throughout the entire occupation of the Southwest from AD 200 onward.

A reader of the paleopathological literature on the American Southwest would, we believe, characterize health in the following manner: Major and persistent nutritional deficiencies resulted from a maize diet; crowded and unsanitary living conditions enhanced the chances of picking up communicable diseases such as gastroenteritis; intestinal parasites were a common and exasperating problem; dental problems including caries and periodontal disease were a major concern; most adults had arthritis and spinal degeneration from carrying heavy loads; parasites such as lice and helminths were common; and infant and childhood mortality was high. A continuum of health problems over time suggests that changes in the patterns occurred, with an increase in diseases associated with large and aggregated populations.

Although this view of health is in the most general sense probably accurate, we argue that much more can be learned from the human remains. Our general statements about prehistoric health leave many questions unanswered: Berry (1983:67), for example, notes for the Rainbow Bridge/Monument Valley Anasazi burials that there is a significant portion of females relative to males, and that this pattern is "associated with large Pueblo III–Pueblo IV towns in the Southwest." Assuming similar mortuary practices for males and females and an overall pattern of compromised health, how did so many females survive their reproductive years relatively unscathed? There are reports in the literature of men and women who lived well into their seventies (Miles 1975)—evidence that runs counter to the "live hard, die young" picture of life in the prehistoric Southwest that has been painted. What proportion of the population actually died because of nutritional anemias? Does nutritional anemia contribute significantly to morbidity in all cases? What are the ranges of variation in indicators of health from site to site? Does the degree of political autonomy have an impact on community health? What portions of the population were most at risk? How did *any* children survive? As Hinkes's (1983) dissertation subtitle ("Trying to Come of Age at Grasshopper Pueblo") suggests, there are still unanswered questions concerning adaptive strategies of infants and children in marginal and harsh environments. Finally, does poor health limit work capacity, affect sociability and group interaction, or significantly reduce reproductive capacity?

A number of specific questions would benefit from regional analyses: Is there a pattern of disease in the Southwest, and has it changed though time? What has been the process of sedentism, and what is the relationship of sedentism to health? What has been the impact of sedentism on population growth? What has been the process of aggregation, and how has it affected the pattern of disease? If there has been an increase in disease, how have the populations responded to the increase in disease load? What was the impact of disease following European contact?

The answers to these questions will require cooperation among researchers in the selection and evaluation of indicators of health and disease. For example, the applications of chemical analysis (of trace minerals, stable isotopes, and DNA) should be undertaken in the context of a set of problems that can be solved in a systematic fashion with input from archaeologists and biological anthropologists.

In order to refine some of the grandiose observations that have been made concerning health and disease trends in the Southwest, it is useful to track the more uncontentious indicators of stress through time and space. In this way, the variability in patterning forms a broad framework for looking at regional differences in health, at the same time providing the highest and lowest prevalence of disease stress. Researchers must recognize the need to generate a body of systematic data that could begin to address the role of health changes in population structure and size.

————— *Acknowledgments* —————

I am indebted to Bob Preucel and Lynne Sebastian for providing critical comments on the presentation of the paleopathology data. Norm Yoffee, Peter Brown, and Alan Goodman read initial drafts and supplied helpful suggestions. Conversations with George Gumerman, Ben Nelson, Paul Fish, Ann Stodder, and George Armelagos have advanced my thinking about the ultimate causes of poor health in the American Southwest.

6

Processes of Aggregation
in the Prehistoric Southwest

LINDA S. CORDELL, DAVID E. DOYEL,
AND KEITH W. KINTIGH

THE TERM AGGREGATION, AS USED HERE, refers to the processes that produce spatial clustering of households, communities, or archaeological habitation sites. Although aggregated settlements did not occur in all parts of the prehistoric Southwest, such settlements do appear in the archaeological record of much of the area sometime after AD 1000. In this paper, we describe the aggregations that took place in the major Southwestern cultural traditions in the theoretical context of some general issues in Southwestern archaeology and anthropology. Our geographic coverage is not exhaustive: we focus on areas within our particular fields of expertise for which there are high-quality recent data.

In some of the more traditional archaeological literature (e.g., Haury 1962a:127), population aggregation is described as a natural consequence of a secure food supply and concomitant social elaboration. Other authors emphasize the difficulties involved in making a living in aggregated communities and propose one or more causal factors underlying the move to large settlements. This perspective was taken by Cynthia Irwin-Williams (1981), who maintained that aggregated prehistoric Pueblo settlements resulted from long-term climatic stress and population-environment disequilibriums. Because the natural environments of the Southwest are generally both risky for agriculture and low in productivity, it is crucial to understand the economic bases of aggregated settlements as well as how and for how long these settlements remained stable over time.

Timothy Kohler (1989) points out that with a mixed agricultural and hunting-and-gathering subsistence base, food producers incur substantial costs for living in aggregated settlements. For prehistoric Southwestern populations that became aggregated, distances to agricultural fields, wild resources, and fuel wood would have increased. Ignoring the size of the settlement itself and assuming a uniform distribution of resources, each doubling of the population approximately doubles the average distance to fields. If resource exploitation is intensified in order to diminish travel costs, there is increased risk of seriously depleting soils and wild food resources. In addition, in the likely absence of efficient human waste disposal, aggregation increases the unknown cost of poorer health and greater infant mortality (cf. Colton 1960). Finally, although social costs are difficult to measure, disputes may be harder to resolve and may have greater consequences among aggregated populations. In light of these difficulties, various explanations have been offered to account for aggregation.

William Longacre (1966:97) considered aggregation a social effort to sustain populations through cooperation in the face of increasing economic uncertainties brought about by climatic deterioration. He suggested that people pooled their labor, and in particular their ability to acquire and share diverse resources. His argument has since been modified by others. The most elaborate evaluation of Longacre's theory was conducted in the Eastern Anasazi area by the Pajarito Archaeological Project (PARP), directed by James N. Hill. PARP attempted to evaluate the response of prehistoric Southwestern society to subsistence stress brought about by drought. Although there were several testable hypotheses related to evaluating subsistence stress in the PARP research strategy, population aggregation was assumed to be one appropriate response.

Hill and Nicholas Trierweiler (1986) argue that specialization in food production, particularly the intensification of agriculture, is one response to stress, and maintain that aggregated populations could most efficiently exploit good localized agricultural land. They also suggest that an aggregated population would be capable of more effective organization of labor and more efficient food distribution. PARP data suggest that there *was* increased intensification of agriculture that could be related to several factors—including climatic change, increased population density, conflict or competition, technological change, or changes in social organization (Hill and Trierweiler 1986; Orcutt 1981).

Fred Plog (1983a, 1983b; Plog et al. 1988) and others (Dean et al. 1985) have developed a different view from that of Longacre. Plog suggested that alliance systems worked to offset periods during which there was high spatial variability in rainfall. According to Upham (1982) and Plog (1989), alliances centered on larger sites are characterized by agricultural intensification, extensive exchange networks, and increased social stratification. Since these systems are costly to maintain, it is argued that they developed when overall regional population densities were great enough to inhibit group mobility. One would thus expect aggregation to coincide with periods of high interlocal environmental differences and increased regional population densities.

Although not related to conditions of environmental stress, a link between population aggregation and intensification of agriculture underlies some interpretations of Colonial period Hohokam settlements (see Cable and Doyel 1985; Wilcox 1979b; Doyel 1988). David Doyel notes that there is localized irrigable land within the Phoenix Basin, and that the investment required to construct and maintain canals and villages placed a premium on labor, which may have stimulated immigration from outlying districts. In this view, population continued to expand after initial aggregation, and more land was brought under irrigation agriculture. At the same time, continued or expanded use of other kinds of farming and subsistence options coexisted with agriculture.

Another position, articulated nearly seventy years ago by A. V. Kidder (1924:126–27), is that aggregation is a response to the need for defense. Recent theories linking aggregation to defense and warfare have been developed by Jonathan Haas (1986, 1989), and from a different but complementary perspective by Hunter-Anderson (1979; and see Kohler 1989). Haas (1989) argues that by AD 1250, continued environmental degradation led to changes in Kayenta Anasazi social organization, including a tenfold increase in the size of villages, indications of closer cooperation among some villages, and the development of warfare and conflict between groups (or clusters) of villages. Haas (1989:506) suggests that the changes in social organization are best understood as the development of tribal polities.

Haas's position is similar to that of Rosalind Hunter-Anderson (1979), who argues that population aggregation was a deterrent to overt hostilities. Her view is that increased population density makes it advantageous to leave buffer zones between aggregated settlements, zones that could be used for hunting and the exploitation of wild plant foods and other resources. An aggregated population could best defend its own agricultural land and resource areas, and would therefore serve as a potential deterrent to encroachment. Because aggregated communities would have a strategic advantage, local groups that were formerly dispersed also would be forced to aggregate.

Kohler (1989) proposes a model that links aspects of the Haas and Hunter-Anderson schemes. Despite the costs of aggregation, he suggests that aggregated communities developed under conditions of increasing population, increased village permanence, and decreased residential mobility. Aggregated communities had a competitive advantage in situations where there was "frequent conflict over claims for agricultural and foraging territory, without the means for either defusing such conflict, or the power to protect their territories against larger competing aggregates" (Kohler 1989:7–8). Kohler's scenario is certainly plausible, but like Haas's (1989) view, it depends on Western notions of territoriality and encroachment. Various modern land claims cases in the Southwest, though potentially biased in some ways, provide a consistent record of overlap in foraging, collecting, and some agricultural land use areas (e.g., Ellis 1974; Ferguson and Hart 1985). Given the spatial unpredictability of some wild resources such as piñon, maintaining exclusive rights of access to a specific territory is not an appropriate long-term strategy.

Discussions of aggregation in all these explanatory models focus on a few key dimensions: population density, the nature of the subsistence base and agricultural technology, paleoenvironmental factors, and methods of social integration.

But information on each of these dimensions is not always available from archaeological data. There are problems in our ability to infer population aggregation, and among the most persistent of these is the question of chronology. Within any one region, it is difficult to know which sites are truly contemporary. Problems of dating are compounded when data from more than one locality or region are synthesized. Phase schemes developed for particular localities are not necessarily comparable, and some are better supported than others by tree-ring, archaeomagnetic, and radiocarbon dates.

Chronological problems are not limited to regional survey data. Making inferences about the process of aggregation requires that we know the contemporary population of single sites. At sites with multiple roomblocks and plazas, the contemporaneous occupation of roomblocks cannot be assumed; in a number of cases, we know that roomblocks were occupied sequentially. Complex building and abandonment sequences are common in the Anasazi area, as shown by analyses of Betatakin, Kiet Siel (Dean 1969), Aztec (Stein and McKenna 1988), Pa'ako (Lambert 1954), Arroyo Hondo (Schwartz 1986), Pot Creek (Crown 1989), Tijeras Pueblo (Cordell 1977, 1980), and other large sites. If anything, these difficulties are compounded in the Hohokam area where dispersed pithouses and courtyard groups were the loci of habitation for most of the prehistoric period. Whether we are dealing with pithouses or aboveground, contiguous-room structures, spacing between structures can vary from one locality to the next. Defining a community is itself problematic (cf. Rohn 1971, 1977, 1989).

It is also difficult to establish the longevity of settlements. The degree of residential mobility among Anasazi and Mogollon populations using pithouses is thought to have been quite high (cf. Powell 1983; Gilman 1987); for the Hohokam area, investigators disagree about the length of occupation of single pithouses. Estimates ranging from 15 years to 100 years have been given for the use-life of a "standard" Hohokam domestic pithouse, and such ranges create great disparities in local and regional population estimates. The same Sedentary period Hohokam villages have been described as housing 500 people and 2,000 people (Haury 1976a; Teague 1984).

Estimating the use-lives of sites with aboveground structures may be no less problematic. Some sites with pueblo architecture seem to have been occupied for only brief periods (Nelson and LeBlanc 1986; Nelson and Cordell 1982), and population estimates may vary by orders of magnitude as great as those for the Hohokam communities. Within an area as well known as Chaco Canyon, for example, estimates of simultaneous population range from hundreds to tens of thousands of persons. In the Chaco case, these disagreements arise between those scholars who consider Chacoan sites to have been primarily ceremonial and those who interpret them as predominantly residential (cf. Hayes 1981; Judge 1989).

In the following pages, we review cultural-historical reconstructions for areas in which aggregation occurred. We emphasize the identification of aggregation and evidence relevant to variables used to explain aggregation. We will be concerned with the dates of aggregation in order to understand it in the context of climatic and environmental factors and regional population densities. We are concerned with ascertaining over what period of time aggregation occurred and whether or not the process appeared to be gradual. We also try to elucidate the economic bases of aggregated settlements in view of the generally low productivity of most Southwestern environments. We discuss the presence of features such as kivas, great kivas, platform mounds, and ballcourts as these relate to the organization of aggregated communities. We realize that the data from our respective areas are not entirely comparable, and though we do direct attention to some differences in the context of each example, most similarities and differences among the areas are discussed following the presentation of case examples.

CASE EXAMPLES

Eastern Anasazi

The Eastern Anasazi region includes the northern San Juan River–Mesa Verde area, and the middle Rio Grande drainage basin. The northern San Juan is the archetypical case of prehistoric Southwestern aggregation cited by Steward (1937). Some comparative information is given here for Chaco Canyon and the San Juan Basin. The Chaco–San Juan area, however, is considered representative of a regional nucleated system, rather than a series of aggregated sites. Following Irwin-Williams (1981), the Chacoan sites are seen to represent a trajectory that was an alternative to the one that led to aggregation. Indeed, it is sometimes suggested that one of the factors leading to aggregation among Eastern Anasazi populations was their reaction to the large Chacoan system. The data discussed here for the Eastern Anasazi are primarily from recent literature (Blevins and Joiner 1977; Chapman and Biella 1977; Cordell 1979, 1989; Crown 1990; Dickson 1979; Hayes 1964; Hill and Trierweiler 1986; Kohler 1989; Orcutt 1981; Powers 1988; Rohn 1977, 1989; Stuart and Gauthier 1981).

The Mesa Verde sequence is often used for the northern San Juan in general (Rohn 1989). The Mesa Verde proper is of interest because it is considered the classic case of gradual cultural change and in situ development and is an area that has been well surveyed and well reported. Recent discoveries have made it clear, however, that the portions of southwestern Colorado that were most densely inhabited by the Anasazi are farther north and west of the Mesa Verde in the McElmo–Yellow Jacket, Montezuma Creek, and Sand Canyon localities. Detailed survey data for these areas are not yet published.

The Mesa Verde Anasazi sequence begins with the Basketmaker III period (c. AD 550–700). Houses were typically shallow pithouses; domesticated plants included corn and beans; and turkeys were either extensively hunted or kept. Sites are usually found on mesa tops as small groups of pithouses. In the subsequent Pueblo I period (c. 700–900), squashes were added to the domestic crops, and cotton was used but not locally grown. Sites consist of long, crescentic rows of rooms and associated pithouse depressions located on the widest parts of the mesa tops in areas of excellent loessic soils. The classic sites of this type are the Pueblo I sites on Alkali Ridge (Brew 1946). Similar large sites are reported for Mesa Verde, the Dolores River valley, and for Yellow Jacket and Montezuma canyons (Rohn 1989:156). Some investigators consider these sites the first instance of population aggregation, but others do not. Rohn (1989), for example, notes that most villages of this period are composed of a dozen or so units consisting of a pithouse and a surface roomblock, but that very small hamlets of one or a few such units are also common. He believes population aggregation occurred after AD 1000—as do we.

Pueblo II sites (c. 900–975) are composed of a few contiguous rooms of un-shaped rock masonry or of *jacal*, with kivas placed well to the south of the line of rooms. Trash areas are well defined in contrast to earlier phases, and sites are generally smaller and more widely spaced than those of Pueblo I. There is some suggestion of local population decline (Hayes 1964). In the northern San Juan area, the apparent decline in population coincides with a worsening in hydrological conditions and with the beginning of elaboration in Chaco Canyon. The period from AD 975 to 1050, considered Late Pueblo II, corresponds to a time of major growth at Chaco Canyon and in the San Juan Basin. At Mesa Verde, Pueblo II sites consist of one-story rows of masonry rooms, with kivas both more formally constructed and closer to the living area than previously. Sites are fewer and more widely scattered, and the first construction of agricultural terraces and retaining walls for fields appear.

Early Pueblo III (c. 1050–1150) (Rohn 1977, 1989), when developments in Chaco were at their height, witnessed the first trend toward aggregation in the northern San Juan. Mean site size doubled from the preceding period. Rohn notes the first occupation of the northern portions of Chapin Mesa, where both mesa tops and benches in the canyon bottoms were inhabited. These locations included "some of the least desirable agricultural lands . . . [suggesting that] . . . their use may indicate pressure on the better lands or their partial destruction through erosion" (Rohn 1977:240). Sites typically have walls of pecked-stone blocks, with the "keyhole"-shaped kiva standard and incorporated in the dwelling area. Towers were more common than previously and often were two or more stories tall. On Mesa Verde, nearly one-third of the sites were located under rock overhangs, and virtually all sites continued to be inhabited in the succeeding Mesa Verde phase (c. 1150–1300), the final phase of occupation for the region.

On Wetherill Mesa, Hayes's (1964) data show that mean site size increased slightly between about 1150 and 1300. Although the increase in average site size is only moderate, variation in site size also increases between 1050 and 1300. In the Mesa Verde region as a whole, however, the largest sites contain about 600 rooms and date to between 1200 and probably 1280 (Varien et al. 1990). Data from the Chuska Valley, the Rio Puerco of the West, and the Acoma area also display greatly increased numbers of rooms per site in the period between 1200 and 1300 (Roney 1990; Fowler, Stein, and Anyon 1987). By 1300, the Mesa Verde and northern San Juan were abandoned by Pueblo builders.

Using the period from 1200 to 1280 as a reference point for aggregation over most of this area, the following observations may be made. Various features indicating agricultural intensification, such as check dams and terraces, long predate aggregation. In addition, although difficult to evaluate quantitatively, it appears that aggregation occurred after the region was relatively "full," in that even marginally productive land had been settled. Various integrating features such as great kivas and tower kivas had been present prior to aggregation. Finally, if the 100-year period is accurate for both aggregation and abandonment, then aggregation occurred relatively quickly and was not a stable condition.

The middle Rio Grande drainage basin includes the Pajarito Plateau, Cochiti, Bandelier, the Caja del Rio, and the Santa Fe, Taos, and Albuquerque archaeological districts. Where possible, we extend our comments to the Galisteo Basin and the upper Pecos. The Early Developmental period (AD 600–900) is characterized by very small pithouse sites (one to three rooms) found at lower elevations near permanent water sources. Sites of this period are rare and often alluviated, and thus lack visibility. The Late Developmental period (900–1200) shows a marked increase in the number of sites, which are distributed over a wide range of elevations and landforms. Sites are still usually small, consisting of small clusters of pithouses or surface rooms, although a few pueblos are estimated to have had as many as 60 to 100 rooms. The characteristic pottery types resemble Chacoan types in design; this was the period during which the Chaco system reached its greatest geographical extent.

The Rio Grande Coalition period (1200–1300) witnessed a great increase in number of sites, including a tenfold increase in the Santa Fe vicinity. Sites are distributed throughout a wide range of landforms and elevations (from below 5,500 ft. to above 7,500 ft.). Water control features and possible fieldhouses are identified in this area for the first time. Although the most frequently recorded sites are small surface pueblos—20 to 30 rooms arranged in rectilinear blocks two to three tiers wide with an informal plaza area and trash mound to the east— there are some much larger sites of up to 250 rooms. The east to southeast orientation of roomblock, open area, and trash mound is fairly consistent, but the presence of a kiva within this arrangement is not. When present, kivas may be round or of Mesa Verde keyhole shape. A common pattern, however, is a rectangular or D-shaped room incorporated within a roomblock but with kiva floor features. The pottery is carbon painted, and some types are virtually identical to those of Mesa Verde. Many sites that reached their greatest size in the subsequent Classic period seem to have been first occupied in the late 1200s (1275–1290). Since most of Chaco Canyon, the Gallina area, and Mesa Verde were being abandoned between 1280 and 1300, there are various potential sources for the Santa Fe-area population increase.

The Rio Grande Classic period (1325–1600) is characterized as a period of both aggregation and population instability. Very large sites were established, but they were not necessarily continuously inhabited for long. With aggregation, there is a clustering of sites at an elevation of about 6,500 feet. Agricultural field types include a variety of gravel-mulch gardens and fields with linear borders and terraces. Abundant limited activity sites suggest intensive use of areas that are no longer the loci of villages. Sites with multiple enclosed plazas are common at the beginning and middle of the Classic; from the middle to the end of the Classic, sites more often consist of massed roomblocks laid out irregularly or in lines. Within these later sites, roomblocks were often constructed by laying out long parallel walls and subsequently dividing the interior space into rooms.

Large Classic sites on the Pajarito Plateau include Tshirigi, with about 600 rooms; Otowi with somewhat fewer rooms; and Tyounyi with about 350 rooms. On the Chama River, Sapawe had about 1,800 rooms; Howiri 500 rooms; Poshuinge 1,800 rooms; and Poseuinge perhaps 700 rooms. Arroyo Hondo Pueblo, near Santa Fe, consisted of about 1,000 rooms. In the Galisteo Basin, Galisteo Pueblo is estimated to have had 1,600 rooms; San Cristobal 1,650 rooms; Pueblo Colorado 1,400 rooms; and Pueblo Shé 1,543 rooms. Multistory Pot Creek Pueblo, near Taos, had an estimated 300 ground-floor rooms.

The Rio Grande glazes, which owe their origin to the Western Pueblo St. Johns and White Mountain red wares, are the characteristic pottery of the Classic period. Black-on-white "biscuit wares" dominate only the northern one-third of the Rio Grande region. Various pueblos were production and distribution centers for the glaze wares at different times. Generally, more production centers existed in the early part of the Classic, and only a few late in the Classic (Warren 1980). Rio Grande glaze ware was also widely traded onto the Plains, and there was a definite expansion of Pueblo population to the east at this time. In addition to pottery, Jemez obsidian was traded widely.

In the Tijeras, Cochiti, Pajarito Plateau, and Arroyo Hondo survey areas, estimated population increased until sometime in the Late or Middle Coalition or Early Classic. Thereafter, population may have declined slightly for these regions, but it also aggregated at a few large sites (cf. Kohler 1989:figs. 1.2a and b). Kohler (1989:4) suggests that population increased throughout this period and that the duration of occupation for habitation sites also increased through time; as yet, there are no data with which to evaluate this assertion. Cordell believes that Late Coalition period sites probably were occupied more briefly than Classic period sites, but suspects that settlements did not become really stable until after European colonization, when frequent village relocation was precluded.

As in the northern San Juan and Mesa Verde regions, in the central Rio Grande drainage agricultural features that suggest intensification, such as fieldhouses and water control features, appear to predate aggregation. Also as in the northern San Juan, sites were established prior to aggregation in all environmental zones, including those marginal for agriculture. The period over which aggregation occurred, AD 1325 to 1600, is considerably longer than that in the northern San Juan, suggesting that aggregation might have been either a more gradual process or an episodic development. Kivas and other community-integration features do not occur with any great regularity until aggregation itself occurs. Furthermore, the production and distribution of ceramics as a potentially specialized craft item postdates the beginnings of aggregation.

The stability of individual aggregated communities is not well known. Most excavated sites seem to have been occupied discontinuously (i.e., Tijeras Pueblo, Arroyo Hondo Pueblo, Pot Creek Pueblo, Pa'ako), or else their size reflects a certain amount of horizontal stratigraphy, with roomblocks being added as others were abandoned. This is especially true of the Galisteo Basin pueblos (Jonathan Haas, personal communication 1990).

About half of the Eastern Anasazi region lies within the Colorado Plateaus, an area for which precise paleoenvironmental data are available (Cordell and Gumerman 1989; Dean 1988a; Dean et al. 1985). These data provide the context and background for various interpretations in which aggregation is seen as a response to particular environmental conditions. Despite a tendency among researchers to generalize the Colorado Plateaus data, Dean (personal communication 1990) cautions that they are not known to be applicable to the middle Rio Grande. Figure 6.1, which provides a visual comparison of temporal variation in tree rings from the Colorado Plateaus and the Rio Grande area near Santa Fe from 1000 to 1600, supports Dean's contention. Unfortunately, detailed hydrological and other paleoenvironmental information for the Rio Grande are not available.

For the Eastern Anasazi region as a whole, investigators frequently have correlated settlement history with paleoenvironmental conditions. The initial expansion of the Anasazi horticultural way of life is seen to coincide with the interval between AD 650 and 850–900, of generally favorable environmental conditions. Although the Chacoan system begins about 900—a time of somewhat depressed water tables and decreased moisture—and may reflect an organizational response to this initial stress, the major period of Chacoan growth and expansion between 900 and 1130 occurs during a favorable paleoclimatic interval. The droughts of 1130 to 1150 coincide with a cessation of building in the canyon, and possibly with the collapse of the Chacoan system.

In the northern San Juan and Mesa Verde areas, the initial impact of major building in Chaco Canyon (c. AD 900–1080) seems to have been a decline in local building that may reflect a loss of population as people moved to the Chaco–San Juan Basin to the south. The large aggregated communities of the Mesa Verde and Yellow Jacket Canyon areas appear in the 1200s, a generally favorable period until the time of the Great Drought. This drought is often seen as the fatal blow to the northern San Juan Anasazi, whose population had steadily increased over the centuries and who had reached the limits of expansion with respect to cultivable land.

While the climate-driven scenario is still viable, a number of investigators are now examining the impact of social factors, such as the development of large, aggregated settlements at the western and southeastern borders of the Chacoan system, on Anasazi abandonment of the northern San Juan. The large and apparently stable southern settlements are seen as pull factors attracting people from the north. Settlement pattern changes in the Eastern Anasazi area have been interpreted as responses to events in Chaco Canyon and the San Juan Basin, either in

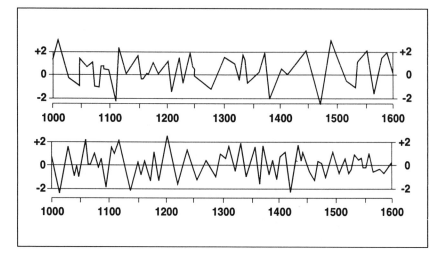

Figure 6.1. Reconstructed precipitation plotted as decade departures in tree-ring widths between AD 1000 and 1600: top, the Colorado Plateaus (after Dean 1988); bottom, the middle Rio Grande (after Rose, Dean, and Robinson 1981).

addition to or instead of being viewed as adjustments to fluctuations in the natural environment. Our current understanding of the Chaco system suggests that it began at about AD 900, became more formalized and expanded between 1050 and 1080, and underwent major geographic expansion between 1080 and 1130. The system itself, although not the estimated population, began to decline between 1130 and 1150.

Population increase in the middle Rio Grande is generally viewed as the result of immigration, first of Chacoans and later of Mesa Verdeans. In the northern districts of the Rio Grande drainage, however, aggregation is seen to occur as a response to the influx of people from the west and northwest, a response that may be the result of competition for agricultural land and access to buffering resources. Alternatively, this aggregation may be a response to environmentally induced resource stress. In the past, the aggregated sites of the northern San Juan have been attributed to warfare and a need for defense, but more recently, they have been seen as a means of removing dwellings from needed arable land.

THE ARIZONA DESERTS

All the problems of determining site size and aggregation discussed above are compounded in the Arizona deserts. In addition, the long occupation spans of many sites, changes in land-use patterns and village layout over time, the lack of visible surface architecture, and problems in determining the functions of some architectural features all limit our understanding of site size and aggregation.

The number of pithouses present at Snaketown, for example, has been estimated to be anywhere from 900 to 7,000 (Abbott 1985:40). Population estimates
for some Classic period compounds may be exaggerated because over 90 percent
of the space appears to have been devoted to activities other than habitation (Doyel
1980). On the other hand, because villages of 1,000 souls were reported by the
early Spanish in the Tucson area, where canal irrigation was used only moderately
(Doelle and Wallace 1988), it seems probable that Hohokam villages exceeding
this size could have existed in the intensively irrigated Phoenix Basin prior to 1400.

Despite these difficulties, new data provide finer resolution for the Hohokam
chronology than was previously available (Cable and Doyel 1987; Dean 1991a;
Doyel 1988; Eighmy and McGuire 1988; Wallace and Craig 1988). Although chronology per se is not a key concern of this paper, it is relevant to the comparisons
with other areas in the Southwest. The following chronology is used here: Pioneer
period (AD 1–700); Colonial period, including the Snaketown phase (700–925);
Sedentary period (925–1075); and Classic period (1075–1450).

The focus of our discussion is the Phoenix Basin, with less attention given the
nonriverine areas. Data from four surveys are relied on: Upham and Rice (1980)
and Canouts (1975) for the Salt River; Debowski and others (1976) and Wilcox
(1979b) for the Gila River. A number of studies of Hohokam village structure were
recently compiled by Doyel (1987a), and regional overviews provide additional information (Doyel 1981; Berry and Marmaduke 1982; McGuire and Schiffer 1982).

The Pioneer period (AD 1–700) began when Late Archaic period people experi-
menting with agriculture moved into the desert basins and integrated floodwater
agriculture into their economic system. During the early Red Mountain phase,
improved agriculture and storage facilities were developed, along with simple
ceramic containers. Settlements probably consisted of small hamlets with 25 to 40
people and fewer than 15 houses. The ensuing Vahki phase witnessed increased
agricultural production and more evidence of social and ceremonial organization. Specialized grinding tools (trough metates and manos) and an increased
frequency of corn remains are reported (Cable et al. 1985). Vahki phase villages
contain plazas and large houses, thought to be residences of village leaders (Cable
and Doyel 1987).

Finally, during the Estrella and Sweetwater phases, grooved and painted pottery were added to the earlier plain and polished red wares. The appearance of
large communal houses at many sites indicates a rapid rate of population segmen-
tation into lineage or other comparable groups, but throughout the Pioneer period,
villages were under 30 acres in area and probably contained fewer than 100 people.

The Colonial and Sedentary periods (c. 700–1075) include the Snaketown,
Gila Butte, Santa Cruz, and Sacaton phases. Numerous villages dating to the early
Colonial period are reported from throughout much of the desert region, especially along the Salt and Gila rivers in the Phoenix Basin. Site size is difficult to
assess, but evidence from Snaketown suggests that the Snaketown phase settlement was 10 to 15 acres in area with a population of 150 people (Haury 1976a;

Wilcox 1979b:101; Wilcox, McGuire, and Sternberg 1981:205). The increase in the number of villages appears to coincide with a commitment to canal irrigation agriculture on the part of the Phoenix Basin Hohokam (Cable and Doyel 1987; Wilcox 1979b). Irrigation probably influenced the reduction of residential mobility because of the longevity of field locations. The investment required to construct and maintain the canals and villages placed a premium on labor, which may have stimulated immigration from outlying districts, as well as the development of more diverse and larger exchange networks. Canal irrigation technology, larger villages, increased ritual elaboration, and population growth all become apparent in the archaeological record at this time, indicating complex relationships among social organization, population, and technology (Cable and Doyel 1985).

Regional survey data reveal an increase in the number of site components during the Gila Butte phase, with village areas in excess of 200 acres common. By the Santa Cruz phase, a number of large villages containing 300 to 500 people existed in the Phoenix Basin, some of which were connected by canal systems. Village segments consisted of groups of house clusters, each with its own cemetery and outside activity areas, surrounding a great central plaza.

Ballcourts and mounds were often located adjacent to the central plaza, and some villages, such as Snaketown, had a concentric settlement plan. Regional integration of these villages was accomplished through a network of several hundred large earthen ballcourts located at primary villages (Wilcox and Sternberg 1983). By the Sacaton phase, some villages exceeded 500 acres in size. Also beginning by the early Colonial period (and continuing through the Sedentary) was a process of range expansion and niche packing, wherein a variety of subsistence techniques and land-use strategies were employed (Masse 1980; Doyel 1981).

During the Classic period, the Phoenix Basin appears to lose centrality within the desert region, and other large populations are located in the Verde, Tonto, San Pedro, Papaguería, and Tucson areas. Unsettled conditions may have existed during the early part of the period (1075–1250), as indicated by numerous stone forts (trincheras) surrounding the region. A number of ancestral sites such as Snaketown and Grewe were abandoned, though Wilcox (1979b:106) reports that along the Gila, at least, the number of new sites equalled the number abandoned.

Throughout the region, some settlements were enlarged; these include Los Muertos, Mesa Grande, Las Colinas, and Pueblo Grande in the Salt River valley and settlements along the Gila River near Casa Grande Ruins (Crown 1987a). Gregory (1987:185) reports that 23 platform mound communities were located along approximately 50 kilometers of the lower Salt River, while 11 such communities were spread over about 60 kilometers along the Gila. By the middle Classic period, the mound sites were separated by a remarkably consistent distance of 5 kilometers.

Site size varies during the Civano phase (1300–1400). Larger sites may have contained more than 30 compounds, scattered over areas in excess of 500 acres and surrounded by trash mounds, cemeteries, and other settlement features. Assuming an average of 20 to 50 people per compound, and assuming simultaneous occupancy, such villages may have contained between 600 and 2,000 people; this estimate excludes any pithouse clusters or social groups living on the fringes of the village areas. Smaller Classic period communities such as Escalante (Doyel 1981) may have contained 100 people in total population. Los Muertos and Casa Grande appear to have retained the concentric village plan of earlier periods, with the largest compounds containing the mounds and big houses surrounded by compounds of lesser size without monumental architecture. Other sites do not exhibit such patterning. Turney (1924) described Pueblo Grande as containing house outlines and mounds covering an area of one mile east to west and two miles north to south, indicating a more dispersed settlement plan.

By the Civano phase, the complexity of Hohokam settlement patterns exceeded that of all previous phases. Each drainage system contained one or more settlement hierarchy, as well as multivillage communities located along the irrigation systems. Many of the communities along the lower Salt River were actually integrated into larger irrigation networks and could be described as megacommunities. Over 500 kilometers of main canals existed around and between these settlements (Masse 1981).

Regionally, long-term population growth in the Phoenix Basin is strongly suggested (table 6.1). Upham and Rice's (1980:80) inventory revealed "a smooth growth process through time for the lower Salt," and the Salt River valley data show component numbers increasing from 9 to 75 between the Pioneer and Classic periods within an area of roughly 1,725 square kilometers. These data indicate the presence of one Pioneer period site every 193 square kilometers. By the Classic period, there was one site every 23 square kilometers, suggesting an eightfold increase in site density. These data cannot be taken at face value, however. Pueblo Grande, for example, had a significant Pioneer period occupation not reported by Upham and Rice, and given lengthy occupation spans, earlier materials at any site tend to lose their surface visibility.

Survey data reveal a great increase in site numbers between the late Pioneer and the early Colonial periods. Wilcox suggests that a 50 percent increase in population may have occurred along the Gila River between the late Colonial and Sedentary periods (Wilcox and Sternberg 1983:238). Upham and Rice (1980) report a 68 percent increase in site components for the lower Salt during the Classic period, a figure which suggests a major shift in settlement trends between the Gila and Salt, with the Salt growing in demographic dominance. At the same time, significant decreases are indicated for the Orme and Buttes localities, where only limited irrigation agriculture could have been practiced.

Despite the great surge in fieldwork during the past 15 years, quantitative data on regional population remain scant. Gregory (1987) inventoried 40 Classic period platform mound communities in the Phoenix Basin; if each of these communities contained between 300 and 1,000 people, the population range would be estimated between 12,000 and 40,000 people. If this figure is doubled to account for nonmound, undiscovered, and outlying sites (an impeachable procedure, to be sure), the result is an estimated population between 24,000 and 80,000—figures which bracket Haury's (1976a) speculative estimate of 60,000. Roughly one-half

TABLE 6.1.

Hohokam settlement data in numbers of components

Period	Orme Reservoir[a]	Lower Salt River[b]	Gila River[c]	Buttes Reservoir[d]	Total
Pioneer[e]	3	9	21	–	33
Colonial	21	29	41	26	117
Sedentary	27	37	46	37	147
Classic	14	75	47	27	163
Total	65	150	150	90	460

[a]Canouts 1975:17–38; only dated habitation sites used, otherwise N = 176.
[b]Upham and Rice 1980:90–93.
[c]Wilcox 1979:95–98.
[d]Debowski and others 1976:104–10; only dated habitation sites used, otherwise N = 250.
[e]Here, the Pioneer period includes the Snaketown phase.

this number would have been located in the 50-kilometer segment of the lower Salt River valley between Granite Reef and the Agua Fria River. Obviously, these numbers are no more than crude estimates.

In sum, it is probable that a number of villages in the Phoenix Basin had populations of 100 by the Colonial period. Growth may have occurred at an accelerated pace due to immigration from surrounding districts. Another period of accelerated growth occurred at the Santa Cruz–Sacaton juncture, when a number of villages probably contained between 300 and 500 people. Truly large villages, such as Snaketown and Cashion, housed more than 500 people at around AD 1000. A number of Classic period villages would also have had populations within this range; several may have exceeded 1,000 people. While real numbers remain elusive, the eightfold increase in site components between the Pioneer and Classic periods identifies population growth as a significant factor in Hohokam culture change. This theme has support in the literature, whether population increase is seen as a result of immigration (Gladwin and others 1937; Haury 1945a; Schmidt 1928; Schroeder 1947) or as a result of internal growth (Grady 1976; Martin and Plog 1973; Weaver 1972).

Some authors envision the Hohokam sequence as one continuous evolution from a simple agrarian pattern to a ranked society by the Classic period. Other models of Hohokam culture change postulate development of social complexity by the late Colonial or Sedentary period. Some question the simple unilineal growth model and envision system collapse and/or reorganization during the early Classic, with a resurgence during the late Classic Civano phase (Doyel 1981).

Nials, Gregory, and Graybill (1989) have published a new regional model of retrodicted streamflow for the lower Salt River valley which addresses the question of how long-term riverine conditions would have affected Hohokam irrigation agriculture. These authors conclude that between AD 900 and 1400 there were at least eight occasions of sufficient river flow to destroy dams and headgates, wash out canal banks, and alter the flow in the riverbed. They further propose that floods at 899 and 1352 probably had devastating effects, resulting in system disuse and abandonment and population dislocation. Geological research (Partridge and Baker 1987; J. E. Fuller 1987) provides independent verification of prehistoric flooding along the Salt and Verde rivers.

Nials, Gregory, and Graybill also point out that some of the largest floods in the Salt River occurred at recognized phase changes in the Hohokam sequence, such as the shift between the Santa Cruz and Sacaton phases and the end of the Classic period. This observation could greatly alter our perception of Hohokam population dynamics and settlement strategies. Instead of a smooth, continuous growth curve, or one with only a few major changes, the sequence could have been marked by significant disjunctures when people were confronted with low frequency, catastrophic events requiring rapid cultural adjustments. Much (but not all) of the site expansion in the peripheries and outside of the Phoenix Basin occurred between 850 and 950, or around the time of the "great flood of 899" (Doyel 1981; Doyel and Elson 1985; Masse 1980); this expansion might have been one result of catastrophic events and subsequent population dislocation from the major rivers. This interpretation is far different from that of simple population growth and range expansion over time.

During the Classic period, subsistence strategies appear to be diverse and exhibit spatial variation. A continuum of such strategies can be documented from the Salt River valley, where highly integrated and specialized irrigation agriculture occurred, to the Gila River area, where a variety of agricultural strategies were employed, to the Santa Cruz Valley where a zonal pattern of resource exploitation included nonriverine agriculture and agave cultivation (Doyel 1988; Crown 1987a; Fish and Fish 1989). During this time extensive rock pile–agave fields, cactus-fruit gathering camps, and other specialized facilities also became common throughout the desert. Some communities may have specialized in the production of certain items: agave and agave fiber at Marana, cotton at Escalante, and ground-stone axes and shell jewelry at Pueblo Grande. It is interesting to note that unlike most of the villages along the Salt and Gila rivers, the Marana mound community in the Santa Cruz drainage did not survive the post-1300 transition. This may have been due to the absence of a strong irrigation base at Marana.

Exchange of both subsistence and nonsubsistence items was very important among the historic Pima and Tohono O'odham (Papago) (Russell 1908; Underhill 1939), and evidence suggests a parallel situation for the prehistoric period. Long-distance trade in exotic pottery is apparent at some sites, especially along the Salt River (Doyel 1989); trade in other commodities such as minerals, stone tools, obsidian, and shell is evident regionwide. The distribution of Salado polychrome pottery over a large area after AD 1300 underscores the operation of an extensive information network. Future research could do well to focus on how much of

the interaction among communities was structured along lines of either cooperation and alliance or competition and hostility (Doelle and Wallace 1988; Fish and
Fish 1989).

At least three periods of accelerated population concentration are identifiable: the early Colonial period (Snaketown phase, c. AD 600–800), the Colonial-
Sedentary transition (c. 925), and the early to middle Classic period (c. 1100–
1350). Each episode is accompanied by changes in material culture and
settlement structure, indicating significant organizational changes. These episodes
of aggregation may have resulted from different causes. In the early Colonial
period, aggregation may have been a response to agricultural intensification and
an increased need for labor. Climatic change altering the source of water available
for irrigation would have intensified the need for rapid mobilization of labor and
resource distribution. Depletion of wood and food resources due to expansion
of agricultural fields into the mesquite zones along the rivers may have further
stimulated agricultural intensification.

The presence between 1100 and 1250 of stone forts on hills surrounding the
basin suggests unsettled conditions, and some large settlements were abandoned
at this time. Since we know little about this period archaeologically, it remains to
be seen if warfare, either local or interregional, was important in stimulating the
aggregation. In general, it is questionable if Hohokam settlement patterns should
be described as highly aggregated at any point in the sequence. Even in the Salt
River valley, where the most dense and nucleated settlements occurred, there were
approximately 20 villages rather than a pattern of fewer but larger towns.

TONTO BASIN AND SOUTHEASTERN ARIZONA

The Tonto Basin is a northern extension of the Sonoran desert biome in central Arizona. Over 600 archaeological sites have been recorded in the basin, with
80 dating to the post–AD 1300 Salado occupation (Wood 1986). Salado populations occupied a series of settlement clusters; the central sites, of which four are
known, had large platform mounds associated with pueblos with walled-in court-
yards. The Rye Creek Ruin, which contained 200 ground-floor rooms, is one such
example. A second level in the settlement hierarchy included platform mounds
enclosed by compounds, similar in structure to Phoenix Basin examples. Three
additional types of settlement existed, including larger pueblos and compounds
exceeding 100 rooms, smaller compounds and pueblos, and special function sites
(Wood 1986). Interestingly, site distribution along the drainages closely mirrors
the regular spacing pattern of platform mounds at every 5 kilometers along the
lower Salt River of the Phoenix Basin, which lies 60 kilometers to the south and
west. Wood (1986:15) estimates a total of between 4,500 and 9,000 rooms for the
Salado settlements, suggesting an overall population numbering between 8,000
and 20,000 between 1300 and 1400.

The Tonto Basin Salado sites provide one of the more dramatic examples of
population aggregation and settlement diversification in Southwestern prehistory.

Many of these communities could have exceeded the larger Phoenix Basin communities in population size, but the dynamics of aggregation in the two areas appear to express quite different growth characteristics. Environmental factors coupled with agricultural constraints may have made the underlying economic base in the Tonto Basin considerably different from that of the Phoenix Basin. These differences, along with the differences in settlement structure, suggest that the function and structure of the two sociopolitical systems were also quite disparate.

A widespread Mogollon-like adaptation characterized southeastern Arizona (east of the San Pedro River and south of the Gila River) between AD 1 and 1000 (Sayles 1945). Architectural diversity is apparent by the Classic period at sites described as compound or courtyardlike (Palo Parado, Tres Alamos, Second Canyon, Ringo Site, Babocomari Village, Kuykendall) and at pueblos (Reeve Ruin). Site size ranged from small (e.g., the Ringo Site, with two or three compounds, and the Reeve Ruin with 30 rooms) to very large (e.g., Kuykendall, with numerous compounds and roomblocks scattered over an area exceeding 40 acres). These sites date primarily between AD 1250 and 1400 and contain variable assemblages of late polychrome pottery, including White Mountain Red Ware and Salado and Casas Grandes polychromes. Given its significant role in post–AD 1250 population aggregation in the southern Southwest, this poorly known region will become increasingly important as demographic studies proceed. At present, it is not clear that sufficient local populations existed to account for the formation of large villages such as Kuykendall. The lack of trash and other characteristics lead Nelson and LeBlanc (1986) to suggest that post–AD 1250 settlements in the region represent "short-term sedentism," a pattern that inflates the number of sites without significantly increasing the size of the population. Explication of regional patterns of aggregation will require consideration of a broad area extending from south-central New Mexico to the Casas Grandes archaeological zone.

Mogollon and Western Pueblo Areas

This summary is based on a selective reading of the published literature, with particular reliance on more recent literature for areas in which it exists. The Mimbres area is of particular interest because aggregated sites seem to have appeared relatively early, during the Classic Mimbres period (AD 1000 to 1150), and because it is one of the few for which site size distributions and detailed population estimates have been published. Blake, LeBlanc, and Minnis (1986:442) summarize the prehistoric sequence leading up to and including the Classic Mimbres period:

> The Early Pithouse period dates from A.C. 200 to A.C. 550 and represents the first substantial sedentary agricultural occupation in the area. . . . The subsequent Late Pithouse period dates from A.C. 550 to A.C. 1000 [and] is marked by . . . the transition from circular to rectangular pithouses, the development of communal structures or great kivas, and increased inter-regional exchange. . . . Next followed the Classic

Mimbres period. . . . The Mimbreños began building cobble-walled pueblos above the surface of the ground. Large sites had as many as six room blocks with up to 50 rooms each. Great kivas ceased to be made, but small kivas, both surface and semi-subterranean, were associated with the room blocks. The Classic Mimbres period ended around A.C. 1130–1150.

The largest sites during the Late Pithouse period had about 125 rooms (table 6.2). Because the period lasted some 450 years, however, the number of contemporaneous pithouses at these sites was probably only a small fraction of the site total. Anyon and LeBlanc (1984) present detailed reconstructions of site size and population during the critical Late Pithouse and Classic Mimbres periods for the Galaz Ruin and a few other excavated sites. They estimate that the Galaz Ruin had 135 rooms during the Late Pithouse period (Anyon and LeBlanc 1984:92) and that 59 pithouses, each with four inhabitants, were occupied at the end of the period (Anyon and LeBlanc 1984:188).

In the succeeding Classic Mimbres period (c. 1000–1150), the larger sites consisted of two to eight roomblocks with totals of 50 to 200 rooms (LeBlanc 1983:105). Although total numbers are again unclear, a substantial fraction of the Classic rooms probably were occupied contemporaneously. Anyon and LeBlanc (1984:188) report that there is little evidence for abandonment of Classic period rooms at the Galaz Ruin prior to site abandonment.

In their demographic reconstruction, Anyon and LeBlanc (1984:188) use as the primary variable the total (or cumulative) estimated floor area occupied during each period (Early Pithouse = 12,904 sq m; Late Pithouse = 23,151 sq m; Classic = 80,405 sq m). They also take into account differing settlement densities by environmental zone, the lengths of the chronological periods, and the use-life of structures (estimated at 75 years for both pithouses and pueblos), and they attempt to correct for Late Pithouse period pithouses obscured by Classic period structures. Their population estimates are derived from estimates of contemporaneously occupied floor areas, assuming 4 square meters per person for the pithouse periods and 6 square meters per person for the periods with pueblo architecture.

Anyon and LeBlanc conclude that there was steady population growth of about 0.3 percent during the Early and Late Pithouse periods, and that this growth continued or accelerated slightly during the Classic Mimbres. They estimate that population at Galaz Ruin grew from 290 at the beginning of the Early Pithouse period to 830 at the beginning of the Late Pithouse period to 3,200 at the beginning of the Classic to 5,133 at the end of the Classic. However, as they recognize, their estimate of the Late Pithouse period floor area is inconsistent with their reconstruction of settlement growth. Maintaining their assumptions about structure use-life and floor area per person, the period's initial population and growth rate would require more than twice the reported floor area.

A reanalysis of the Galaz Ruin data by Keith Kintigh suggests a different picture. Kintigh assumes much shorter use-lives of 20 years for pithouses (see Ahl-

TABLE 6.2.

Mimbres area site size and approximate distribution of number of houses and rooms by period and site size class

Number of Rooms	Sites		Rooms[a]	
	LPH[b]	Classic	LPH	Classic
10	62 (45)[c]	26 (17)	310 (8)	130 (2)
1–24	32 (23)	78 (51)	544 (15)	1326 (23)
25–49	20 (14)	18 (12)	740 (20)	666 (12)
50–125	24 (18)	20 (13)	2088 (57)	1740 (31)
125–200	–	11 (7)	–	1787 (32)

[a]Room counts are obtained by multiplying the midpoint of the site class by the number of sites in that size class.
[b]LPH = Late Pithouse period.
[c]Count and (percent).
Source: Blake, LeBlanc, and Minnis 1986:458.

strom 1985) and 30 years for pueblo rooms, and he does not assume a constant growth rate through the Late Pithouse and Classic Mimbres periods. Rather, he derives the actual cumulative floor area estimated by varying growth rates and initial population of the Early Pithouse period. His reanalysis indicates that the growth rate during the Early and Late Pithouse periods was approximately 0.1 percent—a low but demographically reasonable rate (Hassan 1981). (An initial Early Pithouse period population of about 145 growing at an annual rate of 0.1% to a population of 324 at the end of the Late Pithouse period fits the cumulative floor area estimates from both periods quite well.)

Using any growth rate consistent with the Late Pithouse period floor area figures, one must conclude that there was a population explosion during the Classic Mimbres period. An annual population increase of between 2.0 percent and 2.25 percent over the 150-year period (to a final population of 6,318) is required to account for the cumulative Classic Mimbres room area. It seems unlikely that internal growth could be sustained for 150 years at these rates, suggesting that there is either a major problem with the cumulative floor data or that there was substantial in-migration during the period.

During the Late Pithouse period, larger sites lack apparent internal subdivisions and seem to contain only one contemporaneous communal structure, suggesting that the communal structure functioned at the site level of social integration. In Mimbres Classic period villages, public architecture includes walled plazas and either kivas or large surface rooms associated with individual roomblocks; unwalled plazas appear to be the only site-oriented public spaces (Anyon and LeBlanc 1980:264). The appearance of two apparently hierarchical levels of ceremonial structure within a village might indicate an increase in organizational complexity within Mimbres society (Minnis 1985b).

Aggregation in the Mimbres area, then, is associated with the transition from

pithouses to aboveground architecture, an increase in maximal site size, and a
change in the site size distribution. Further analysis of the published demographic
data suggests that the architectural and organizational transition was associated
with a major demographic shift, from low to very high population growth. Minnis (1985b) argues that agricultural features are first noted in the Classic period,
perhaps indicating that agricultural intensification occurred at some time during
the Classic. His thorough environmental analysis suggests that the early part of
the Classic was unusually predictable and unusually advantageous for agriculture,
while the latter part of the period was notably unpredictable and unfavorable for
agriculture. If aggregation occurred early in the Classic, as seems likely from the
above analysis, it would appear that the initial aggregation was not a response to
stress.

Between AD 1000 and 1150, and contemporary with the Chaco and Mimbres
phenomena, generally similar settlement pattern sequences are found in several
areas outside of the Mimbres Valley, within the culture areas generally identified
as Mogollon and Western Pueblo. At about the same time as in the Mimbres Valley,
the dominant form of residential architecture shifted from pithouses to aboveground masonry habitations elsewhere in the Mogollon area, as well as along the
Upper Little Colorado, at Zuni, and in the area of the Hopi Mesas. Pithouses with
surface storage rooms remained characteristic of the Hopi Buttes and middle Little
Colorado River valley, and small pithouse villages were found in the Verde Valley
(Fish and Fish 1977).

During this period (1000 to 1150), kivas are found in the areas generally regarded as Anasazi, including Hopi and Zuni. The appearance of great kivas at Zuni
has long been recognized as associated with the Chaco Phenomenon, and increasingly, great kivas farther to the west are being recognized as Chacoan manifestations (Fowler, Stein, and Anyon 1987; Lekson et al. 1988). In the Mogollon area,
great kivas have a much longer history. We should heed the cautionary comments
of Anyon and LeBlanc (1980) and Haury (1985), however, that although they share
a name and are probably both ceremonial structures, Mogollon and Anasazi great
kivas have notable differences and should probably be treated as distinct entities.

Clustering of sites around great kivas (which are either isolated or associated
with small villages) is characteristic in the Mogollon area during this period
(Accola 1981; Peterson 1988; Bluhm 1960; Stafford and Rice 1980) and is reported
in the upper Little Colorado River valley (Longacre 1964). But there is considerable variation in the closeness of associated site clusters to Chacoan great kivas.

Maximum site size appears to be on the order of 10 to 20 rooms at this time in
the Reserve area (Accola 1981), the Tularosa Valley (Wendorf 1956), the Pine Lawn
Valley (Bluhm 1960), the upper Little Colorado River valley (Longacre 1964), and
in the Forestdale Valley (Haury 1985; Stafford and Rice 1980). In contrast, it is
argued by Whittlesey and Reid (1982) that the Grasshopper Valley did not support permanent year-round settlements at this time. Near Zuni the overwhelming
majority of sites have fewer than 20 rooms, but a few seem to have as many as

80 rooms. The largest of these, Village of the Great Kivas (Roberts 1932), is a well-known Chacoan outlier; another, Kiatuthlanna (Roberts 1931), is argued by some to have been associated with Chaco as well. It appears, however, that non-Chacoan sites occasionally reach similarly large sizes (Fowler 1980).

During the 150-year period following AD 1000, increased numbers of sites are reported in most areas, and it has been argued that populations grew substantially (Bluhm 1960; Longacre 1964), although the impact on these conclusions of the differential visibility of pithouse and pueblo architecture is unclear.

Aggregated sites generally appear within the (non-Mimbres) Mogollon area between AD 1150 and 1300, the same period in which Devil's Park (Peterson 1988) was abandoned and the Pine Lawn Valley virtually abandoned (Bluhm 1960). Along the middle San Francisco River (Accola 1981) and in the Tularosa Valley (Wendorf 1956), however, the process of population consolidation into large pueblos began in the phase from about 1150 to 1250 or 1300. Comparatively few sites are dated to this interval, but these sites generally have more than 100 rooms.

In the Forestdale Valley, Haury (1985) reports that one 75-room site, AZ P:16:9, dates well into the 1200s and that the large site of Tundustusa was established in the 1200s and grew to 200 rooms during the next century. Turkey Creek Pueblo, in the Point of Pines region, is a 335-room site dated to the mid-1200s (Lowell 1986, 1988). The architectural plan indicates that it grew by accretion from a number of separate roomblocks into a large, contiguous-walled pueblo surrounding a square plaza.

In contrast, during the late 1200s in the area around Grasshopper, dispersed settlements clustered around focal communities that had about 20 rooms and a plaza and were located near good agricultural soils. Here, large-scale aggregation occurred late but very rapidly, starting in the early 1300s. Before its abandonment c. 1400, Grasshopper Pueblo, situated on the largest plot of arable land in the area, grew to 500 rooms. Small sites did not disappear in the area, however; rather, a wide range of site sizes is evident (Whittlesey and Reid 1982).

Longacre (1964) reports 8- to 40-room pueblos along the upper Little Colorado between 1100 and 1300, with a general decrease in the number of sites but an increase in average site size. His reconstructed population peaks at about AD 1200. In the early 1300s, there were only 10 large towns, containing from 50 to upwards of 100 rooms, geographically restricted to the two major drainages.

In the Zuni area, the first sites with more than 60 rooms (excepting Village of the Great Kivas) appear some time after 1175, and perhaps as late as the mid-1200s. As with several other areas considered, the largest sites very rapidly increased in size by almost an order of magnitude. The Scribe S site, with a well-dated occupation restricted to the mid-1200s to perhaps 1280, has about 500 rooms in several roomblocks dispersed on a ridge. The Hinkson Site (Kintigh 1990a) is similar in size, also has multiple roomblocks strung out along a ridge, and has a similar ceramic assemblage, but contains more evidence of a somewhat earlier occupation. Unlike the Scribe S site, however, Hinkson has a two-story "great house" with banded masonry of pecked and ground sandstone, a 33-meter-diameter unroofed ceremonial structure, and prehistoric roads. A number of other sites with similar configurations and ceramic dates have been identified and described by Fowler, Stein, and Anyon (1987) in west-central New Mexico and east-central Arizona. These sites appear to be the earliest clearly aggregated sites in the areas in which they appear.

By the mid- to late 1200s, the multiple roomblock sites like Scribe S and Hinkson were abandoned, and large, apparently planned pueblos (Watson, LeBlanc, and Redman 1980) (as well as a few large unplanned pueblos) began to be built along the middle and upper Little Colorado River, along the Mogollon Rim, at the Hopi Mesas, and at Zuni. These sites range in size from 100 to 1,400 rooms, and sites with 400 or more rooms are not uncommon (Kintigh 1985).

Many, if not most, of these large, late Western Pueblo sites are plaza-oriented and have kivas, but some evidence suggests that there are more rooms per kiva than in earlier periods. Near Zuni, several early planned pueblos appear to have associated large round ceremonial structures, but this architectural form drops out of the archaeological record by about AD 1300. It seems clear that by early in the 1300s the overwhelming majority of the population lived in large, aggregated pueblos. In some areas, including the upper Little Colorado and Zuni, small sites datable to this period completely disappear from the archaeological record. In other areas, notably Chavez Pass, small sites have been argued to continue (see Kintigh 1988 for a fuller account of this transition).

Two striking observations can be made about the post-Mimbres/post-Chacoan aggregation in the Western Pueblo area. First, the temporal range is relatively narrow: The earliest clearly aggregated sites (with a lower limit of 100 rooms) seem to appear early in the 1200s, and by very early in the 1300s either an aggregated settlement pattern or abandonment is clearly the rule and appears to be universal. The second striking thing about these data is that, at least as we see it archaeologically, aggregation does not appear to be a gradual process, with sites getting progressively larger over a century or more. Instead, aggregated sites of from 5 to 25 times the size of the previously largest sites seem to appear within one or a very few generations. Although quantitative data are not widely available—with the exception, perhaps, of Grasshopper (which is also atypical in other ways)—it appears that the number of smaller sites diminishes substantially with aggregation.

Although the authors who provide comment agree that population increase preceded aggregation, demographic data on a much larger spatial scale are needed to evaluate population trends concomitant with these widespread and approximately contemporaneous initial aggregations. Similarly, comparable subsistence data that would allow us to compare subsistence strategies or carrying capacity are not available.

DISCUSSION

As we indicated at the outset of this chapter, current models of aggregation require information about population density, subsistence economy, agricultural technology and intensification, paleoenvironmental factors, and methods of social integration. Even having limited ourselves to geographic areas with good data bases, we cannot discuss all of these dimensions for each region, and we clearly feel most comfortable with the Mogollon and Anasazi data. The problems of operationalizing a definition of aggregated settlement in the context of a *ranchería* pattern elude us, and the additional complexities of dealing with pithouse communities that are also somewhat dispersed on the ranchería model—as is the case in the Late Pithouse period Mogollon and the Hohokam prior to the Classic—make this situation highly intractable.

Nevertheless, it seems to us that of the cases we consider here, the Hohokam pattern is most like an Old World model of incipient social complexity and also perhaps most appropriate to Longacre's original statements about aggregation. That is, arable land and particularly irrigable land is highly localized in the Arizona desert, and either increasing population density or a diminishing resource base combined with increasing population would lead to efforts at intensification. The type of intensification that appears most often is irrigation and expansion of the irrigation networks, efforts that both require and can support further population increases. It is worth recalling here that Kohler's (1989) remarks about the costs of aggregation (like those of locational geographers) assume that resources are uniformly distributed on the landscape. Such an assumption is unreasonable for much of the Southwest, and for the Hohokam system and irrigable land, no such assumption can be made.

With the Hohokam Classic, aggregation in the desert took a form that is more readily apparent to those of us who work in the mountain or plateau areas. As Doyel suggests, the economic base of this period of aggregation is not restricted to reliance on irrigation agriculture, and it included the kinds of activity exemplified by the large Classic period Hohokam community of Marana: a combination of canal irrigation, a variety of dry-farming techniques, and the production and exchange of agave fiber. In their discussion of the Marana community, Paul Fish, Suzanne Fish, and John Madsen (1989) argue that the aggregated population enabled Marana to capture diverse economic strategies, thus providing an overall reduction of risk. This analysis of the economy of the Marana community is closer to some economic geographic models for aggregation.

Although from a theoretical perspective, many economic geographers view dispersed settlement as the most efficient means of sustaining agrarian communities, in cases where a variety of field types exist, it may be efficient to locate centrally (Smith 1976). In addition to following the Marana pattern, other Classic Hohokam communities also intensified their agricultural efforts. Still other Classic Hohokam communities seem to have intensified trade. That some of these communities also lacked stability (as reflected in longevity) is both disturbing and interesting from a theoretical standpoint. The message we derive from the Hohokam data is that the Hohokam exhibited far more diversity in economic bases and in settlement trajectories than older scenarios would have led us to believe.

Questions about aggregation are relevant to a general discussion of the development of social stratification. For the past ten years, Southwesternists have debated the idea that complex political structures, particularly social and economic hierarchies, are required in large aggregated settlements with evidence of extensive trade and agricultural intensification (see Upham, Lightfoot, and Jewett 1989). Yet even those who argue most eloquently for periods during which there were local political hierarchies and regionally interacting "elites" have difficulty reconciling their view with the lack of archaeological expression of economic differentiation. There are no archaeologically visible, well-fed, conspicuously consuming groups of elites, and most Anasazi and Western Pueblo aggregated settlements appear to have been modular and unstable over the long term (Johnson 1989). As we have noted, however, there are problems in interpreting prehistoric social organization and in making assumptions about prehistoric land use. Rather than dismiss the idea that politically complex societies existed prehistorically in the Southwest, we prefer to attempt to separate the process of aggregation from that of developing political complexity.

One way to gain insight into the process of aggregation is to examine our data in light of Johnson's (1989) theories of scalar stress. Johnson (1989) suggests that for efficient decision making, there is a limit of about 6 to 14 participants. If we assume that nuclear or extended family households were the low-order building blocks of Southwestern communities, and that leaders of households served as participants in community-level decision making, then settlements with consensual decision making would be limited to about six households. Communities of more than six or so households would need some higher-level decision-making structure. Johnson suggests that either simultaneous or sequential hierarchies develop as a result; with either one, he maintains, the upper limit on community size should increase dramatically. To evaluate the costs and benefits of aggregation, then, one must specify the group incurring that cost or receiving that benefit. In a sequential hierarchy, the costs and benefits should be comparatively equally shared because of the lack of concentrated power. In a simultaneous hierarchy, the benefits often will be reaped by the elites and the costs will be borne by the remainder of the population.

Following up on Johnson's (1989) discussion archaeologically, we would interpret aggregated sites as those with evidence of more than about six contemporaneous households. How to recognize a household, knowing that household size may have varied substantially both spatially and temporally, remains a question; it may be possible to escape the use of arbitrary cutoffs through examination of archaeological data from various areas and times. In the Zuni case, examination of histograms of the sizes (number of rooms) of sites with pueblo architecture revealed a range of from 1 to 1,400 rooms but showed a marked paucity of sites with between 60 and 120 rooms. Kintigh (1990b) argued that this size distribution reflects the dichotomy between sites with simple and more complex decision-making processes. We would not suggest that the same breakpoint would necessarily be found elsewhere, but distinct gaps in the site size histograms that are consistent with Johnson's organizational distinction may well be useful indicators of differences that can be called nonaggregated and aggregated sites.

For the Anasazi and Mogollon areas, we feel more comfortable defining aggregation as a settlement strategy to be examined independently of questions of political complexity. We are encouraged by the operational model that focuses on jumps in settlement size; yet, even looking at numbers of rooms (and holding organizational considerations temporarily in abeyance), we note differences among the regions examined. In the Mesa Verde and Kayenta areas, for example, large sites seem to be aggregates of households that may be definable architecturally, with modular courtyard groups or "plaza groups." In the aggregated communities of the Pajarito and upper Rio Grande and upper Pecos areas, however, the architectural indications of household are more subtle (Habicht-Mauche and Creamer 1989): long lines of rooms, the major walls of which are built at the same time, with interior space subdivided later. It is the organization of labor that seems to be quite different here; as indicated above, the differences in organization between Betatakin and Kiet Siel should not be minimized.

We have noted that for the Santa Fe district and Mesa Verde (and probably Chaco), water control features were present before community aggregation occurred. If Longacre's theory of aggregation counteracting stress is correct, at least initial steps toward agricultural intensification must have been taken prior to aggregation. With respect to timing, we note that in the Mimbres area, aggregation appears to occur at approximately AD 1000 to 1050. Virtually everywhere else—the upper Rio Grande, Galisteo Basin, Zuni, and so on—it becomes the rule at about 1275 to 1290, although the first occurrence may be earlier. According to our understanding of the paleoclimatic data of the Colorado Plateaus (Dean, this volume), the 1000-to-1050 period experienced neither decreased rainfall nor lower groundwater tables. It does coincide with a period of increased spatial variability of rainfall, as Fred Plog (1983a) suggested. The interval from 1275 to 1290, on the other hand, is nearly coincident with the Great Drought on the Colorado Plateaus, though apparently not with an increase in spatial variability in rainfall.

Finally, although we recognize that there is a correlation between aggregation and increased population density in any area, we are wary of falling into the trap of "Cardboard Darwinism" (Gould 1987; Vayda 1989). To begin to unravel the issues involved in the aggregation process, we need a much better understanding of the economies of the aggregated sites in the Southwest than we now have.

7

Toward an Explanation
for Southwestern "Abandonments"

PAUL R. FISH, SUZANNE K. FISH,
GEORGE J. GUMERMAN, AND
J. JEFFERSON REID

 INTEREST IN THE CIRCUMSTANCES SURROUNDING ABANDONMENT of habitation sites is as old as archaeology itself. With even cursory knowledge of an area, it may be evident that remains of some periods are predominant and those of others are minor or absent. The largest and most elaborate sites can be seen to have experienced periods of development and growth, eventually to have been forsaken. The topic of abandonment has had wide appeal to archaeologists and the public alike, engendering visions of dramatic events and collapsing societies. Although there undoubtedly were instances of precipitous calamity, the archaeological record of the American Southwest more often suggests that abandonments occurred as the result of cumulative human decisions made under changing conditions in the social and natural environment.

Because particular decisions concerning abandonment are interwoven with cultural and environmental factors unique to each case, we adopt the broadest perspective of abandonment as a cultural phenomenon: abandonment is viewed as part of a larger process that includes both leaving one area and relocating to another. Abandonment decisions are seen as solutions to problems. The perceived outcome of abandonment must have been considered more acceptable, under given circumstances, than remaining in the same location; therefore, conditions in the area of destination, as well as in the area being abandoned, would have affected the timing and manner of departure.

Our discussion of abandonment includes several approaches. First, a general model is offered for regional abandonments in late prehistoric times. We believe this model describes tendencies embodied throughout the Southwest and provides a framework for analyzing exceptions. Data in the form of maps for sequential chronological intervals are assembled in order to facilitate preliminary evaluation of this model. Next, inferred causes for abandonments at site, local, and regional levels are discussed. The integration of abandoning populations at destinations and later utilizations of abandoned areas are briefly considered. Finally, case studies of abandonments at increasing scales are examined for the vicinity of Grasshopper Pueblo (Mountain Mogollon), the Tucson Basin (Hohokam), and the Colorado Plateaus (Western Anasazi).

THE ARCHAEOLOGICAL DEFINITION
OF ABANDONMENT

Abandonment is defined archaeologically as the absence of evidence for habitation of any magnitude or duration in a locus of previous habitation. Significant reduction of earlier resident population is a corollary. Temporally, abandonment behavior may be so compressed as to constitute a brief event or so extended as to represent a trend or process; such distinctions may be difficult to discern in the archaeological record. Populations utilizing or remaining in the abandoned territory have low archaeological visibility.

Abandonment is a phenomenon of variable geographic scale, and has been so treated in the Southwestern literature. Cordell (1984) identifies site, local, and regional scales as typical foci of study. Cultural and ecological factors most relevant to abandonments at small scales may be different in kind and frequency from factors shaping abandonment phenomena at more encompassing scales. Site abandonments are commonplace throughout Southwestern prehistory, abandonments of locales such as valleys are less frequent, and regional abandonments are most infrequent. Factors influencing smallest-scale abandonments account for larger-scale phenomena through repetitions only if there are sufficient elements of causal interrelationship and locational and temporal synchronicity.

Even where contemporary site and local abandonments are so widespread as to create regional patterns, different scales of archaeological analysis result in insights into different aspects of the overall phenomenon. Studies focused at the levels of sites, locales, or regions experiencing abandonment tell us about environmental and cultural factors affecting the persistence and success of populations in those respective units. However, variables limited to negative conditions such as subsistence stress in abandoned areas represent incomplete data for reconstructions in which factors such as rearrangements of long-distance trade networks are considered.

Smaller scales of analysis are most relevant for documentation of disadvantageous circumstances that may have precipitated abandonment decisions. They may also provide evidence bearing on relocation, such as preexisting exchange relationships. Nevertheless, the larger process of abandonment, including alternatives and outcomes, can be fully understood only at scales encompassing both points of departure and destination.

Regional rather than more circumscribed abandonments have been selected as the primary subject of our discussion because we wish to examine potentially pan-Southwestern patterns and relationships. The fact that regional abandonments cluster in relatively late prehistoric time, when they are also geographically wide-spread, suggests commonality in at least some attributes. Conditions particular to each abandoned region may have largely governed the specific timing and nature of abandonment behavior, but they seem insufficient to explain the essentially pervasive distribution and temporal concentration of these events.

The term "region" lacks a very precise definition in Southwestern usage and in archaeology generally. In the sense we use it here, it might be loosely equated with major ceramic or topographic subdivisions of Southwestern traditions (Kayenta Anasazi, Tucson Basin Hohokam, Mountain Mogollon, etc.). To meet the criteria for regional abandonment, a significant fraction of such a region must be affected. Extents of regional abandonment as great or greater than archaeologically defined instances are represented by early Spanish descriptions of *"despoblados"* in various parts of the Southwest, although post-contact factors influencing these later depopulations are largely noncomparable.

A GENERAL MODEL FOR SOUTHWESTERN ABANDONMENTS

We wish to explore the proposition that large-scale abandonments across the Southwest in late prehistoric times can be related to the development of organizational modes enabling relatively denser, more integrated populations, and to the areally intensified production underlying these aggregates. The relationship between aggregated configurations and regional abandonments is not necessarily one of direct cause and effect. In some instances, units of aggregated living may have developed in place without marked effect on populations elsewhere. However, the development of such aggregates provided new alternatives to outlying groups experiencing social or environmental stress. At times, aggregated entities also may have contributed to pressures on smaller enclaves in surrounding regions.

Around AD 1000, "experiments" with denser populations, intensified production, and more integrated and inclusive territorial units were underway in a few areas such as Chaco Canyon and the Phoenix Basin. Subsequently, abandonments on a regional scale begin to cluster broadly in time. Isolated cases appear by AD 1150 to 1200 and occur widely at AD 1300. By 1350, numbers of large areas lack archaeologically recognizable habitation sites of any size and duration.

When regional abandonments became widespread, between AD 1200 and 1400, a number of relatively aggregated configurations in riskier and more limited environments for intensification disappeared, including examples involving the Mogollon of the Grasshopper vicinity, the Hohokam of the northern Tucson Basin, and the Kayenta Anasazi in northeastern Arizona. During the same period, concentrations of denser population shifted toward areas capable of supporting intensified agriculture and particularly riverine irrigation. It is assumed that these aggregated units based on intensive production absorbed some significant proportion of formerly more dispersed populations.

Cordell and Gumerman (1989) have identified intervals in Southwestern pre-history bounded by "hinge points," a concept of rather limited chronological ranges during which change occurred between one set of characteristic modes of behavior and a following set. Regional abandonment, and the larger phenome-non to which we suggest it relates, exhibit some parallels with this model. An integral relationship between regional abandonment and aggregated configura-tions develops prior to a chronological threshold and then comes to be widely expressed across a number of Southwestern regions during the following interval. Aggregation and intensified production do not "diffuse" across the Southwest, but the organizational solutions and structures that facilitate these developments and link them with regional abandonments are shared and cumulative over time. Suc-cessive aggregated units build on the organizational innovations and productive technologies of their predecessors.

The organizational legacy of even ultimately unsuccessful sociopolitical enti-ties is a topic recently explored for state level civilizations (Yoffee and Cowgill 1987), but the basic observations are applicable to the Southwest as well. By an additive process, the repertoire of institutional stances and productive arrange-ments for aggregated living should have grown through time and become increas-ingly viable for denser populations and more integrated territorial units. Paren-thetically, we should make it clear that pronounced hierarchy and linearization (cf. Flannery 1972a) appear not to have been the primary structural arrangements underlying aggregation in many parts of the prehistoric Southwest. Elaborated and pervasive kinship systems, including elements of fictive kinship when nec-essary, and comprehensive sodality structures are prominent among the range of Southwestern solutions in ethnographic situations.

With respect to abandonment and relocation, critical attributes of aggregated configurations can be identified in both social and economic spheres. Organi-zational structures had to be sufficiently flexible to provide newcomers access to the means of production such as land and water, to assign them social roles, and to mediate interactions among the enlarged, more heterogeneous member-ship. Furthermore, aggregated configurations had to be productively expandable in order to absorb the increased labor of abandoning groups—and with it, to sup-port the higher population total.

Initial frameworks for aggregated living and intensified production had to be in place before abandoners could consider such alternatives. Absorption may have entailed greater labor inputs or lower production per unit area than in home-lands, but with possible tradeoffs in increased subsistence security and survival through the stress initiating abandonment. From the viewpoint of existing ag-gregates, abandoning groups may have represented a potential for new labor and productive expansion. In cases such as the Phoenix Basin, Zuni, the Tonto Basin, the Rio Grande pueblos, or Casas Grandes, emigrating personnel may have been utilized readily in riverine irrigation and other labor-intensive or differentiated subsistence activities, including farming or extractive specialities, or farming in adjacent and more marginal uplands.

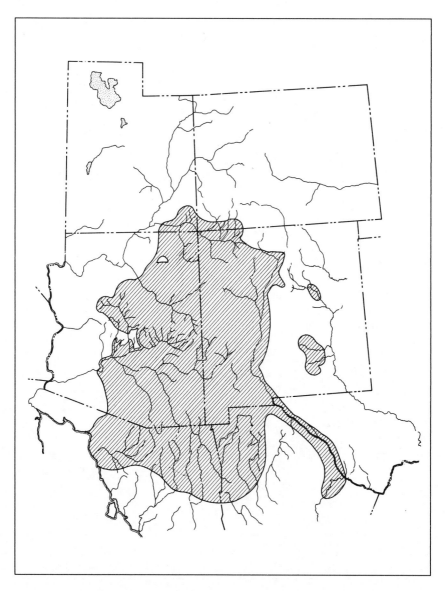

Figure 7.1. Distribution of Southwestern agricultural peoples, AD 1275 to 1300.

Maps of the greater Southwest have been prepared to illustrate the broad-scale patterns that are the basis for the inclusive model of regional abandonments (figs. 7.1, 7.2). Chronological precision must be qualified by the lowest common denominator in the southern Southwest, where tree ring correlations are generally unavailable. Furthermore, these maps reflect broad-brush geographic generalizations based on data provided by individuals listed in the acknowledgments. It is

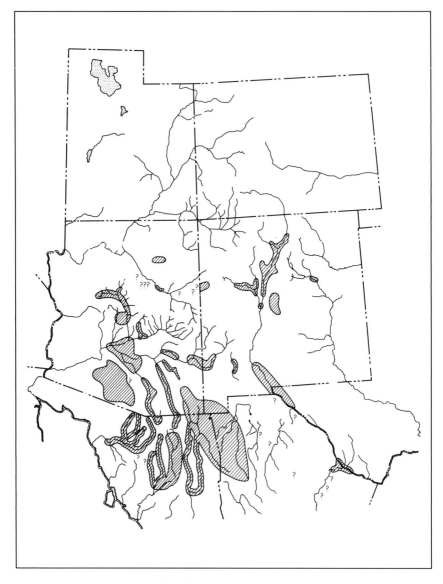

Figure 7.2. Distribution of Southwestern agricultural peoples, AD 1400 to 1425.

doubtful that even this modest number of contributors could reach consensus on
details.

At AD 1100, virtually uninterrupted occupation occurred across the entire
Southwest. Figure 7.1 shows the distribution of occupations during early Pueblo III
times at approximately AD 1275 to 1300. Figure 7.2 compares the distribution
during the mid-Pueblo IV period, or about AD 1400 to 1425. This second map can

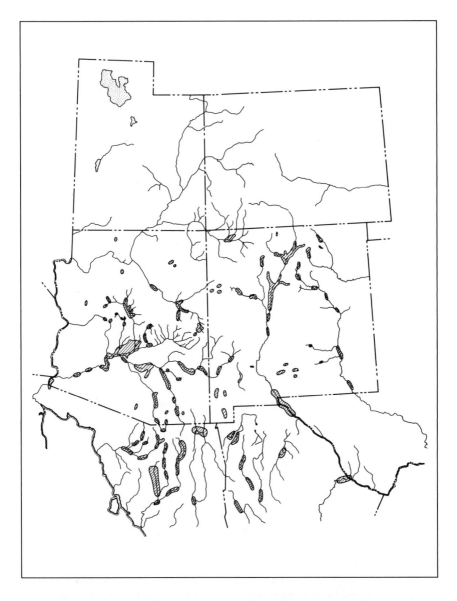

Figure 7.3. Distribution of gravity irrigation in the Southwest prior to AD 1900. (Compiled from British Museum Library n.d.; Water Resources Institute 1953; U.S. Government 1901. For northern Mexico, modern gravity irrigation canals—as shown on Comisión de Estudios del Territorio 1:50,000 topographic maps—were used as proxies for historic systems in areas where other information was lacking.)

be compared to figure 7.3, compiled to show the distribution of historic irrigation in the earliest part of the fifteenth century, when simple gravity systems were most common and few permanent dams were in place. A general congruence can be seen between figures 7.2 and 7.3. However, it is also apparent that aggregated configurations with the potential for riverine irrigation were not uniformly distributed or equally accessible to prehistoric inhabitants of all Southwestern regions.

PROCESSES OF REGIONAL ABANDONMENT

In the literature, Southwestern abandonments have been treated predominantly from the point of view of negative or "push" factors in the area of departure. A number of models or causal agents have been advanced for abandonment decisions, although few could be perceived to apply consistently across the Southwest as a whole. Environmental deterioration is a case in point. Two separate winter and summer weather systems create clinal patterns in the seasonal distribution of annual precipitation from north to south and east to west; origin and timing of additional limiting factors to agriculture and critical rainfall therefore are not uniform across Southwestern regions. For example, Hohokam of the Phoenix Basin irrigated from the Salt and Gila rivers, with high flows fed by winter precipitation from Pacific fronts in the uplands above the Mogollon Rim. Summer rainfall, on the other hand, was the primary source of agricultural water for Hohokam to the south, where sustained flows in intermittent or ephemeral watercourses were concentrated in that season by storms from the Gulf of Mexico (Fish and Nabhan 1991).

Cultural vectors such as intrusive ethnic groups (e.g., Ambler and Sutton 1989), intergroup conflict (e.g., Doelle and Wallace 1991; Wilcox and Haas, this volume), trade realignments (e.g., Spoerl and Gumerman 1984; Wilcox and Haas, this volume), and domino effects (e.g., Upham 1982) can seldom be convincingly expanded to pan-Southwestern levels that incorporate both the upland and southern desert culture areas.

The manner of abandonment is a class of information unique to each area of departure and may be instructive for understanding both spheres of the abandonment process. The Anasazi leaving northern Black Mesa, for example, apparently knew where they were going, and their destination was only a short distance away. In the many years of excavation, no more than two or three whole metates were found in the contexts of the final period at Black Mesa (Gumerman 1984:109); all had been removed from mealing bins, and only completely worn or broken ones remained. Even with ubiquitous raw materials and informal, easily manufactured styles, it was considered worth the effort to carry these heavy objects to the new location. Portable material culture in general is scarce in this final stage of occupation.

In contrast, when NA7519 in the vicinity of Navajo Mountain was abandoned, metates were propped against walls and deliberately broken. Not only did these departing Anasazi not want to be burdened, they also seem to have had no expectation of future return and they did not want others to use their metates (Lindsay et al. 1968). Betatakin and Kiet Siel provide another well-documented contrast between abandonment behaviors, with the former case simultaneous and comprehensive and the latter markedly more gradual and individual (Dean 1969, 1970). With sufficient numbers of such fine-grained studies, consistency or variability in modes of abandonment within and between regions might be established.

The role of destinations in abandonment decisions is hard to isolate. It requires consideration of evidence from broader territory and has been relatively neglected. Typically, chronological precision and methods for distinguishing cultural identity are inadequate to link conclusively the relevant populations and areas. Nevertheless, expectations concerning destinations must have strongly influenced abandonment behavior. The timing of abandonments during late prehistory can be viewed as the outcome of an interplay between conditions in previous homelands and the availability and perception of alternatives. Regions affected by similar sets of adverse factors (e.g., the Anasazi on the Colorado Plateaus) may have experienced relatively synchronous abandonments. However, in few cases has it been suggested that abandonment resulted in simple replications of prior settlement patterns in more favorable environments elsewhere. Where aggregated settlements served as destinations, their subsequent development was also affected by abandonment decisions.

The range of solutions for the integration of abandoning populations into existing aggregates is poorly understood. Ethnographically, Puebloan cases include preservation of incoming group identity by accretion as separate clans (e.g., Hopi and Zuni) and the acceptance of ethnically distinct groups conditional to fulfilling particular functions or roles (the Tewa on the Hopi Mesas). Unfortunately, analogies for non-Puebloan groups of the greater Southwest are less plentiful and illuminating. Almost certainly, anticipated methods of incorporation at destinations would have influenced the staging of abandonments. Related persons abandoning and arriving en masse might be more apt to achieve acceptance as a group, while single or a few households might be assimilated into existing organization. In all but the most catastrophic cases of abandonment, negotiations between abandoners and inhabitants at destinations likely preceded departures.

WHAT'S HAPPENING OUT THERE?

Just as regional abandonments can be viewed as part of a larger process that includes relocation, the issue of low level, succeeding occupations or utilizations of abandoned areas can also be construed as closely related. Questions arise as to how residual populations might be characterized, to what degree they were disjunct or retained the organization and personnel of the previous populations, and how they did or did not relate to the aggregated settlement systems joined by at least some of the former regional occupants.

These questions have been the subject of recent debate. One position downplays population loss and identifies problems of archaeological visibility as creating perceptions of markedly lower densities. Although there are insights to be gained from the concepts of "power" and "resiliency" or their terminological equivalents (Upham 1984, 1988; F. Plog 1983b; Stuart and Gauthier 1984; Tainter and Plog, this volume), it is difficult to support the contention that shifts to resilient or mobile, diversified, and nonintensive strategies in later prehistoric time account for population reductions of the magnitude usually identified as regional abandonments. Criticisms have been leveled at the archaeological evidence invoked to indicate the widespread presence of groups with resilient strategies (Sullivan 1987; Adams and Adams, n.d.). Although resilient strategies of the sort documented in post-contact times may have been practiced by reduced and poorly visible populations in some abandoned areas, other forms of continued utilization might also produce a relatively insubstantial archaeological record.

Another possibility for the origin of dispersed populations in abandoned areas is the influx or territorial expansion of groups having dissimilar, often extra-regional, ethnic affiliation. Extractive rather than strongly agricultural economies in these cases may partially reflect cultural patterns. An example of such an interpretation is the discussion by Ambler and Sutton (1989) of Numic groups living among San Juan Anasazi and exerting a key negative force in the eventual Puebloan abandonment of the region. Although the post-contact Southwest is replete with instances of mobile raiders who are ethnically distinct from their agricultural victims, there are also examples of more mutually advantageous and regularized relationships. These sorts of interactions, best documented at the edges of the Southwest, have been studied ethnographically and investigated in late prehistoric contexts (Kelley 1952; Ford 1972; Spielmann 1983; Snow 1981).

In some abandoned areas, artifactual evidence links items of material culture to points of origin in aggregated settlements. These items, largely ceramic, could have been traded to ethnically distinct occupants—newcomers (as in Ambler and Sutton 1989) or long-resident "Querechos" (Upham 1982)—but are often regarded as indicating the presence of persons from the manufacturing group. These linkages become somewhat more complicated, of course, if intermediary trade contributes to the presence of distinctive wares in either aggregated settlements or abandoned areas.

For the time span following AD 1350 in many parts of the Southwest, the difficulties of recognizing and interpreting archaeological evidence pertaining to periods of abandonment are compounded. The manufacture of localized styles in decorated ceramics declines, while trade wares and pan-regional styles rise in prominence. By latest prehistoric time, a number of widespread ceramic types apparently circulate from relatively restricted locales of manufacture (e.g., Jeddito/Sikyatki, Ramos, and perhaps some Salado polychromes) yet may represent the major chronological markers in geographically distant areas. Where tiny percentages of late diagnostics occur at multicomponent sites, it may be virtually impossible to distinguish between fleeting visits and more substantial late occupations in which decorated diagnostics are at minimal levels. Precision in ceramic and all other dating in the post–AD 1350 era for much of the Southwest is also low due to the paucity of well-controlled excavations in large late sites and of tree ring or other absolute correlations.

All of the foregoing possibilities may have contributed to ephemeral remains postdating major regional abandonments. Variability across the Southwest should be expected in this as in all other aspects. There has been little exploration, however, of potential modes of utilization more integrally linked with contemporary and adjacent population aggregates. Small-scale farming and gathering in the most favorable locales, for example, could have provided short-term but critical supplements during episodes of agricultural calamity, such as flood damage to canals. Depleted natural resources in the vicinities of aggregated populations also may have occasioned extractive activities in outlying areas. Former occupants would be likely to specialize in hunting, gathering, or quarrying in former home territories. Rights to land and resources in abandoned areas may have been retained, with such continuities structuring use of sparsely settled hinterlands by members of aggregated settlements. At Hopi, for example, periodic visits are made to distant boundary markers of ancestral clan land (Page 1940; James 1974).

CASE STUDIES

Case studies illustrate perspectives on regional abandonment in three major cultural traditions of the Southwest. The studies represent differing geographic scales and bodies of relevant data. Issues that can be and are addressed reflect variability in available evidence and in the interests and theoretical orientations of the authors.

THE WESTERN ANASAZI CASE STUDY

The Western Anasazi case study area (fig. 7.4) is artificially bounded and was chosen because it crosscuts natural and cultural boundaries, has examples of the wide range of demographic trends for the entire Anasazi region, and has been differentially but relatively well studied. There is considerable variability in the edaphic and physiographic situations of five subzones: Navajo Mountain, the Long House–Klethla Valley area, Black Mesa, the Hopi Buttes, and the Little Colorado River.

Western Anasazi Environments. The Navajo Mountain subzone has limited soil development, and surface water is scarce. The Long House–Klethla Valley environment is more dissected, and though often narrow, some canyons have thick deposits of alluvium and many carry perennial flows fed by springs. The Black Mesa uplands have areas of deep alluvium, with few reliable water sources; surface water is more plentiful in the mesa's southern interior and along its southern extremities near the Hopi villages. The Hopi Buttes study area is eroded sandstone

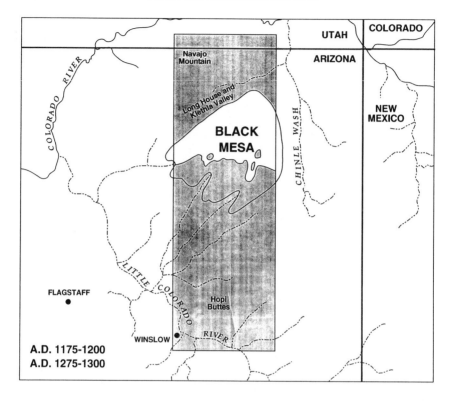

Figure 7.4. Distribution of agricultural settlements in the Western Anasazi case study area, AD 1175 to 1300.

and volcanic badlands with very little potable water and no major drainage system. The Little Colorado River subarea is the lowest and hottest; though locally quite wide, the floodplain would have been risky for large-scale, labor-intensive irrigation systems because of potential flooding (Lightfoot and Plog 1984).

Demographic and Social Trajectories in the Subzones.   From about AD 1000 to 1150, the entire study area was occupied by people living in small habitation sites seldom containing more than 20 rooms. There is little indication of supravillage organization. It is the first period of substantial, year-long occupation for much of the upland Western Anasazi country. Overall, it is a period when the area of occupation is dramatically increased, population rises, and the distinctiveness of the material manifestations are locally enhanced.

This same interval witnesses ameliorating environmental conditions. Groundwater tables are rising, and after the first years of the eleventh century precipitation is greatly increasing and consistent throughout the area (fig. 7.5). Favorable conditions permit a wide variety of strategies to succeed in diverse, spatially discrete environments. These strategies would inhibit the need for large-scale

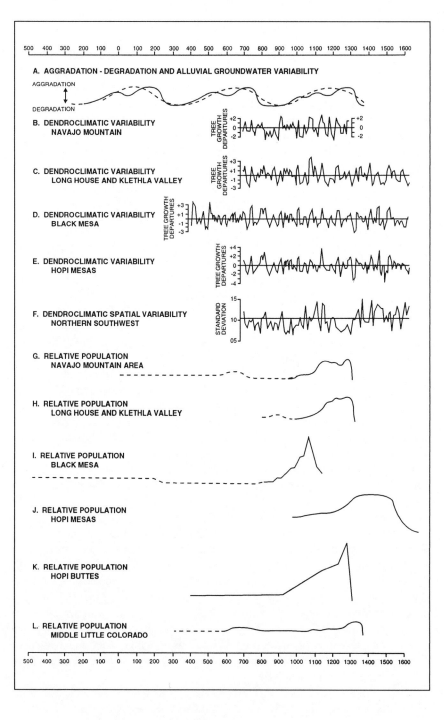

Figure 7.5. Environmental variability and population curves for the Western Anasazi.

socioeconomic networks and would facilitate the development of localized traditions. Exchange networks seem to shrink, and more-or-less economically independent hamlets fill almost all available habitats. There is no evidence for investment
in intensive agricultural techniques. It should be noted that it is this period in the
Eastern Anasazi area which saw large-scale developments in Chaco Canyon.

After AD 1150, there was a slight decrease in the water table levels, an increase in erosion, decrease in precipitation, and shrinkage in the area occupied.
The northeastern and central part of the Black Mesa subarea is without permanent habitation. The abandonment of these uplands echoes similar trends in the
huge Grand Canyon and Virgin Tradition regions to the west. Higher elevations,
locations with little surface water, and areas where it is difficult to collect and
store water are abandoned. The Hopi Buttes, an exception to this rule, may have
continued to be occupied because their settlement pattern and social organization
were adapted to the dispersed wild resources on which the people were highly dependent. Hopi Buttes inhabitants developed an extensive suprasettlement network
centered on a ceremonial site in an attempt to cope with the dispersal necessitated
by their unusual emphasis on gathering (Gumerman 1988). In other areas, particularly the Navajo Mountain zone, a period of agricultural intensification ensues
(Lindsay 1961; Lindsay et al. 1968; Sharrock, Dibble, and Anderson 1961).

Concerns for domestic water supplies after AD 1150 are indicated by the clustering of sites around natural surface water and reservoirs (Dean, Lindsay, and
Robinson 1978). The Long House–Klethla Valley area experienced major population growth due to influx from the uplands. Even in the valleys, the populations
began to be concentrated in the upper parts of the drainages as arroyo cutting
made it difficult to farm the lower reaches (Dean 1969; Dean, Lindsay, and Robinson 1978). The result of this process was a discontinuous population distribution
characterized by fewer but larger sites, separated by areas without permanent
habitation. In sum, the century from AD 1150 to 1250 seems to be characterized
by population movement and experimentation in different organizational forms
in an attempt at dealing with a deteriorating environment.

From AD 1250 to 1300, a period of falling water tables and increased erosion,
there was a greater reliance on agriculture and the greatest evidence for agricultural intensification. The Navajo Mountain segment has the largest concentration
of soil and water conservation and control devices, probably because such invest-
ments were unnecessary in the Long House–Klethla Valley subarea (Gumerman
and Dean 1989), where site clusters are concentrated in locales with low potential
for arroyo cutting and where alluvial groundwater is forced to the surface. Sites
in both the Navajo Mountain and the Long House–Klethla Valley subareas seem
to situated in a "line-of-sight" fashion, and there is some indication of internecine
conflict (Haas and Creamer 1985)

Beginning about AD 1300, there was a severe drop in the water table, the onset
of a major arroyo cutting cycle, and a major decrease in precipitation. The entire
northern part of the study area became unsuitable for permanent habitation. The

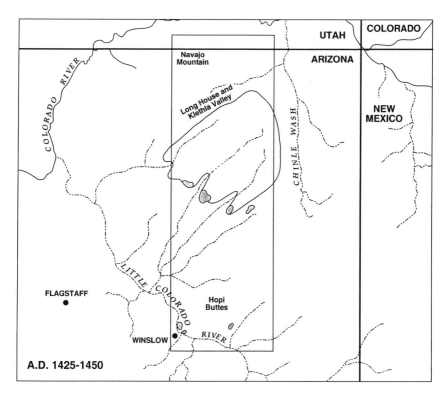

Figure 7.6. Distribution of agricultural settlements in the Western Anasazi case study area, AD 1425 to 1450.

abandonment of much of the uplands seems orderly. Most portable artifacts were taken, and doors were sealed. The Navajo Mountain, Long House–Klethla Valley, and Hopi Buttes subareas were emptied of permanent population at this time, and the people undoubtedly moved to the southern end of Black Mesa. Other areas where surface water was still present, such as Tsegi Canyon, were simply unsuitable for agriculture because headward arroyo cutting, which had begun earlier, intensified and hindered water delivery to the field systems. Clearly, the complex social order that had developed since the AD 1000s demanded a certain level of population density to be sustained. Once a critical portion of the population left, it was necessary for a complete exodus or the total transformation of the social form as it had developed. The southern edges of Black Mesa and a few locales of surface water along the Little Colorado River were still occupied and had substantial concentrations of populations.

In terms of environment and location of population, the situation at AD 1450 (fig. 7.6) was not much different than it was in AD 1300, although the sites are usually much larger, often numbering several hundred rooms. What had changed was the social order of the Western Anasazi. The movement of population, the obvious series of major settlements, changes in subsistence strategy, and organizational decisions that had to be made in that century and a half meant major social transformations throughout the Anasazi world. Decisions may have been as much conditioned by the existing social situation as they were by the natural environment. The transformations that appeared in Pueblo IV, exemplified by new artistic forms and ideological changes with the introduction of the katsina cult, may have been affected by the severe subsistence stress brought on by the deteriorating environment and the concentration of population (Adams 1981, 1991; McGuire 1989; McGuire et al., this volume).

Sometime after about AD 1450, only the villages on the Hopi Mesas were inhabited. Presumably, environmental conditions were such along the Little Colorado River that villages could still be supported, although there is evidence to suggest that major flooding destroyed portions of sites and canal systems, and the managing of water may have been a persistent problem (E. Charles Adams, personal communication 1992). It is the Hopi villages, which depended more on intermittent forms of irrigation from seeps and springs, not those villages dependent on large streamflow, which have survived to this day.

THE TUCSON BASIN HOHOKAM CASE STUDY

The case study region for the Hohokam in the low deserts of southern Arizona lies along the lower reaches of the Santa Cruz River. The Tucson Basin proper, a 45-mile stretch between the San Xavier Reservation and the town of Marana, is the center of a red-on-brown variant within the Hohokam ceramic sequence. Average annual rainfall is between 9 and 12 inches, and perennial surface flow is confined to limited stretches of the river and its major tributaries.

At the chronological precision of ceramic phases, settlement history from systematic survey is available for 800 square miles in the northern basin (Fish, Fish, and Madsen 1989, 1990; Fish and Fish 1990). An area dramatically abandoned during the early Classic Tanque Verde phase lies within this study area, as do some of the later Classic clusters of aggregated settlements that are likely destinations. Full coverage data from the Marana Community, an integrated territorial unit of multiple sites, permits a quantified assessment of population dynamics prior to abandonment and an exhaustive distribution of post-abandonment activities.

Preclassic Settlement and Abandonment Evidence. Sites of all periods in the northern Tucson Basin are concentrated in two bands along the valley axis. One linear array follows the Santa Cruz River, including both irrigable floodplains and lower valley slope alluvial fans suitable for floodwater farming. The second band follows the mountain flanks in a broad swath along the upper valley slope and its adjacent upland edge. This settlement emphasis remains stable until the Classic period, with sites somewhat variably dispersed throughout the two topographic bands according to greater or lesser local opportunities. Separate Preclassic communities, each containing central ballcourt sites, cover 27 square miles in the band of settlement along the river and 22 square miles on the upper valley slope, respectively.

Preclassic abandonments (prior to AD 1100) of a regional scale have not been identified in the Tucson Basin, although there are instances of areally restricted abandonments of multiple sites. One such example involves a group of four sites along the northern Santa Cruz River whose arrangement suggests a shared canal line. Abandonment of these sites by the Classic period could be the result of localized change in river morphology, as has been suggested for one portion of the southern basin (Doelle, Dart, and Wallace 1985; Waters 1988), or could be correlated with population reorganization and aggregation at the beginning of the Classic period.

Early Classic Settlement and Abandonment Evidence.   Near the beginning of the Tanque Verde phase of the Classic period at about AD 1100, accelerating aggregation and reorganization becomes apparent (Fish, Fish, and Madsen 1989). Sites span the valley slope between the two previous communities, which coalesce into a single new territorial entity centered on a platform mound site. The early Classic Marana Community encompasses both a larger territory (56 square miles) and more numerous sites than its combined Preclassic precursors (fig. 7.7). A new level of architectural differentiation can be distinguished among Classic habitation sites in the unequal distribution of substantial adobe structures and compounds, as well as the unique occurrence of a platform mound.

Because structure numbers cannot be tabulated from surface indications with Hohokam architecture, square meters of habitation area serve as a reasonable proxy for chronological comparison of population. Approximately 2,300,000 square meters are recorded in the two Preclassic communities, while early Classic occupations total 6,100,000. This contrast becomes greater if relative duration is considered; although the Tanque Verde phase is poorly dated by absolute methods (Eighmy and McGuire 1989; Dean 1991), it clearly represents a shorter interval than the Preclassic time span. Some Preclassic sites are no longer occupied in the following period and may have contributed former population to areas more densely settled during Classic time. Nevertheless, the greater magnitude of habitation area in Classic sites by a factor of three implies substantial growth of the existing population or the inclusion of persons from outside the confines of the prior two communities.

Contemporaneous with the development of the larger, more aggregated, and more differentiated early Classic community is widespread evidence of intensified subsistence production (Fish, Fish, and Madsen 1990). Indeed, such intensification must have been a prerequisite for supporting the enlarged population. Agriculture is expanded into hydrologically marginal and previously unused land of the middle valley slope, and agricultural features proliferate along the mountain flanks. Drought-resistant agave, planted in fields of rockpile features, becomes a more important crop in the expansion of cultivation beyond optimal locations (Fish et al. 1985). Settlements appear in poorer floodwater situations along the

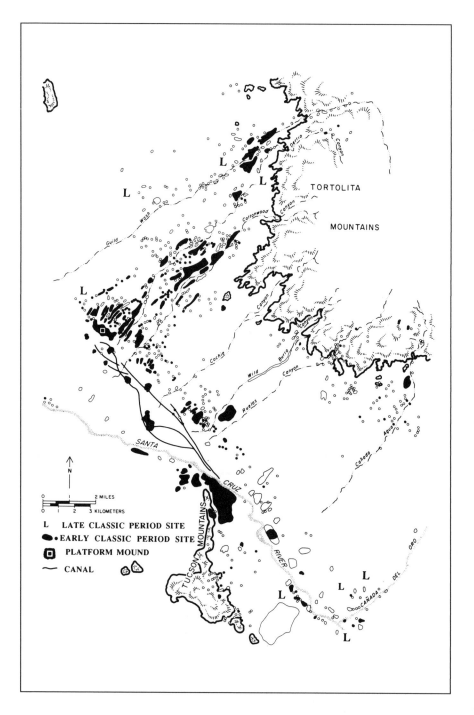

Figure 7.7. Distribution of early (AD 1100–1300) and late (1300–1450) Classic period settlements in the northern Tucson Basin.

edge of the lower valley slope and are serviced by a canal constructed at this time. Intensification can also be recognized in nonagricultural production by the occurrence of huge extractive sites in portions of the middle slope containing dense saguaro cactus.

Identifiable habitation ceases by about AD 1350 throughout the 56-square-mile extent of the Marana Community, a segment of the Tucson Basin continuously inhabited since the beginning of the Hohokam sequence. The abandonment of this large area appears generally synchronous as measured with the low resolution of Hohokam ceramic phases. Salado polychromes, the markers for the transition from the Tanque Verde to the following late Classic Tucson phase, are exceedingly rare and virtually absent from contexts suggesting residence (see fig. 7.7).

No environmental trigger for this abandonment is apparent. Locally derived environmental sequences are unavailable for the Tucson Basin, and in a reconstruction from tree ring records above the Mogollon Rim by Graybill (1989), summer precipitation, the critical factor in Tucson agricultural production, was found to be surprisingly complacent between AD 750 and 1350. Systemic disruptions of Salt River canals are posited at about AD 1350 (Nials, Gregory, and Graybill 1989) due to flood-induced changes in Phoenix intake locales. The morphology and seasonal flow regime of the Santa Cruz is not similar to that of the Salt River, but even in the event of parallel flood damage, occupation and production could have continued in the long-standing mountain flank settlements of the Tucson community.

This early Classic Marana Community could be viewed as an instance of aggregated living and intensified production in an environment with natural upper limits for subsistence. A riverine irrigated core may have contributed disproportionately to the supply of annual crops for the whole community. River flow is not perennial in this area, however, restricting the magnitude and productivity of canal systems compared to those on the Salt and Gila rivers and even those on perennial, upstream stretches of the Santa Cruz to the south. The diversity of agricultural production in the community implies that a residential population could have persisted in parts of it under any conceivable environmental scenario. Nevertheless, a consensus for abandonment was reached by all inhabitants. In this sense, the decision to abandon can be viewed as a social as well as an economic choice among a large population whose strong interconnections are emphasized by such joint action.

Late Classic Settlement and Abandonment Evidence. Figure 7.8 shows that the abandonment phenomenon of the later Tanque Verde phase is of a truly regional scale and involves more than a single multisite community unit. The absence of residential occupations between the midpoint of the Tucson Mountains and the southern edge of the Picacho Mountains (800 square miles) has been established by systematic survey coverage. Areas to the north and south that continue to be occupied into the period marked by Salado polychromes are indicated by the distribution of large sites of the late Classic.

Barring catastrophic population loss, it is reasonable to assume that inhabitants of the northern Tucson Basin were incorporated into late Classic settlement concentrations to the north and/or south. It further follows that productive capacities in these areas must have been sufficient to absorb the increased labor force as well as to satisfy the greater consumptive demands. A necessary correlate of this heightened aggregation is the development of social structures capable of integrating significant increments of immigrants and maintaining stability in the face of higher numbers in closer proximity. A case can be made that later Classic settlements occur in situations with potential for agricultural intensification. Large sites in these areas also exhibit remains suggesting highest residential densities for any period and the greatest investment in public architecture of presumed integrative function.

Large late Classic (Tucson phase) sites in the southern Tucson Basin are situated along stretches of the Santa Cruz with perennial surface flow or along major tributaries with extensive upland watersheds supplying reliable agricultural water; historic gravity irrigation was practiced in the vicinity of all these site locations. Each of the late southern sites in figure 7.8 is known to have had multiple compounds. At the three sites where preservation allows meaningful assessment, densities of surface remains are maximal for any time period and a platform mound is present. During this period in the southern Tucson Basin, there is a decrease in numbers of small sites (Doelle, Huntington, and Wallace 1987), and the large sites correspond to locations in which productive intensification through irrigation was a possibility with an increased labor pool.

Late Classic sites to the north of the Tucson Basin occur in proximity to the Picacho Mountains. Five sites with platform mounds are found in areas with long histories of habitation; they also represent the largest and densest occupations. One of these sites is adjacent to the Santa Cruz; the others are located along watercourses which are ephemeral but have watersheds of significantly greater size than Santa Cruz tributaries in the abandoned northern segment of the Tucson Basin. A relatively unusual number of large reservoirs demonstrates a potential for water management to prolong availability. The three northern sites are from 9 to 15 miles from the preeminent site of Casa Grande and may be integrated into its sphere in some manner.

Late Classic Utilization of Abandoned Areas.   Distributional data pertaining to a continued presence in the abandoned territory illustrate the difficulty of understanding relationships between such remains and inhabitants of contemporary settlements in surrounding areas. Figure 7.7 shows the northern Tucson Basin distribution of sites with Salado polychromes, the only chronological diagnostics for Hohokam occupations of the later Classic. Each of the few sites yielding polychromes within the former early Classic community contains at most a handful of sherds; all are small sites that lack assemblages suggesting substantial habitation during late Classic or earlier times. Because diagnostics are typically rare at small sites and because polychromes may be trade items, late Classic utilization of the

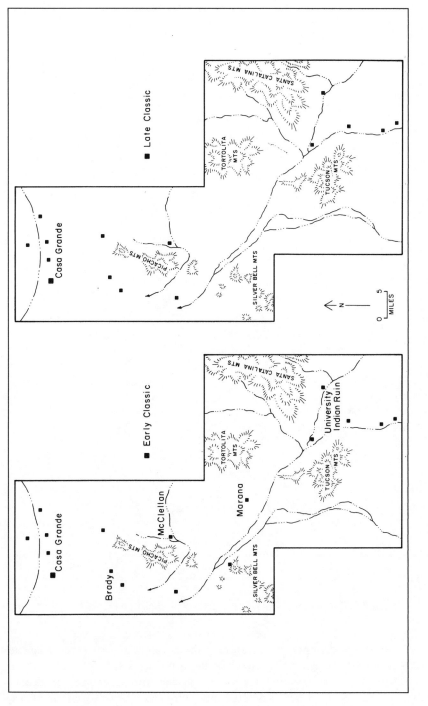

Figure 7.8. Distribution of early and late Classic period platform mound sites in southern Arizona.

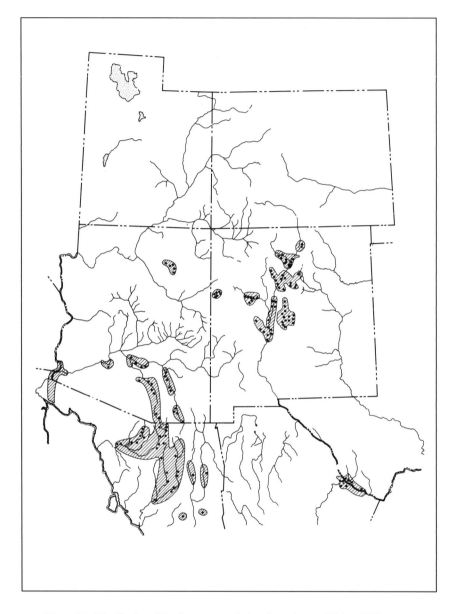

Figure 7.9. Distribution of Southwestern agricultural peoples, AD 1600 to 1700.

area could be underrepresented. However, these wares occur consistently in late sites of all sizes to the north and south of the abandoned area.

The distributional patterns suggest an ephemeral presence based on extractive activities or travel between north and south. Near the Tortolita Mountains, co-occurrence of polychrome sherds and projectile points on one small site may indicate hunting. Two lines of evidence raise the intriguing possibility of continued use of rockpile fields for agave production in the previous community. A late Classic radiocarbon date was obtained on agave from a roasting pit in a large field. Additionally, a small site at the northern edge of a series of these fields yielded polychrome sherds associated with a relatively diverse lithic assemblage. Because agaves require less direct tending than annual crops, it is possible that at least a reduced level of production might have been maintained by former community residents or other persons living at a distance, perhaps in conjunction with seasonal fieldhouse residence. Distances of late Classic settlement clusters to either the north or south would have permitted such exploitation of the intervening abandoned area.

Two Abandonments in the Grasshopper Region

Two episodes of abandonment in the Grasshopper region of east-central Arizona illustrate the high information value of small-scale, long-term studies of abandonment processes. More significantly, the investigation of small-scale abandonments goes beyond categorizing abandonment phenomena to permit estimates of other, more critical, behavioral processes and parameters.

In the first episode—the apparent abandonment of the Cibecue Valley by AD 1300 as populations aggregated on the adjacent Grasshopper Plateau—we may identify both "push" and "pull" forces acting on the same population. Examining these forces together allows us to evaluate the contribution of environmental and social factors.

In the second episode—the certain abandonment of the Grasshopper Plateau and region by AD 1400—we emphasize changes in the behavioral system that make abandonment decisions inevitable. These linked abandonments, occurring within little over a century, underscore the need to investigate processes of behavioral change with reference to characteristics of specific cases of relatively high resolution.

Late Pueblo III Period Settlement, AD 1250–1300.   Small settlements of up to 20 to 25 rooms were dispersed throughout the central portion of the Grasshopper Plateau and along upper Cibecue Creek and its tributaries; occupied landforms ranged from terraces above creeks to the pediment overlooking the Cibecue Valley to prominent ridge and hilltops. There is no patterned use of ridge tops sufficient to suggest positioning for protection. Settlements cluster near agricultural soil, with the largest settlement in each group serving as a focal community. In the vicinity of Grasshopper Pueblo, for example, three settlement clusters have been identified (cf. Graves, Holbrook, and Longacre 1982): one focuses on Chodistaas, one on Grasshopper Spring, and one on the small pueblo obliterated by the fourteenth-century construction of Grasshopper Pueblo. Settlement clusters also characterize the Cibecue Valley. This pattern is the local expression of the long-term, mountain pattern of dispersed communities, which in the eastern mountains (Forestdale Valley and Point of Pines) center on settlements with a great kiva and in the central mountains on settlements with an enclosed plaza-courtyard.

A subsistence routine of hunting, gathering, and gardening required social group mobility that would have taken local residents to above the Mogollon Rim as well as into the deserts along the Salt River to the south (see Graybill and Reid 1982). Additionally, procurement of mountain resources (salt, hematite, chert, steatite, wild plants and animals) by nonlocal people would have increased the opportunity for social interaction as it also contributed to their familiarity with the Grasshopper region.

An Apache land-use model for mountain landscapes around Grasshopper is an appropriate framework for beginning to conceptualize the settlement, subsistence, and demographic fluidity of the AD 1200s (see Goodwin 1942).

Process and Event in the Abandonment of the Cibecue Valley.   Population density in the Cibecue Valley as well as throughout the Grasshopper region increased as the result of two processes: (1) inmigration of populations from above the Mogollon Rim and, perhaps, the desert; and (2) a decrease in residential mobility by the long-term inhabitants. Population movement into the region was, at least in part, a result of widespread demographic shifts on the Colorado Plateaus. The Maverick Mountain occupation at Point of Pines Pueblo is the best known example of such a movement of plateau people into the mountains at this time (Haury 1958).

Aggregation of people into large pueblo communities occurred earlier in surrounding regions than in the Cibecue Valley. Forty miles to the east of Cibecue there are 100-room pueblos with late thirteenth-century ceramic assemblages; to the north above the Mogollon Rim is the Pinedale Pueblo, which serves as the type site for the Pinedale phase (Haury 1985:391–92); to the west in the Sierra Ancha there are tree-ring dated thirteenth-century cliff dwellings, which attest the movement of northern peoples into the mountains (Haury 1934); and to the southwest around present-day Lake Roosevelt there are large communities with late thirteenth-century black-on-white ceramics. The ceramics and architectural layout of some of these communities implicate both indigenous mountain populations and populations from plateau and desert areas.

The movement of nonmountain peoples into the Cibecue Valley and the Grasshopper Plateau and the buildup of aggregated communities elsewhere in the mountains had several effects on the local people. First, the long-term pattern of residential mobility was constrained, with the result that settlements came to be occupied full-time. This level of residential stability was probably achieved in the AD 1280s at the height of the Great Drought (AD 1276–1299). Second, increased population density and the presence of displaced peoples would have increased competition for resources, thereby creating an atmosphere of social and economic uncertainty. For the residential kinship groups in small settlements of the Cibecue Valley and Grasshopper Plateau this competition may well have been heightened by the threat posed by the surrounding aggregated communities. That social uncertainty and potential threat of raids may have reached a dangerous level is suggested in the fact that all three of the excavated settlements of this period that were burned (Chodistaas, Grasshopper Spring, and P:14:197) are on the Grasshopper Plateau.

Abandonment of Cibecue Valley and Aggregation on the Grasshopper Plateau. People living in small, vulnerable communities at a time of demographic change and economic uncertainty abandoned the Cibecue Valley in response to the pressures of local competition for resources and the threat posed by already aggregated communities. They joined others on the Grasshopper Plateau. This settlement and organization reconfiguration for defense is supported by a number of observations

First, the Cibecue Valley and surrounding pediment, which had been occupied extensively during the late Pueblo III period, was not occupied during the AD 1300s except for the Cibecue Creek Pueblo of 40 to 60 rooms (because access is prohibited, there are insufficient data on when the pueblo was established). The valley was abandoned by the resident population as aggregation began on the Grasshopper Plateau, though it may have continued to be used for farming by the inhabitants of Pueblo communities on the eastern edge of the Grasshopper Plateau. Abandonment of the well-watered Cibecue Valley for the uplands of the Grasshopper Plateau, which today lacks permanent surface water, suggests that the move was not undertaken to improve agricultural conditions. The founding of pueblos along the perimeter of the Grasshopper Plateau and on high, defendable landforms also suggests both an initial and a continuing concern with maintaining a defensive posture. The directional trend in this positioning is toward the south and west, away from the Cibecue Valley. Finally, there is evidence that population aggregation forced organizational solutions to permit cooperation among divergent residential kinship groups of similar and dissimilar ethnic traditions. The community decision-making hierarchy of Grasshopper Pueblo was structured by restricted sodalities. The prominence of the Arrow Society in a sodality hierarchy is consistent with a settlement configuration stressing defense (Reid 1989; Reid and Whittlesey 1982, 1990; see Jorgensen 1980:226–40).

Pueblos on the Grasshopper Plateau. The trickle of change that had characterized population dynamics prior to AD 1300 became a torrent after this date. The 18-room Chodistaas Pueblo—the largest pre-1300 community on the Grasshopper Plateau—was replaced within a generation by Grasshopper Pueblo, which was rapidly approaching 500 rooms. A change from 200 to 2,000 rooms reflects a dramatic population increase on the Grasshopper Plateau. Settlement changes also included occupation of a broader range of landforms; this was the first significant occupation of cliffs and promontories where sites represent a mix of habitation and redoubt. Continuation of defensive concerns is also suggested by the placement of pueblos on hilltops or otherwise defendable locales.

The Grasshopper Plateau hosts ten pueblos (excluding Oak Creek Pueblo) of greater than 35 rooms, or an estimated total of 1,321 out of the nearly 2,000 pueblo rooms assigned to the AD 1300s. The distribution of pueblo size suggests a ceiling of between 120 and 140 rooms per pueblo. The main pueblo at Grasshopper—with three distinct roomblocks of over 100 rooms, each with an associated plaza—might best be viewed as a coming-together of three pueblo communities of the 120- to 140-room range. This range may represent a recurrent size threshold for communities with simple village organization.

Pueblo location is interpreted to be a function of proximity to agricultural land and defensive positioning along the plateau perimeter. The two processes operating in this expanding settlement system were (1) differential community growth during regional population expansion, a niche-filling phenomenon; and (2) a return by at least some of the regional population to a dispersed settlement system based on residential moves (Reid 1989; Tuggle, Reid, and Cole 1984).

Growth at Canyon Creek Pueblo: Mobility Response to Agricultural Shortfalls. The best-documented case for pueblo growth from regional population expansion is Canyon Creek Pueblo, a cliff dwelling of 120 rooms (Haury 1934; Reynolds 1981; Graves 1982, 1983). Graves's analysis indicates an initial temporary occupation beginning in AD 1327, with pueblo growth reaching its maximum shortly after 1340.

Stockpiling of construction timbers prior to establishment indicates an expectation of movement to that locality (Graves 1982:111–16), perhaps in anticipation of the need to expand and diversify cultivated land while maintaining a small-settlement defensive posture. One supposes that pessimistic prehistoric farmers were not misled by a period of abnormally high precipitation (between AD 1300 and 1325) and sought, therefore, to buffer an inevitable crash by preparing for the establishment of satellite communities. Initial room construction at Canyon Creek in AD 1327 followed closely a crash in the precipitation regime (AD 1325) and coincided with peak population at Grasshopper Pueblo (Reid and Graybill 1984). Degradation of the mule deer population (Olsen 1940) and an increase in subadult nutritional stress (Hinkes 1983) are inferred for this period.

The founding of Canyon Creek Pueblo suggests that these farmers had (1) a short response time to exercise a mobility option for subsistence management and (2) an ability to monitor rather closely alterations in precipitation. One suspects that the condition being monitored was annual agricultural productivity and its effect upon short-term food storage. The lag time (2–3 years) between the precipitation crash of AD 1325 and the actual occupation of Canyon Creek in AD 1327 could reflect the stored-food margin (see Burns 1983). Although other management options—such as increasing labor per unit of land, expanding hunting and gathering territory, and local exchange or redistribution of food—could have operated with short-term effectiveness, the Canyon Creek case points toward the existence of a tradition of precipitation awareness and behavioral response that could be translated rather quickly into management options rooted in residential moves to bring more land under cultivation (Reid and Graybill 1984).

Abandonment of the Grasshopper Plateau. At its peak, probably in the mid-1300s, the population on the Grasshopper Plateau may have been near the maximum carrying capacity for the agricultural technology of the inhabitants. No evidence exists to indicate attempts at agricultural intensification by upgrading technology from dry farming to irrigation (Tuggle, Reid, and Cole 1984). That irrigation was an option in the environment of the Grasshopper region is demonstrated by Apache agriculture of the historical period.

Defendable locations of major pueblos, networks of small, butte-top pueblos, and the extensive use of cliffs for unobtrusive storage suggest a continuation of economic and social uncertainty, but there is no evidence of conflict of the kind necessary to cause abandonment of the region. The regional expansion in settlement is equated with a 30-year period of below-average precipitation beginning in AD 1325. Increased physiological stress among subadults during this time at Grasshopper Pueblo supports an inference of periodic subsistence shortages (Hinkes 1983) resulting from a dependency on agriculture (Decker 1986) forced by the degradation of the mule deer population and of wild plant resources (Reid and Graybill 1984).

An increasing commitment to residential stability, to village rather than residential kinship group organization (see Jorgensen 1980), and to agriculture was played against the background of an agriculturally limited upland environment, one not farmed by the Apache today. Makeshift adjustments probably continued until the people of the Grasshopper pueblos realized that the mountains of east-central Arizona were ill suited over the long term to growing dependable crops for a large population, at which time they left.

Summary

To summarize, the Cibecue Valley was abandoned at AD 1300 as aggregation began on the Grasshopper Plateau. Both processes—abandonment and aggregation— are linked to population and settlement reconfiguration in response to the need to maintain an adequate defense and to protect food stores. The move from a valley of greater agricultural potential to a plateau of less potential suggests that protection of personnel and stores was of greater importance in the decision to move than were subsistence-related factors.

The most visible organizational response to population aggregation into villages was the creation (or redefinition) of restricted sodalities. A renegotiation of land use patterns also must have accompanied aggregation on the Grasshopper Plateau.

Population expansion and increasing dependence on agriculture were accelerated by a decrease in precipitation below the long-term mean during the period AD 1325 to 1355. Effective mechanisms of monitoring agricultural productivity— probably incorporated as ceremonial knowledge—and of reacting quickly to agricultural shortfalls combined with game management effectiveness under conditions of continued population growth to produce a reliance upon agriculture that, in general form, survived into historical times in localities with a predictable water supply. Moving—abandoning one area for another—to bring additional and, in some instances, more marginal land into cultivation may be the inexperienced prehistoric farmers' least-cost first solution to production shortfalls and the chronic cause of most abandonments in late prehistory.

The Grasshopper Plateau and surrounding region were abandoned by pueblo villagers by AD 1400. We do not know where the people of Grasshopper went, although the nearby Lake Roosevelt area is a likely spot for at least some of them. If so, it is reasonable to expect there to have been continued resource procurement within the Grasshopper region much like what occurred during centuries prior to AD 1300.

Social and economic uncertainty due to rapid population increase and threats of raids, critical to the abandonment of Cibecue Valley and to aggregation on the Grasshopper Plateau, were complicating factors in the final abandonment of the Grasshopper Plateau that inhibited a return to small, vulnerable pueblo settlements. Resumption of an in-place, mobile, hunting-gathering-gardening strategy was also denied by the degradation of wild plant and animal resources, especially mule deer.

There is no compelling evidence that abandonment of the Cibecue Valley, the Grasshopper Plateau, or the Grasshopper region was due to either (1) a breakdown of trade-exchange networks; (2) the collapse of political organization or the failure to implement necessary social organizational or structural adjustments; (3) disease; or (4) catastrophe. These two episodes of abandonment prompt one to step back from the customary context of questioning of prehistory to ask not why these peoples departed but why after a well-established tradition of small-group mobility they came to rest in large pueblo communities at all.

DISCUSSION

Parallels to many of the forces and conditions initiating late prehistoric abandonments must have occurred throughout regional chronologies. However, earlier solutions to such stresses failed to produce archaeological patterns of regional scale in which residential occupations were virtually lacking; populations increasing even at low rates over time may have eventually eliminated a number of earlier options. Regional abandonments became widespread in an era of increasing alternatives in the form of aggregated settlements which possessed the potential for organizational and productive expansion.

The linkage of regional abandonments with aggregation and intensified production in the late prehistoric Southwest has validity only as a model of the broadest scope. Likewise, the tendency for late settlement aggregates to coincide with riverine irrigation must be viewed as a pattern with pan-Southwestern expression, but one strongly tempered by appropriate local opportunity.

The behavioral trends embodied in the general model undoubtedly could be overridden by a variety of region-specific factors. In the Mountain Mogollon case study, inhabitants left the relatively aggregated settlements of the Grasshopper Plateau under conditions of environmental degradation and subsistence stress.

Large, late Western Anasazi sites on irrigable but flood-prone lands along the Little Colorado came to be abandoned. Tucson Basin Hohokam departed en masse from the Marana Community, in spite of the fact that sectors of their diverse territory would have remained productive under any environmental scenario. Natural and cultural limits that were eventually exceeded challenged the long-term stability of particular aggregated entities. However, accommodation to prior levels of concentration and integration may have facilitated the ultimate incorporation of members into even more highly aggregated systems such as the Lake Roosevelt settlements for the Mountain Mogollon or the dense, late Classic Tucson communities for the Hohokam.

Sometime in the fifteenth century, additional areas with the densest regional populations, most interlinked productive technologies, and among the strongest evidence for a degree of hierarchy (most notably Casas Grandes in Chihuahua and such sites as Mesa Grande and Los Muertos in the Phoenix Basin) experienced disruptions and were also abandoned. It is difficult to document end points in these sequences, but recent reanalysis of absolute dates suggests that terminal occupations approaching AD 1500 are plausible (Dean 1991; Eighmy and McGuire 1989; Dean and Ravesloot 1993). Roles for disease and other factors of European contact in at least the final decline of these systems would appear to be increasingly realistic considerations.

The early historic distribution of aboriginal agriculturalists in the Southwest (see fig. 7.9) reveals a further shrinkage from Pueblo IV times (fig. 7.2) into zones centered on irrigable stretches of major streams (fig. 7.3). The correlation between irrigation and Indian occupation is heightened, of course, through a selection of such locales by the Spanish for missions. In that missions and other early settlements were predominantly associated with existing aboriginal populations, these historic patterns can be seen as having roots in late prehistoric trends.

Any model that attempts to address complex cultural processes at a pan-Southwestern scale must be highly generalized. The modeling of regional abandonments as part of a larger phenomenon, which included new alternatives in aggregated living, is of this nature. This model is of such schematic form as to have little power in explaining variability in abandonment events across the Southwest; to analyze regional variability, it is necessary to control conditions in the respective areas of abandonment and destination. However, this formulation of linkage leads to clear programmatic goals for achieving greater understanding of the total phenomenon than we have had in the past. Efforts must be focused on tracing the destinations of abandoning populations and examining their subsequent integration into aggregated settlements, or on identifying their deployment into other distributional and geographical arrangements. Such goals will necessarily entail innovative approaches to chronological refinement, rigorous sourcing studies of artifacts, comprehensive survey at regional scales, and renewed excavations at large, late settlements. Without relation to outcomes, regional abandonments remain half-told stories awaiting a conclusion.

8

Strong and Weak Patterning in Southwestern Prehistory
The Formation of Puebloan Archaeology

JOSEPH A. TAINTER AND FRED PLOG

 UNTIL RECENT YEARS, many prehistorians viewed Southwestern archaeology as a squeezed orange. The area had been explored for over a century, and many sites had been excavated. The range of material variation was thought to be known, and cultural-temporal sequences had been developed. Southwestern prehistory was interpreted as a unilineal progression from mobile foragers to sedentary agriculturalists. Puebloan society of the historic era was thought to be the culmination of an unbroken continuum from the independent, self-sufficient, egalitarian Pueblos of the prehistoric period.

Yet Southwestern prehistory has been much rethought, and archaeologists now can consider a very different picture. Southwestern societies, rather than progressing unilineally toward the historic Pueblos, seem in various times and places to have evolved toward complexity, collapsed, abandoned their territories, and started somewhere else to evolve toward complexity again. Rather than being uniformly egalitarian agriculturalists, early Puebloans may sometimes have been differentiated by rank, influence, and occupation. Instead of being autonomous and self-sufficient, villages seem to have been integrated into regional interaction spheres and alliances, through which their economic well-being was enhanced. The ancient Southwest, in this view, is not a squeezed orange; it was a dynamic place of such complexity that we are only now learning to ask intelligent questions about it.

Some of these questions represent a return to fundamentals. Surprisingly, after a century of work, we find ourselves asking again, What is the nature of the Southwestern archaeological record? In the past we tended to describe this record in terms of its most salient characteristics: the development and intensification of agricultural systems; the establishment of ceramic traditions; and the evolution of large Puebloan communities. It is becoming apparent, however, that by focusing on such conspicuous features we have developed a reconstruction of prehistory that is wrong because it underemphasizes important elements of variation (e.g., Cordell and Plog 1979; Plog 1983b). For example, although the evolution of large pueblos is to most people the essence of Southwestern prehistory, in fact large pueblos were statistically rare. The average size of a Southwestern site is only 6.5 rooms (Plog 1983b:310). An accurate prehistory must look beyond the salient features and take into account the people—and the time periods—for whom conspicuous characteristics were not the norm.

To develop a prehistory that is not limited to salient characteristics, we must recognize dimensions of variation that have previously been little explored. Some of these dimensions, which we will discuss to varying degrees, are as follows. The first, *degree of structure,* is an overarching concept that encompasses many of the other dimensions. For some times and places, the Southwestern archaeological record is highly structured, with characteristics such as formal architecture, rich assemblages of elaborate artifacts, and strong covariation among elements. Chaco and Mimbres are examples of highly structured systems, but in the Puebloan Southwest they represent perhaps the extreme range of the phenomenon. Our syntheses of Southwestern prehistory are largely based on such patterns (Cordell and Plog 1979). This is unfortunate, for the Southwest also shows unstructured systems where residences were ephemeral, artifact assemblages meager, and statistical patterning minimal. One of us has elsewhere referred to this phenomenon as strong and weak patterning (Plog 1983b).

Strong patterns may never have dominated Southwestern prehistory for very long. Even during times when there were strong patterns—for example, when large towns were built—there were also people generating a weakly structured archaeological record. A classic example is the Hosta Butte phase occupation of Chaco Canyon itself. The small sites that characterize this phase are so different from the great Chacoan towns that the two occupations were once thought to be temporally distinct. Strong patterning, we emphasize, was not always the norm for Southwestern prehistory. Very often it was an exception that we need to explain.

Second is the concept of *ranking.* The traditional wisdom is that, for most of prehistory, the Southwest was occupied by egalitarian foragers or farmers. Yet it has become evident that during certain times and places, vertical differentiation evolved (e.g., at Chaco [Tainter and Gillio 1980:100–113; Schelberg 1982]; and at Gran Quivira [Tainter and Levine 1987:50–51]). Where ranking did develop, though, it was of short duration (no more than a few generations) and may not have led to true stratification. Partly for this reason, few Southwestern archaeologists can even agree on how to recognize ranking.

The third dimension, *complexity,* is a quantity, a characteristic of societies that we can and should measure. One of us previously characterized complexity as being generally understood to refer to such things as the size of a society, the number and distinctiveness of its parts, the variety of specialized roles that it incorporates, the number of distinct social personalities present, and the variety of mechanisms for organizing these into a coherent whole (Tainter 1988:23). This approach is similar to one taken earlier by Fred Plog (1974).

A complementary approach follows the work of John L. Casti (e.g., 1986) in focusing on diversity and predictability. Complex systems are characterized by diverse, nonoverlapping structures; they manifest much unpredictability or inconsistency. Knowing one part of a complex system does not allow one to predict the remainder. Simpler systems, on the other hand, are characterized by redundant, predictable behavior, and much of what one observes can be reduced to a single, underlying structure such as the kinship system.

This conception of complexity offers an interesting perspective on Elman Service's (1962) classification of societies in evolutionary stages: bands, tribes, chiefdoms, and states. As we have each indicated elsewhere, the typology is not really useful, but for the purpose of illustration we can contrast the societies at the extremes—bands and states—with those in the middle—tribes and chiefdoms. Tribes and chiefdoms are the sort of middle-range societies that initially formed the basis of anthropology. They are characterized by the kinds of normative behavior that bring joy to social scientists. Bands and states, on the other hand, exhibit diverse behaviors. Bands *permit* diversity, which is necessary to survival by foraging. States *generate* diversity in the form of many roles, personalities, and institutions. It is curious that although most humans have been members of bands (an enduring form) or states (an overpowering form), anthropology has mainly focused on the middle-range societies, which are rare in our history.

Systems can be so complex that they appear unstructured. Classic examples are turbulence in air or in a fluid. This phenomenon has gained much prominence lately under the rubric of "chaos" theory (e.g., Crutchfield et al. 1986; Gleick 1987; Gordon and Greenspan 1988). Some of its principles are (1) apparently deterministic processes can yield unpredictable results, and (2) processes with seemingly random elements can yield quite structured results. Later we will discuss in detail an archaeological case in which the interaction of highly structured variables actually yields weak, unpredictable patterns. We refrain from labeling the phenomenon "chaotic" (in part because the term in popular usage means "unstructured"), but it seems at least superficially analogous to some of the phenomena discussed by chaos theorists.

A matter overlooked entirely in earlier studies of complexity is its cost. Complex social systems are costlier to maintain than simpler ones. Cost is a major factor, for it both inhibited the evolution of complexity and caused complex systems periodically to collapse (Tainter 1988). Whereas earlier archaeologists saw complexity as a natural consequence of human creativity, reliable food supplies, and leisure time, today it is impossible to study complexity without inquiring into the costs and benefits of participating in complex systems.

A fourth dimension is *regional integration*. One of the most exciting developments in recent years is the recognition that, at times, the Southwest witnessed the development of political and economic systems that spanned large areas. The best-known of these is the Chacoan system (to be discussed below), but it may be only the most visible of what was once a recurrent phenomenon (Plog 1979, 1983b; Upham, Crown, and Plog, this volume). Sometimes termed "alliances"

(Plog 1983b), these regional systems were a major factor in producing strong patterns in the archaeological record.

Finally, there is the concept of *modularity*. Simple systems, following Casti (1986), are repetitive and predictable. Gregory Johnson (1989) recently reminded us that this was the nature of many Southwestern societies, which he calls "modular" societies because they are made up of similar, repetitive units. Many large pueblos do seem to have consisted of an aggregated series of smaller social modules. Although this observation has antecedents as far back as the Mindeleffs (V. Mindeleff 1891; C. Mindeleff 1900), it is a useful reminder that strong patterns can be produced by organizations that were not hierarchical.

Two archaeological sites may help to illustrate what Johnson means by the term modular. One is Kiatuthlanna (Roberts 1931), a famous site in east-central Arizona. It is formed of a series of units, each of which consists of a kiva surrounded by small (storage) and large (habitation) rooms. Kiatuthlanna contains three such blocks. A second example is Yellow Jacket, in southwestern Colorado (Rohn 1989). It is a later, very large site, consisting of dozens of Kiatuthlanna-like units. These two sites exhibit a pattern that is horizontal and modular, not overtly vertical or hierarchical. Similar units repeat. The repetition may be at the level of a small site (Kiatuthlanna), a large site (Yellow Jacket), or even the settlement pattern of a large area.

Some prehistorians have felt that we will find in the archaeological record kinds of organization and behavior not observed ethnographically. The modular pattern described by Johnson is the best case of which we are aware. It seems to reflect an extreme degree of simplicity (*sensu* Casti 1986) or normative behavior. A single pattern is repeated over and over.

One of us (Plog 1978) has suggested that Western Pueblo clans are also repetitive units. They allow for rapid change in response to environmental contingencies. In this respect, what social anthropologists call clans may have had a material counterpart in modular units such as Johnson sees. Easily broken and easily reformed, they made the ideal basis of villages in a risky environment.

STRONG AND WEAK PATTERNS

What links these diverse concepts, for archaeologists, is the idea of strong and weak patterning. Strong archaeological patterns are produced by societies that are hierarchical; that are complex; that are highly modular; that engage in normative behavior; and that participate in regional systems. Weak archaeological patterns are produced by societies that are acephalous; that are undifferentiated; that engage in diverse behaviors; and that are relatively independent (table 8.1). As we have said, systems may be so highly complex that they appear unstructured. Such systems are termed chaotic.

Strong patterning gladdens the heart of any archaeologist. Strong patterns provide the stuff to fill both museum displays and data tables. Weak patterns evoke a contrary, often negative, reaction. One of us (Tainter) recalls a conversation with

TABLE 8.1.

Elements of strong and weak patterning

Attribute	Strong Pattern	Weak Pattern
Site characteristics	Some large, planned, centralized sites	Predominence of small sites
Ceramic production	Specialized, localized; much trade	Unspecialized; mainly local use
Ceramic pattern	Clear association of types and areas	Great variation through time and space
Architecture	Homogeneous styles at larger sites	Expedient, diverse
Trade goods	Substantial quantities at larger sites; many exotics	Limited quantities; mainly utilitarian
Agriculture	Intensive	Extensive
Social organization	Vertical or strongly modular	Egalitarian, diverse

Source: F. Plog 1983b:311, with modifications.

a Southwestern archaeologist who had recently worked in Australia. To him, Australian archaeology was like 40,000 years of the Archaic—all on the surface, and with no diagnostics. Few of us would want the challenge of decoding such an unstructured record.

When, inadvertently, we do happen upon a weakly structured archaeological record, our reaction is often puzzlement, ad hoc interpretation, or a conclusion that the data are incomplete. In cultural resource management, the reaction to weak patterning is often to declare a site insignificant—not worthy of preservation or study. Those who synthesize prehistory tend to see an evolution from weak to strong patterns, and to characterize later prehistory as increasingly structured. Yet weak patterning is a major part of the archaeological record. Indeed, during the four million years or so of hominid evolution, what our ancestors left behind was primarily one weak pattern overlaid by another.

As a rule, even during times when strong patterns were produced, weak patterns did not disappear. They continued as people engaged in expedient behavior, or as less-complex peoples lived about the peripheries of more complex societies (Adams 1978; Stuart and Gauthier 1981). Early hierarchies, however structured they may have been, were typically imposed on older, tribal forms of organization (Claessen and Skalnik 1978). Regional systems overarched but did not immediately supplant local ties. Where vertical systems emerged they were often made up of societies that had been, and substantially remained, modular (Simon 1965). Thus what appears in the archaeological record as a high degree of structure will almost always be the result of interaction between strong and weak patterns.

To interpret the archaeological record without overemphasizing salient characteristics, we must realize that the record is not a unilineal progression toward more structure and stronger patterns. It is a series of fuzzy sets in which weak patterns overlie weak patterns; strong patterns emerge, interact with weak patterns, and disappear; and weak patterns again become dominant. Strong patterning presents archaeologists with an attractive but deceptive trap.

We will illustrate these points by discussing a well-known case: the Chacoan system of northwestern New Mexico. What we see in this area is a Puebloan archaeological record which is strongly patterned, reflects a strongly patterned environment, and yet has at its periphery one of the more chaotic, unstructured records of Puebloan prehistory. We will show that these strong and weak patterns are both intelligible within the concepts we have discussed. We will also find that examining this matter in detail leads us to question some of the fundamental notions of Southwestern prehistory.

THE CHACOAN SYSTEM

The term "Chacoan system" is one of the most conceptually neutral of several names given to the strongly patterned Puebloan archaeological record of the San Juan Basin. The Chacoan system was situated in a highly structured (i.e., redundant, not patchy) environment and participated in exchange systems extending south into what is now Mexico. Yet Chaco is paradoxical: the interactions among complex behavior, a strongly patterned archaeological record, a highly structured environment, and ties with other complex societies produced, across large areas of the Southwest, a weak, unpatterned record that has confused generations of archaeologists. This curious situation can be illuminated by a brief discussion of Chaco.

The San Juan Basin is a relatively dry, flat, featureless plain surrounded by fertile river valleys and high-relief, well-watered uplands (Tainter and Gillio 1980:115–16; Judge et al. 1981:68; Judge 1982:8; Tainter 1982). At the center of the basin is its major topographic feature, Chaco Canyon. The canyon is almost a small "island" of topographic and resource variety in a "sea" of topographic and ecological homogeneity. It captures runoff from a wide drainage basin—crucial in the arid Southwest—but is characterized by a short growing season and some of the poorest soils in the region (Judge et al. 1981:68; Schelberg 1982:105; Powers, Gillespie, and Lekson 1983:289.

In an environment not well endowed for subsistence agriculture, there developed what seems to have been the most complex system of regional hierarchical organization in the prehistoric northern Southwest. Called by such terms as the Chacoan Interaction Sphere (Altschul 1978), the Chacoan Alliance (Plog 1983b), or, as here, simply the Chacoan system, it was characterized across the San Juan Basin by distinctive, large pueblos called "great houses" or "Chacoan towns." These pueblos display Chacoan masonry and architecture; the importation and consumption of exotic sumptuary goods, raw materials for building and manufacture, and probably food; and a road network linking outlying Chacoan communities

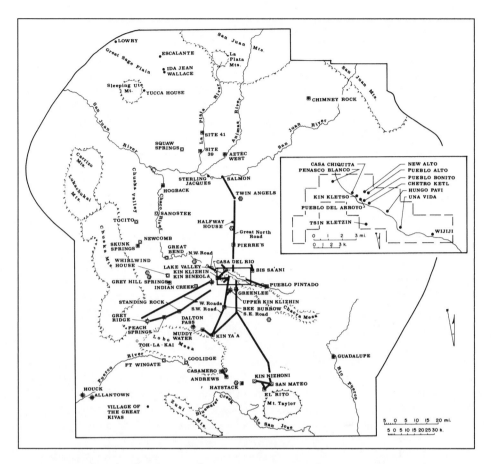

Figure 8.1. The Chacoan regional system, AD 1050 to 1175 (after Powers, Gillespie, and Lekson 1983:2). (Courtesy of the U.S. National Park Service)

to the central canyon (fig. 8.1) (Marshall et al. 1979; Kincaid 1983; Powers, Gillespie, and Lekson 1983).

The most compelling interpretation is that the Chacoan system was a ranked, hierarchically organized, regional network of trade and perhaps other forms of resource exchange (Tainter and Gillio 1980:100–113; Judge 1982; Schelberg 1982; Powers, Gillespie, and Lekson 1983).[1] The evidence for hierarchical organization is provided by (1) differential community investment in a few large, planned, elaborate great houses that are in many ways unique in the Southwest; (2) importation and consumption of exotic sumptuary goods, including ornate pottery vessels, macaws, and items manufactured from turquoise, shell, jet, and quartz crystal; (3) the presence of a minority of burials associated preferentially with such sumptuary goods; (4) clear evidence of labor mobilization in great house construction, road building and maintenance, and transport of goods; and (5) the overwhelming association of items (2) and (3) with great houses, to the exclusion of the hundreds of small, architecturally simple villages in the San Juan Basin. This last item suggests that elite residence was specifically linked to the great houses (Tainter and Gillio 1980:100–113; Schelberg 1982; Lekson 1984; Akins 1986).

Evidence for trade and perhaps other kinds of resource exchange includes (1) the centrally focused road network (Ebert and Hitchcock 1973; Kincaid 1983); (2) the importation of 150,000 to 200,000 beams to roof the canyon's great houses; (3) the importation of over 40,000 pottery vessels and perhaps also their contents to one canyon site alone (Pueblo Alto); (4) the presence in quantity of exotic goods, particularly very large amounts of turquoise; and (5) indications that maize not locally produced was consumed at the major canyon site of Pueblo Bonito (Schelberg 1982).

That such a system would evolve in the San Juan Basin is not surprising. A large population living in a marginal, arid, fluctuating, and unpredictable environment will depend vitally on what William Isbell (1978) has termed an "energy averaging" system. As the name implies, such a system serves to even out the effects of fluctuations in localized productivity. Energy averaging can ameliorate either temporal or spatial fluctuations. The former is often achieved by storage facilities, the latter by building exchange alliances with groups experiencing different production cycles (e.g., Vayda 1967; Bean 1972).

A fundamental economic problem in the interior of the San Juan Basin was that with a great deal of topographic homogeneity over broad areas, finding interaction partners who had different production cycles would have been difficult. Everyone in a locality would experience roughly the same cycle of highs and lows. The solution was to form exchange relationships with groups at the margins of the basin, who had different resources and production cycles and access to high-relief, well-watered uplands and productive agricultural valleys. From perhaps as early as AD 500 (well before the Chacoan system achieved its final, famous form), populations in the central basin were trading extensively with areas at the basin's margins to the southwest of Chaco Canyon. By the first part of the tenth century, trade had become more formalized, craft specialization emerged, and great houses began to be built in the canyon and in a few outlying areas (Judge 1979:902–4; Judge et al. 1981). During the eleventh and twelfth centuries, the Chacoan system was at its height, but it collapsed by about AD 1200 (Schelberg 1982).

The Chacoan system, with its roads for transport, its social hierarchy able to command distant resources, and its multitude of storage rooms in great houses (Marshall et al. 1979), seems to have been able, if not designed, to aggregate, store, and reallocate resources. Chaco Canyon, situated in the center of the San Juan Basin, would have been the most efficient, least-cost location from which to administer a basinwide economic system. Not surprisingly, for important segments of prehistory, it appears to have been the center of the Chacoan economic universe (Tainter and Gillio 1980:100–113).

The spatial extent of the Chacoan system can be understood as a solution to two problems: minimizing the travel and transport costs associated with resource exchange (cf. Lightfoot 1979), while satisfying a need for maximum resource variety. The Chacoan system extended outward in nearly all directions from the basin's center until the variety requirement was fulfilled, and then stopped. Once maximum variety was achieved at the margins of the San Juan Basin, further expansion would have been costly and pointless (Tainter and Gillio 1980:100–116; Tainter 1982, 1984).

STRONG AND WEAK PATTERNS IN THE CHACOAN SYSTEM

The existence and extent of the Chacoan system exerted a strong influence on the character of the archaeological record. In particular, it has conditioned many of our traditional ideas about the entities called Anasazi and Mogollon, and about how the remains of these entities are distributed in space. In the older literature, Anasazi and Mogollon are referred to as "cultures" or "traditions" (e.g., Haury 1936; Reed 1946; Wheat 1955). The "boundary" between them is generally considered to extend across west-central New Mexico and east-central Arizona, at about the latitude of Acoma Pueblo.

Although the Chacoan system is a classic example of what we call a strong pattern, its periphery shows a surprising lack of structure. At the southern periphery, Anasazi and Mogollon assemblages mix, intermingle, and change. There is no strong statistical pattern. Sites display varying proportions of brown- and graywares; sites with Anasazi-like architecture are found near ones with Mogollon-like features; and these characteristics change over time (e.g., Ruppé 1953; Dittert 1959; Frisbie 1982; see also Stewart 1980). Archaeologists interested in cultural classification have found the region impossible to pigeonhole. This situation has led to various ad hoc interpretations. Some scholars call it a "marginal" area, whose fluctuating characteristics are to be explained by variations in the diffusion of Anasazi and Mogollon "influences" and by the repeated immigration of Anasazi and Mogollon culture-bearers (e.g., Ruppé 1953; Danson 1957; Dittert 1959; Bullard 1962; Berman 1979; Frisbie 1982).

In recent years it has been shown that such interpretations lack both logical and empirical foundations (Tainter and Gillio 1980; Tainter 1982, 1984, 1985; Tainter and Levine 1987). Moreover, the mixed assemblages in the Anasazi-Mogollon transition zone can be accounted for more rigorously and parsimoniously as resulting from the interaction of strong patterns and highly structured systems. We illustrate this by discussing some classic archaeological puzzles: the mixing of Anasazi and Mogollon cultural characteristics in the Acoma, Albuquerque, and Zuni areas. First we will describe the archaeological puzzles, and then offer explanations for them.

The Weak Patterns

The Acoma Area. Cebolleta Mesa, in the middle of the traditional Acoma area, has been extensively studied by Reynold Ruppé (1953) and Edward Dittert (1959). There are striking differences in the archaeological assemblages of northern (Los Pilares) and southern (Los Veteados) Cebolleta Mesa, and these assemblages change through time. Southern sites tend to average about 25 percent brownwares, while northern sites average 10.1 percent (Ruppé 1953:83). Ruppé suggests that "brown wares are a hallmark of the Mogollon area, and when found outside the area, can be accepted as indication of contacts or influence" (1953:82).

When a site, in this framework, shows a larger percentage of brownwares than its neighbors (as Los Veteados sites occasionally do), it is interpreted as the result of small southern groups having drifted into the area (Ruppé 1953:84). The Kiatuthlanna phase (AD 800–870), for example, shows almost no brownwares, while in the succeeding Red Mesa phase (870–950) assemblages become more diverse: 17 percent brownwares in the south, 5 percent in the north. An entry of Mogollon people is accordingly postulated (Ruppé 1953:107, 115).

For the Cebolleta phase (950–1100), Ruppé and Dittert see a major Mogollon influx. One Los Veteados site displays 50 percent brownware sherds, several sites show about 20 percent, roughly half contain 5 to 10 percent, and only one settlement lacks brownwares altogether. In Los Pilares, by contrast, brownwares total less than 5 percent overall and are entirely absent on more than half the sites (Ruppé 1953:122). Dittert sees resemblances in this period between some Los Veteados architecture and that of the Mogollon Alpine Branch, and he postulates a large influx of southern people (1959:543–44).

The succeeding Pilares phase (1100–1200) continues these trends. Southern sites are often made of adobe and are oriented more often east-west than north-south. Nearly all contain brownwares. Northern sites are of masonry, are oriented primarily north-south, and display brown paste ceramics less than half the time (Ruppé 1953:340–42; Dittert 1959:548). Dittert proposes that site-unit intrusions account for such variations in the White Mound and Cebolleta phases, and trait-unit intrusions are responsible in the Pilares phase (1959:575–76).

The Albuquerque Area. The Albuquerque area of the Rio Grande valley, a few kilometers beyond the southeastern edge of the San Juan Basin, has always been an archaeological puzzle because of the diversity of its remains. Although perhaps predominantly northern in character, this archaeological record also displays a sustained frequency of southern characteristics. Reinhart (1967:209–32) believes that as early as the Late Archaic (after c. 1000 BC), hunting populations moved into this area from the south. Pithouse sites of later times in the Albuquerque area are notable for the percentages of brownware ceramics they display, and also for architecture that occasionally bears a resemblance to Mogollon forms (Allen and McNutt 1955; Peckham 1957; Schorsch 1962; Vivian and Clendenen 1965; Frisbie

1967; Wiseman 1976). Ford, Schroeder, and Peckham (1972) see the area immediately to the south as a shifting boundary between cultural and linguistic groups (but see Eidenbach 1982). Frisbie suggests that the Albuquerque area was "one of the main regions for cultural transmission between north and south" (1982:20).

A brief discussion of some Albuquerque-area pithouse sites will illustrate the pattern. Basketmaker III/Pueblo I (c. AD 500–900) pithouses excavated by Stewart Peckham (1957) on the east side of the Rio Grande display a dominance of Lino Gray sherds, but with proportions of Mogollon brownwares that range from 3 percent to more than 27 percent. At least one pithouse displays a short, stepped, lateral entrance similar to some early Mogollon pithouses. The floor of this house contained, as northern sherds, 65 Lino Gray and one Lino Fugitive Red, and as southern sherds, one Alma Plain and two San Francisco Red. On the opposite bank of the Rio Grande, Theodore Frisbie (1967) excavated three pithouse villages of the same period. One pithouse showed Mogollon-like features, including an inclined lateral entryway, floor grooves, and a groove isolating the pithouse center. Mogollon sherds on these sites range from 15.8 percent to 72.8 percent of the total undecorated collection. A Basketmaker III pithouse a few miles south along the river contained only 4.7 percent brown- and redwares, along with an antechamber reminiscent of some Mogollon examples (Schorsch 1962).

The Zuni Area.   The third puzzle to be discussed is the changing character of the Zuni archaeological record, from Chacoan Anasazi to Mogollon Western Pueblo (Reed 1946, 1948b, 1950; Johnson 1965; LeBlanc 1989a). Zuni and Acoma, along with the Hopi pueblos, are generally regarded as the descendents of what has been called the Western Pueblo Archaeological Complex (Reed 1948b), or Western Pueblo Culture (Johnson 1965). Johnson places the development of Western Pueblo Culture in the mountains of west-central New Mexico and east-central Arizona around AD 1000. Its universal features, he suggests, include plaza or multiple-court layout, extended inhumations, the ¾ grooved ax, and turkey hunting rather than keeping.

During the Basketmaker III to early Pueblo II period (c. AD 400–1000), Zuni ceramic assemblages consisted of such Anasazi types as Lino Gray, Kana-a Black-on-white, Kiatuthlanna Black-on-white, and White Mound Black-on-white. Forestdale Smudged, a Mogollon type, is also present but is common in Anasazi sites of this period. No redwares have been observed (Marshall n.d.; Dodge, Pearson, and Ferguson 1977). Although the archaeological characteristics of this period suggest Chacoan relationships to many investigators (e.g., Reed 1955:179), Wasley (1960b:32–34) believes that Mogollon "colonies" existed throughout the area at this time.

In the later Pueblo II to early Pueblo III periods (c. 1000–1150), Chacoan great houses and roads were built in the eastern Zuni area (Roberts 1932; Marshall et al. 1979; Powers, Gillespie, and Lekson 1983), formally incorporating the region into the Chacoan system. Yet redware ceramics and square kivas indicate concurrent social and economic ties to the south. By the fourteenth century, however, there was a significant change. Western Pueblo characteristics, such as extended inhumations, appeared throughout the Zuni region (Johnson 1965), and it is from this time that the area becomes distinctly part of the Western Pueblo complex. Correspondingly, Zuni abruptly loses its northern character. Whereas the Acoma and Albuquerque areas show continuous mixing of northern and southern characteristics, what we see at Zuni is a sudden end to northern features and concomitant shifting to a western orientation.

UNDERSTANDING THE WEAK PATTERNS

Weak patterning in the Anasazi-Mogollon transition zone is not the puzzle that generations of scholars have thought. Nor does it need to be explained by a deus ex machina like diffusion or migration. To the contrary, it is an expectable result of the development, operation, and collapse of the Chacoan system.

The Acoma Area. What we see in the Cebolleta Mesa area is that beyond the southern edge of the San Juan Basin, Anasazi characteristics begin to give way to Mogollon forms. It is no coincidence that this corresponds with the southern edge of the Chacoan system. The population of the southern San Juan Basin had access to high-relief, upland terrain in the San Mateo and Zuni mountains and to productive alluvial farmlands in the Red Mesa valley. These people would have achieved maximum economic advantage by interacting preferentially with populations experiencing different production regimes. This in essence meant the formation of exchange ties with San Juan Basin populations to the north. To the south were populations offering only more of what groups at the southern basin margin already had: high-relief terrain. Extended exchange relationships to the south would have offered little advantage in resource variety and economic security. Exchange relationships in this direction were consequently never as frequent or as formalized as those to the north. The material symbolism that facilitated and reinforced such relationships reflects this fact. As one proceeds south of the San Mateo and Zuni mountains into areas superfluous to the Chacoan exchange system, archaeological materials come less and less to exhibit Anasazi characteristics, and more and more to display Mogollon properties. The result is an apparent "boundary," but a boundary that reflects trade, interaction, and the integration of ecological diversity rather than unified cultural traditions (Tainter and Gillio 1980:115–16; Tainter 1982:7–8).

The Albuquerque Area. The Basketmaker III/Pueblo I pithouses of the Albuquerque area largely predate the formal architecture and roads of the Chacoan system but correspond in time to the earlier basin exchange networks noted by Judge (1979). The archaeological record, though, appears to indicate a lack of sustained social and economic ties between these areas. Herein lies a clue to the archaeological puzzle of the Albuquerque region. Why was the Albuquerque area (apparently) not formally integrated into the basin exchange system? The Rio Grande valley contains agricultural lands, foraging territories, and high-relief terrain that presumably would have been advantageous to a basin energy-averaging system. Why were formal economic ties not then established?

Viewed from the perspective of the central San Juan Basin, the answer is evident. To a central basin population looking outward, the riverine resource base of the Rio Grande was duplicated by another productive riverine area that lay in the same direction but was much closer: the Rio Puerco. The valley of the Rio Puerco lies off the southeastern edge of the basin, between the basin and the Rio Grande valley.

The Chacoan network included much of the central Rio Puerco valley, for one of the earliest great houses (Guadalupe Ruin, dating from the tenth century AD [Pippin 1987]) is located here. Viewed in this way, once the Rio Puerco was incorporated into the basin exchange system, inclusion of the central Rio Grande valley would have been superfluous and costly. Hence it was never strongly integrated into the San Juan Basin network, and so at least in the early Puebloan era does not exhibit the overwhelmingly Anasazi character of much of northwestern New Mexico.

Why then is the area not more easily classifiable (for those so inclined) as Mogollon? This can be approached by reversing the question: why should the Albuquerque area have been Mogollon? What advantages would result from strong economic ties, and cultural sharing, to the south? Quite simply, there do not appear to have been very many. No major resource variety would accrue from such ties, for the agricultural and foraging potential of the Rio Grande valley is much the same immediately north or south of Albuquerque. No great increase in subsistence security would result from a north-south interaction network. Some interaction along this axis did occur, but clearly not of such a nature as to influence overwhelmingly the character of the archaeological record.

It seems, therefore, that the early agriculturalists of the Albuquerque area participated in at least two interaction networks: a northwestern-oriented one focused on the San Juan Basin (the predecessor of the Chacoan system), and a southern-oriented riverine one. These populations were not strongly integrated into the first network, while the second was never of major importance. Thus, the peculiar geographical situation of these populations led to the formation of an archaeological record which reflects occasional, rather than sustained, interaction in both directions, as local conditions made necessary or advantageous (Tainter 1984). The result was the puzzling, weakly structured archaeological record that characterizes the area.

The Zuni Area.   The development of Western Pueblo archaeological characteristics in the Zuni area is fully understandable within the framework espoused here. The critical factor was the Chacoan collapse. With the demise of the Chacoan system by the early thirteenth century and the subsequent abandonment of the San

Juan Basin, the focus of Zuni interaction had to shift from the north to the west, toward the large population centers along the Little Colorado River (cf. Upham 1982). The resulting archaeological record appears superficially to reflect spatial expansion of Western Pueblo Culture (and has been so interpreted), but it is more completely and parsimoniously seen as an economic realignment made necessary by the collapse of the Chacoan system (Tainter and Gillio 1980:93–94; Tainter 1988:178–87).

SUMMARY AND CONCLUSION

The emergence of a San Juan Basin exchange system, its formalization in the Cha-coan network, and its disappearance with the Chacoan collapse account for much that has seemed puzzling in the Anasazi-Mogollon transition zone. From at least AD 900 to 1200, and perhaps from 500 to 1200, much of what we perceive as the strongly patterned Anasazi character of northwestern New Mexico was a function not of a shared culture but of social and economic interaction.

The weak pattern of mixed and changing assemblages that we see along the southern margin of the San Juan Basin reflects variable and shifting participation in the Chacoan system and its antecedents. In the Acoma area we see shifting interaction between north and south. In the Albuquerque area we see a weak pat-tern, which arose because the early agricultural populations of this area did not participate in a strong economic network. And at Zuni we see early participation in the Chacoan system, followed by an economic reorientation to the west after the Chacoan collapse.

What we find at the southern edge of the San Juan Basin is a weak, unstruc-tured archaeological record resulting from the interaction of strong patterns and highly structured systems. The driving force was the San Juan Basin itself. The basin and its periphery of fertile river valleys and well-watered uplands is a highly structured environment. The basin itself is flat and redundant (predictable and not patchy), but at its edges these characteristics terminate abruptly with the transition to riverine and mountain settings. There is nothing equivocal about this pattern: it is a definitive structure to which all occupants of the basin have had to adjust.

When populations were sedentary and sufficiently dense, the San Juan Basin required specific economic and social adjustments. With reduced mobility, eco-nomic ties between the basin and its periphery were needed for subsistence security. These in turn called for a hierarchical, centralized system of economic management, which was the most parsimonious way to monitor and direct a basinwide system of exchange. The result was a strongly patterned archaeologi-cal record: sites and artifacts are easily classified; spatial distributions are highly distinctive; and statistical patterning is clear (e.g., the association of exotic items with great houses). It was inevitable that an archaeological record this structured would once have been interpreted as a distinct cultural tradition.

A chaos theorist might have predicted that this strong patterning would pro-duce, in places, a lack of distinctive structure. Perhaps this is characteristic of boundary phenomena in general. In the Chacoan case specifically, the weak patterning at the system's periphery is the logical result of an economic and social response to the San Juan Basin and its environs. The economics of exchange and transport dictated that the Chacoan system could expand only so far, and where it stopped, the archaeological record ceases to be strongly patterned.

Two very important lessons emerge from this case study. One is that when prehistory is written as an abstraction from strong patterns, places where such patterns are not found can only produce interpretive consternation. The literature of the southern Chacoan periphery demonstrates this clearly. Our tendency to label and classify exacerbates this problem: if we cannot call something Anasazi or Mogollon, we spend decades trying to figure out why it cannot be pigeonholed. Writers of prehistory have to realize that such phenomena are not aberrations. The Anasazi-Mogollon transition zone, for example, covers at least 50,000 square kilometers, an area much too large to ignore. Weak patterns are the essence of much of prehistory and cannot be left out of our generalizations and syntheses.

A second lesson concerns the archaeological phenomena that we call Anasazi and Mogollon. In our traditional syntheses, these are thought to reflect unified cultural traditions. Our analysis leads to what many will regard as a heretical proposition: that the notion of Anasazi and Mogollon as cultural traditions has outlived its usefulness and, indeed, never was correct. In northwestern New Mexico at least, what we call Anasazi is an archaeological pattern which resulted from an economic and social response to the San Juan Basin and its periphery. It is not a cultural tradition. The material similarities that define the Anasazi phenomenon are only partly a result of cultural transmission between generations (the essence of a cultural tradition). These similarities reflect more strongly such things as the movement of goods and marriage partners; emulation of sumptuary behavior among elites; and adoption of common symbols to reinforce exchange ties (Tainter 1982, 1984). Thus, we can no longer speak of Anasazi and Mogollon cultures, for that is simply not what they were.

These terms have blinded us to much behavioral variation, as in the areas we have discussed. It would be greatly beneficial if they simply dropped from use. We are under no illusions, of course, that this will happen any time soon. Cultural classification is nearly as ingrained among Southwestern archaeologists as pottery classification (but see Dean 1988c and Speth 1988). We are reminded of a remark once make by Christopher Hitchens in regard to classificatory thinking: "The best that can be said for this method [classificatory thinking] is that it economizes on thought. You simply unveil it like a Medusa's head and turn all discussion into stone" (1988:301). Unfortunately, the Anasazi and Mogollon concepts have turned archaeological discussion into such hardened stone that we suspect eons of criticism will be needed to free us of them.

------- *Notes* -------

We express our appreciation for comments on earlier drafts of this paper to Robert McC. Adams, Linda Cordell, George Gumerman, Robert Preucel, Jefferson Reid,

Lynne Sebastian, Bonnie Bagley Tainter, and Steadman Upham. This paper culminates research that we have each pursued over several years. Finding our interests converging, we agreed to collaborate for this advanced seminar. I greatly regret that Fred was not able to see the fruition of our work in this volume.

—J. T.

1. Despite recent advances in understanding San Juan Basin archaeology, some Chacoan scholars are now venturing revisionist interpretations. As summarized by Judge (1989), these views seem to be converging on an interpretation of Chaco Canyon as a (nearly) vacant ceremonial center and of Chacoan society as not distinctively ranked. Some of the elements of this revision (which is fully presented only by Judge) are that (1) Chacoan great houses held few persons relative to their size, or may even have had no full-time residents; (2) Chaco was the site of periodic ritual gatherings of peripheral people, who perhaps went there on formal religious pilgrimages; (3) these pilgrims housed themselves in the otherwise empty (or nearly empty) great houses during their canyon sojourns; (4) turquoise had a religious metaphor and was sought by the pilgrims from canyon artisans; and (5) Chaco dominated ritual and controlled turquoise, its medium of expression. Several things need to be said about this emerging model.

First, the vacant ceremonial center is an old notion in American archaeology. It has typically been applied where there are imposing ruins about which we know little. Proponents of the view that Chaco Canyon great houses were such places might keep in mind that where this notion has been closely scrutinized, it has been thoroughly discredited. The classic case is the southern lowland Maya, whose "vacant ceremonial centers" are now known to have been cities (Haviland 1970). The image of contented Maya peasants cheerfully building vacant ceremonial centers is the product of a bygone era, and of popularization. Yet the image of contented Anasazi peasants cheerfully building vacant great houses is no more compelling.

Second, among pilgrimage sites for which we have historical knowledge—such as Rome, Jerusalem, and Mecca—there does not seem to be a case where the pilgrims enjoyed better housing than the local people. To the contrary: religious pilgrims have very often been preyed upon by unscrupulous officials, merchants, innkeepers, and thieves. Those who suggest that Chacoan pilgrims occupied the empty great houses while most canyon residents did not must explain why Chaco would be so anomalous in this respect.

Third, the idea that pilgrims occasionally lived in the great houses is crippled by the same logical flaw as Hayes's (1981:68) suggestion that captives were kept in such places (Tainter 1991:184). The notion is unfalsifiable, and so its acceptance is a matter of faith. It is of course logically impossible to demonstrate that pilgrims *didn't* stay in great houses.

Fourth, the roads, great houses, transport of commodities, and support of high-ranking individuals indicate a level of labor investment in the Chacoan system well above the norm for the Puebloan Southwest. If the purpose of this investment was to obtain finished turquoise pieces, then the people of the San Juan Basin were paying a very high price to get some trinkets. One does not have to postulate that the Anasazi had much economic rationality to question the logic of this reconstruction. Archaeologists who argue that prehistoric people behaved irrationally, as the Chacoan revisionists are implicitly arguing, must assume the responsibility of explaining why. To suggest that the archaeological record can be explained by irrationality is no more logical than to suggest that it can be explained by diffusion, or migration, or self-aggrandizement, or any other deus ex machina.

Finally, one of the arguments of the Chacoan revisionists is that there were fewer people residing in great houses than we previously thought. This finding is used to downplay Chaco as hierarchical and complex, since fewer great house residents would mean fewer elites. Yet scholars who have worked to quantify hierarchy and rank differentiation have pointed out that lowering the proportion of elites to nonelites actually raises the degree of status differentiation (e.g., Harary 1959). Archaeologists who want to downplay the hierarchical nature of Chaco are, ironically, producing results that indicate quite the opposite.

9

Alliance Formation and Cultural Identity in the American Southwest

STEADMAN UPHAM, PATRICIA L. CROWN,
AND STEPHEN PLOG

 AS OUR TITLE SUGGESTS, we are interested in two things in this paper. First, we want to examine the nature of social, political, and economic integration among prehistoric groups in the American Southwest. Integration, perforce, means a combination and articulation of separate and diverse elements—a unification, coordination, consolidation, incorporation. In the prehistoric Southwest, social, political, and economic integration took place on many different levels—household, village, pan-village, region, panregion—and in many different ways. We are, however, specifically interested in only one kind of integration: the process of alliance formation as a means of integrating diverse groups occupying widespread regions. Second, we are, of necessity, faced with the task of identifying alliances within and between distinctive cultural groups. That is, the prehistoric groups we study are presumed to have been united through the sharing of a common culture. This latter "necessity" stems more from the way Southwestern prehistory has been written, however, than from any desire on our part to be entrapped by inflexible designations of archaeological cultures.

We recognize, however, that archaeologists begin and end their work with a common assumption about the existence of archaeological cultures and the relationship of an archaeologically defined culture to the conceptual meaning of the term "culture." As contained in the orthodoxy of the introductory textbooks of our field, this assumption is both basic and simple:

> By investigating groups of prehistoric sites and the many artifacts in them, it is possible to erect local and regional sequences of human cultures that extend over centuries, even millennia. (Fagan 1988:31)

To the archaeologist, culture is based largely on the material items found in a site. More specifically, it is common practice for archaeologists to refer to identical or

similar assemblages from two or more sites close to each other in time or space as
evidence for a particular culture (Knudson 1985:94).

> Over the years, archaeologists have chosen to begin their inquiry by
> provisionally adopting a simplified, purposively streamlined concept of
> culture. Some time ago, archaeologists stumbled upon a powerful pos-
> tulate: Temporal variability is best reflected by shared, modal aspects
> of culture. It is difficult to overemphasize how important this simple
> conclusion has been to practicing archaeologists. (Thomas 1989:252)

We do not dispute the wisdom of the reasoning reflected in the above quota-
tions (although perhaps we should have years ago!). The three of us have duly written about the three primary archaeological cultures of the Southwest—Hohokam,
Mogollon, and Anasazi—and have sought to describe and explain the evolution of
these "cultural systems." All of us have talked about "cultural developments" during certain phases or periods in the regions where we work and have described
specific episodes of culture change or continuity. Unfortunately, we now find that
the assumptions we share about the existence of these cultures bind us inextricably to a narrow course of interpretation.

The narrowness of this course was illustrated recently in an article written by
Ronald Atkinson (1989), an Africanist who works among the Acholi and neighboring peoples of East Africa. Atkinson, "working with unconscious, nonnarrative
traditions as well as the more accessible and commonly utilized narrative ones"
(1989:22), examines the evolution of Acholi ethnicity and culture prior to the beginning of the colonial period. Like most anthropologists, Africanists interested in
tracing the tribal identities of different African groups have usually identified distinctive cultures first and have then sought to analyze and explain the evolution
of social, economic, and political institutions rooted in those cultures. Contrary
to prevailing anthropological wisdom, however, Atkinson argues that the Acholi
adopted a common ethnicity and cultural identity only after previously unaffiliated groups embraced a new form of political and economic organization:

> It was the acceptance or rejection of [a] new sociopolitical order that
> ultimately determined ethnicity, language, and many social and politi-
> cal practices, and not the other way around. (Atkinson 1989:26)

Such a conclusion is directly relevant to the common assumption regarding
archaeological cultures noted above. When similarities of material culture are
identified in regions, archaeologists usually begin with the assumption that such
similarities derive from the sharing of a common culture which arrived with the
people and within which the institutions and practices of the people evolved; in
other words, that groups who shared the same culture also shared the same political institutions, subsistence patterns, and social organization. Atkinson shows that
this situation may, in some cases, be entirely reversed.

In many respects, the Acholi and the East African cultural milieu they occupy could not be farther from the American Southwest and its native peoples. On the other hand, the evolution of Acholi ethnicity and culture holds important lessons for the prehistorian, especially for scholars interested in the formation of large social aggregates that archaeologists have conveniently referred to as "cultures."

The introduction and spread of the new sociopolitical order and the emergence of a recognizable Acholi culture is a long and complex process that is described by Atkinson in detail (1989). Considerations of space preclude a full accounting of this process, but the central points can be summarized as follows:

1. The basic mechanism in the spread of the new sociopolitical order was the forging of alliances among neighboring groups. The rulers of these new polities possessed prestige and social position because they were economically successful. Their system of tribute and redistribution allowed for the buffering of agricultural risk among the polity's lineages and allowed the polity to establish connections with other groups organized similarly.

2. The spread of a common language occurred, in part, because of "political alliances, economic cooperation, and marriage ties" and "because new structures and activities associated with the chiefs were not present before" (Atkinson 1989:28).

3. The most important single element in the spread of the new political order and in the adoption of a common language was trade. The principal commodity in circulation was iron, and iron deposits did not exist in the Acholi region. The Acholi actively participated in local and regional trade networks in which tobacco, foodstuffs, ostrich-egg beads, and ostrich feathers were traded for iron commodities. Alliances were forged to solidify trading relationships

4. Periodic droughts and food shortages made it advantageous for groups not yet incorporated into polities to join, since membership offered the opportunity of economic support during bad agricultural years. Moreover, incorporation into the new political order facilitated entry into local and regional trade networks and provided a series of potential allies. Membership in the new order provided a "larger group of closely associated village lineages with which to hunt, go on trading expeditions, or exchange women" (Atkinson 1989:25).

Atkinson goes on to explain how membership in the new order gradually distinguished members from nonmembers and that as the new order spread, it became the social, political, cultural, and linguistic mainstream. Members of the new order, however, did not refer to themselves by a single term or common name, preferring instead to retain their traditional cultural and ethnic designations. But through time the social, political, economic, and linguistic homogeneity of the region became noteworthy, and in the 1860s outsiders began to refer to the inhabitants of these polities by the collective term Shuuli. This term was transformed in usage to Acholi, the name now used to refer to the people and culture of this East African region.

ALLIANCES AND SOUTHWESTERN CULTURES

To an archaeologist studying the Acholi, the record of material culture would undoubtedly show the existence of an Acholi "culture" long before these ethnically
and culturally diverse groups ever shared a common language or unified system
of beliefs, values, and knowledge. Yet the initial assumption would be tied to the
notion that such a "culture" existed. To our knowledge, no Southwestern archaeologist has seriously entertained the notion that the archaeological record of the
Southwest does not contain the material residues of Hohokam, Mogollon, or Anasazi cultures. Rather, more nearly the opposite is true: depending upon the geographic area in which one works, the beginning assumption is that groups that
possessed a distinctively Anasazi, Mogollon, or Hohokam culture can be reconstructed from the archaeological record. From the patterning of material remains,
local and regional similarities or differences can be identified, and from them one
can develop, describe, and explain cultural sequences for these groups. Finally,
one can study from these cultural sequences, the emergence of distinctive social,
political, and economic forms within a single cultural tradition.

If Atkinson is correct, however, the initial assumption about a "culture" having
existed is misleading; sometimes the archaeological record contains the remains
of disparate cultural and ethnic groups who at different times and in different places may have participated in the same political and economic systems—
thereby interacting in both cooperative and competitive ways—but who did not
share a common culture. We believe it may be productive to entertain such a
notion and to begin with the initial proposition that bounded archaeological cultures did not exist in the Southwest. We do this because the belief that a "culture"
existed at a given time and place carries with it powerful ideas about common history, adaptive uniformity, and sociopolitical and economic homogeneity that may
be unwarranted.

Consequently, our beginning assumption in this paper is that when homogeneity in material culture exists within or between regions, it signifies only that
interaction and the sharing of information, goods, and possibly people occurred.
Depending on the intensity, extent, and duration of the patterning and the kinds,
quantity, and distribution of specific items of material culture, it may also mean
that interacting groups participated in a common social, political, and economic
system. If such a pattern was also widespread and persisted for an extended period
of time (i.e., a few generations), we believe the conditions are met for the characteristic of group organization that we term "alliance," a concept we explore below.
Outside of written records or detailed oral histories, however, we know of no way
to determine if a common language or culture was ever a part of the archaeological patterns we now identify.

TABLE 9.1.

Language diversity and intelligibility in the Southwest

Group	Language Family	Subfamily Branch or Language	Other Groups Speaking Mutually Intelligible Dialects
1. Hopi	Uto-Aztecan	Hopi	None
2. Zuni	Zuni	Zuni	None
3. Acoma	Keres	Western Keres	4, 5–9
4. Laguna	Keres	Western Keres	3, 5–9
5. Santa Domingo	Keres	Eastern Keres	6, 7–9
6. San Felipe	Keres	Eastern Keres	5, 7–9
7. Santa Ana	Keres	Eastern Keres	8, 5–9
8. Zia	Keres	Eastern Keres	7, 5–9
9. Cochiti	Keres	Eastern Keres	5–8, 3
10. Taos	Tanoan	Northern Tiwa	11
11. Picuris	Tanoan	Northern Tiwa	10
12. Sandia	Tanoan	Southern Tiwa	13–14
13. Isleta	Tanoan	Southern Tiwa	12–14
14. Ysleta del Sur	Tanoan	Southern Tiwa	12–13
15. Santa Clara	Tanoan	Tewa	16–19
16. San Juan	Tanoan	Tewa	15–19
17. San Ildefonso	Tanoan	Tewa	15–19
18. Nambe	Tanoan	Tewa	15–19
19. Tesuque	Tanoan	Tewa	15–18
20. Hano	Tanoan	Tewa	None?
21. Jemez	Tanoan	Towa	None
22. Pima	Uto-Aztecan	Tepiman (Pimic)	23
23. Papago	Uto-Aztecan	Tepiman (Pimic)	22
24. Walapai	Yuman	Upland (Pai)	25–26
25. Havasupai	Yuman	Upland (Pai)	24–26
26. Yavapai	Yuman	Upland (Pai)	24–25
27. Mohavi	Yuman	River Yuman	28–29
28. Yuma or Quechan	Yuman	River Yuman	27–29
29. Maricopa	Yuman	River Yuman	27–28

SOUTHWESTERN CULTURES AND THE ETHNOGRAPHIC PRESENT

Our beginning point in this paper is the material record that signifies connectivity between groups. But before considering the nature of that connectivity in prehistory, it would be wise to consider briefly the cultural and linguistic diversity of native peoples in the Southwest as it has been recorded during the "ethnographic present."

We hold to the assumption that language is a fundamental symbol of cultural and ethnic identity: that linguistic boundaries often coincide with cultural ones. Table 9.1 provides a listing of contemporary Southwestern groups based on languages spoken and mutual intelligibility of the dialects in existence during the ethnographic period. We realize that these ethnographic data probably provide a very poor analog for understanding language diversity and the potential extent of cultural homogeneity in the prehistoric Southwest (cf. Upham 1982, 1987). Population loss and other severe colonial disruptions have dramatically altered the sociopolitical and economic character of all Southwestern groups. We know, for example, that some groups (e.g., Sobaipuri) became extinct during the early colonial period; these do not appear in table 9.1. The "cultural integrity" and maximum spatial extent of other groups have been affected by resettlement and population relocation. As in other New World areas, these conditions of contact have probably reduced overall linguistic and cultural diversity among Southwestern groups.

Yet we believe the data in table 9.1 are still instructive. Despite the effects of the contact period, the following conclusions can be drawn from the table: linguistic diversity is great given the relatively small geographic extent of the American Southwest, and mutual intelligibility of dialects spoken is low across the entire region. For each of the 29 groups listed in the table, the average number of other groups speaking mutually intelligible dialects is three, with mutual intelligibility limited to close neighbors. The greatest number of other groups speaking mutually intelligible dialects is eight, all in the Keres language family and all between neighboring groups. The fewest number of other groups speaking mutually intelligible dialects is zero (the Hopi, Zuni, Hopi-Tewa, and Jemez).

While these data must be viewed with caution, it is clear that the idea of a common culture across traditionally defined archaeological regions like the Anasazi, Mogollon, and Hohokam is problematic in the absence of a mutually intelligible symbolic system (i.e., a common language). These data indicate that the Southwest is best viewed as a culturally and linguistically heterogeneous region that is populated today by distinct cultural and ethnic groups. The modern Southwestern cultural landscape, then, appears to parallel the pre-Acholi landscape of East Africa. But we know that this kind of cultural heterogeneity is not evident in the material record, at least on the scales at which that record is examined by archaeologists. Consequently, to begin to penetrate higher-order formulations that may impinge on the idea of "cultural identities," we believe it is imperative to focus on variation in the degree to which patterning is present and to isolate "strong patterns" (F. Plog 1984) in the material record of regions that may signify cooperation and competition among groups at a supraordinate level. In the remainder of this paper we attempt to identify strong patterning in the archaeological record and to chronicle the evolution of the social correlate of that patterning, a phenomenon we refer to as the process of alliance formation.

A SPATIAL STRUCTURE FOR UNDERSTANDING THE CONCEPT OF ALLIANCE

If the landscape of East Africa were examined prior to the emergence of a distinctive Acholi "culture," one would see the many settlements of localized lineages existing as dispersed, politically autonomous villages. These villages would be surrounded by agricultural fields and would be spaced so as to maximize agricultural productivity and minimize intervillage conflict. Yet the need for mates and commodities not available at the local level would necessitate social and economic relations between villages. These relationships might be quite formal, but they probably existed only among a few localities. As the spread of the new sociopolitical order affected more and more local populations, however, the network of connections between villages would become more pronounced and widespread, and the material manifestations of these connections—shared material culture— would create distinctive distributional patterns.

Unfortunately, the kinds of studies that might inform us of these changes have not been done for the Acholi. As Atkinson describes the evolving system, however, organizational units formed that were distinguished by constellations of unique material traits and the sharing of ideas, information, and commodities. This synergy led to increased homogeneity in the adaptive patterns of the cooperating lineages. In the Southwest, we do not know the organizational details of past sociopolitical orders as we do for the Acholi. Instead, we are able to define unique spatial and organizational units on the basis of shared material culture— the strong patterns alluded to above. Consequently, we must work from these details toward the organizational structure of the systems we study.

Steadman Upham and Lori S. Reed (1989) have recently examined a series of concepts used by archaeologists to examine strong patterns in the archaeological record, and we borrow liberally from their analysis in the following discussion to provide a framework for discussing alliances in the Southwest. Upham and Reed begin by considering the concept of "regional systems." The use of the term "regional system" has gained currency among Southwestern archaeologists as a way to describe both the spatial structure of settlements and the interactive ties that linked various settlements across a particular landscape. Upham and Reed argue that this conflation of settlement structure and interaction derives from one of the first method statements developed for regional analysis that was read widely by archaeologists (Smith 1976). This combined usage is found in the description of the "Hohokam regional system," and the dual meaning is also embodied in the idea of a "Chacoan regional system" (cf. Judge and Schelberg 1984). Operationally, such conflation may be heuristically useful, but when possible it may be preferable to decouple settlement structure from interaction in describing strong patterns in the archaeological record. For example, for different areas of the Colorado Plateaus and Mogollon Rim country we refer to aspects of settlement structure by using the term settlement cluster, and to elements of interaction by relying on the concepts of province, alliance, or social network.

In the southern deserts of Arizona, archaeologists have used different terms to describe settlement structure and interactional patterns. They have used the concept of regional system, for example, in conjunction with "core-periphery" models. The core-periphery model has been used in various forms for at least six decades in the Southwest, deriving originally from what David Wilcox (1980) has referred to as the Gladwinian model (cf. McGuire 1991). But the economic and political relationships posited by core-periphery models again conflate settlement structure and interaction. Randall McGuire (1991) has critically examined the core-periphery model in relation to the distributional data for different classes of artifacts and architectural features. His work suggests that variability in both core and peripheral regions—shifting boundaries, different local developmental histories, and the variable demographic circumstances of different groups—render the idea of an organizationally uniform core and periphery untenable. Unfortunately, too little work analyzing the regional structure of settlement outside of the Salt-Gila core area has been completed to decouple settlement structure from interaction in a manner that is comparable to analyses for regions in the central and northern Southwest. Moreover, the *ranchería* style of settlement over much of the southern deserts and the emphasis in many areas on irrigation agriculture pose problems for conventional quantitative analysis of settlement patterns that employ point pattern analysis and areal measures of connectivity and association. As a result, the following discussion of spatial structure may appear uneven.

Research to define spatial variation in the distribution of settlements at regional scales has a relatively long history in Southwestern archaeology (Kidder 1924; Martin and Plog 1973; McGregor 1965; Willey 1953; Wormington 1947). Yet only within the last decade have archaeologists formalized this work to be able to talk about discrete organizational units above the level of a single drainage or restricted geographic area (Cordell 1984; Hantman 1984; Lightfoot 1984; F. Plog 1979; S. Plog 1980b; Riley 1987; Upham 1980, 1982; Wilcox 1981a). Efforts to define regional settlement organization for portions of the central and northern Southwest have been made by several archaeologists (Earls 1987; Kintigh 1985; Lightfoot 1984; Marshall and Walt 1984; Upham 1982, Upham and L. Reed 1989, Upham, Lightfoot, and Jewett 1989). Most of this research has focused on the late periods of prehistory—the thirteenth through sixteenth centuries. In several of these studies, a key operational concept is that of settlement cluster, a quantitatively derived measure of spatial association whose roots extend back to the work of Spicer (1962). Spicer used this term to refer to groups of proximate settlements (both pueblos and rancherías) which shared common threads of economy, religion, and politics and were subject to the programs of enforced reduction employed by the Spaniards. Upham (1982:58) adopted Spicer's terminology to refer to clusters of settlements that form spatially discrete entities, and that concept and terminology have now been used in other analyses. Map analysis of settlement clusters across the plateau and montane regions suggests an average size of about 2,500 square kilometers.

Several settlement pattern analyses have also been conducted at the regional level for different areas of the southern deserts. Most such work, however, has focused on the analysis of settlement along canal systems in the Salt-Gila Basin, or on the analysis of the canal systems themselves (Ackerly, Howard, and McGuire 1985; Crown 1987a; Gregory and Nials 1985; Neitzel 1984; Nicholas 1981; Nicholas and Neitzel 1983b; Nicholas and Feinman 1989; Upham and Rice 1980). Concepts analogous to those used in the central and northern Southwest, such as settlement cluster or province, do not exist.

A concept that *is* used, however, is that of "irrigation community," a term applied to groups of contemporaneous settlements situated along the same major canal system (Crown 1987a; Doyel 1977; Gregory and Nials 1985). Considerations of water management and the organizational demands of canal construction and maintenance are viewed as causal factors in the formation of these irrigation communities. At the present time, however, there is no consensus about the degree of regional integration of these communities in the Salt-Gila Basin (Ackerly 1982; Crown 1987a; Nicholas and Neitzel 1983b; Wilcox 1991c). Though no consensus exists about the degree of integration between communities in the Salt-Gila Basin, few researchers would disagree that a regional system existed that was centered on a Salt-Gila "core area." In the core-periphery model, which we discuss below, the distribution of artifact and architectural styles indicates that sociopolitical and economic alliances united groups residing in the Salt-Gila core in varying ways to populations in nine distinct peripheral regions (cf. Wilcox 1979b, 1980; Wilcox and Sternberg 1983; McGuire 1991). Alliances, then, have again been posited by archaeologists as a mechanism that united spatially separate groups in economic and sociopolitical relationships.

ALLIANCES AND SOCIAL NETWORKS

During the late periods of prehistory, settlement clusters in the central and northern Southwest were regularly spaced on the landscape at intervals of approximately 50 to 70 kilometers (Jewett 1989; Upham and L. Reed 1989; Upham 1982). Such regularity signifies that social factors were operating within and between regions to shape the spatial configuration of these units. Similar claims have been made for communities in the southern deserts, especially in the Salt-Gila core area (Upham and Rice 1980). The notion that social factors operate to determine settlement locations is certainly not new. Social and economic geographers have been telling this to other social scientists for the last several decades (e.g., Zipf 1949; Christaller 1966; Losch 1954), and some archaeologists have used geographic models based on measures of social distance to advantage (e.g., Blanton 1975; Flannery 1976; Hammond 1974; Hodder and Orton 1976; Renfrew 1977; and others).

Models based on social distance are derived from empirical studies that focus not only on the demands of market and transportation, but also on issues related to site catchment (cf. Vita-Finzi and Higgs 1970). Social distance models based on this latter concept are usually predicated on some notion of minimum distance between neighboring settlements and are driven by assumptions about adequate living space to pursue subsistence needs without encountering undue competition. Social distance models based on considerations of market and transportation, on the other hand, are usually predicated on notions of optimal spacing between settlements to facilitate the distribution of goods, services, and information. At the foundation of each of these concepts of distance is the notion of managing human interaction within and between neighboring populations.

One of the most interesting, but controversial, attempts to contextualize the nature and extent of interaction during this period is reflected in recent attempts by archaeologists to deal with the concept of alliance (Cordell and F. Plog 1979; F. Plog 1984; Upham 1980, 1982, 1987). Some of the controversy may stem from confusion over the anthropological baggage associated with the term "alliance," or by the way it has been associated with interpretations of sociopolitical complexity in the Southwest. The term has been used in exactly the manner that formal alliance theorists intend, however, and ideas that spring from the theory about alliance formation and exchange (Lévi-Strauss 1969:233–310 et passim) have been used by archaeologists to broaden discussions of regional system formation and connectivity between regions.

Lévi-Strauss's ideas of exchange include both the more conspicuous exchange of marriage partners and, at a higher and more inclusive level, the exchange of all forms of material and information. In fact, his elucidation of alliance formation and generalized exchange is embedded in a conception of information theory that includes both material and nonmaterial (read "symbolic") dimensions. Consequently, when a claim is made that an alliance of fourteenth-century settlement clusters "may have involved the establishment of affinal kin ties, the transmission of esoteric knowledge, and the exchange of . . . material" (Upham 1982:157), that claim rests on correlations in archaeological data used in conjunction with a structuralist definition of the alliance concept.

For archaeologists, the foundation of the alliance concept resides in the ability to demonstrate that persistent, high levels of exchange and interaction took place over a wide region, and that such exchange involved the transmission of specialized commodities that may not have been available to all members of a given population. The inference that mate exchange and the transmission of information took place in conjunction with the exchange of goods is based on (1) an incredibly large number of ethnographic case examples in which long-term, persistent material exchanges are accompanied by the exchange of marriage partners (see Lévi-Strauss 1969), and (2) the fact that the exchange of information is embedded in stylistic messages contained in the goods themselves (cf. S. Plog 1980b; Wiessner 1983; Wobst 1977). Such stylistic messages are contained in both the design and form of commodities and—as H. M. Wobst, Stephen Plog, and Polly Wiessner have shown—can function as symbols to demarcate group identity. Warren DeBoer (1984) has demonstrated the ease with which many such design components travel and has modeled boundary effects based on design variability. Such boundaries have clear implications for the formation and maintenance of alliances.

In the following section of this paper, we explore the concept of alliance in different geographic areas of the American Southwest using the spatial and organizational frameworks gleaned from the previous theoretical sections and from our discussion of alliance formation and sociopolitical development among the Acholi.

THE SOUTHERN DESERTS OF ARIZONA

As noted previously, the "regional system" concept is firmly established in the literature of the southern deserts of Arizona (Wilcox and Shenk 1977; Wilcox 1979b, 1980; Wilcox and Sternberg 1983; Crown 1987a). The arrangement of certain kinds of highly distinctive architectural features, ballcourts, and the limits of exchanged red-on-buff ceramics serve as baseline measures of regional system boundaries (Wilcox and Sternberg 1983; Wilcox 1985; Crown 1987b, 1989). Although prehistorians have identified a regional system/alliance system using these attributes, the issues of how the system developed, the nature of interaction within the area, and why the system collapsed remain.

THE SALT-GILA BASIN REGIONAL SYSTEM

There is substantial evidence for interaction between groups occupying the southern deserts long before construction of the earliest ballcourts between AD 775 and 850. Sites with pithouse architecture, storage features, trash accumulations, cemeteries, and horticulture indicate that a largely sedentary farming lifestyle had developed in southeastern Arizona by 1000 to 500 BC (Huckell 1987). The presence of shell ornaments on these sites suggests interaction and exchange with populations to the southwest of the Tucson Basin. Pottery occurs in southern Arizona by AD 300, and a decorated pottery tradition begins after 450. As illustrated by the distribution and frequency of dated red-on-buff ceramics outside of the Salt-Gila Basin and the variety of exotics within the Salt-Gila Basin (Doyel 1987b; Crown 1989; Doelle and Wallace 1989), the limits of exchange between groups residing in the southern deserts and surrounding populations widened (as indicated by the distribution) and probably intensified (as indicated by the frequency) through time (Crown 1984, 1989).

Ballcourts appeared in the Salt-Gila Basin and in adjacent areas at essentially the same time after AD 775, and Wilcox (1991d) has argued that the system of ballcourts developed to ameliorate discrepancies in access to food and exotic trade items brought about by population increases that accompanied the development of irrigation agriculture at the end of the Pioneer period (prior to AD 775). Population in areas with irrigable land grew at a more rapid rate than in surrounding areas, altering the nature of existing exchange and interaction networks. The ballcourt system then arose in response to these changes, providing a ritual context for sustained interaction. Other researchers have suggested that environmental uncertainty, perhaps particularly the destruction of canals by a flood in the late 800s, stimulated groups to intensify contacts with outsiders in order to reduce risk and diversify their subsistence base (Masse 1991).

From a beginning of only six (documented) courts at AD 850, 28 additional courts existed by approximately AD 1000, and by the end of the early Classic period (AD 1250), 206 courts had been constructed at 165 sites in Arizona (Wilcox

1991d). After this time, no additional courts were constructed, and existing ball-courts apparently were no longer used. Their occurrence at a restricted number of sites suggests that whatever ritual or other activity occurred at the ballcourts drew populations from surrounding sites without ballcourts. The ballcourts probably provided a mechanism for interaction and exchange in material goods, food, marriage partners, and services/labor of various types (Wilcox and Sternberg 1983). Exchange of goods and services in connection with ballcourt ritual supplemented previous exchange networks based largely on kinship or trading partner ties (Wilcox 1991d:176).

At its height, the area encompassed by the ballcourt network included the region from Flagstaff in the north to the southern Arizona border, and from the San Simon River in the east to Gila Bend. Part of the regional system/alliance model entails the concept of a "core" area surrounded by a periphery or rings of peripheries (McGuire 1991; Wilcox 1980; Wilcox and Sternberg 1983). Although originally formulated to distinguish the area with the purest manifestations of distinctive traits (the core) from areas receiving "diffused" ideas or migrants from this core (the periphery), the core-periphery model has more recently described a system of political and economic alliances between populations within the regional system (McGuire 1991). The proliferation of ballcourts between AD 800 and 1100, in particular, is viewed as signaling the emergence of a formalized system of relations and interaction between core and periphery populations. This system is very different from earlier organizational structures. The widespread exchange of goods and the apparent shared ideology manifest by the spread of ballcourts indicate greater levels of interaction among groups participating in this alliance than among these groups and outside populations.

Populations in some outside areas (for instance, the Papaguería [Masse 1991]) clearly exchanged goods, interacted with core area groups, and shared other items of material culture, however, but did not have ballcourts. Populations in yet other areas exchanged goods and interacted with core area groups at low levels, but possessed very different kinds of material culture (e.g., groups occupying the Mimbres drainage). Whatever the reasons for the patterning found, it appears that ball-courts alone should not be used to define participation in an alliance system in the southern deserts. Other indicators of shared style, technology, forms, and ideology must be incorporated. While the presence of a ballcourt certainly may indicate participation in the system, absence of ballcourts should not be taken to indicate lack of participation (Masse 1991). Other axes of variability must be examined.

The degree of integration of populations in the "ballcourt alliance" is not clear. Wilcox (1979b; Wilcox and Sternberg 1983) has argued that the network of ballcourt communities was economically integrated through the exchange of high-value goods. Elite households at the ballcourt sites may have exchanged rare exotics (copper bells, pyrite mirrors, macaws, shell trumpets, rubber balls) that cemented marriage alliances and helped in dispute negotiation (Wilcox and Sternberg 1983:212–14). This exchange network may have extended into Mesoamerica, incorporating core area groups in an even broader alliance network (Wilcox and

Sternberg 1983; Nelson 1981, 1986; McGuire and Howard 1987; Doyel 1987b), but some researchers have questioned the evidence for this kind of elite exchange (Seymour 1988; Crown 1989).

The ballcourts may indicate the emergence of a shared ideology, and some aspects of style and material culture over this broad area appear to have been shared as well. Despite the presence of ballcourts and these shared elements, however, sites in the alliance exhibit some difference in material culture, subsistence practices, site structure, and burial practices (Crown 1989; McGuire 1991:31). Such evidence tends to suggest considerable diversity in the system. Evidence is lacking to indicate that this area was ever unified by a common culture or uniform ethnic identity. Rather, shared styles and ideology appear to have been incorporated into distinct local systems. It is also the case that the Salt-Gila Basin and surrounding areas never operated in concert politically or economically. No single site or portion of the area coordinated interaction and exchange. Goods and information— and probably people—certainly moved within this acephalous alliance network, but not in an equivalent fashion. Populations within the Salt-Gila Basin received different kinds and quantities of exotic goods differentially, with the patterning reflecting both a site's position in the site hierarchy and its geographic locale within the basin.

The major drainages in the basin may have provided porous boundaries for exchange networks with surrounding populations (Crown 1984, 1985, 1989; Doyel 1987b), resulting in differential access to different kinds and quantities of intrusive pottery found at sites north of the Salt, south of the Gila, and between the rivers. It is likely that with increased data this patterning of bounded exchange networks within the Salt-Gila Basin will appear even more locale-specific, and that exchange with surrounding groups will be found to have been organized at a level no higher than sites sharing an irrigation system or utilizing a single ballcourt—the idea of "community" discussed earlier (cf. Crown 1984). Patterning in the differential distribution (cf. Upham, Lightfoot, and Feinman 1981) of intrusive goods is apparent in the Tucson Basin, as well (Doelle and Wallace 1989), and such patterning seems to be linked to the ballcourt system. Groups in southern Arizona, although sharing many elements of material culture, were not fully integrated in a political or economic sense. At most, small clusters of sites were linked to surrounding populations, and all populations did not interact in an equivalent fashion with groups either within the alliance or outside of it. Groups in the peripheries interacted with the core groups in differing ways and, as noted by McGuire (1991), groups in the peripheries diverged from one another and from those in the core over time.

The regional system and the alliance network discussed above collapsed in the early AD 1100s. A number of factors have been implicated in the collapse, including environmental perturbations, a response to the collapse of surrounding alliance networks in the San Juan Basin or the Mimbres Valley, and changes in the availability of or access to specific resources. Further research is needed to discern the processes leading to widespread abandonments (of both peripheral areas and parts of the basin) and the restructuring attendant on this collapse.

The sequence of development of the Salt-Gila regional system appears to parallel the case of the Acholi in many ways. First, the regional system seems to have been formed when a number of previously unaffiliated groups in both core and peripheral areas forged alliances to ameliorate local imbalances in resource production (cf. Wilcox 1991d). Variation in material culture, subsistence strategies, mortuary practices, and settlement of allied groups in both core and periphery suggest that the regional system was composed of culturally and ethnically distinct populations. Second, large quantities of nonutilitarian goods (especially shell) appear to have moved throughout the alliance system as exchange ties with neighboring groups were solidified. Further research on the distribution of exchanged items may shed light on the nature of connectivity between allied groups. Finally, the spread of a shared ideology appears to be indicated by the adoption of ritual associated with ballcourts (Wilcox and Sternberg 1983). We would also suggest that the distribution of stone effigy vessels and palettes may be associated with the sociopolitical structure of the regional system, in much the same way that royal drums and other items served as markers of the new sociopolitical order of the Acholi. The distribution of palettes and stone effigy vessels may thus delimit the extent of alliance ties in the regional system.

Despite the collapse of the regional system, large populations continued to occupy the Salt-Gila Basin. Major changes in settlement structure took place, and platform mounds emerged as the architectural marker of a new network of relations among populations occupying the Salt-Gila core. The move of some individuals to habitation on top of these mounds late in the thirteenth century indicates an increased level of social complexity (Gregory 1982; Wilcox 1991c; although see Nelson 1986 and Doyel 1977, 1980, for a contrasting view). Individuals holding leadership roles were probably vested with authority to allocate land and water as an increasingly complex irrigation system developed to sustain the agricultural needs of large, sedentary basin populations (Ackerly 1982; Gregory and Nials 1985; Nicholas and Neitzel 1983; Crown 1987a). A more even distribution of exotic goods throughout the basin suggests greater equivalence in interaction with surrounding populations, although there is still no evidence for political or economic unification of basin populations (Ackerly 1982; Crown 1987a). This system broke down after AD 1350, perhaps due to catastrophic flooding and destruction of the canals (Nials, Gregory, and Graybill 1989). The Salt-Gila Basin was largely depopulated after this time.

THE TUCSON BASIN REGIONAL SYSTEM

Defined as one of the "peripheries" of the Salt-Gila core, the Tucson Basin has a significantly different culture history than does the Salt-Gila (Doelle and Wallace 1989). Following collapse of the Salt-Gila regional system in the early AD 1100s and the decline of both the ballcourt system and red-on-buff pottery manufacture, distributions of red-on-brown pottery suggest the emergence of a new regional system and network of alliances (Doelle and Wallace 1989; McGuire 1991). This new system appears to have had the Tucson Basin as its "core" and probably spanned the area from northern Sonora to north of the Tucson Basin. The inclusion of the Salt-Gila Basin in this regional system, however, is a matter of debate. Tanque Verde Red-on-brown pottery is found in high frequencies in the Salt-Gila Basin after AD 1150, but at least some of this material appears to have been manufactured locally (Crown, Schwalbe, and London 1985), suggesting information flow from the Tucson Basin as opposed to the direct exchange of goods. As noted by William Doelle and Henry Wallace (1989:4), this reversal in the flow of ideas and information between the Tucson and Salt-Gila basins is perhaps the strongest indicator we have of the changing nature of alliance ties through time.

Doelle and Wallace (1989:38) also argue that warfare was an important component of thirteenth- and fourteenth-century interaction in southern Arizona and that platform mounds are evidence of a political hierarchy capable of effecting alliance formation and controlling conflict. Evidence for conflict is found in hillslope settlements and defensive refuges, the construction of compounds, and abandonment of "buffer" zones between areas of aggregated settlement. Before such a system of alliances took hold in the Tucson Basin, however, there may have been a decrease in ritual control over competition and social differentiation, resulting in increased conflict and differentiation (Doelle and Wallace 1989:28). Consequently, the network of alliances can be viewed as a stabilizing force in the development of regional sociopolitical and economic relations.

ALLIANCE FORMATION AND THE SALADO POLYCHROMES

Early alliance systems in the Salt-Gila region are best defined by the exchange of objects and distribution of specialized architectural features. In contrast, later alliances in the southern deserts and the rest of the Southwest are defined by the production of highly decorated, stylistically uniform pottery over a broad area. In both cases, the widespread exchange of information and goods is indicated, but the later alliance systems are considerably greater in size than those of previous times. Debates concerning the meaning of the Salado phenomenon result in part from confusion about the existence of a Salado "culture" with the production of Salado polychrome pottery.

Two definitions of the so-called Salado culture exist, one based on geographic locale, the other based on a polythetic definition of a suite of traits. The Gladwins (1930:3) defined the Salado as "the people who colonized the upper Salt River drainage," that is, the Tonto-Globe area of Arizona. In subsequent years, a lengthy list of traits was developed to identify these Salado people (Gladwin and Gladwin 1935:27; Haury 1945a:207; Gladwin 1957:264; Steen 1962:68; Cartledge 1976:97), and it included the manufacture of the Salado polychromes. As Salado polychromes were found to occur over much of the greater Southwest, however, the list of traits accompanying the pottery that were presumed to be indicative of a Salado culture also grew. Many researchers viewed the presence of Salado polychromes in particular areas as evidence of "Salado" migrations from the Tonto-Globe area (Franklin and Masse 1976; LeBlanc and Nelson 1976:77–78; Mayro et al. 1976), and the Salado were less often identified as strictly a Tonto-Globe "people." Other researchers viewed the pottery distributions as indicative of widespread exchange from the Tonto-Globe area (Haury 1945a, 1976a:82; Schroeder 1952:330; Johnson 1964; Wasley 1966; Lindsay and Jennings 1968; Doyel 1976:33, 1977; Grebinger 1976:45; Weaver 1976:24).

Two approaches to the Salado problem have changed these views. First, several archaeologists have examined the occurrence of Salado "traits" in sites identified as Salado (Gumerman and Weed 1976; Weaver 1976; Nelson and LeBlanc 1986). Their results indicate considerable variability in what is designated "Salado"; more-over, only a single trait, Salado polychrome pottery, is common to all of these sites. Second, research conducted to assess the locus of production for the Salado poly-chromes demonstrated that the manufacture of Gila Polychrome, one of the most common Salado types, took place throughout the Southwest (Wallace 1954; Danson and Wallace 1956; Martin and Rinaldo 1960:186–95; DiPeso 1976; LeBlanc and Nelson 1976:75; Crown 1983:302; Lightfoot and Jewett 1984; Crown and Bishop 1987). Demonstrable production of this pottery over an area bounded by Hopi and Zuni on the north and Casas Grandes on the south, and stretching from Gila Bend, Arizona, to eastern New Mexico, negates the "Tonto-Globe outlet for pottery exchange" model. It also calls into serious question all migration models involving the Salado. As LeBlanc and Nelson (1976) point out, the Tonto-Globe area could not produce enough emigrants to populate the large area in which the pottery is found, particularly since population in the Tonto-Globe area was also apparently increasing. If the only distinguishing trait for the Salado phenomenon is the presence of the Salado polychromes, then clearly the idea of a Salado cul-ture is untenable.

More importantly, Salado polychromes were manufactured by indigenous populations over much of the greater Southwest, and their presence has impor-tant implications for the formation of alliances and regional integration during the fourteenth and fifteenth centuries (cf. Upham 1982; Upham and L. Reed 1989). While other aspects of material culture are not unified, the production of essentially identical pottery indicates a breakdown of stylistic boundaries that de-marcated groups occupying widespread regions throughout the Southwest during the preceding one thousand years. Information on pottery manufacture and de-sign was unquestionably shared over this broad area, and certain material objects suggest shared symbols of status as well (particularly turquoise-encrusted Glycy-meris shell frog and bird pendants [see Wilcox 1987; McGuire 1991]). The degree of connectivity between populations indicated by the manufacture of an essen-tially identical pottery style is a different kind of phenomenon than is previously seen in the Southwest.

The Salado polychromes have long been interpreted as emblems of an ethnic group or segment of society holding leadership roles (Schmidt 1928:297–98; Haury 1945a:43–44; Hayden 1957:201; Gerald 1976:68–69; Rice 1986; Wilcox and Sternberg 1983); again, we note that strong similarities with the Acholi case are suggested. The sociopolitical meaning of Salado polychromes might be interpreted in the same manner that Atkinson describes the core elements of the new sociopolitical order among the Acholi, especially the significance of possessing royal drums (Atkinson 1989:22; see also our earlier discussion of the Acholi). This proposition, however, is difficult to assess in the absence of detailed intra- and intersite distributional data for different regions. But if Salado polychromes functioned like Jeddito Yellow Ware, which has been used to identify a Jeddito alliance (Upham 1980, 1982), then the existence of a managerial elite may be suggested. Like the Jeddito alliance, however, strong, regional sociopolitical and economic integration of populations—that is, centralized political leadership—would not be a characteristic of an alliance marked by Salado polychromes.

As early as 1980, researchers suspected the existence of a Salado alliance (e.g., Upham 1980:273), but they did not specify its spatial extent or identify its organizational parameters. Wilcox (Wilcox and Sternberg 1983:244–45) recently argued that a Salado regional system existed as a "weakly integrated system of exchange among a large series of small-scale regional systems," and that integration of these small-scale systems occurred through alliances of individuals (as councils) representing each small regional system. He has also suggested that the Salado polychromes were exchanged between the elites of these small-scale regional systems, elites who were linked by intermarriage (Grebinger 1976; Mayro et al. 1976; Graves et al. 1982; Wilcox 1987, 1991d). The turquoise mosaic frogs and birds may have been symbols of a "special office" shared among many ethnically distinct groups (Wilcox 1987:140), and Gila Polychrome may have been a symbol of "membership in an elite kin group" (Wilcox 1987:172; see also Gerald 1976). Wilcox argues further that the regional reorganization of the Southwest in the century following AD 1250 was partly stimulated by increasing conflict that led to the establishment of "military alliances which were cemented by elite intermarriages" (Wilcox 1987:143): conflicts over land and water rights within the Salt-Gila Basin, for instance, may have prompted inhabitants of sites along individual canal networks to seek outside military assistance.

> A continuous network of cross-cutting ties of elite marriage may be what integrated this vast interaction sphere for a century or more after AD 1250 to 1300. . . . Each linkage in the network of alliances may have been quite fragile and easily broken as advantage was sought in another direction. Archaeologically, the palimpsest of these shifting connections resulted in the appearance of a widespread interaction sphere. (Wilcox 1987:145)

If these interpretations are correct, the stylistic unity of Salado polychromes does indicate sociopolitical and economic integration of populations residing over a large portion of the Southwest.

We believe other possible explanations for the stylistic unity should be explored. It is possible, for example, that such unity is tied to the emergence of a regional cult (Werbner 1977). The frequency of Salado polychrome vessels in many sites is too high and their contexts of recovery are too widespread to indicate that they were solely symbols of membership in an elite kin group (unless this kin group occupied essentially an entire site). Regional cults incorporate groups that differ in language, culture, and natural resources; they stress peace and engender the flow of goods, services, information, and people across ethnic boundaries (Burger 1988:114; see also Smith and Heath-Smith 1980). Such a cult might emerge in response to the strains apparent following collapse of the Salt-Gila regional system or demographic disruptions indicated by the widespread movement of populations in the late thirteenth century (cf. McGuire 1986). Whatever the exact nature of the Salado alliance, it collapsed by AD 1450, a collapse that was accompanied by widespread abandonments of many of the areas in which the pottery is found. Flooding of irrigation networks in the Salt-Gila Basin (Nials, Gregory, and Graybill 1991), creation of a buffer zone between the populations of the Tucson Basin and hostile Yavapai groups to the north (Doelle and Wallace 1989), warfare, declines in net productivity on a macroregional scale, or population/resource imbalances (Wilcox 1988a) might all have contributed to the collapse of the Salado alliance.

The three alliances defined for prehistoric southern Arizona differ in several important respects, and it is important to remember that all three are defined on the basis of material culture distributions. The patterning found, although clearly significant, admits a number of interpretations. The tendency in recent years has been to interpret distributions of ceramics and architectural features as indicative of elite intermarriages, political connectivity, elaborate exchange networks, and political/economic alliances. Although these phenomena may indeed characterize the process by which culturally and ethnically diverse groups occupying widespread regions are integrated, the case of the Acholi of Uganda suggests that it may not always be so. Groups can remain more or less localized in a social and political sense and still be part of a wider economic sphere; groups can remain politically autonomous and still function as full-fledged members of an alliance. Thus, alternative explanations to those listed above should be sought and considered.

THE CENTRAL AND NORTHERN SOUTHWEST

The fact that groups can remain socially and politically localized and still be part of a wider economic sphere is illustrated well by the course of prehistory in the central and northern Southwest (Cordell and Plog 1979; F. Plog 1984; Upham 1980, 1982). Although the concept of alliance is invoked primarily in discussions of the post–AD 1000 period in these regions, it is important to recognize that all groups, regardless of their size and complexity, ally themselves with other peoples and that such relationships minimally provide important sources of mates, information, and energy (whether in the form of cooperative labor or access to natural resources). Thus, it is not unusual to read ethnographies of organizationally simple, nonhierarchical hunting and gathering groups in which individuals marry, trade, and interact with nearby kin as well as with genealogically unrelated people whose primary residence area lies tens if not hundreds of kilometers away (e.g., Wiessner 1977). Consequently, it would be surprising if similar networks of alliance and integration did not characterize the central and northern Southwest from the earliest periods of human occupation. The significant questions about alliances in the region, therefore, are not if they existed, but how they changed over time in association with cultural processes such as demographic change, agricultural intensification, and shifting economic relationships.

Given the above proposals, it is not surprising that there are indications of regional connections or networks during the Paleo-Indian and Archaic periods (Wills 1988a). Alliances and alliance networks exist at varying spatial scales and levels of complexity. Unlike the case of the Acholi, which represents the upper extreme of both scale and complexity, groups in the Southwest before the emergence of village life may have forged alliances that linked dispersed, mobile populations into wider networks of solidarity. There is, for example, a decrease in the extent of the Paleo-Indian style zones as the Archaic begins, likely the result of the significant reductions in mobility that accompanied the development of an economic base in which gathered plants played a much more important role. Despite the reduction in mobility, Wills (1988a:88) notes remarkable similarities in projectile point styles over broad areas in the Early Archaic. Such stylistic homogeneity signals the widespread sharing of information that could only result from relatively frequent intergroup contact. During the Middle Archaic there is a significant increase in stylistic variability that appears to be associated with population growth, increased competition for resources, and the need for boundary maintenance mechanisms. The trend toward greater stylistic variation was reversed during the Late Archaic, perhaps as group boundaries became established and group movements became more predictable in both time and space (Wills 1988a:88–89). The marked reduction in frequencies of nonlocal lithic raw materials between the Paleo-Indian period and AD 1 are also consistent with arguments for significant reductions in the extent of regional alliances.

PITHOUSES AND PUEBLOS

As Atkinson notes for the Acholi, the forging of alliances can be accompanied by important social, political, and economic transformations among the participating groups. We believe that one of the most significant transformations during any period in Southwestern prehistory was associated with what archaeologists refer to as the "pithouse-to-pueblo transition" (henceforth PPT), typically dated between approximately AD 500 and 900 in the northern Southwest. (We note that this "transition" was not a uniform process across the region and that pithouses as a style of dwelling persisted well into the thirteenth century [see Stuart and Farwell 1983].) The switch from subsurface to surface dwellings during that period is probably the most visible indication of culture change, but it was only a product of more important social, political, and economic evolution. Of the latter, increasing reliance on a trio of cultigens—corn, beans, and squash—has received the most attention from archaeologists. Cultivated plants were known to Southwestern peoples and were certainly an important contributor to yearly food supplies by at least 1000 BC, but the PPT marks the development throughout most of the region of an adaptation in which agriculture became primary, structuring hunting and gathering activities (rather than vice versa). That development, in turn, was only possible given associated changes in group organization, technology, and politics. The lag between the initial appearance of cultigens and significant dependence on agriculture is thus primarily a matter of sociocultural evolution, rather than an indication of the presence or absence of suitable natural environmental conditions (S. Plog 1990a).

Among the most important of the social, political, and economic changes were (1) the increasing exploitation of ceramics for processing cultivated foods (particularly after the foods were dried and stored [Ford 1968]); (2) a reduction in local obligations to share food and other resources (or, conversely, the increasing ability of family groups to accumulate resources); (3) the establishment of permanent villages occupied during all seasons of the year; (4) an increase in group ownership or control of land and the use of symbols (e.g., cemeteries) to legitimize that control; and (5) an increase in external exchange that was correlated (and likely associated) with increasing evidence of formalized ritual structures (LeBlanc 1982; S. Plog 1990a). As Richard Lee (1979:412–13) has argued, there are fundamental contradictions between the sharing ethic central to hunting and gathering societies and the saving of resources that is equally critical in farming and herding societies (see also Hegmon 1991). The transition from subsurface to surface dwellings, although likely promoting efficiency in certain tasks (Gilman 1987), is thus regarded by us as a fundamental part of a social, political, and economic transformation, marking the need and ability of individual groups to control the increasing quantities of cultivated plants and to store those products in close association with residences.

The above-mentioned social transformations are relevant to the concepts of alliance and integration in at least two important ways. As noted above, external exchange likely increased with agriculture and sedentism as a means of maintaining ties to both resources and land in other areas (Braun and Plog 1982; Hantman 1983). Such ties would have been both possible and necessary given the increased production and productive variation associated with greater dependence on agriculture and the relatively short-term occupation of most settlements (Hantman 1983; Ahlstrom 1985) and use of nearby fields. Productive variation may have increased the desire for access to food in other areas, while short-term occupations would have required access to areas with alternative fields. The development of formal ceramic exchange networks in the Four Corners region involving San Juan Red Ware and the development of broad stylistic zones as exemplified by the Lino and Kana-a decorative styles are two examples of this selection for stronger external ties.

Locally, it is likely that new mechanisms of conflict resolution evolved as settlement stability increased, mobility declined, and disputes could no longer be resolved by people "voting with their feet" (Lee 1979:367). And the likelihood of disputes may have increased with reduced sharing and greater accumulations of resources by small social units. Increasingly formalized ritual activity may have been one of the mechanisms of resolving conflicts. Intergroup exchange also has its competitive, conflict-creating side, possibly explaining the association of exchange and formalized ritual noted above.

Thus, we see the increasing appearance of ceremonial structures—kivas—in the archaeological record along with larger storage facilities constructed adjacent to dwellings. The association of these elements define the "Prudden units" or "unit pueblos" so characteristic of the ninth and tenth centuries in the northern Southwest. In other words, basic aspects of the social transformations that accompanied (and allowed) increased dependence on agriculture suggest both increased integration and the existence of alliances. In many respects, the spread of this new adaptation on the Colorado Plateaus parallels the spread of the new social order among the Acholi, although the scale and complexity of this Southwestern case does not match the East African example. But the emergence of a new economic system based on agriculture, the increase in ritual activity associated with kivas, the architectural similarities of villages, the development of formalized ceramic exchange networks, and the existence of broad stylistic zones suggest that the connectivity between groups and the sharing of goods, information, and people had reached new levels.

Although further increases in integration and alliances, as well as other aspects of organizational complexity, were not inevitable once the above changes had evolved, they were certainly more probable for many reasons. Sedentism and agriculture have clear impacts on fertility rates (S. Plog 1986a). The potential for population growth greatly increases, and if population growth occurs, there are more people to manage. More importantly, there is more surplus labor, more information to be digested, more disputes that need to be resolved, more competition for land and food, and more opportunities for disparities to arise in access to basic resources. Individuals or groups who are capable of filling such roles would thus be selected for, promoting social differentiation. Increasingly formalized ritual activity also can result in differential access to ritual knowledge, and access to and possession of ritual knowledge is one path to political power (Upham 1982; Whiteley 1986:70).

The hypothesized association of exchange and ritual implies a fundamental difficulty in separating ritual power from economic control. In many parts of the world, early political leaders appear to have been individuals closely connected with or in control of religious leadership and ritual knowledge (e.g., Adams 1956:228). In the case of the Acholi, new hereditary leaders were able to gain and maintain power because they controlled individual lineage heads (see Atkinson 1989:22–28). These lineage heads were the main ritual leaders of the localized polities, and their power and prestige were often enhanced by affiliating with the new order. Consequently, we argue that disparities in access to ritual knowledge must be placed on an equal footing with inequalities in control of food or other resources as a factor that may promote increased political centralization and organizational complexity.

There is some evidence that the potential for greater organizational complexity was realized as the PPT unfolded. Large sites like Alkali Ridge (Brew 1946) that contain sizable sets of storage, habitation, and ceremonial rooms appear to be directly linked to the development of formal exchange networks. The fact that such sites exist in the region where the production of San Juan Red Ware was likely centered is at least suggestive of increasing organizational elaboration associated with exchange. Despite such evidence, the transformations that accompanied the PPT do not mark a pinnacle of development or the maximum extent of alliance networks in the central and northern Southwest. Instead, they largely set the stage for the diverse processes that created more complex organizational patterns during the next several hundred years of the prehistoric period.

LOCALIZED ALLIANCE NETWORKS AND CHACO CANYON

During the decades that immediately followed the PPT there appear to have been few major changes in aspects of alliance and integration. The tenth and early eleventh centuries are often characterized as ones of steady population growth and upland expansion, a characterization that is an accurate generalization for the period as a whole. By AD 1050–1100, agricultural communities were distributed throughout most of the northern Southwest. But neither growth nor upland expansion were continuous; rather, they were irregular processes with episodes of growth and upland expansion followed by periods of decline and contraction (e.g., S. Plog 1986a). The irregularity of the processes and the amount of land available, particularly at the beginning of the period, may have made consolidation of any type of power, control, or leadership difficult. Diverse adaptations that allow unbalanced exchange (Schneider 1975) also can contribute to the development of hierarchy, and that diversity may have been lacking in the period immediately following the PPT (though present during the transition and after AD 1100, a point to be considered below). We thus see little evidence of political centers during the tenth and early eleventh centuries; it is difficult to think of an area of the central and northern Southwest that stands out in any way.

Better information, however, is available for the period after approximately AD 1030, a date that marks another significant transition point in the prehistory of the northern Southwest. The subsequent sixty-year period exhibits a pattern of population growth in virtually every portion of the area, growth that is perhaps unprecedented during the entire prehistoric period in both rate and magnitude. By AD 1090–1100, Pueblo occupation of the northern Southwest probably reached its widest spatial extent (e.g., Lipe 1970:112–13). In at least some local areas, rates of population increase are so high that they cannot be explained by local changes in fertility or mortality. Therefore, significant population influxes must have occurred, though the movements may have been over short distances (cf. Upham

1988). These growth rates are not correlated with any of the climatic indices regarded as important in some recent studies (e.g., Dean et al. 1985), although favorable climatic conditions certainly would not have hindered the growth process (S. Plog and Hantman 1990). The lack of significant correlations between environmental and cultural change and the clear existence of strong interareal correlations in aspects of cultural processes suggest that change during the period was largely a cultural phenomenon involving local, regional, and interregional alliance formation.

Evidence of change in aspects of alliance ties can be found at a variety of spatial scales. Within regions, there were trends toward more localized networks during the period, a process termed "tribalization" by David Braun and Stephen Plog (1982). Although exchange intensity (i.e., the per capita amounts of exchanged goods) did not follow a consistent pattern, lithic raw materials imported from areas most distant from any particular locale decreased in a relatively continuous manner. Conversely, a relative increase in materials from more proximate sources is indicated. Toward the end of the period, there is also evidence of increasing centralization of exchange activity: much higher frequencies of nonlocal ceramics occur at large sites with ritual structures, even in areas where the largest sites had no more than 10 to 15 rooms (S. Plog 1990a).

These localized networks appear to be similar to the kinds of systems found in the "peripheries" of the southern deserts after AD 500. Different local demographic histories, different local subsistence strategies (especially involving the degree of dependence on agriculture), and different stylistic patterns in the distribution of material culture all point to processes that linked different local populations into larger cooperating units. Overall patterns in the distribution of stylistic characteristics followed a somewhat similar trend as regional ceramic styles (the basis of the "branches" defined by Colton [1939]) developed. These styles differ from those of both earlier and later periods in that they lack strong patterns of association among design attributes, a characteristic of styles that convey messages of social group affiliation and identity (S. Plog 1990b). In at least some areas, nonlocal styles that can be argued to be symbols of regional alliances are concentrated more heavily at sites with ritual structures (S. Plog 1990a). Thus, a variety of evidence is consistent with the hypothesis that more localized, but better integrated networks developed during the period (see also Braun and Plog 1982).

In addition to organizational changes at local scales, significant alterations occurred in the nature of regional alliances. The most noteworthy developments unfolded in Chaco Canyon, where massive amounts of labor were required for the construction of great houses, roads, and outliers. The roads and outliers in particular provide the first unmistakable evidence of a highly integrated, centralized, and sizable regional network. Stylistic markers, particularly Dogoszhi-style ceramics, suggest that participation in the Chacoan network extended even farther than the area defined by roads and outliers. That hypothesis is supported by precise correlations between processes of change (e.g., in population levels, ceramic assemblages, and the intensity of construction activities) in both Chaco and distant areas (S. Plog 1986b). In many of these distant areas, community size, exchange intensity, and public buildings were markedly different from Chaco, but Chacoan-style ceramics coexisted with ceramic types that had evolved from local traditions. The complexity of regional alliances thus greatly exceeded those of earlier periods, with a hierarchical arrangement clearly centered on Chaco.

Important questions exist about the nature of these alliances and the structure of the regional organization. Some archaeologists have interpreted Chaco as the center of a regional redistribution system that developed during a period of significant spatial variation in climate and, presumably, in food production. Such interpretations assume or imply considerable sociocultural complexity, including significant stratification or ranking. But as studies of material exchange and outliers have generally failed to suggest any clear-cut patterns of artifact redistribution (e.g., Cameron 1984:144; Powers, Gillespie, and Lekson 1983:343; Toll 1984:130), other interpretations have been developed.

In the most common alternative proposal, Chaco is seen as a religious or pilgrimage center with only a small resident population. Strong associations of Chacoan decorative styles with ritual structures in areas distant from the canyon (S. Plog 1990a) are consistent with the hypothesized importance of the canyon as a ritual center. Some who favor this perspective argue that it refutes proposals of significant sociocultural complexity by explaining the great houses, road networks, and outliers as a religious, as opposed to economic, phenomenon. To propose that the great houses or roads of Chaco were built for ritual purposes and therefore do not imply a significantly different level of sociocultural complexity, however, ignores the strong interrelationships that exist between religion, politics, and economics in virtually every society—prehistoric, ethnographic present, or contemporary—to which Chaco can be reasonably compared (see also Powers, Gillespie, and Lekson 1983:303). Thus, although we have much yet to understand about the specific nature of the Chacoan network, it seems clear that developments in the Chacoan system indicate a level of integration and regional alliance in the Southwest that has no parallel during earlier periods.

The development of the regional network centered on Chaco Canyon marks the beginning of a period in which centers of other regional networks developed in the central and northern Southwest. Ceramic data indicate that regional connections existed between such centers, meaning that increased connectivity existed between plateau and montane populations. Increasing evidence indicates that toward the late eleventh and early twelfth centuries, the focus of regional networks in northwestern New Mexico and southwestern Colorado shifted northward to sites along the San Juan (Toll 1985; Stein and McKenna 1988). H. Wolcott Toll (1985:421, 423, 487), for example, notes that most of the "outliers" north of Chaco Canyon postdate AD 1086, and by the early twelfth century there are more "Chacoan" sites in the north than in other sections of the network. Two concurrent changes in stylistic motifs also occurred: (1) reductions in mineral-paint wares decorated with the characteristic hatching motifs; and (2) increased use of carbon-painted ceramics with decoration characteristic of the northern San Juan and Mesa Verde regions (Toll 1985:429–30). Such changes may signal a shift in the center of the network from which information emanated.

This period also saw the shift to McElmo-style architecture in the canyon, a change that suggests a redefinition of public architecture (Toll 1985:487). It should be emphasized that the above changes did not necessarily involve northward movements of population, although the measurement of small- or large-scale population movements is difficult given existing chronological control. Rather, the shifts in the location of regional centers seem to involve a number of considerations: a change in the production focus of certain material items, the introduction and spread of new stylistic and architectural symbols, and perhaps the adoption of a different political and ideological system.

Although regional centers and regional systems can be identified, it should be emphasized that these systems or networks were not tightly bounded or controlled. Unlike the case of the Acholi, individual alliance networks in the Southwest maintained their own identity through the use of distinctive stylistic markers. When the full range of evidence regarding information and material exchange is examined, the data indicate that local populations were participating in a diverse set of networks. Toll (1985:451) notes that the source of Chacoan redwares was from the north at a time when the network had more of a southern and western orientation. Sources shifted to the south, however, as a more northern orientation of the network developed. Similarly, data from east-central Arizona (Hantman 1983, 1984) and northern Arizona (Hegmon 1986; S. Plog 1986b:319) are consistent with the hypothesis of diversification in alliances. Jeffrey Hantman (1983, 1984) argues that the maintenance of long-distance alliances was an important risk-reduction strategy for agricultural populations in the northern Southwest.

The late eleventh and early twelfth centuries began of a period of regional abandonments. Although Chaco and the northern San Juan may not have been depopulated, many local areas had begun to lose population in the late 1000s and were abandoned by AD 1130. This process started well before the much-discussed climatic changes of the twelfth century; the latter changes therefore were apparently not the stimulus. As the center of the Chacoan network shifted northward, competing centers developed in other parts of the northern Southwest, especially in the Rio Grande region, as they were bolstered by influxes of groups from nearby localities that were abandoned. By the middle of the thirteenth century, population clusters and regional centers existed in several areas, including the Rio Grande valley, Mesa Verde, Acoma, Zuni, Hopi, and across the southern Little Colorado drainage and Mogollon Rim country to the Verde Valley. Only some of these areas survived two additional periods of regional abandonments, first in the late thirteenth century and again in the late fourteenth and early fifteenth centuries.

LATE PERIOD ALLIANCES

Upham and L. Reed (1989) have shown that by the late fourteenth century there was a more or less continuous distribution of settlement clusters across the central and northern Southwest. Yet there were also far fewer settlements and significantly greater degrees of population aggregation—a pattern that is unique to this latest period of Southwestern prehistory. Moreover, highly distinctive ceramic traditions developed, and elaborate exchange networks linked populations across the region. These developments suggest that quite formal regional alliances had developed and that important changes were occurring in the nature of local integration.

Some of these changes at the local level have been described as increases in the complexity of local decision-making organizations that involved the centralization of leadership functions and the development of economic inequalities and social stratification (Cordell and F. Plog 1979; Upham 1982; Lightfoot 1984; Upham and F. Plog 1986). At the regional level, however, such changes appear discontinuous over space, and no pan-Southwestern sociopolitical or economic system developed. Instead, large regional alliances demarcated populations in different areas. One such alliance, the Salado alliance, has already been described. Another, the Jeddito alliance, has been described elsewhere by Upham (1982). The structure of this latter alliance differs markedly from the Salado alliance in that it appears that Jeddito Yellow Ware, a highly distinctive coal-fired pottery, was made in only a few locations (Upham 1982; Bishop et al. 1988) but was traded widely.

In the Rio Grande region, no clear-cut distributional patterns are apparent, but preliminary distributional analyses suggest that at least two, and perhaps three, major stylistic zones can be demarcated. These stylistic zones are defined by biscuit and glaze ware ceramic traditions, and perhaps by the localized distribution of Jemez Black-on-white. Generally, "biscuit ware pottery occurs primarily in the Abiquiu-Chama and Jemez Springs settlement clusters, whereas Rio Grande Glaze Ware, especially Glazes A through C, are found in the assemblages of all other settlement clusters, sometimes as the dominant bichrome or polychrome type" (Upham and L. Reed 1989:67).

This distributional pattern was first recognized by A. V. Kidder (1915), who noted that biscuit wares had a more northern distribution than glaze wares. He noted further that biscuit and glaze wares were differentially distributed on large sites, with biscuit wares predominating on large sites of the Pajarito Plateau such as Otowi, Tsankowi, and Tshirigi, and glaze wares being more common in large pueblos such as Puye, Tyounyi, and Yapashi. Kidder speculated about these broad stylistic zones but concluded that more work was needed to resolve the complex distributional patterns.

Unfortunately, such work has not yet been completed. Previous physicochemical characterization of these wares (Honea 1973; Shepard 1942; Warren 1970, 1979), however, has suggested probable production loci and the extent of exchange during the fourteenth and fifteenth centuries. More recently, Lori Reed (1990) has conducted additional source work on the Rio Grande glaze wares using x-ray diffractometry. This work allows limited speculation about the structure of alliances during this period.

The distinctive spatial distributions of these ware groups, with the highest concentrations occurring in core areas surrounding the zones of production, provide evidence of stylistic boundaries and interaction between populations occupying sites in the different production zones. Some biscuit ware is found on sites in the Pecos, Galisteo Basin, and Albuquerque settlement clusters; some Rio Grande glaze ware occurs on sites in the Abiquiu, Chama, and Jemez Springs settlement clusters. As we noted previously, however, the foundation of the alliance concept rests in the demonstration of high levels of interaction and trade, and in the differential distribution of specialized commodities that may not have been available to all members of a given population. Because analyses are preliminary, we cannot demonstrate that the above conditions are satisfied for the biscuit and glaze wares. Although the work of Anna Shepard (1942) and Helene Warren (1970, 1979) has clearly established restricted zones of production and widespread exchange for the Rio Grande glazes, we do not yet know enough about the stylistic characteristics of this pottery to offer a conclusion about the existence of alliance networks. One tentative conclusion that can be drawn on the basis of the ceramic stylistic and distributional data, however, is that style zones in the northern Rio Grande appear far less pronounced than those defined by Jeddito Yellow Ware or the Salado polychromes.

CONCLUSION

In this paper we have described a number of different alliance systems that operated at different times in the southern deserts of Arizona and in the central and northern Southwest. There are tantalizing pan-Southwestern temporal correlations in the development of these alliance systems, and we are tempted to seize upon these correlations to discuss pan-regional sociopolitical and economic issues. At this point, however, too little is known about the organizational structure of participating groups, the likely points of articulation between different regional alliances, or the synchronous or serial development of different alliance networks. Yet we note that by AD 900 in different areas of the Southwest, the move to ally with one's neighbors apparently affected groups from the Salt-Gila drainage to Chaco Canyon; by the early AD 1100s the alliances born of those needs had been replaced by other more localized alliance systems. Similarly, the emergence of the Salado and Jeddito alliances, and the apparent differences between them, suggests an opposition that may ultimately find its roots in intergroup conflict and regional warfare. Discussion of these points, however, is premature.

Earlier in this paper we indicated our preference for discarding the traditionally defined cultural labels that are used in the Southwest to describe the developmental sequences of different groups. We selected this course of action because our reading of Southwestern prehistory leads us to conclude that the ideas of common history and cultural homogeneity carried by terms like Hohokam, Mogollon, and Anasazi are antithetical to describing and explaining change. We have sought to demonstrate our conclusions regarding this point by showing how local groups with different demographic characteristics, subsistence strategies, mortuary practices, and settlement patterns joined together in alliances to buffer environmental risk, obtain mates, and exchange goods and information. These events are not unique to specific areas of the Southwest; rather, they are typical of most Southwestern regions. Although the scale of alliance systems varied markedly through time, we believe that alliances can be defined for virtually all time periods.

To illustrate the kinds of connections we believe may have existed in some parts of the Southwest at certain times, we have leaned heavily on the prehistory and history of the Acholi of Uganda. The Acholi provide the quintessential example of how dispersed local groups who did not share a common culture or language forged alliances with their neighbors. These alliances were predicated on the adoption of a common sociopolitical order and the development of important economic connections that allowed the Acholi to acquire key resources and buffer environmental risk. Moreover, these alliances were signaled by the sharing of key elements of material culture that were stylistically unique. The regional distribution of these key stylistic elements thus defined the spatial extent of the alliance system that ultimately came to mark a distinctive Acholi ethnicity and culture.

In this context, we believe the example of the Acholi can be brought home to the Southwest: the processes by which autonomous local groups were linked into larger cooperating networks is a key to explaining the course of Southwestern prehistory. Although we do not know the extent of ethnic and linguistic diversity in the prehistoric Southwest, we suspect it was great. Moreover, we suspect that the distribution of key stylistic markers like ballcourts, hatched designs on black-on-white pottery, the Salado polychromes, or Jeddito Yellow Ware are actually masking cultural heterogeneity while signifying union within a larger alliance network. Most importantly, however, we believe it is far more fruitful to begin with an idea of cultural heterogeneity and adaptive variability—even at the seemingly benign level of identifying groups as either Hohokam, Mogollon, or Anasazi—and to presume that a common ethnicity and cultural identity emerged only after (if at all) previously unaffiliated groups embraced a new form of social, political, and/or economic organization embodied in the distinct alliances we have described.

10

The Scream of the Butterfly
Competition and Conflict in the Prehistoric Southwest

DAVID R. WILCOX AND JONATHAN HAAS

 THE QUESTION OF WARFARE or competition and conflict in the prehistoric Southwest is an empirical issue. In this paper, we explore the current state of knowledge about this issue, arguing that such processes did exist and that explanations of the evolution of Southwestern societies must reckon with them. Our objective here is not to present such a reckoning, but rather to assemble data that document the reality of conflict and competition in the prehistoric Southwest and to appeal for greater consideration of these important variables.

The issue of competition and conflict hinges in large part on what social units were potentially in contention, and on what their ideologies were. Were individuals, households, superhouseholds, villages, regional systems, multivillage polities, states, or empires in competition with one another? The nature of competition and conflict clearly depends on the nature of the players and their objectives.

Similarly, the assessment of any sample of data from the archaeological record is contingent on our interpretation of its social and ideological context. If a burial with a projectile point in its back dates to a period when only band-level societies existed, the possible explanations for this episode of violent behavior are more limited than they would be if the burial dated to a time-space context characterized, for example, by multivillage polities separated by no-man's lands. A nasty little murder may be the best explanation in either case, but many more alternatives must be considered in the latter case than in the former.

A review of the evidence for warfare, raiding, violence, and conflict in the prehistoric Southwest reveals bouts of conflict at different times and places. This is unsurprising, given the prevalence of conflict and warfare among ethnographically known tribal populations and the extensive evidence of warfare in the Southwest in the historic record (Ellis 1951; Dutton 1963; Jones 1966; Dozier 1970; Haas and Creamer 1993; Creamer and Haas 1991). The nature, intensity, duration, extent, causes, and effects of prehistoric competition and conflict in the region, however, remain unclear.

The data do indicate that tribal-level warfare was probably not always endemic throughout the Southwest. In all the subregions there are long periods with no signs of conflict or warfare in settlement patterns, burial populations, or art. Reduced levels of conflict or fear of competing neighbors may have been periodically achieved due to the successful spread of religious ideologies or the formation of economic alliances (e.g., ritual congregations) (Bean and Vane 1986:663). The absence of evidence, of course, does not prove the absence of warfare. But those periods during which the people were not preoccupied with defensive site locations and there are no signs of violence in skeletal remains stand in sharp contrast to the periods that evidence such preoccupation and conflict. Therefore, although we may not now be able to make absolute statements about the presence or absence of warfare, we can make direct interpretations about periods of significantly greater and lesser warfare.

None of the models of competition and conflict discussed here applies across the Southwest as a whole. Each seeks to shed light on the processes identified in a particular area, but none adequately accounts for the broader patterns that characterize the available data. Why were some periods and some areas more violent than others? Why did the individualistic pattern of head-hunting and stockaded households that appears to characterize the early centuries AD cease in Pueblo II/ Classic Mimbres/Sedentary Hohokam times? Why do no-man's lands emerge, and what are the social and political processes that produce them? What, in short, accounts for the *evolution* of systems of competition and conflict in the greater Southwest? To answer these questions, the kind of generalizations arrived at here must be examined in the context of Southwestern prehistory as a whole. Although such a synthesis is beyond the scope of this paper, several preliminary observations can be formulated.

EARLY DATA AND MODELS

The idea that many Pueblo sites were defensive or defensible was first proposed by American observers in the nineteenth and early twentieth centuries (Hodge 1877; Holmes 1878; Morgan 1881; Bourke 1884:285; Cushing 1892; Hewett 1906; Jeançon 1912). Some of the early observers (for example, Amiel Whipple [Foreman 1941:191]) were trained military officers who were impressed by the relatively inaccessible locations of these sites and by certain architectural characteristics—high walls without doorways, "loop holes," walls across mesas, and the like—that could have made attack difficult. Early excavations also revealed some bodies with projectile points in them (Wormington 1947), bodies without heads, or burials with skulls only (Roberts 1931:169); a "war club" was also found (Judd 1952). Many of these features are universal in the record of human conflict (Rowlands 1973; Ferguson 1984; Vencl 1984; Otterbein 1985).

J. A. Jeançon (1912), in his excavations at Pesedeuinge in the Chama Valley, found that the pueblo had been burned and that it contained a body whose "skull was crushed by a large stone that almost filled it." Jeançon concluded that "the whole place was destroyed by enemies who drove out those of the inhabitants that they could and, after killing the rest, set fire to all portions of the buildings that would burn" (Jeançon 1912:30). Later work in the Chama Valley showed that it remained unoccupied for centuries, until in the late 1200s a series of plaza-centered palisaded fort sites was built (Peckham 1981; Beal 1987). Many of the later Pueblo IV sites were either strongly fortified or exhibit evidence of violence (Wendorf 1953; Beal 1987), suggesting that these sites occupied a perilous frontier. The area was abandoned shortly before Coronado's entrada in AD 1540.

Direct evidence of violent death was found repeatedly in the earliest generations of archaeological exploration of the Southwest. The first reported excavation in Arizona was conducted by George Banghart in the Chino Valley north of Prescott; in a burned room containing several bodies he "satisfied himself that the occupants . . . were besieged and murdered" (*Arizona Weekly Miner* 1872; see also Hodge 1877:189–90). In a Basketmaker II site, the Wetherills found "spear-points between the ribs, stone arrow-heads in the backbone, a great obsidian spear driven through the hips, crushed skulls and severed limbs" (Prudden 1897:61; see also Prudden 1896:560; Hurst and Turner 1990). In a late Pueblo III site near Petrified Forest, Hough (1903:313) found a mass grave with burned and fractured human bones; he concluded that "undoubtedly here was evidence of cannibalism" (this conclusion has recently been confirmed by Christy Turner [personal communication, 1989]). Pepper (1920) reports another case of cannibalism from Peñasco Blanco in Chaco Canyon.

Even more remarkable is a statement made by Pedro Pino, the former governor of Zuni, who told John Bourke in 1881 that human sacrifice was once widely practiced by the Pueblos:

> In the days of long ago (*eu el tiempo de cuanto hay* [before the Spanish entrada]) all the Pueblos, Moquis, Zuni, Acoma, Laguna, Jemez, and others had the religion of human sacrifice (*el oficio de matar los hombres*) at the time of the Feast of Fire, when the days are shortest. The victim had his throat cut and his breast opened, and his heart taken out by one of the Cochinos (priests); this was their 'oficio' (religion), their method of asking good fortune (*pedir la suerte*). (Bourke 1884:196)

To our knowledge, Pino's statement has never been critically discussed in the anthropological literature. How credible is it? We believe some kind of sacrifice is plausible. A kiva mural at Pottery Mound (Hibbin 1975:67–69) arguably shows a sacrificial scene, with an adult female as the victim. In the 1920s, two Mimbres pots were found with nearly identical scenes showing a priest in a horned serpent costume holding a knife in one hand and a decapitated human head in the other; a zigzag line connects the head to a headless body lying next to the priest

(Fewkes 1923:pl. 13; LeBlanc 1983:pl. 76). The highly unusual death assemblage in Pueblo Bonito—consisting of the disarticulated skeletons of women and children who were successively interred in two arguably sacred areas of the site (Fritz 1978) above the floors under which six fully extended adult male burials were found (two of them the turquoise-rich burials under Room 33) (Pepper 1909; Judd 1954; Akins 1986)—could also have resulted from periodic human sacrifice (Wilcox 1991a; for similar assemblages, see also Morris 1924; Lister 1965:13–29). If we take seriously the possibility that ritual human sacrifice was practiced in the Southwest, as it was in many parts of North America (see Trigger 1991:559), we must next ask who was sacrificed—and consider the possibility that the victims were captives.

Nomad Versus Pueblo: Kidder's Theory

To A. V. Kidder (1924), the issue was not "Are these sites defensive?" but "Who was the enemy?" Kidder opted for Athapaskans, postulating that these hunter-gatherers—clearly intrusive into the Southwest (see Wilcox 1981a)—were responsible for forcing the Pueblos first to aggregate into large settlements and then to abandon vast areas.

The theme of "enemy peoples"—warlike hunter-gatherers from outside the Southwest who attack and oppress peaceful farmers—has been an enduring one in the Southwestern literature (Reagan 1931; Jett 1964; Ambler and Sutton 1989). Numic speakers from the Great Basin, however, have replaced Athapaskans as the "enemy" in most of these models. If in fact there were local hunter-gatherer populations within the Southwest (Stuart and Gautier 1981; Upham 1984; Fetterman and Honeycutt 1990), other scenarios are also logically possible. In particular, "hill people," who may have been only marginally agricultural, may have engaged in regular raiding against the valley or basin peoples (see Dyson 1985); such may have been the relationship, for example, between the Piedra-Rosa-Largo-Gallina populations and Chacoan people (see Hall 1944).

A different approach to the issue of farmer/hunter-gatherer interactions has been developed in studies of protohistoric Pueblo-Plains relationships (Kelley 1952, 1986a; Gunnerson 1956; Wilcox 1981a, 1984, 1991b; Spielmann 1982; Baugh 1982, 1984, 1986). Kelley (1952), in an elegant paper, showed how trade and raid interactions could alternate as environmental conditions fluctuated. Spielmann (1982) has applied ecological theory, invoking the concept of "mutualism" to account for the interactions. Baugh (1984) and Wilcox (1984, 1991b), in contrast, have applied a version of world systems theory, reaching substantially different conclusions from Spielmann (1991a).

Pueblo Versus Pueblo: Linton's Theory

The first sophisticated anthropological model of competition and conflict in the Southwest was proposed by Ralph Linton in 1944. In a mere five pages, Linton deftly argued against the nomad-raid model and in favor of internecine conflict among Pueblo villages. Taking the defensive character of Pueblo III Anasazi sites as his initial premise, Linton (1944) pointed out that recent anthropological and archaeological studies had shown that (1) it is improbable that nomadic food gatherers were warlike; (2) the nomads were vastly outnumbered by the Pueblos; (3) the nomads were less organized than the Pueblos; and (4) "both [the] folk-lore of the Pueblo people and their behavior prior to the final Spanish conquest [1696?] seem to indicate that they were . . . quite ready to assume the offensive when occasion offered" (Linton 1944:30; see also Jones 1966):

> The American nomad raider had to come and go on foot, and the Ana-sazi warriors, numerous and fresh from the village, must have been formidable in pursuit as well as in defense. That the nomads were able to wear down the Anasazi settlements and eventually to drive out their inhabitants by successive attacks is, under the circumstances, highly questionable. (Linton 1944:30)

Considering the issue further, Linton (1944:31) looked for skeletal evidence of violent death, which he thought indicated "neighborhood brawls rather than foreign invasions." "Finally, if the nomads forced out the Anasazi, we would expect them to occupy the land taken, but in fact there is a long hiatus before we have any evidence of nomad occupation in these areas" (Linton 1944:31). (This argu-ment remains sound today, even if we accept the new dates for Athapaskan (or Ute) occupation in the upper San Juan after AD 1450 [Hogan 1989; Brown 1990].)

As an alternative, Linton (1944:31) suggested that internecine strife accounts for the defensive character of cliff dwellings:

> Most tribal wars are intermittent. . . . The rapid growth of population which took place in the area from Basketmaker III well into Pueblo III coupled, toward the end of the period, with soil exhaustion and re-current droughts must have resulted in bitter competition for any good agricultural land still available. *This competition might be expected to be especially severe between adjoining communities, where land which had been seized could be exploited from the established pueblo.* There must have been an increase in neighborhood wars, like that which later wiped out Awatobi, and such mass attacks may well have been preceded by years of bickering and reciprocal raids on crops. (Linton 1944:31; empha-sis added)

Having stated his hypothesis, Linton then claimed that it was both coherent and fruitful:

> The building of fortifications by one group would necessitate similar action by other groups, and the accumulation of defensive works, may, perhaps, be interpreted as a sort of armament race undertaken both for immediate safety and in preparation for the time when the communi-

ties would have to join battle for the dwindling fields on which their existence depended. (Linton 1944:30–31)

Cumulative soil exhaustion and droughts (not warfare) seemed to Linton to be the principal cause for abandonment. If the Anasazi had also rather thoroughly hunted out the game, these conditions would have made the area uninhabitable; hence, the hiatus of occupation is explained.

THE LARGO-GALLINA DATA SET: A CASE STUDY

The generation that experienced World War II was much influenced by Linton's arguments. Other scholars began to take seriously the possibility of violence and conflict as causative factors (Bennett 1946; Reed 1948; Ellis 1951; Woodbury 1959). After the war, excavations by the University of New Mexico's archaeological field school in the Gallina area, high in the mountains near the Continental Divide in northern New Mexico, produced the most convincing and diverse evidence yet documented for violence during Pueblo III (Upham and P. F. Reed 1989). We present these data here as a coherent case study and a contrast to the thematic approach adopted below.

Clearly, dozens of Gallina people were murdered (Blumenthal 1940:12; Hibben 1948; Bahti 1949:55; Pendleton 1952:149; Green 1962:154; Green 1964:35, 39; Chase 1976; Mackey and Holbrook 1978; Mackey and Green 1979). Supporting data include multiple mass burials with arrows embedded in them, a shark's tooth embedded in an ilium, a stone axe embedded in a skull, and cut marks on bone. The burials were found in burned towers or houses; many of the towers of the Gallina sites are visible from one another (Sleeter 1987). A recent probabilistic survey (Mackey and Holbrook 1978:47) found that of 183 habitation sites, 62 (34 percent) were burned and 127 (69 percent) had a defensive (or defensible) location, and that of 116 Gallina skeletons, 49 (42 percent) have been found unburied on the floors of burned habitation structures.

Sleeter's data on interconnections among the Gallina pueblos fall into three groups that appear to correspond with three of the five settlement clusters he defined (Upham and P. F. Reed 1989:155). The evidence for warfare has been attributed to neighbor fighting neighbor (Schulman 1950; Green 1964:36; Mackey and Green 1979). Paralleling Linton (1944), Mackey and Holbrook (1978; Holbrook and Mackey 1976) attribute abandonment of this area to reduced crop success due to decreasing effective moisture. The possibility of conflict with people in neighboring regions also merits consideration.

ARCHITECTURAL DATA SUPPORTING COMPETITION AND CONFLICT

Before discussing more recent models of conflict and competition, we examine in greater detail the data that provide the empirical basis for such arguments: first, architectural data, and then five other classes of archaeological data that indicate the reality of competition and conflict. The distribution of masonry towers has long been seen as a basis for inferences of warfare in the prehistoric Southwest (Schulman 1950). Malcolm Farmer (1957) also included "palisades," "forts," hill-slope "retreats" (trincheras), "fortified villages," and "guard" villages in his typology of "defensive systems." We briefly discuss each of these architectural classes.

TOWERS

Networks of isolated masonry towers, towers connected to kivas by tunnels, or towers otherwise incorporated into masonry roomblocks are known to the west in the Hovenweep area of southeastern Utah, to the east in the Gallina country (and possibly the Chama), and to the south in Canyon de Chelly. Between these boundaries, they occur in the Sand Canyon, McElmo Canyon, Johnson Canyon, and Mesa Verde areas.

Towers have long been known to be intervisible, and systematic studies have been completed in the Gallina (Sleeter 1987) and Hovenweep areas (Dallas 1977 cited in Winter 1981). At Hovenweep, Dallas found that: "each of the towers could be seen from at least two others, and that some of them could be seen from more distant mesa top ruins, which in turn could be seen from other suspected towers many miles away. [Dallas] proposed that this demonstrated a long distance signal network that could have been used for defensive purposes" (Winter 1981:31)

Intervisibility would have facilitated signaling between sites, and signaling systems are often constructed in times of danger (Sawyer 1982:78). Most towers date to the thirteenth century AD (Winter 1981; Sleeter 1987; Rohn 1977; Ahl-strom 1985), but some of those in the Mesa Verde region and the Chaco system were built as early as the late 1000s and early 1100s (Rohn 1977:239; Lekson 1984; Stein and McKenna 1988).

Interestingly, towers are distributed in a series of contiguous areas within the greater Mesa Verde region and, contemporaneously, in the nearby Gallina area (Schulman 1950:290). What lies in between are the lower Largo, Piedra, and Pine drainages, which were all wholly abandoned by AD 1125 (Mera 1935; Hall 1944; Eddy 1966, 1977). Clearly, the Gallina set is distinct from the rest and is inter-nally differentiated into several intervisible tower systems (Sleeter 1987; Upham and P. F. Reed 1989). What remains unknown (but knowable) is whether or not there are also, within the greater Mesa Verde region, distinct *sets* of intervisible tower sites that are not intervisible from one another. Haas and Creamer (Haas 1989; Haas and Creamer 1993) have documented such a boundary within the Kayenta region southwest of Mesa Verde (see below), and it seems likely that such boundaries will be found in the Mesa Verde region as well. If so, the general picture may be one of a large series of discrete settlement clusters, with formal systems for communication within each cluster. Political alliances among the vil-lages in each group would thus appear likely.

An alternative interpretation of towers is offered by Arthur Rohn (1977, 1989), who suggests that they were ceremonial structures. Rohn states that "too many of the towers stand among other residential and ceremonial buildings making them ineffective sentinels, most are closely associated with adjacent kivas, virtually all exhibit the same masonry found in kivas (and different from domestic room masonry), and some isolated towers occupy settings consistent with known shrines" (Rohn 1989:149).

Let us examine this argument. Rohn presents no quantitative data and makes no attempt to experiment, as did Winter (1981) and Sleeter (1987). It is significant that many towers are connected to kivas by tunnels, or are otherwise associated with kivas, and that many are built using a similar masonry style, but other interpretations of these data are possible. Consider, for example, the circular structures archaeologists call kivas, which are widely thought to be "ceremonial" structures—that is, architectural spaces dedicated to ceremonial activity. Lekson (1988) and Cater and Chenault (1988) have shown that these circular structures quite probably were primarily habitation structures. It follows, then, that it would be eminently sensible to have a tunnel as an escape hatch into a defensive tower from one's principal habitation (see also Mackey and Green 1979). We conclude that the association of towers with kivas strengthens, rather than weakens, the defense hypothesis.

PALISADES

Increasing numbers of substantial wooden stockades have been excavated in recent years. Hall (1944) first reported Rosa phase stockaded settlements that date in the mid to late 800s (Ahlstrom 1985). Others dating to the subsequent Piedra phase (AD 880–950) were later found along the lower Piedra River in the nearby Navajo Reservoir District (Eddy 1966; Ahlstrom 1985). Basketmaker III palisades have also been found in the Mesa Verde region (Carlson 1963; Rohn 1975), and recent contract archaeology projects are revealing more that date from Basketmaker III and later (Kuckelman and Morris 1988; Larry Hammack, personal communication 1989). A stockaded farmstead dating to the early 1100s was excavated by Seaman (1976) in the Gallina country (see Stuart and Gauthier 1981:43).

All of the stockaded sites cited above were farmsteads where a nuclear or extended family lived. In the Piedra phase along the lower Piedra River, a central pithouse was rebuilt in place many times, evidencing a settlement duration of several generations (Eddy 1966). Similar patterns are apparent at other stockaded sites (Rohn 1975). If the palisades did serve a defensive function, it was most likely to enhance a household's ability to defend the productive agricultural land in the vicinity of the settlement. But how common were such palisades? We agree with Rohn's position on this:

> Either most prehistoric Basketmaker-Pueblo settlements had no stockade, or archaeologists have consistently failed to discover them. I favor

the second alternative, especially for the older sites, because excavators generally restrict their efforts to the visible or productive features. I am inclined to believe that a great many, if not most of the Basketmaker III through Pueblo II settlements once were surrounded by stockades. (Rohn 1975:117)

Palisades appear in the Kayenta area (on Black Mesa) in the early 1100s (Shirley Powell, personal communication 1989) and in the late thirteenth century: Lindsay (1969) reports a ring of postholes surrounding the pithouses of Neskahai Village in the Glen Canyon area. Clearly, more broad-scale stripping (an excavation technique to look for postholes) of sites is needed to test Rohn's hypothesis.

But were the palisades really intended for defense? One suggested alternative is that they were needed to mark household boundaries or to keep children, dogs, or turkeys inside the farmyard (Walt 1985; Rohn 1989:149). The large size of the posts used, however, and their number, would have entailed a huge amount of construction work for a single household. As possible turkey pens, the massive palisades differ considerably from the flimsy *jacals* used to make well-attested turkey pens, where noticeable deposits of turkey droppings (or their residues) are found. Finally, supposing that the palisades were turkey pens would imply that the humans lived in the same space as the turkeys. Jean Pinkley (1965:71) tried this at Mesa Verde and does not recommend it: "The birds were arrogant, defiant, noisy, dirty pests, and we decided, for their own good and for the sake of our sanity, that steps had to be taken to drive them back to the wilderness." But the attempt failed, and Pinkley (1965:72) concludes that the Anasazi had no alternative but to "corral them at night and herd them during the day." Palisades, then, if designed with turkeys in mind, were more likely intended to keep turkeys out than to keep them in! Most likely, however, their primary purpose was to keep out dangerous humans, not annoying fowl.

FORTS

"Forts" were first reported in the Flagstaff and Walnut Creek areas by military observers in the nineteenth century (Whipple in Foreman 1941). One of the sites reported by Whipple (and Fewkes 1912) has recently been mapped (fig. 10.1). Colton (1939a, 1946) and Hargrave (1933, 1938) studied a number of other "fort" sites both east and west of the San Francisco Peaks in the Sinagua and Cohonina areas, respectively. Comparable sites are found in the Verde Valley (Schroeder 1947), Agua Fria (Cushing 1892; Wood 1978; Spoerl 1984), the Prescott area (Hodge 1877; Page 1970; Austin 1977; Ryan 1988), and the Aquarius Plateau west of Prescott (Colton 1939b). Austin (1977) showed that sets of these sites in the Prescott area are intervisible, as are some along the Agua Fria (Spoerl 1984). Recent work by the Museum of Northern Arizona/Northern Arizona University archaeological field school in the Cohonina area has shown that some of the walled-plaza

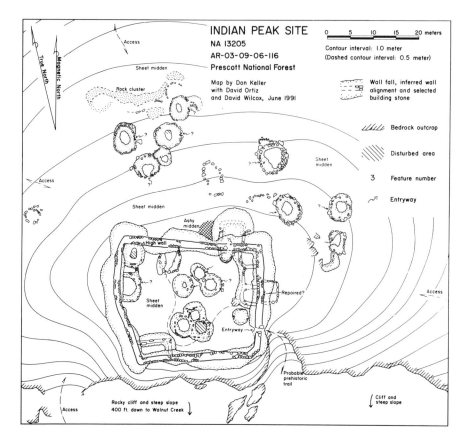

Figure 10.1. Map of the Indian Peak Fort Site along Walnut Creek, west-central Arizona.

sites are intervisible (Michaelson 1988), and we have confirmed earlier reports that they date in the 1000s (Remley 1989). Most Sinagua forts date to the Elden phase (Colton 1946), which Wilcox (1986a) places at AD 1150 to 1250.

Most of these fort sites are located on a high prominence; they usually have a massive wall surrounding three or four sides of a central plaza. Some have room-blocks associated; others do not. Some have plentiful quantities of artifacts; others only a few. Where adequate settlement data are available, such sites in the Cohonina area are found to be the largest in their localities and time periods. Some of these sites are judged to be more defensible than others in terms of ease of access, openness, and so on. We hesitate, however, to conclude that all such sites were in fact forts; their diversity still defies ready interpretation, and some might be shrines or places of religious retreat.

If we focus on the Elden phase sites, however, and notice their association with "fortified sites" like Wupatki or Citadel Ruin and the cliff dwellings of Walnut

Canyon, the fort interpretation has more appeal. Skeletal evidence for violence has also been reported from this region (Smith 1952:20, 53, 67, 179–80; Ezell and Olson 1955; Fay and Klein 1988; Turner and Turner 1990).

Forts are also reported in other parts of the Southwest. Tsiping, Riana, Palisade, and Leafwater are all famous forts in the Chama Valley at the north end of the late prehistoric Pueblo distribution (Hewett 1906; Peckham 1981; Beal 1987). On the south end of the Pueblo domain, Late Elmendorf phase sites are in highly fortified positions, with a wide no-man's land to the south (Marshall and Walt 1984). The expansion of Glaze A sites into that no-man's land was protected by having the largest site (San Pascual) located at the south end of the distribution; a new no-man's land then occurred farther south (Marshall and Walt 1984; Wilcox 1991b).

HILL-SLOPE RETREATS

Trincheras (Sauer and Brand 1931) are another class of feature long thought to be defensive refuges (Blackiston 1908; Cushing 1892; Hayden 1957; Fontana, Greenleaf and Cassidy 1959; Di Peso 1974a; Gregory 1979; Spoerl 1984; Gerald 1990). They occur in southern Arizona (Stacy 1974), northern Sonora (Pailes 1980), and northwestern Chihuahua (Di Peso 1974a). Many of the Chihuahuan sites are walls across drainages and are certainly agricultural terraces (Herold 1965; Luebben, Andelson, and Herold 1986); other stone walls that occur near the foot of hill slopes may also be agricultural (Sauer and Brand 1931; Fish, Fish, and Downum 1984).

David Wilcox (1979a, 1979b, 1987, 1988b, 1989b; Wilcox, McGuire and Sternberg 1981; Wilcox and Sternberg 1983) has championed the hypothesis that the hilltop trincheras in many cases were defensive features. In a two-year quantitative study of the dry-laid walls on Tumamoc Hill in Tucson, he found that their morphology and distribution is best explained by a warfare or defensive refuge hypothesis: (1) although only about half a meter high, the walls would have afforded good protection from bow-and-arrow attack from below; (2) the cleared space behind the walls would have given defenders a natural advantage in hand-to-hand combat with attackers standing on the treacherous loose rock of the revetment wall; (3) the greatest numbers of walls are on the gentlest slopes, and the fewest on the steepest; and (4) wall openings are designed in such a way that defenders could control access (Wilcox 1979a).

Alternative hypotheses were also considered and rejected, among them the possibilities that the walls may have marked trails or agricultural plots. If the cleared space behind the wall was the objective, the features may have been trails, except that several such spaces led into cliff faces. A few areas of deep soil are present, suggesting the possibility of agricultural plots, but the vast majority of the spaces, though cleared, are also rocky (Wilcox 1979a). Efforts to test the feasibility of agriculture on the hill continue to be made (Fish, Fish, and Downum 1984; Katzer 1987; Fish and Fish 1989).

Another class of hill-slope retreats has also been identified. Mimbres sites dating to the early pithouse period (AD 200–650) are characteristically found on high, isolated buttes, often some distance from the nearest watercourse (LeBlanc 1983; Anyon 1984). It is not known if any of them were palisaded. Following the introduction of the bow and arrow in this area, settlement location shifted down into the river valleys (LeBlanc 1983:45; see also Blitz 1988). Similar settlement shifts during the same general time period are also reported farther north (Irwin-Williams 1973; Stewart 1980; Hayes 1981; Haury 1985).

FORTIFIED VILLAGES AND HAMLETS

Farmer (1957:250) defines "fortified villages" fairly broadly: they are "so arranged that the village layout formed a defensive unit. It may or may not include such features as defensive walls, palisades, retreat alcoves, towers, or forts." They may also be located on a high point of land or in a cliffside rockshelter. Though he has in mind mainly Pueblo III and IV large pueblos, Farmer (1957:255) also includes the large Chaco sites (see also Morris 1939:43; Judd 1959:7; Judd 1964) and Hohokam Classic period compounds. The Fortified Hill Site in Gila Bend (Greenleaf 1975) would also qualify.

Most of the sites included in this class were formed by the aggregation of multiple household units. After AD 1250 to 1300 they most often consisted of a central plaza enclosed by the roomblock and connected to the outside world by a narrow corridor (Reed 1956; Adams 1989). "The plaza lay-out inside a high unbroken exterior wall, and the sizable force of warriors which such towns could muster, would have put them in far more favorable positions than when [they were] small and openly constructed" (Woodbury 1959:131).

No doubt the plazas were increasingly important as centers of ceremony (Haury 1950; Reed 1956), but that was also true in the Southeast at this time (Morse and Morse 1983; Walthall 1980; Smith 1986). Southeastern sites had palisades around them, some settlements had been burned to the ground, and in many places regional abandonment occurred or no-man's lands opened up between settlement clusters that were over a day's walk apart (Morse and Morse 1983; Hudson et al. 1985; Dye and Cox 1990; see also Engelbrecht 1985). Identical processes occurred in the Southwest (see below), but large Southwestern pueblos did not often have palisades because their high outside walls were a perfect substitute for them.

GUARD VILLAGES

The most famous instance of a "guard village"—a settlement established to inhibit access to a larger cluster of settlements—is Hano, a Tewa site on First Mesa at Hopi (Dozier 1954; Farmer 1957). *Genizaro* settlements in New Mexico during the eighteenth century, where war captives were forcibly settled, were also guard villages (Dozier 1970), and Farmer (1957:255–56) suggests that several sites near Chaco Canyon (such as Pueblo Pintado and Tzin Kletzin) may have been guard villages as well. Jeançon (1922) identified a site controlling access to Chimney Rock Pueblo as a guard site. The "Guardian Pueblo" occupied in the thirteenth century in the Glen Canyon area blocks access to the community of sites on Segazlin Mesa and is a good example of this type of site (Lindsay et al. 1968). The strategy thus may be quite old in the Southwest and should be discernable in numerous settlement systems.

FIVE OTHER CLASSES OF DATA

Five other classes of data support the hypothesis that competition and conflict existed in the prehistoric Southwest: (1) artifacts; (2) burned sites; (3) skeletal evidence; (4) rock art; and (5) no-man's lands. We shall argue that the cumulative weight of these data strengthens the likelihood that conflict was endemic in the Southwest in several periods but perhaps less common in others. Another way to study conflict is to map the distribution of different site classes on regional or macroregional scales, looking for patterns of systemic interaction best explained in terms of competition and conflict (e.g., see Johnson 1973). Though the latter approach is beyond the scope of the present paper, we touch on it at several points, and it would be worth examining in this way the distributional parameters of the data assembled here.

ARTIFACTS

Atlatls and darts, bows and arrows, axes, and even sharks' teeth have been implicated as implements of murder in the Southwest. Clearly, however, all of these items could have been used for other purposes and are not, in themselves, evidence for conflict or competition (Peckham 1965; Grant 1979; Vencl 1984; Geib and Bungart 1989; Rohn 1989). Shields and "fending sticks" are another matter. Fending sticks are light, curved sticks about 1 to 1.5 m long that occur in dry cave deposits dating before AD 450. Experiments (Geib 1990) have shown that they work beautifully to fend off darts thrown with an atlatl. Shields became necessary once the bow-and-arrow appeared in the Southwest at around AD 450. Arrows shot with a bow move more rapidly and have greater penetrating power than do darts (Frison 1978).

The data on shields or body armor are diverse. Several Pueblo II or Pueblo III basketry-shield specimens have been found (Morris and Burgh 1941:41, 51). An anthropomorph with a quiver, painted on a Mimbres bowl, holds a shield with a butterfly symbol in one hand and a spear in the other (Bentley 1988:58). Though Rohn (1989:149–50) claims that early historic Pueblo and Plains shields were ineffective, he cites no supporting evidence. The use of body armor is suggested by a Mimbres design (Peckham 1965) and by a matched set of five bone ribs 133 mm to 165 mm long with holes drilled a short distance from each end that were found at Poshu Pueblo in the Chama Valley (Jeançon 1923:26).

Other artifactual support for conflict or competition is rare (Rohn 1989), but a

Mimbres pot showing arrows embedded in a human figure (Jelinek 1961) is worth mentioning. It should also be recalled that it was the artifact assemblage associated with the so-called magician burial from Ridge Ruin, an Elden phase site in the Flagstaff area, that led Hopi informants to tell McGregor (1943) that the burial was that of a war chief. Fewkes (1926:12–13) also interpreted decorated bone hairpins found near Young's Canyon in the Flagstaff area as what the Hopi call *herunka*, which were worn by warriors; similar artifacts have been found in burial contexts in many late prehistoric Southwestern sites (see Wilcox 1987:127–28).

Another "warrior" grave, found by Earl Morris (1924:192–95) in Room 178 at Aztec, had a large painted basketry shield with a wooden handle associated with a large male skeleton. Also present were two axes whose shapes suggested to Morris (1924:194) "that they were intended for use as weapons rather than as tools." (Jeançon [1923:18] similarly reports that bipointed axes called *tzii-wi* by the Tewa were used only for war.) A long knife of red quartzite lay in front of the left hand of the Aztec burial (Morris 1924:194). Similar knives are common in the archaeological record of the northern Southwest (Guernsey and Kidder 1921:15; Cole 1990:175, 183). Lengthwise across the Aztec warrior and above the shield a wooden object was found that "tapers from a handle at one end to a fairly broad blade at the other. It may have been a digging-stick, but one cannot escape the impression that it would have been serviceable if used as a sword" (Morris 1924:195). Randall Morrison suggests that similar wooden implements found in Chaco Canyon were swords (personal communication to Stephen Lekson, 1970s).

Burned Sites

Many factors may account for burned structures and even for totally burned sites (Cameron 1990). A regional pattern of high percentages of burned settlements, particularly when they also contain good floor assemblages or burned bodies, has been regarded as evidence of warfare (Morris 1939; Mackey and Holbrook 1978). Earl Morris, summing up his many years experience excavating in the La Plata–Animas area of the northern San Juan, concluded that "through Basket Maker III and Pueblo I catastrophic conflagrations were widespread. Rare is the dwelling of either of these ages which does not show signs of burning, and far more frequently than not a great proportion of the possessions of the occupants was destroyed by the blaze" (Morris 1939:41).

Although the presence of humans in these burned houses was extremely rare, Morris (1939:42) regarded the pattern of burning as good evidence of "troubled times." A strikingly different pattern was present during Pueblo II and early Pueblo III: "After Pueblo I, in that portion of the San Juan country which my observations have included, signs of fire and destruction do not again become frequent until well toward the close of Pueblo III [in the 1200s]" (Morris 1939:42). The late Pueblo III burning was usually associated with the removal of goods first, though Morris also documented several instances of violent death during the Pueblo III period (Morris 1939:42).

A recent library study by Catherine Cameron (1990) confirms the pattern seen by Morris (see also Rohn 1989:150; Schlanger and Wilshusen 1990), but Cameron argues against the warfare interpretation. Examination of her tables, however, shows that half of these burned sites did have intact floor assemblages, which increases the probability that the occupants were caught unawares by the event. Experiment has shown that it is not easy to burn a pithouse (Wilshusen 1986). Thus we conclude that the warfare hypothesis is still a strong contender as an explanation for these data.

We have assembled a far from exhaustive list of villages that may have been wiped out or attacked:

> The Coombs Site, south-central Utah, AD 1050–1200 (Lister, Lister, and Ambler 1960);

> Jones Ranch Road sites, between Manuelito Canyon and Whitewater Arroyo, 1100s and early 1200s (Anyon, Collins, and Bennett 1983:757);

> Horse Camp Mill Pueblo, west-central New Mexico, late 1200s (McGimsey 1980);

> Point of Pines Pueblo, east-central Arizona, late 1200s (Haury 1958);

> Chodistaas, Grasshopper Spring, and AZ P:14:197 (ASM), Grasshopper Plateau, late 1200s (Fish et al., this volume);

> Palisade Ruin, Riana, and Leafwater Ruin, Chama Valley, 1300s (Beal 1987);

> Gila Pueblo, central Arizona, late 1300s (Gladwin 1957);

> Kuaua Pueblo, central New Mexico, circa 1400 (Dutton 1963:25);

> Te'ewi and Pesedeuinge pueblos, Chama Valley, early 1400s (Wendorf 1953:46; Beal 1987).

We are confident that a careful search of the literature would turn up many more cases like this.

SKELETAL EVIDENCE

Several of the burned sites listed above also had skeletal assemblages that support the claim of warfare (Lister, Lister and Ambler 1960 [in the late 1000s component]; McGimsey 1980:38–42; Wendorf 1953:46; Anyon, Collins, and Bennett 1983:757). The case of Te'ewi is especially interesting because the physical anthropologist Eric Reed (1953) examined the bone:

> At least twenty-four adult and sub-adult individuals, possibly more, are represented—all males, and mostly very young men. There are also six small children or babies. None of these are "burials" in the usual sense; they were not deliberately laid-out inhumations, flexed or extended,

with accompanying offerings. Instead, they evidently are people who died where they were found in the burning of the kiva. (Reed 1953:104)

Six individuals were found above the fallen and burned roof; many showed signs of burning or violence (Wendorf 1953:46). Reed goes on to say that

a good many bones are broken and crushed, or appear chopped off— not, however, sufficiently frequently and definitely the latter, I believe, to justify a positive assertion that these people were killed by enemy action and flung into the kiva which then was fired. This intriguing thought is certainly a possibility, but I feel that the equally dramatic picture of the young men struggling to escape from the burning cere- monial chamber must also be suggested. (Reed 1953:104)

More details of the chopped-off bones would greatly improve this picture; the hypothesis of a tragic accident provides no explanation for even one occurrence of such an event, whereas the hypothesis of a devastating attack does. The latter hypothesis might also explain why the bodies found above the roof fall were not subsequently buried.

Arrow or dart points embedded in skeletons are pretty clear evidence of vio- lent death (Prudden 1897:61). Again, our list is not exhaustive, but it is interesting to find even this many cases: Morris 1919:185; Morris 1939:42; Guernsey and Kidder 1921:5; Cosgrove and Cosgrove 1932:25; Roberts 1940:136; Worming- ton 1947:71–72; Wormington 1955:87–88; Judd 1954:257; Shutler 1961:49; McGimsey 1980:169; Wiseman 1982; McKenna 1984:355.

Axe blows without the axe are less certain evidence of violence because a hole in a skull could be caused by several processes and physical anthropolo- gists have only rarely evaluated these cases. Several Basketmaker skeletons in the Prayer Rock district had their heads bashed in, and in one case healing had oc- curred (Morris 1959:222, 226). One of the two richest burials known from Chaco Canyon (the two males buried below the floor of Room 33 at Pueblo Bonito) had its head bashed in (Akins 1986:116). So too did several skeletons at Yellow Jacket (Rohn 1989:151), the skull of a young girl in Site 616 on Mariana Mesa (McGimsey 1980:41, 169), 25 skulls in a room at a Pueblo III site near Yucca House (Morris 1939:42), five bodies on the floor of a Pueblo III kiva at a site on the east branch of the Mancos River (Morris 1939:42), and three adults which were stretched out full length with their arms outspread at a Pueblo III site in the Animas Valley (Morris 1939:42). Scattered human bones have been found in Pueblo III rooms at the West Pueblo at Aztec, the Old Fort south of Farmington (Morris 1939:42), and at the Guadalupe Ruin (Pippin 1987:119). Two skeletons with crushed bones and two with broken necks are reported from TA 18 in the Rio Grande de Rancho area (Green 1963). Haas and Creamer (1993) found an isolated skull with its fore- head bashed in at a pithouse village dating to the late thirteenth century in the Klethla Valley in northeast Arizona.

One of the most dramatic cases of a Basketmaker II massacre was found by the Wetherills in Grand Gulch (Hurst and Turner 1990). Two later massacres are also known, one of which—in Battle Cave across from Antelope House—was reported by Ann Morris from Canyon del Muerto:

> Above the deepest [Basketmaker II] burials we found clear evidence of a dreadful prehistoric massacre. There were a large number of broken and cracked skulls. The nature of the fractures showed them to have been made with heavy stone axes—even children and babies had not been spared this brutality. There was one old lady who had been done to death in this summary fashion in the final hand-to-hand stage of the fighting who had in the preliminaries been shot with an arrow. It had pierced her left side at an angle from below. (Morris 1933:217)

Another massacre is reported by Paul Martin from southwestern Colorado in the "proto-Mesa Verde" Charnal House Tower:

> In the northeast corner we came upon a veritable mass of bones, which covered an area greater than six square feet. These bones represented individuals who had probably been killed or who had all died at the same time from other causes. However that may be, the bones were literally flung into this corner, one skeleton lying across another, in great confusion. One skull, to our great surprise, was covered with hair, which to all appearances, was thickly matted with blood. No other bones could be found for this skull nor for two others. There were in all eleven adults, three of which were females, and three infants. (Martin 1929:26)

Sometimes data on embedded projectiles or axe blows are not available (due to cremation of the dead, for example; but see Creel 1989). At other times, they are ambiguous: an illustration of this is found in the Hohokam area, where direct evidence for conflict and competition is rare (Fish and Fish 1989) but where two out of the five Classic period platform mounds that have been excavated had burials in them that might have resulted from violence. One (at Las Colinas) had an arrowpoint in the stomach cavity; two others (buried together at La Ciudad) had large holes in the skulls, one of which had a fragment of a stone axe associated with the hole (Saul 1981; Wilcox 1987:123). Is this a coincidence? Certainly that possibility cannot be excluded, but we believe the probability of such repeated coincidences would be exceedingly small.

Scalping is documented at both Chaves Pass and Grasshopper ruin, two fourteenth-century pueblos (Allen, Merbs, and Birkby 1985; see also Friederici 1907; Parsons 1924; Dutton 1963:81–97, 201–204). Trophy skulls with trepanning holes (for suspension) are known in the Southwest only from Paquimé (Casas Grandes) (Di Peso 1974; Ravesloot and Spoerl 1989). Skulls buried alone or headless skeletons, however, are much more widely distributed. In a Pueblo I site in the Kiatuthlanna district, Zuni River drainage, Roberts (1931:169) found a skull "without additional parts of the skeleton" in a ventilator shaft. He comments further that "the careful burial of two crania was noted at a Pueblo I site in southwestern Colorado" (Roberts 1930:163) and that "diggers have occasionally reported the finding of a headless skeleton" (Roberts 1931:169). One of the best documented cases of this sort was found in 1937 in Chaco Canyon, "on the floor of Kiva 6 in Site Bc51, just the skull alone, with a fracture on the te[m]ple and marks as of a stone knife at the base of the skull" (Kluckhohn and Reiter 1939:38–39). At least these reserachers looked for cut marks; would that all of these cases had been carefully examined by physical anthropologists!

Similar finds have been reported in the Hohokam and Mogollon areas. Cushing (1892) found a seated burial without a skull at Los Hornos, a Hohokam site in the Salt River Valley; Halseth (1936) states that "skull burials are reported from several places in and adjacent to the Hohokam region. I have found some here [at Pueblo Grande]"; and the skull was missing in eight out of 48 cases in burials from Mogollon Village (Haury 1936; Reed 1948). At the Swarts Ruin, the Cosgroves (1932:25) found that 160 of 1,009 burials were "disturbed." Some of these disturbances were clearly attributable to later intrusions, but many cases of only skull burials were found. Anyon and LeBlanc (1984) discuss the probability that a small group of headless skeletons and isolated skulls at the Galaz Site on the Mimbres River were deliberate burials.

Repeated cases of skull or skull-less burials are also reported from the Anasazi area. Gladwin (1945:58) found five well-preserved skeletons lacking heads and an isolated skull burial in Red Mesa phase contexts in the Red Mesa Valley. Reed (1948) states that a detached skull was found at Aztec by Civil Works Administration workers in 1933–34 and that Tom Onstott found headless skeletons in 1948 excavations in Frijoles Canyon. Rohn (1977:240) reports several isolated skull burials on Chapin Mesa in late Pueblo II contexts. A mass burial of approximately 29 bodies in Room 59 at Wupatki (early 1200s) contained only one skull, two hyoids, and four first-cervical vertebrae, but no cut marks were found on any of the 17 mandibles (Turner and Turner 1990). In the Taos area, four burials were found at Blumenschein's (1958) Site 103, which dates in the period AD 1100–1300.

A unique find in a much earlier context was the painted skin of an adult head with a string attachment found lying under the left shoulder of an 18-year-old female Basketmaker II mummy (Kidder and Guernsey 1919:74, 190–92); Kidder and Guernsey interpret the specimen as a trophy. Reagan (1933:57) also reports two prehistoric trophy scalps from a cave in the Fremont area along Nine Mile Canyon.

Numerous cases of disturbance in Basketmaker II cist graves have been reported, and most involve the removal of the crania (Kidder and Guernsey 1919; Guernsey and Kidder 1921:37; Nusbaum 1922; Lockett and Hargrave 1953; Morris 1959:219–20, 227–30). The explanation for this prehistoric removal of crania is uncertain. Possibly later people were searching for the shell beads that often occur in great quantities in these Basketmaker burials (Guernsey and Kidder 1921; Morris 1959:219–20), but such beads were not always taken (Lockett and Hargrave 1953; Morris 1959:304). Perhaps a form of witchcraft is involved (Jeffrey Dean, personal communication 1989). Alternatively, the heads may have been removed before the burials were interred. Examination of one specimen from Woodchuck Cave at the Museum of Northern Arizona revealed that the cranium was evenly removed just above the atlas vertebrae and that the neck area (in contrast to the rest of the body) was black, suggesting that the blood welled out when the head was cut off.

Interestingly, Roberts was absolutely unwilling to consider the obvious hypothesis of head-hunting: "There is nothing in the finding of the skulls in Colorado or at the Long H Ranch [Kiatuthlanna] to imply that the people could be considered, in any sense of the word, head hunters" (Roberts 1931:169). Head-hunting, however, was a widespread cultural practice in northern Mexico (Beals 1932, 1933, 1943) and California (Kroeber 1925:844; Beals 1932; Loeb 1932), and it could well have occurred in the Southwest as early as Basketmaker II and as late as the fourteenth century at Paquimé (Ravesloot and Spoerl 1989). Beals reports of the Acaxee in the mountains of eastern Sinaloa:

> Warfare was of two kinds—a community affair, the warriors going forth in bands, and a type of head-hunting, small parties waylaying the unwary on trails or in their fields, with the object of securing victims for cannibal feasts. Santaren says the reason for so many wars was that the people did not recognize any political heads to compose differences between the various groups. Wars were often between those of the same language. (Beals 1933:16)

Human sacrifice may also account for decapitation (Cosgrove and Cosgrove 1932:25).

Cannibalism has also been demonstrated to have occurred repeatedly in the American Southwest, from Basketmaker times to the protohistoric period (Hough 1903:313; Turner 1983). The physical anthropologist Christy Turner II and Jackie Turner have identified and studied the greatest number of cases of this practice (Turner and Morris 1970; Turner 1983, 1989; Turner and Turner 1990; see also Morris 1939:75; Reed 1948 [for a Patayán case found by Gordon Baldwin in 1947]; Bennett 1966a, 1966b; Flinn, Turner II, and Brew 1976; Hartman 1975; Nickens 1975b; Luebben and Nickens 1982; Nass and Bellantoni 1982; Olson 1966; Smith 1952; Rice, Hantman, and Most 1982; Fetterman, Honeycutt, and Kuckelman 1988; White 1991). Their identifications are based on the co-occurrence of the following criteria: cut marks, split long bones, burning, and anvil marks (Turner 1983; Turner and Turner 1990).

ROCK ART

Sally Cole (1984) has shown that the famous Green Mask site in Grand Gulch pictures a Basketmaker era head skin remarkably like the one found by Kidder and Guernsey (1919). Many other rock art depictions of flayed head skins are also known from southeastern Utah, some with the carrying loop and others worn by anthropomorphic figures (Cole 1985, 1989, 1990). Together with the assemblages of Basketmaker mummies without heads (Lockett and Hargrave 1953; Morris 1959) and the Basketmaker III evidence for palisaded sites, these data indicate a widespread Basketmaker pattern of head-hunting. Its motivation may in part have been religious, the flayed skins perhaps being a celebration of Xipe-Totec-like beliefs concerning the fertility of corn, a newly adopted cultigen in Basketmaker II times.

Although a few "battle scenes" have been reported (Reagan 1931:177; Jennings 1978:137, 139; Yohe, Sutton, and McCarthy 1986), the evidence for conflict and competition apparent in post-Basketmaker rock art consists mainly of "shield-bearing warriors" and the famous "trophy heads" displayed in the so-called Classic Vernal style found in the Uinta Basin of northeastern Utah (Reagan 1931; Beckwith 1935; Wormington 1955; Schaafsma 1971, 1980; see also Castleton and Madsen 1981). A "headhunter" scene is also present in Snake Gulch north of Grand Canyon (Greg Woodall, personal communication 1989). The shield-bearing warrior motif appears to be a horizon style dating to late Pueblo II and Pueblo III (Cole 1990; Loendorf 1990).

The Uinta Basin rock art is particularly interesting. Large anthropomorphic figures are shown holding heads and sometimes shields. They quite clearly pertain to the Fremont period, which Ambler (1966b) would date to the eleventh and twelfth centuries (but see Marwitt 1986:169). The rock art in the area immediately to the north and south of the Uinta Basin is distinct (Schaafsma 1971, 1980; Cole 1990). Contrasts in contemporaneous Archaic projectile point styles (Holmer 1985) also suggest that an ancient cultural boundary separated the Uinta Fremont populations from Plains-related groups to the north. We may wonder, then, if the trophy heads are an early instance of war propaganda that proclaimed the hubris of one of these populations vis-à-vis the others.

NO-MAN'S LANDS

No-man's lands are zones between settlement clusters that are habitable but not occupied. The suggestion that they are "everyman's lands" (a proposal of Jeffrey Dean's) is an important alternative hypothesis and implies that a variety of ephemeral "limited activity" sites should be present in them. No-man's lands are often interpreted as administrative (political) boundaries or as buffer zones that inhibit conflict due to the transportation costs that crossing them creates (Rowlands 1973; Johnson 1973:145–46). H. P. Mera (1935, 1938, 1940) was the first to document systematically a series of no-man's lands over 20 miles wide among the protohistoric Pueblos living along the Rio Grande. More recently collected settlement data arguably supports Mera's conclusions (Wilcox 1991a; see also Preucel 1987).

Steward (1941) was the first archaeologist to recognize that the Glen Canyon area may have been a no-man's land from late Basketmaker to middle Pueblo II.

His view is supported by many later studies (Aikens 1966:53; Matson, Lipe, and Haase 1988:259; Rohn 1989; Fairley 1989:119–20; Hegmon 1990). In the area characterized by the White Mesa variety of Piedra Black-on-white ceramics (Hurst, Bond, and Schwindt 1985), Fetterman and others conclude that "based on survey evidence it appears that Cottonwood Canyon and nearby Elk Ridge, Milk Ranch Point, Allen Canyon and Chippean Ridge served as home to a large population of Anasazi people during the period AD 800–900. Interestingly, much of the rest of what is now known as southeast Utah appears to have been abandoned during this time" (Fetterman, Honeycutt, and Kuckelman 1988:5).

In northeast Arizona, Haas and Creamer (1991) found a 15-kilometer gap between the occupations in two adjacent valleys. This gap had been occupied relatively continuously up until the late thirteenth century, and its appearance corresponds to the wholesale movement of people in this region into defensive site locations.

Upham (1982) and Jewett (1989:385) have shown that Pueblo IV settlements in Arizona occur in clusters, with "buffer" zones in between "that are nearly always greater than 20 or 25 kilometers, yet rarely exceed 70 kilometers in width, requiring 2–3 days to cross." The nearest neighbor of sites in a cluster is rarely more than 20 kilometers distant, and more often less than 10 kilometers (Jewett 1989). Mera's broad survey results document similar relationships for Pueblo IV settlements in New Mexico, and comparable relationships are present among late prehistoric sites in the Southeast (Hudson et al. 1985; Dye and Cox 1990).

No-man's lands have recently become more clearly documented in the Hohokam area, where they also emerge after AD 1100 (Debowski et al. 1976; Canouts 1975; Wilcox and Sternberg 1983; Wilcox 1988b; Wilcox 1989b; Fish and Fish 1989; Doelle and Wallace 1990, 1991). Dramatic changes in the structure of Hohokam settlement networks were thus brought about. Anomalous abandonments of sites like Snaketown (Haury 1976), Sacaton (Wasley 1960c), and Olberg in the Gila Valley (Wilcox 1979b), and Las Cremaciones (Wilcox 1985), Van Liere, and Cashion (Antieu 1981) in the Salt Valley can now, perhaps, be explained. As in other areas of the Southwest at this time, settlement clusters were forming. The expanding importance of platform mounds was one aspect of this process. By AD 1200, three distinct settlement clusters are apparent in the Phoenix Basin (fig. 10.2): one centered on Pueblo Grande in the lower Salt Valley, and two smaller ones in the middle Gila Valley, one of which was headed by Casa Grande (Wilcox and Shenk 1977; Wilcox 1988b). The radius of most circles shown in figure 10.2 is 22 miles, the distance it is said a person can travel on foot in a day (Drennan 1984).

The complexity of the fourteenth-century political landscape sketched in figure 10.2 is highlighted by the no-man's lands and spacing of distinct multisettlement polities. Abandonment of a 25-mile-wide zone of arguably still productive land between the Phoenix and Tucson basin *aggregates* of site clusters came about shortly before AD 1300 (Wilcox 1988b; Doelle and Wallace 1991; see Fish et al., this volume). Doelle and Wallace (1990, 1991) and McGuire (1991) have proposed that the Tucson Basin populations were already becoming culturally distinct

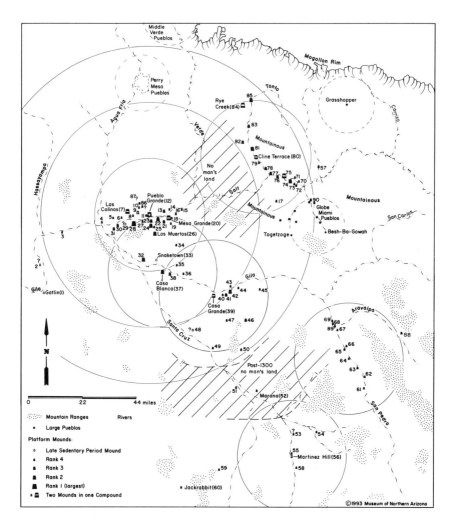

Figure 10.2. Distribution of known late prehistoric platform mound sites in Arizona
(after Sauer and Brand 1930; Gregory and Nials 1985; Wood 1986; Gregory 1987; Wil-
cox 1988b; Archaeology in Tucson 1990; Alan Dart, personal communication 1991).

from the Phoenix Basin ballcourt system as early as AD 1000. Once these regional
systems broke down into distinct site clusters, new forms of political integration
came about. We suggest that the Salt River polity in the late 1200s incorporated
the middle Gila River ones into a complex polity and was actively pursuing other
fields of conquest when the no-man's land between the Phoenix and Tucson basins
was formed. The rank order in both the size of compound mounds surrounding
platform mounds and the size of the platform mounds themselves supports this
model (Wilcox 1988b, 1991a) (fig. 10.2).

Key to figure 10.2:

1. Gatlin
2. Enterprise Ranch
3. Morocco
4. Pueblo Pointente
5. Pueblo del Alamo
6. Pueblo del Rio
7. Las Colinas
8. Casa Chica
9. La Ciudad
10. Casa Buena
11. Dos Casas
12. Pueblo Grande
13. Pueblo Ultimo
14. Mesa 3:5 (GP)
15. Crismon
16. Pueblo Moroni
17. Las Sierras
18. Casa de Nephi
19. Casa de Mesa
20. Mesa Grande
21. Las Acequias
22. Plaza Tempe
23. Pueblo del Monte
24. Los Hornos
25. Los Guanacos
26. Los Muertos
27. Las Canopas
28. Pueblo Viejo
29. Las Cremaciones
30. Pueblo Primero

31. Villa Buena
32. Hidden Ruin
33. Snaketown
34. Sonoqui
35. Lower Santan
36. Upper Santan
37. Casa Blanca
38. Sweetwater
39. Casa Grande
40. Pueblo Bisnaga
41. Adamsville
42. Florence
43. Escalante
44. Pueblo Pinal
45. Tortilla
46. Tom Mix
47. Brady Wash
48. Toltec
49. AZ A:6:39 (ASM)
50. McClellan
51. Robles
52. Marana
53. Jaynes Station
54. University Indian Ruin
55. Martinez Hill North
56. Martinez Hill
57. Cherry Creek
58. Zandarelli
59. Coyote Mountains
60. Jackrabbit

61. Second Canyon
62. High Mesa
63. Debbies
64. Big Bell
65. Camp Village
66. Leaverton
67. Buzan
68. Ash Terrace/Camp Grant
69. Flieger Ranch
70. Meddler Point
71. Pyramid Point
72. Livingston
73. Pinto Point
74. Schoolhouse Point
75. Armer Ranch
76. Porter Springs
77. Rock Island
78. Bourkes
79. Horse Pasture
80. Cline Terrace
81. Encino
82. Park Creek
83. VIV
84. Rye Creek
85. Gisela
86. Leos
87. Grand Canal
88. Haby Ranch
89. AZ BB:2:3 (ASM)
90. Wheatfields

RECENT MODELS

During the last decade there has been a renewed interest in theories of conflict and competition in the Southwest (Mackey and Green 1979; Wilcox 1979a, 1989b; Hunter-Anderson 1979; Hill and Trierweiler 1986; Haas 1986, 1989, 1990; Preucel 1987, 1988; Orcutt, Blinman, and Kohler 1990). Two distinct research approaches are discernable. Wilcox (1989b) and Haas (1989, 1990) begin with conceptions about the boundedness of social units that are able to act in their own interests; they then examine the politics of threat and counterthreat that these units mount against one another (see also McGuire 1991). Haas has applied these ideas to the Kayenta area, seeking to understand the emergence of tribal formations and the ways that environmental adversity affects their behavior. Wilcox, on the other hand, has concentrated principally on the Hohokam, but he has begun to explore the possibilities of warfare as an important causal variable in the Flagstaff area (Wilcox 1986a) and among the protohistoric Pueblos (Wilcox 1981b, 1984, 1991b).

Rosalind Hunter-Anderson, James Hill, and Hill's students Nicholas Trierweiler, Robert Preucel, and Janet Orcutt postulate that aggregation and the formation of "buffer zones" is a conflict reduction strategy. Hunter-Anderson (1979) derived her version of these ideas from a comparison of ethnographic cases, especially the work of Hickerson (1962); she concludes that "the common link among these cases is the competitive strategy of withdrawal from contested zones for residential purposes and exploitation of the uninhabited space by small logistical forays." Aggregation thus is viewed as a means of reducing competition for resources. Hunter-Anderson applied these ideas to account for settlement patterns discovered in the southern Pajarito Plateau as part of the Cochiti Reservoir project (Biella and Chapman 1979). A little later, Hill began a project on the northern part of the Pajarito Plateau and developed an approach quite similar to Hunter-Anderson's (Hill and Trierweiler 1986; see Cordell et al., this volume). Jan Orcutt later worked on the Dolores Project and applied similar ideas to an interpretation of the aggregation of the earliest (Pueblo I) network of true villages, where each "village" had 100 or more people (Orcutt, Blinman, and Kohler 1990; see also Kane 1989). This model owes much to the independent reasoning of Tim Kohler (1986).

Robert Preucel (1987, 1988) completed his dissertation on the Pajarito Plateau data. In general, Preucel (1988:xix) argues that "the larger the population aggregate, the farther the average farmer must travel to secure farmland. In addition, . . . mobility strategies are strongly influenced by territorial circumscription."

As the Pajarito Plateau filled up with populations in the late Coalition period (AD 1275–1325), the frequency of seasonal agricultural circulation substantially increased. A dramatic settlement reorganization occurred in the early Classic period (AD 1325–1450) when two site clusters of large pueblos (averaging 400 rooms) were established in defensible locations on mesa tops overlooking broad, relatively well-watered canyons (Preucel 1988:141). "The abundance of field houses may indicate a relatively peaceful existence with little inter-village warfare" during this period (Preucel 1988:269). In the following century, however, competition intensified and the settlement pattern shifted to a linear series of evenly spaced pueblos (every 5 km) averaging 250 rooms each. "The reduction in the number of seasonally occupied sites may have been due to an increase in inter-village hostilities during this period," concludes Preucel (1988:269). By AD 1550 (the time of the first Spanish entradas), the plateau was completely abandoned.

In a conclusion that would have pleased Ralph Linton, Preucel argues that:

> The process of aggregation [which initially reduced competition] . . . was costly. While it provided security from raiding and warfare, it required the use of more labor-intensive agricultural strategies to provision the larger populations. This intensification [in this area] appears to have taken the form of the "field house strategy"—rather than irrigation agriculture—due to the virtual absence of permanent streams on the

plateau. However, this response was successful only for a short period of time. Crop failures are the probable causes for the eventual abandonment of the plateau at the end of the Middle Classic phase. (Preucel 1987:26)

DISCUSSION

Although there has been some recognition of the presence of prehistoric competition and conflict in the Southwest for well over a century, there has been very little research explicitly aimed at understanding the role of conflict or warfare in the evolution of Southwestern cultural systems. Yet these are complex phenomena that can have rippling effects on many different aspects of cultural systems and the archaeological record. Without trying to place all the evidence of defense, conflict, violence, and so on in direct historical or ecological perspective, we would like to offer several considerations that must be included in efforts to explain patterns of human behavior in the prehistoric Southwest.

First, competition and conflict need not be glaringly obvious in the archaeological record to have played a critical role in the historical trajectory of a particular cultural system. Tribal warfare, by its very nature, is relatively low level: large-scale pitched battles are a rare exception; casualties are low; there are no armies and few if any specialized weapons; hit-and-run raiding is common, organized attacks and sieges are not (see Turney-High 1949; Otterbein 1985). Anyone doing ethnoarchaeology in tribal societies known to have warfare would be hard pressed to find indications of massive fortifications, soldier cemeteries, or dead and mangled bodies lying about. At the same time, however, the relatively low level of conflict does not necessarily translate into low societal impact. There is violence, death, burning, and pillaging. People subject to the endemic threat of such conflict can be expected to modify their behavior to minimize the negative effects through passive and active postures or offensive and defensive strategies (see Boulding 1962).

A related issue that needs to be considered is that not all tribal warfare is the same. It is likely that the Southwest witnessed many different kinds of warfare in the course of two thousand or more years. Again, drawing from the ethnographic record, warfare may be carried out for revenge, to steal resources, to steal wives, to acquire slaves, to drive a competing group off of choice lands, or to enhance the prestige of the warriors. Patterns of warfare may or may not include killing people, the destruction of property, or the formation of boundaries between groups. A cycle of warfare may be short term or long lasting, internecine or intertribal. Furthermore, the advantage that could be taken of ecological conditions varied from place to place: it was not possible to build cliff dwellings without large caves or overhangs, or hill forts without appropriately located hills. Because of warfare's many faces, we cannot expect to find in the archaeological record some common, discrete set of identifying variables that will serve as a universal material "marker."

Recognizing both the low level and the complexity of tribal warfare, we can consider more specific ways in which competition and conflict should be incorporated into research on patterns of behavior in the prehistoric Southwest. Settlement patterns can be significantly affected by warfare. There is evidence from across the Southwest that at various times the people moved into defensible locations. With this kind of defensive strategy, site location might not follow traditional environmental parameters. Defensively located sites may not be near water or arable land; they may also be very hard to find and seriously underrepresented in the existing survey data base. In the Kayenta area, for example, a survey designed to look explicitly for defensively located sites discovered major populations in areas that had previously been thought abandoned (Haas and Creamer 1991). Thus, on a methodological level, surveys, room counts, population estimations, and settlement pattern models all have to take explicit account of the possible impact of warfare and defensive settlement strategies.

Just as defensive sites are underrepresented in some surveys, competition and conflict are underrepresented in some explanations of broad patterns in the cultural development of the prehistoric Southwest. Specifically, inadequate attention has been paid to the potential role of warfare in trying to explain patterns of both aggregation and abandonment. We do not mean to resurrect the simplistic argument that warfare played a unicausal role in stimulating aggregation or abandonment, but rather to argue that warfare was part of the causal "formula" behind both processes.

Again, turning to the Anasazi area as an example, there is a clear pattern of aggregation occurring in the Pueblo III period, most commonly in the thirteenth century. This was the time when people throughout the northern Southwest were moving from dispersed villages of a few dozen families into much larger villages of 50 to 1,400 rooms (see Dean 1969; Marshall et al. 1979; Kintigh 1985; Fowler, Stein, and Anyon 1987). Although myriad models have been presented to account for this process, few of them allow for a significant role to be played by warfare. Yet our review of the data for competition and conflict presented above demonstrates that the period from AD 1250 to 1300 is one in which evidence for warfare is most apparent and widespread—a time in virtually all parts of the subregion when we see the most evidence of violence, burned sites, and markedly defensive settlement strategies.

The concurrence of evidence for aggregation and warfare in the thirteenth century is not just coincidental—it is connected. Warfare offers a highly parsimonious, if perhaps only partial, explanation of why people would have banded together into physically larger communities. The phrase "United we stand, divided we fall," though perhaps trite, seems glaringly relevant to the late Pueblo III period. What better reason for the Anasazi to aggregate into large, very crowded walled towns than because there was safety in numbers? Large villages are not an efficient way to exploit shrinking resources in a hostile environment. The pattern of aggregation does not fit a maximization model and is not a particularly adaptive strategy in the face of the twelfth- and thirteenth-century conditions of increased erosion and lower overall precipitation. Even if the population was forced to cluster around remnant zones of arable land and water sources, such circumstances do not induce people to live together in one village.

Faced, however, with conflict, raiding, or predation of some sort, a dispersed population that aggregates is making an eminently logical choice. The advantages of sheer numbers coupled with increased defensive capabilities (in terms of defending a village site) would outweigh the disadvantages of poor sanitation, crowding, and increased distance to fields. This strategy was apparently first adopted in the Anasazi area during late Basketmaker and Pueblo I times (Kane 1989; Orcutt, Blinman, and Kohler 1990). Considerable evidence for Basketmaker violence and fortified homesteads suggests the social context in which such aggregation took place.

The Anasazi data point to a strong pattern of correlation between aggregation and warfare, and they raise the prospect of a cross-cultural causal relationship between these same two phenomena. The insight offered here is that in our efforts to explain the process of aggregation in any part of the Southwest (or elsewhere, for that matter) it will be highly profitable to consider, incorporate, or rule out the potential role of warfare in bringing together large groups of people in large, packed villages.

A similar argument can be made for abandonment. Though the idea is still floating around that intrusive nomadic groups preyed upon the resident horticulturalists of the Southwest and drove them away from their homelands (see Ambler and Sutton 1989), there is little ethnographic or archaeological evidence to support it. It seems more productive to look at warfare between resident Southwestern groups, as argued by Linton (1944), as one of a complex of variables that contributed in different combinations to patterns of both local and regional abandonment. Warfare limits residential mobility by small groups, removing that option in times of environmental stress. This in turn can lead to overexploitation of local resources and can exacerbate the effects of a natural erosional cycle. Warfare also greatly reduces the effectiveness of a strategy of deploying isolated fieldhouses to exploit scattered plots of arable land (see Preucel 1988). Warfare thus reduces the range of options available to a settled population and promotes wholesale abandonment, both to get away from one's enemies and to find greener pastures.

In arguing for much greater consideration of the presence and effects of competition and conflict in the greater Southwest, we are not trying to say that warfare was a monocausal agent placing a black hand on the evolution of cultural systems in the region. Indeed, warfare itself must be seen as an effect of a combination of environmental, demographic, and political variables. The role of warfare also must be seen only in the context of the particular historical circumstances of a local, regional, or macroregional community. If we are ever to understand the complex and dynamic patterns of human behavior in the Southwest, we must begin factoring warfare into all of our equations. Not to do so would be like trying to understand the modern American economy without considering the military. But just as all American economists do not study the military, all Southwestern archaeologists should not be expected to study warfare. We do, however, have to stop turning a blind eye to the unavoidable conclusion indicated by the evidence for two thousand years of conflict and competition all across the Southwest and must fully consider its potential role in the evolution of the prehistoric Anasazi, Mogollon, and Hohokam peoples.

——— *Acknowledgments* ———
Special thanks go to George Gumerman for asking us to write this paper and for his sensitivity and wonderful assistance in helping us to complete it. Originally, Stephen Lekson was invited to participate in this project;he provided valuable input but in the end chose not to appear as an author. Great assistance was provided by Dorothy House and her assistants in the Museum of Northern Arizona Library. Jodi Griffith drafted the two figures. Support for the fieldwork for figure 10.1 and the drafting of both figures was provided by Deborah Dosh, Kinlani Archaeology. Helpful comments were received from Miranda Warburton, Phil Geib, Richard Wilshusen, Roger Anyon, Joan Mathien, Greg Woodall, Todd Bostwick, Christian Downum, Winston Hurst, Margaret Lyneis, Christy Turner, Phil Weigand, Timothy Kohler, Douglas Craig, Victoria Clark, Winifred Creamer, Henry Wallace, and others. We also thank George Gumerman, the volume reviewers, and Jane Kepp for valuable comments. For errors and faulty interpretation, we alone are responsible.

"The scream of the butterfly," the paper's title, is taken from the song "When the Music's Over" (aka "The End") on the album "Strange Days" by Jim Morrison and The Doors.

11

Drawing the Southwest to Scale
Perspectives on Macroregional Relations

RANDALL H. MCGUIRE, E. CHARLES ADAMS,
BEN A. NELSON, AND
KATHERINE A. SPIELMANN

 THE SPANISH LEGEND OF THE SEVEN golden cities of Cíbola died
with the return of the Coronado expedition to Culiacán, Mexico, in
1542. Thirty years later, new rumors circulated in the Chichimecan
mining frontier of northern New Spain, tales of a *"nuevo México"* to
the north of the land of the Chichimecs, a country similar to the México of the
Aztec. In 1581 nine Spanish soldiers and three Franciscan friars left the mining
town of Santa Barbara, in what is now southern Chihuahua, to seek out this other
México. For fifty days they trekked across the lands of the Chichimecs, arriving
at last at a pueblo of forty-five houses set amidst fields of corn, beans, and squash
(Hammond and Rey 1966:141). The Spaniards named this land *Nuevo México*.

The Spaniards engaged in a bit of hyperbole by calling the pueblos of the Rio
Grande valley a Nuevo México, but their notion does give order to spatial differences in culture and adaptation. The numbers of people and the size of towns in
the area paled in comparison to the great cities of the central highlands of Mexico,
the *mesa central*. The region was, however, markedly unlike the Chichimeca, that
land of barbarians that lay north of an east-west line from Culiacán to Monterrey.
The Chichimeca was arid, and its people, the Chichimecs, moved from place to
place, grew few if any crops, and lacked clothing and fine pottery. Nuevo México
was better watered, and its people lived in fixed towns of large houses, intensively
farmed well-established fields, and made fine cotton clothing and pottery (Beals
1932:134–35).

The Spanish notion of a Nuevo México created an entity quite different from
Mesoamerica, yet more like Mesoamerica than the other cultural entities that
ringed it. Today we place this region in the Southwest culture area, which modern scholars have extended far beyond the limits of the Spanish Nuevo México.
The modern notion of the Southwest springs from the same types of comparisons

that the Spaniards drew, and we still define the area in terms of houses, pots, and fields. As usually described, the Southwest culture area encompasses those regions north of Mesoamerica where people lived year-round in villages or towns, made pottery, and grew corn, beans, and squash. The limits of agriculture mark the edges of this area on all sides except the south, where the Southwest blends into Mesoamerica, the source of the triad of crops used to define the region.

The question of macroregional relations with the prehistoric Southwest has traditionally been answered by viewing some relations as internal to the Southwest and others as external. Such discussions typically concern how or where to draw a boundary around the Southwest as a culture area; that is, how to define what is in and what is out. In this paper, we propose instead a dynamic perspective that views the Southwest not as a spatial unit but as a set of social relations between cultural groups. This approach does away with the idea that some relations are internal and others external; instead, such social relations appear and work differently at different scales. The issue of the Mesoamerican connection in the Southwest requires us to look at relations at a macroscale that extends from the Valley of Mexico to Chaco Canyon. It also compels us to examine more local relations on a more restricted scale in order to understand specific aspects of this connection: for example, the katsina cult among the late prehistoric Pueblos (AD 1250–1500). At a continental scale, the western, northern, and eastern boundaries of the Southwest look sharp and clear, but when we examine each border in turn, it becomes fuzzy, ever fluctuating, and arbitrary.

INSIDE AND OUTSIDE THE SOUTHWEST

Whether we see the spatial variation in the past in terms of bounded units or of relations affects how we order, interpret, and write prehistory. For the last fifty years archaeologists have tended to study Southwestern prehistory in terms of bounded units, a notion that compels us to fill in all of the space on the map. But the cultural stuff we wish to study, such as adaptations, social groups, trade, and style, does not spread evenly or completely over the map. Drawing lines emphasizes the edges, where the things we wish to study are in fact the most indistinct. In giving cultural relations a hard edge they did not have, we work against a dynamic view of Southwestern prehistory, and by defining our object of study as a spatial unit, we project the Southwest as a culture area into time periods that long predate such a cultural pattern.

The idea of a Southwest culture area starts with the notion of a Pueblo Southwest much like the Spaniards' idea of a Nuevo México (Goddard 1913; Kidder 1924; Wissler 1917, 1938). During the first half of this century, scholars enlarged the Southwest to take in far more than the pueblos, but they never reached agreement on the extent and nature of the region (Beals 1932, 1944; Gladwin and Gladwin 1935; Haury 1936, 1962a; Jennings 1956; Kirchoff 1943, 1954; Kroeber 1939; Reed 1964; Sauer and Brand 1931; Willey 1966). Most authors seem to agree that the culture traits they use to define the area sprang from a climax, or hub, and then spread out over the region; some stress the study of this hub, and others emphasize the borders of the area. All envision the area as having both a cultural and an environmental basis, but they argue over the relative importance of these factors to the existence of the area.

Since the late 1960s most archaeologists have turned away from debates about cultural areas to ecological studies of resources and technology. They elevated the environmental aspect of the culture area notion to the main focus of research and primarily asked questions that could be answered in very small parts of the area. The *"pochteca"* theorists were the major exceptions to this trend (Di Peso 1968, 1974a, 1974b; Kelley and Kelley 1975; Weigand, Harbottle, and Sayre 1977; Riley and Hedrick 1978; Lister 1978; Reyman 1978; Pailes 1980).

The archaeological trends of the 1980s moved us away from the study of how people made a living in a local area to questions about how areas in the Southwest were linked and how these linkages helped shape the prehistory of the region (Altschul 1978; Upham 1982; F. Plog 1983b; Plog, Upham, and Weigand 1982; McGuire 1989; Schroeder 1981; Minnis 1989). These trends once again raise the issue of what was the nature and extent of a Southwestern culture area.

WORLD SYSTEMS THEORY

Much of the theory behind the new focus on the Southwest as a whole seems to be directly—or, more often, indirectly—inspired by the world systems perspective of Wallerstein (1974, 1980; see Whitecotten and Pailes 1986; Upham 1982; Wilcox 1986b; Plog, Upham, and Weigand 1982; Kohl 1987). Wallerstein leads us to ponder how the growth of cores stems from the creation of peripheries and nudges our focus from diffusion and adaptation to interaction and dependency. In world systems theory, core and periphery are not spaces but social relations, and societies are no longer bounded spaces but dynamic entities begotten and transformed by the unequal economic relationships of a larger system. Core areas dominate this system and forge the economic relationships that create the great diversity needed to link a region as a whole.

The strict use of world systems theory in our study of the prehistoric Southwest could be seriously misleading, as it is highly unlikely that the Southwest was ever as economically or politically integrated as this model assumes. The technology available to move bulk items, for example, would have allowed the regular circulation of foodstuffs over distances of only 50 to 60 kilometers (Lightfoot 1979; Hassig 1988:64). Using these distances as radii of movement suggests that food distribution networks could have covered areas of 7,800 to 11,232 square kilometers. The Chaco interaction sphere had an area of over 53,000 square kilometers (Altschul 1978) and lies over 1,500 kilometers north of the northernmost Mesoamerican center. The "alliances" proposed by Fred Plog (1983b) cover areas of 15,000 square kilometers or more. It would be a mistake to take these figures too literally, but they do give us some idea of how limited bulk commodity distribution networks could have been in the prehistoric Southwest. The cultural subareas of the Southwest must have been primarily self-provisioning. They were linked to other regions by a trade in preciosities. Trade in preciosities will link areas and can lead to cultural convergence and dependencies that can form the locus of cultural change. Such trade will not, however, lead to large-scale functional convergence and uniform peripheries because the local ecological relations remain primary.

Peer Polity Interactions

A number of archaeologists working in Europe have proposed the notion of peer polity interaction as an alternative to a world systems approach (Renfrew 1986), and some archaeologists in the Southwest have recently applied this idea to Southwestern prehistory (Minnis 1989a). The model of peer polity interaction emphasizes a scale of analysis intermediate between the local and the interregional. The stress on interactions within a region assumes that these are of greater importance to cultural change than are the region's external links.

We would agree that the scale of analysis defined by the peer polity model is an important one for looking at cultural change. The processes that occur in local river valleys or basins are often too restricted, and those operating at the level of the whole of the Southwest or the Southwest and Mesoamerica are too grand to account for most of the changes in prehistory. In addition, we doubt that the Southwest was ever a single network of peer polity interaction, believing instead that at any given time multiple networks could have existed.

There are dangers, however, in framing our present concern with external relations in terms of an either/or choice between a peer polity or world systems model. When we look at the effect of external relations on Southwest societies, as we do with the late Pueblos, we need to do so in the context of relations and processes at the intermediate scale of the peer polity model, but this model gives us little or no guidance on how external relations articulate with or affect process at this scale. At the largest scale, the examination of Mesoamerican–Southwestern interactions, the model is useful because it dismisses simple theories of long-range domination of the Southwest by Mesoamerica. Beyond that point, however, the peer polity model runs the risk of being a new isolationism that frames research questions in a way that obscures any significant impacts long-range interactions may have had on the prehistory of the Southwest and gives us only the idea of "emulation"—a new term for the old notion of influence—to account for Mesoamerican traits in the Southwest.

Beyond a Theory of Internal and External Relationships

If we think of the Southwest as a set of relations between social groups and admit that the boundaries of these relations are fuzzy, then it is no longer useful to frame our inquiry in terms of inside and outside. Instead we need to ask, What is the process of change in these relations? What makes some social groups central to this process, while others remain peripheral? And how does our study, and the nature of the relations we see, change as we vary the scale of our analysis?

We cannot assume that cultures will exist as bounded units, but we can look for a dynamic process of inclusion and exclusion within a complex web of social relations. The existence of distinct cultural boundaries is a phenomenon that requires explanation. We have to ask if and why distinct cultural boundaries came into existence, rather than simply assume they will exist. When the Spaniards arrived in the Southwest, they encountered a complex amalgam of languages, cultures, and adaptations that resisted their efforts to categorize Southwestern Indian people into distinct *provincias, reynos,* and *naciones* (Spicer 1962:8–10; Naylor 1983). As Spicer (1962) recounts, the fuzzy boundaries that the Spaniards encountered hardened into distinct bounded cultures in response to Spanish colonial policies.

The formation of alliances, or any form of bounded group, includes some people but at the same time excludes others. We have to ask, then, why some social groups become central to webs of relations and thereby delineate others as peripheral or external. Kroeber explained this phenomenon with a model of invention and diffusion: a central area was one in which many new traits were invented and from which they diffused. The model is inadequate because it only describes the process and does not tell us why invention occurs in the culture climax or why other groups should accept the traits generated in the climax. Furthermore, what we want to look at are complexes of behaviors, and such complexes do not tend to be nicely bounded in space. In world systems theory, a social group becomes "core" because of its functional position in the international division of labor; other groups are constituted as peripheral in this division. In both theories, centrality results from a single factor—tradition or economics—and all other aspects of the social group follow from this aspect.

We are uneasy with the idea that the various centers we see in prehistory always resulted from tradition or economic position. Centrality may be a product of a variety of factors. A social group may be central because of its position in a web of religious, economic, or political relations, and one group may be the center for one set of relations (e.g., religious), while a different group is the center for another set of relations (e.g., economic).

A more important problem with the core-periphery contrast is that it assumes that all groups and relations can be ranked. As the notion of peer polity interaction suggests, this is a questionable assumption. A great number of contrasts can be made between social groups based on linguistics, culture, adaptation, religion, and so on, and these distinctions may be ranked or not (Marquardt and Crumley 1987:11).

How we place a social group, as central or peripheral, depends in part on the scale at which we examine the web of social relations and what aspects of the social world we choose to look at. In the context of Southwestern prehistory, we may wish to speak of Chaco Canyon as a center, but in terms of the Southwest and Mesoamerica, the entire Southwest must be thought of as a periphery.

In the Hohokam Classic period the Phoenix Basin was not a center for stylistic innovation, but it did have a more intensive agricultural system and greater social differentiation than surrounding areas (McGuire 1991).

Marquardt and Crumley (1987:2) speak of the "effective scale" of research: that being "any scale at which pattern may be recognized or meaning inferred." As we change the effective scale of our analysis, we frame a different web of relations. The unevenness in these relations will disappear at a different scale as a new pattern of unevenness appears. Social groups also live and act in a world of varying scales, and their position vis-à-vis others changes as their scale of reference changes. Our choice of an effective scale, therefore, brackets an area for study allowing us to view a particular set of social relations while denying us access to sets visible at other scales. Also, we will find that some theoretical models are more informative at one scale and others at a different scale, so that our choice of models in part depends on the scale of our analysis.

The prehistoric world we wish to understand was a complex product of the intersection of all these scales. The impact of different external relations was quite variable across time and space. Thus, our studies of prehistory need to be multi-scalar. As we change scales, the boundaries that seemed sharp at one level become fuzzy and disappear; what was external at one level becomes internal at another. At the highest scale, we need to look at the relationship between Mesoamerica and the Southwest, two regions that were not as tightly integrated as some have thought but whose historical processes of change were by no means unconnected. At a lower scale, we ask how long-range relations affected the development of the late prehistoric Pueblos. Here, important concepts and symbols drawn from Mesoamerica were reworked into a religious system that was and is distinctively Pueblo. Finally, we look at relations on the edges of the Southwest, where external relations appear much more localized in extent and importance.

THE MESOAMERICAN CONNECTION IN THE SOUTHWEST

The nature of the Mesoamerican connection in the Southwest lies at the heart of one of the basic issues in North American archaeology (fig. 11.1). It is clear that interaction occurred between the Southwest and Mesoamerica, but it is not clear to what extent the events and processes we see in the Southwest were determined by events and processes in Mesoamerica (Wilcox 1986b). Most previous discussions have treated this as an issue at the highest regional scale, with little regard to how these long-range relations would have been played out at different scales: that is, how relations at the highest scale would have connected with local relations to produce the patterns of change that we see. The highest scale is the level of a world system, and we must question if such a system existed and what the nature of the linkages in that system were. At the local or regional scale, we must ask how these higher-level linkages figured into the relations between cultural groups or polities that were situated close to one another in a single region.

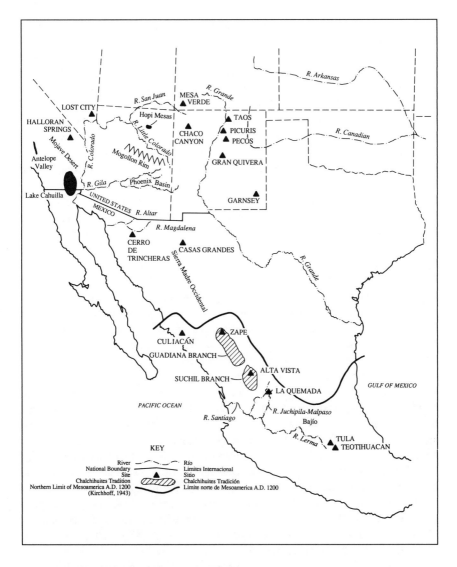

Figure 11.1. Map of the Southwest and Mesoamerica.

SOUTHWESTERN–MESOAMERICAN RELATIONS

The debates about the nature of Southwestern–Mesoamerican relations have been polarized between scholars who see direct intervention in the Southwest by Meso-american agents (Kelley and Kelley 1975) and others who see less direct links and who consider relations within the Southwest to be primary (McGuire 1980; Schroeder 1981; Plog, Upham, and Weigand 1982; Mathien and McGuire 1986; Wilcox 1986b). As a result of this debate, few archaeologists now posit pochteca setting out from the Valley of Mexico with bags of trinkets designed to entice Southwestern peoples into reorganizing themselves at higher levels of sociopolitical integration. Some researchers, however, still argue that Mesoamerican-based groups or individuals entered the Southwest and directly affected the development of the region (Di Peso 1983; Foster 1986; Kelley 1986b; Weigand 1988). These direct intrusion models contain several essential ingredients that must be present for any account of such macroregional relations: appropriate geographic scale, an assessment of timing, and a postulation of mechanisms that could account for seemingly serial or synchronous changes in widely separated cultural groups. We present here an alternative model that also contains these ingredients, that fits the empirical evidence better, and that relates macroregional and local relationships.

The Southwestern farming traditions were the northernmost expressions of a change that began by 200 BC with the advent of the Chupícuaro tradition in the Bajio. This tradition was the basis for later distinctive developments in West Mexico and the Southwest (Braniff 1974; Florance 1985; Kelley 1976). Chupícuaro and its derivatives first spread westward along the Lerma-Santiago River basin and then northward into the piedmont zones and prominent drainages of interior Guanajuato, Jalisco, Zacatecas, and Durango, and later (leaping a gap of arid and rugged territory) into Arizona and New Mexico, edging finally into Utah, Colorado, Chihuahua, and Sonora. A simultaneous or possibly later set of transformations occurred along the coastal strip seaward of the Sierra Madre Occidental, involving parts of Jalisco, Nayarit, and Sinaloa.

The Mesoamerican influences that archaeologists associate with this economic and social transformation range from the basic (maize, pottery) to the subtle (highly stylized and transformed iconographic elements). Kelley (1966) and Braniff (1974) have traced striking ceramic similarities from Chupícuaro through Morales, Malpaso, Chalchihuites, and Hohokam. Foster (1982) identifies a pattern of stylistic parallels in brown wares that he labels the Loma San Gabriel–Mogollon continuum. Wilcox (1986c) uses the distributions of languages and the Mesoamerican ball game to connect the northern periphery of Mesoamerica and the southern Southwest. Each of these continua suggests a somewhat independent set of links. There exists a general agreement that the strongest relationships occur in the Hohokam area (Brand 1943; Haury 1943, 1945b; Kelley 1966; Kelly 1943; McGuire 1980; Wilcox 1986b).

The above aspects of the "Mesoamerican connection" correlate with the advent of settled village life, a widespread and highly generalized process. Overlying that process is the appearance of regional centers in certain places at certain times. These regional centers are large towns (such as Casas Grandes) or clusters of towns (Chaco Canyon and the Phoenix Basin Hohokam) with public architecture, irrigation networks, and sometimes roads that suggest social organization on a supravillage level. The appearance of Southwestern regional centers was the northernmost echo of a process of changing relations within and among societies that began earlier and with greater intensity much farther to the south. In both

Mesoamerica and the Southwest, however, major segments of the population lived outside the sway of such centers, and farmers and nomads were always present.

Ignoring the temporal dimension momentarily, we can examine the distribution of regional centers in Mesoamerica along the same corridors as the spread of the farming traditions. A dense concentration of regional centers organized as city states existed in the Basin of Mexico. Westward along the Lerma-Santiago drainage, the density of regional centers dropped, the level of social organization declined, and centers occurred primarily in the riverine and lake zones. Up the Juchipila-Malpaso and three parallel drainages, there was a decline in both the size and frequency of major centers as the terrain became more arid to the north and the streams diminished in size toward their headwaters. Such peripheral centers as La Quemada and Alta Vista were surrounded by tight clusters of associated secondary centers and villages, and then by large gaps with no evident sociopolitical complexity—presumably the territories of small-scale agriculturalists, hunter-gatherers, or both. Large portions of these intervening territories were in fact not arable and could only have served as hunting and gathering territories for the centers, or more likely as home ranges for other, more mobile societies.

The Southwestern regional centers appear as additional instances of a broad pattern in which centers diminished in frequency and scale toward the arid lands of the north. In the Southwest, as in several other areas of the northern Mesoamerican periphery (e.g., Chalchihuites), regional centers were relatively isolated from one another. Yet the Southwest was not just one more Mesoamerican island.

The degree of sociopolitical complexity in the Southwest was lower in both the horizontal and vertical dimensions. But in both dimensions the degree of development appears to have been considerably less than in peripheral Mesoamerica. Distinctions of rank, as expressed in personal adornment, domestic architecture, and possession of exotic items, were far less elaborated in the Southwest than in peripheral Mesoamerican societies. Also, overall community or polity size and rank-size variation within polity settlement systems appear much less developed in the Southwest than in the Mesoamerican periphery.

The differences in social organization were not simply differences of degree but appear more as differences of kind. The social systems of the two areas are analogous to two families of languages that had some cognates but different deep structures. We suspect that the Southwestern societies were fundamentally consensus based, while the Mesoamerican societies comprised definitive hierarchies. A good illustration of the contrast can be found in the organization of ceremonial facilities in Southwestern versus Mesoamerican sites. In Anasazi and Mogollon sites, kivas were usually located in public plazas, not in association with specific dwellings, or often, in the case of great kivas, away from habitation areas altogether. Mounds in the Hohokam and Casas Grandes areas also seem to have been separated from dwelling areas, although in the Classic period of the Phoenix Basin residences on top of platform mounds were most likely occupied by community leaders. In contrast, the more monumental altars, temples, and pyramids of peripheral Mesoamerican peoples were integral parts of elite residential compounds. These differences, we feel, may be indicative of very different patterns of access to sacred information and social surplus.

The social surroundings of regional centers also differed between the Southwest and peripheral Mesoamerica. Regional centers in the northern periphery of Mesoamerica were separated from one another by distances of 150 to 200 kilometers and often had only hunter-gatherers as neighbors. The series of polities that ran from Jalisco to Durango (Juchipila-Malpaso-Suchil-Guadiana-Zape) exemplifies this pattern. Each of these centers appears to have directed an independent polity that was a tight cluster of settlements surrounded by an area of very low population density. To one side of this string of polities was the Sierra Madre Occidental, a rugged and inhospitable zone; to the other side were the deserts of the Gran Chichimeca. We know less about the coastal centers of the "Mixteca–Puebla route" (Kelley 1985, 1986b), but we assume a similar pattern of isolated polities, based on the wide spacing of such sites in the narrow coastal plain. Along both the interior and coastal strips, marked gaps with little archaeological evidence of villages or towns separate those areas that are labeled Mesoamerican from those that are considered Southwestern. In the interior, the gap appears in far northern Durango and southern Chihuahua (Brooks 1971); along the coast, it occurred in northern Sinaloa and southern Sonora (Sauer and Brand 1931; McGuire and Villalpando 1989).

In contrast to the empty spaces in the northern Mesoamerican periphery, the gaps between the Southwestern regional centers were filled with an amalgam of culturally variable but fundamentally similar agriculturalists, mostly egalitarian but considerably more populous and sedentary than their counterparts in northern Mexico. Within that amalgam were rare nuclei of social elaboration. The major regional centers—Chaco Canyon, the Hohokam, Casas Grandes and the Pueblo IV towns—are heightened expressions of larger patterns that together made up the patchwork of ethnic and organizational variability that we call the Southwest. Most archaeologists have assumed that whatever external relations the Southwest had with Mesoamerica must have been mediated through those anomalous, organizationally variable regional centers.

The relative infrequency of regional centers in both the Southwest and the northern periphery is even clearer when we consider the temporal dimension. The history of events suggests that the formation of regional centers in the Southwest was part of a broad process that also included expansion of the Mesoamerican periphery.

The general pattern in the Mesoamerican periphery is one of an advance and retreat of regional centers from about AD 500 to 1350. In the northern periphery as well as in the Southwest, the isolated regional centers were not contemporary with one another but were associated with different waves of this advance and retreat. The La Quemada and Alta Vista polities, for example, were largely contemporary with one another, but the Guadiana branch of the Chalchihuites came later (Kelley 1985). In the Southwest, Sedentary and Classic Hohokam were contemporary with Chaco and Casas Grandes, respectively, but the latter two did not overlap with one another. The Spaniards arrived during a period of retreat, when only mobile hunters and gatherers lived in many of the Classic and early Postclassic period northern Mesoamerican centers.

Direct intrusion theorists postulate that entrepreneurs caused the Mesoamericanization of the northern periphery and the Southwest. We prefer to see long-distance exchange as a correlate or consequence of social process rather than as a cause. The various Southwestern societies must have been self-sufficient and organizationally distinct from their counterparts in the Mesoamerican periphery. Even if exchange was an important part of the economy, the Southwestern societies would have had no apparent reason to reorganize themselves around production for distant polities. Such production could not have increased their subsistence base, nor could Mesoamerican polities have dispatched armies over the great distances separating the centers to collect tribute payments. We do not wish to ignore the role of long-distance exchange or to disavow evidence of ideological affinities among societies north of the Lerma-Santiago; rather, we seek to set economic variables alongside those of society and tradition in the hope of developing more holistic explanations.

There are empirical as well as theoretical reasons for continuing to question the direct intrusion interpretations. New evidence from La Quemada, a peripheral center that figures prominently in these scenarios, raises doubts about some of the postulated links in the trade system. Weigand (1978, 1982) portrays La Quemada as a Toltec outpost designed to aid turquoise trade with the Southwest, arguing that the site must have been constructed rapidly by foreign sponsors because the local labor supply would have been inadequate to construct the massive ramparts, defensive walls, and road system. Weigand proposes that La Quemada linked the Toltec capitol of Tula with Chaco Canyon, in an imperial network of rare resource trade dating from about AD 900 to 1100.

Recent excavations at La Quemada (Jiménez Betts 1989; Nelson 1990), however, revealed no Toltec material. Nor does the chronological evidence from ceramic vessels and figurines support the idea that Toltecs founded the site. Rather than having been built in a burst of foreign-sponsored construction activity around AD 900, the site seems to have been built over hundreds of years, beginning perhaps in the late 400s. The excavations recovered no turquoise from the site, although Weigand, Harbottle, and Sayre (1977) trace turquoise recovered earlier from La Quemada to the Cerrillos source in New Mexico.

These new data do not rule out a role for La Quemada in a grand Toltec system of rare resource acquisition; nor do they rule out political dependency of the site upon the Toltecs. They do, however, raise questions about direct Toltec intervention as a force in the founding of La Quemada and about the existence of an imperially organized exchange network involving Chaco Canyon.

If we reject direct intrusion models of Southwest–Mesoamerican relations, what kinds of models are more appropriate? We do not wish to deny the importance of economic ties based on preciosities, even though we may not accord them explanatory primacy. It is undeniable that certain rare items were moving very long distances, and with them symbols that seem to have been prominent in some Southwestern and Mesoamerican cultures.

World systems theory (Wallerstein 1974) avoids conceiving of societies as bounded entities and allows for the simultaneous possibilities of autonomy and relatedness. An especially intriguing aspect of world systems theory is the notion of "structural underdevelopment." This notion holds that because the core-periphery relationship is one of exploitation, the economy of the periphery is depressed while the core grows. Growth of the periphery may actually be inversely related to that of the core, accelerating positively only after the periphery is released from the dependency relationship.

The notion of structural underdevelopment may have implications for the growth of regional centers in the Mesoamerican periphery and the Southwest. Nelson (1993) has suggested that the growth of regional centers in the northern Mesoamerican periphery during the period AD 650 to 1100 was related to the disintegration of Teotihuacán and its replacement by a number of smaller centers. That disintegration, which had ended by about AD 750, may have left behind a series of low-visibility systems of rare resource extraction (Weigand 1982), which local peoples gained more control over with Teotihuacán's decline. Once free of tribute obligations, peripheral polities could have used surpluses for local growth, underwriting what we think to be an advance of Mesoamerica's northern "frontier."

We do not mean to imply that Teotihuacán itself was directly involved in resource extraction in the Southwest, and we are quite certain that it was not. Rather we suggest that the appearance of regional centers in the Southwest could have been part of a broad process that began with the liberation of peripheral Mesoamerican polities from core control. As more peripheral centers developed, they in turn created conditions in which other small-scale, independent polities could arise, possibly in part to serve the adjacent southern center's demands for exotic goods. In each case these processes worked themselves out at a local level with interregional relations existing between proximate centers and not necessarily across the entire chain of centers. The Southwestern regional centers would then be the ripples that remained from a wave that began centuries earlier and two thousand kilometers away.

To accept such an explanation, we must assume a larger investment by Teotihuacán in the procurement of prestige goods than some archaeologists would allow (Sanders, Parsons, and Santley 1979; Blanton and Feinman 1984). Another prerequisite is the demonstration that each area where complex societies appeared had something to contribute to a world economy. The outstanding case for such an argument is Chalchihuites, where an extensive system of mines cannot be accounted for by local demand (Weigand 1968, 1982). Other possibilities come to mind: Chacoan turquoise (but the source is not close to Chaco), Hohokam shell (again the source is distant from the ostensible production center), and so on. At present we do not have adequate data to evaluate either how important prestige goods were to core societies or the role of peripheral societies in making them.

Another possible explanation, again related to the demise of the core policy of Teotihuacán, is that the elites and craft guild members of that center dispersed to the peripheries when the Teotihuacán elite began to lose its hold (Stark 1986). Although Toltec legend records such a dispersal from Teotihuacán, no clear evidence shows that it could have affected areas as distant as the Southwest. Such an explanation also does not fit with the fact that the various regional centers in the Southwest appear over a period of several centuries. Our attempts to relate developments in the Southwest to those in Teotihuacán must deal with distances of up to two thousand kilometers and periods of up to three hundred years.

The most plausible approach seems to be to assume that some common, replicable process occurred repeatedly in the whole chain of societies. Each instance may have facilitated another, though each instance was largely independent and generated by local actors. If we accept that changes in social relations do not necessarily have only economic determinants, that social and ideological variables also have a role to play, then our explanations can have both uniformitarian and idiosyncratic elements.

The conditions for the transmission of Mesoamerican cultural elements to the Southwest were probably set up when agriculture made possible the accumulation of social surplus; that is, production beyond the subsistence needs of the producer that is appropriated by individuals or social groups (Gledhill 1978; cf. Bender 1985; McGuire 1989; Saitta 1988). The manipulation of that surplus to create social obligations and dependencies, however, revolved around local personalities, the appropriate timing and severity of local crises, and local moves to adopt hierarchy as opposed to other solutions to social problems.

Once social differentiation existed, those in leadership roles would naturally seek ways of legitimizing their authority (Flannery 1968). Such legitimization would come primarily from the leaders' ability to handle recurring problems (food shortages, threats from other groups), which would be achieved by calling upon stored wealth and the obligations of protégés (McGuire 1989). A secondary but important source of legitimization might have come from the adoption of the symbolic canons of existing systems of authority (Helms 1979).

In the case of the Southwest, the established systems of rank and authority were to the south, and their trappings were certain styles of adornment, architecture, exotic raw materials, and sacred knowledge of agricultural cycles, rain, astronomy, and warfare. The meaning of these symbols was often transformed in the Southwest, but even if the meanings differed, the symbols retained power because of their connection to the south. Such symbols and esoteric knowledge also existed in the Southwest, but leaders could enlarge their images by increasing their store of them, while simultaneously expressing their identification with other leaders. Yet these leaders would not be well served by clothing themselves entirely in symbols of foreign extraction; it was important to express a commitment to the local community and to maintain local group identity. To adopt Mesoamerican symbolism wholesale would be to betray that local commitment. Also working against wholesale adoption was the fact that the local system of authority was only vaguely like that of Mesoamerican societies. Too, there were symbolic dialogues to be conducted with societies in the Plains, the Great Basin, and beyond the Colorado River.

We feel that an accounting along these lines is more satisfactory than direct intrusion models because it does not overburden exchange as an explanatory variable. Pochteca, if they existed prior to Aztec times and traveled as far as the Southwest, were simply conduits for a flow of information and goods that aided processes of maintenance and change in social relations within and among Southwestern societies. We suggest that macroregional "external relations" can best be understood by reference to those local social relations, their traditions and ideologies, and their active uses of material culture for legitimization and reinforcement.

THE LATE PREHISTORIC PERIOD

As we shift our scale downward and look at the late prehistoric period, circa AD 1250 to 1500, of the upper Southwest we see changes in Pueblo society that reflect influences from Mesoamerica. In this context the assumptions of core-periphery appear fallible, however, and instead we see roughly equivalent social groups interacting within a geographic region. Social relations were fluid, and contacts and borrowing were extensive and extended. There is no question that the source of much of this borrowing lay to the south of the traditional Pueblo area, but the things that were borrowed were reworked and used to transform Pueblo society on a local level.

At about AD 1300, Pueblo people abandoned the seven-hundred-year-old Anasazi tradition of decorating white ceramics with black designs and began producing yellow, red, and orange wares. People from northern Chihuahua to the central Rio Grande valley to the Hopi Mesas began adding reds and whites to the traditional black designs. Dynamic asymmetric forms emphasizing birds—especially parrots and raptors—and snakes replaced the tight geometry and symmetry of earlier Pueblo ceramic decorations (Carlson 1970, 1982).

The buff-, tan-, yellow-, red-, or orange-based polychromes with bird motifs occurred in a variety of types: Ramos Polychrome at Casas Grandes, El Paso Polychrome along the lower Rio Grande, Gila Polychrome in the Salado area, Fourmile Polychrome above the Mogollon Rim in east-central Arizona, Matsaki Polychrome in the Zuni area, and Sikyatki Polychrome in the Hopi region. The common parrot motif (Hays 1989), along with macaw and parrot remains found in many post-1300 pueblos above and below the Mogollon Rim, further suggests connections beyond the "regional" level. Many local groups used a distinct set of symbols that crosscut the conventional boundaries Southwestern archaeologists draw around ethnic groups. The ultimate origins of the bird/snake iconography lie deep in

Mesoamerica, but they marked distinctive regions in the Mogollon and Anasazi traditions.

The symbolism of this new iconography clearly sprang from a new belief system, but conquerors did not force these beliefs onto an unwilling, subject people (McGuire 1980; Schroeder 1981). Rather, local peoples took up these ideas or beliefs, interwove them with their existing cosmology and in so doing remade their religion and social organization. In Chihuahua or points south the roots of this system may have lain in Quetzalcoatl or Chac, but in the Pueblo world, the belief system became the katsina cult (Adams 1991).

Thus from about AD 1250 to 1400, or the fall of Casas Grandes, an extensive system of exchange transferred items and ideas from the sedentary cultures of Chihuahua north to Hopi and the central Rio Grande. Pueblo settlements became quite large and surprisingly similar in layout. This network of interaction spanning tens of thousands of square miles was seemingly at a more intensive level than during any other prehistoric period, with relations that crosscut archaeological traditions and included Chihuahuan, Salado, "Western Pueblo," and remnants of the Anasazi traditions. This new set of social relations introduced ideas and artifacts into the traditional Pueblo (Anasazi) heartland and laid the cultural foundation for what we today call Pueblo Indians.

The key to this change was not, however, that "southern" ideas were moving north. This had almost always been the case. Nor did the northern people merely layer the new information on top of existing patterns. In reality, much more happened. The Southwestern peoples absorbed the new information and transformed their culture—not in the image of the south, but in a uniquely Puebloan fashion. Although connections and influence were certainly external, the mechanisms fostering and finally accomplishing change were internal. The late thirteenth century witnessed a transformation in Pueblo settlement and society that forever altered traditional Anasazi patterns and replaced them with patterns that were still in place at the Spanish conquest and remain in place, albeit altered by European contact, to the present.

Watson Smith (1971) noted a strong stylistic influence from both the north and the south on the thirteenth-century ceramics from the western mound at Awatovi. Although the center of Anasazi population had been north and east, first in Chaco and later in Mesa Verde during the eleventh through thirteenth centuries, a gradual shift was occurring. Depopulation of the Four Corners region began in the twelfth century as many groups moved south into already-peopled areas (Eddy, Kane, and Nickens 1983; Lekson 1986; Steen 1966). As population shifted, as new contacts developed between groups, and as adjustments were made, the internal dynamics of Anasazi tradition began to change.

This population movement extended across much of the Southwest. Haury (1958) has documented a migration to Point of Pines from the Kayenta Anasazi area in the late thirteenth century. Di Peso (1958) noted a similar migration as far south as the San Pedro River valley south of Tucson at about the same time. Carlson (1970, 1982) detected the effect of northern polychromes (Kayenta Anasazi) on upper Little Colorado River polychromes (White Mountain Red Ware) in the late 1200s. Clearly, not only ideas, but also people, were moving southward as part of the great depopulation of the Four Corners in the late 1200s.

The cause of movement was probably resource based. The drought and erosion cycle that began in the late 1200s reduced the subsistence resource base in the highly populated Four Corners area (Euler et al. 1979; Dean et al. 1985). This depleted base could not support a population already at or near carrying capacity, and at least some people were forced to leave.

As populations moved into better-watered *refugia*—such as the Little Colorado River valley, the Mogollon Rim, and the Rio Grande valley—village size and layout changed markedly. Before AD 1250–1300, settlements were generally small (less than 50 rooms) and lacked a formal plaza area. By AD 1350, people lived in pueblos with more than 200 rooms and with one or more plazas totally enclosed by rooms.

Great kivas frequently were associated with the larger thirteenth-century settlements along the Mogollon Rim and in the upper Little Colorado River valley. These structures probably integrated the several social segments of the local community or even social segments of nearby communities. As settlements increased in size, however, the enclosed plaza replaced the great kiva and became the integrative structure used to serve the enlarged population of the aggregated settlements of the fourteenth century and later (Haury 1950).

These developments were primarily internal. Population aggregation was a product of the internal dynamics of Pueblo society and the changing physical environment. An evolving social organization sought to integrate the diverse segments of a community into cooperative rather than competitive systems that sustained aggregation. Moieties and sodalities crosscut the small-society social organization based around lineage and clan. Vivian (1990) traces the roots of the Eastern Pueblo moieties to Chaco Canyon before AD 1000, and the moiety system undoubtedly evolved in the context of sustained aggregation along the Rio Grande valley. Thus, according to Vivian and other scholars, the moiety system clearly developed locally.

We now call the socially integrative system developed in the upper Little Colorado River area between AD 1275 and 1325 the katsina cult (Adams 1991). Its evolution during a time of transition in population size and makeup, village size, and village layout suggests that these elements were all linked. According to Adams, the cult acted to integrate Western Pueblo society, allowing it to cope with immigrants and potential conflict for limited resources (Adams 1989, 1991). The cult plays the same role in modern and historic Western Pueblo society, where it is the only sodality that crosscuts all social groups of a pueblo.

Although the katsina cult developed in the upper Little Colorado River area at about AD 1300, the elements comprising the cult did not originate in that area. In fact, the cult contains a rich body of iconography and associated artifacts suggesting southern sources of contact and influence.

Cult icons appear on rock art, pottery, and kiva murals over much of the

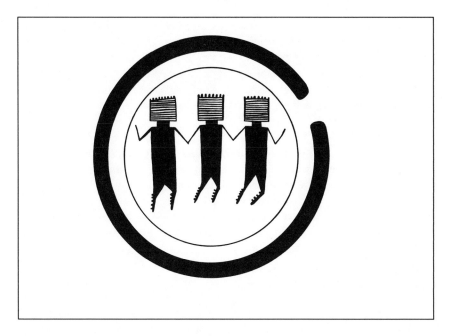

Figure 11.2. A Jeddito Black-on-yellow bowl from Homol'ovi II, with three katsina figures, apparently dancing. (Drawn by Kelley Hays, Arizona State Museum collections)

Southwest (fig. 11.2). Common motifs appearing on pottery in the AD 1300s include parrot/macaw and snake/serpent motifs. Abstract representations of these motifs appear in ceramics from northern Mexico (Casas Grandes and Chihuahuan polychromes) through southern New Mexico, central Arizona, and northeastern Arizona. These ceramics not only are decorated with similar motifs, but also use polychrome designs on buff or brown backgrounds (Carlson 1982; Adams 1991). Similarly, the late AD 1200s saw images of parrots on rock art and live birds traded from northern Mexico, probably Casas Grandes. The kiva murals of the time also have designs with a distinct Mexican flavor, used as background features to typical Puebloan elements and figures.

Artifacts that appear in the thirteenth and fourteenth centuries with northern Mexican/southern Arizona origins include stone or ceramic griddles (*comales* or *piki* stones), the loaf-shaped shaft smoother, shoe-form ceramics, and possibly rectangular ceremonial vessels and stone paint palettes (Adams 1991:90–94). As with the iconography, this artifactual assemblage points to substantial influence from northern Mexico.

Thus the thirteenth and fourteenth centuries saw drastic population shifts in the Anasazi world, along with changes in settlement pattern, land use, and village layout. These new patterns characterized Pueblo people prior to Spanish contact, and some survive today. The populations that moved to the southern and eastern edges of the Anasazi world established new contacts and even new alliances.

For the Eastern Pueblos, these contacts were primarily with the Plains tribes to the east (Riley 1987). The Western Pueblos focused southward, whence came new religious ideas and symbols via Salado peoples (Adams 1991)—ideas and symbols that were compatible with the agrarian cultures of the Pueblo peoples and carried with them the luster of foreign authority. When the stresses of the late 1200s and early 1300s beset the Pueblos, they drew on these ideas and reworked them to form the katsina cult.

Born in the upper Little Colorado River area, the katsina cult spread rapidly into neighboring regions—from the Rio Grande–Galisteo area on the east to the Homol'ovi–Hopi area on the west. After seven centuries of change, the cult still plays an active and interactive role in Pueblo culture. The cult facilitated the re-definition of social relations between groups, allowing them to merge effectively into large villages, and helped enforce relations with groups to the south. Although those relations were severed by AD 1500, their influence on Pueblo society is still visible in the twentieth century.

ON THE BORDERS OF THE SOUTHWEST

Topographic and vegetational changes can be used to define the eastern and western edges of the Southwest, but these factors are of little use in delineat-ing a northern border to the region. On the east, the Plains end with the Pecos Basin and the Raton Plateau, whose shortgrass vegetation is in marked contrast to the piñon-juniper woodlands and montane forests of the southern Rockies, Glorieta Mesa, and Sacramento Mountains (Fenneman 1931; Shelford 1963; Wil-liams and McAllister 1979:6–7). On the west, the Colorado River marks the boundary between the Sonoran and Mojave deserts and sets a convenient western limit to the Southwest (McGuire and Schiffer 1982:14; Warren 1984:340). On the north, the boundary between the Southwest and the Great Basin cuts across the Colorado Plateau with no clear environmental break or change (Cordell 1984:23).

Although the ecological borders of the Southwest are fairly easy to define on the west and east, the cultural borders remain fuzzy in all directions. At various times in prehistory no border appears to exist, and biologically as well as cultur-ally the Southwest grades into adjacent areas. During other periods, ethnic groups and adaptations in these two areas are quite distinct, but even then, defining bor-ders is risky because of the great amount of exchange of people and social relations across these boundaries. As we have said, the boundaries that looked so clear at a continental scale simply fade away when viewed on a regional scale.

THE ARCHAIC

Even at a continental scale, however, such boundaries do not exist during all time periods. Jennings (1964) speaks of an archaic Desert culture that extended from the Great Basin south across the whole of the Southwest. Irwin-Williams (1979) argues for the existence, by 3000 BC, of four interactive traditions in Arizona and

New Mexico: the Pinto Basin, Cochise, Oshara, and an eastern tradition. She refers to these four traditions collectively as the Picosa and contrasts them with the Archaic of the eastern United States, northern California, and the Columbia Plateau. During the Archaic period, no cultural boundary existed along the Colorado River: the Pinto Basin tradition extended from the Pacific halfway across Arizona, where it merged into the Cochise and Oshara traditions (McGuire and Schiffer 1982:176–79; Cordell 1984:157–79). The eastern tradition extended into central Texas, where it met with the eastern Archaic, and the Oshara tradition extended northward almost to the Columbia Plateau. In the Archaic, then, the physical space that would later hold the Southwest was not a distinct entity but part of a much larger network of cultural relations that extended from the Pacific coast on the west to central Texas on the east, and from the Columbia Plateau on the north to an indeterminate point in the Bajio of Mexico on the south. Some two thousand years after the appearance of these traditions, patterns of interaction shifted and the Southwest came into being as a cultural area.

PLAINS–PUEBLO INTERACTIONS

In the Southwest–Plains border area of eastern New Mexico, adaptations have fluctuated between an emphasis on horticulture and reliance on pure hunting and gathering. Eastern New Mexico archaeology is often considered neither Puebloan (because physiographically it is Plains) nor Plains (because the material culture was often Puebloan). Although the data from this area remain spotty (Stuart and Gauthier 1981), we can tentatively reconstruct the flux in adaptations.

From around AD 900 to 1400/1450, scattered populations practicing a mixed hunter-gatherer and horticultural subsistence strategy lived in eastern New Mexico (Glassow 1980; Jelinek 1967; J. H. Kelley 1984; Rocek and Speth 1986; Stuart and Gauthier 1981). Wendorf and Reed (1955) have argued that these horticulturalists were Puebloan farmers who moved onto the Plains, but other researchers suggest that they were indigenous populations who took up agriculture, adopted some of the technology of their Pueblo neighbors, and traded with them for certain items (Snow 1981, 1984; Rocek and Speth 1986).

At the same time as these farmers were dwelling on the plains of eastern New Mexico, small, dispersed horticultural populations, known as the Panhandle Aspect, lived along the Canadian River drainage in western Texas and Oklahoma. The Puebloan pottery, Jemez Mountain obsidian, and small quantities of turquoise and shell beads that occur on Panhandle Aspect sites confirm interaction between west Texas and eastern New Mexico. Tools of Alibates dolomite from the Texas Panhandle and pieces of bison bone from the Plains also occur in small quantities at contemporaneous Rio Grande pueblos (Spielmann 1983; Lintz 1991). Plains–Southwestern interaction during this time period appears fairly diffuse, and Lintz (1991) interprets it as a strategy of alliance formation among individual trade partners, perhaps to offset variations in local food production.

By AD 1350 this interaction intensified. Lintz (1991) argues that the southern

Plains became drier, causing Panhandle Aspect peoples to focus more on hunting and gathering and less on agriculture. Trade with Southwestern populations is thought to be another means these people used to acquire food under increasingly difficult climatic conditions. In the end, however, agriculture ceased to be viable, and farming ended in the Texas Panhandle.

At the same time that farming ends in west Texas, farming sites also disappear from the archaeological record of eastern New Mexico. Jelinek (1967) has proposed that Puebloan farmers in the middle Pecos Valley moved onto the Plains and became bison hunters in response to an increase in bison herd size in the fourteenth century; he postulated, moreover, that the historic Kiowa were the descendants of these hunters. The Kiowa language is related to Tanoan, the language group of many Rio Grande pueblos. More recently, Speth and Parry (1980) have used data from the Garnsey site, a fifteenth-century bison kill in southeastern New Mexico, to argue that bison herds on the southern Plains were not as attractive or reliable a resource as Jelinek thought. They do not dispute the transition from horticulture to hunting and gathering in the area, however, though the transition may have occurred later than originally thought, perhaps in the fifteenth century (Rocek and Speth 1986).

Snow (1984) has pondered the fate of the northeastern New Mexican farmers. He revives an argument once made by Hawley (1937) and Trager (1967) that the Tanoans may have been non-Anasazi part-time horticulturalists on the western edge of the Plains, some of whom moved westward in the fourteenth and fifteenth centuries to become part of Puebloan society, while others remained on the Plains and became the present-day Kiowa.

Although none of these scenarios is supported by enough data to make a strong case, all illustrate the lack of a discrete border between Plains and Pueblo cultural systems in the late prehistoric period. Populations in the eastern Southwest/western Plains share similar cultural inventories and adaptations. Moreover, there appears to be clinal variation in biological characteristics from the eastern Southwest into the western Plains (Rocek and Speth 1986). The only clear difference in the material culture of these groups appears to be that "Plains" sites contain cord-marked, paddle-and-anvil ceramics while "Pueblo" sites yield coil-and-scraped brown wares and black-on-white ceramics. Much has been made of stylistic signaling through pottery design, but we question the wisdom of drawing boundaries based on a single trait.

A watershed of sorts in Plains–Southwest relations occurs in AD 1450. Prior to this date, fairly dispersed populations living by a mixture of hunting, gathering, and horticulture occupied both the Plains and the Eastern Pueblo areas. After this time, the Pueblo people lived in large, aggregated pueblos with an emphasis on farming, and only hunters and gatherers resided on the Plains. These hunter-gatherers may include both the descendants of former horticultural populations and the ancestors of modern southern Athapaskan peoples who moved into the void left by the horticulturalists (Brugge 1983); the Athapaskans were to some degree specialized bison hunters who developed trading relations with the Pueblos (Spielmann 1983, 1991a).

With the arrival of hunter-gatherer populations at the eastern border of Southwestern farming populations, the intensity of Pueblo interaction with Plains groups increased dramatically and the interaction had a greater effect on the large pueblos of the Rio Grande area. Plains nomads annually exchanged quantities of bison meat, fat, and hides for Puebloan corn, cotton blankets, jewelry, and ceramics. This exchange took place at the eastern border pueblos of Taos, Picuris, Pecos, the Galisteo Basin, and Gran Quivira; it resulted from what Wilcox (1984) terms a multiethnic division of labor and what Spielmann (1986, 1989, 1991a) argues was a mutualistic system in which farmers and hunters benefited through the exchange of complementary staple resources from different ecozones. Plains–Pueblo exchange also provided the eastern border pueblos with bison hides, which they used to participate in the pan-Southwestern inter-pueblo trade network.

CALIFORNIA–SOUTHWEST INTERACTIONS

Indian populations west of the lower Colorado River in the Mojave desert never adopted agriculture, but they did make pottery and lived in brush-and-*jacal* structures much like those found in the western Southwest. The lack of corn agriculture would place these peoples in the California cultural area, while the ceramics would place them in the Southwest. The placement of these people in a California culture area is in part an arbitrary decision that makes the cultural area congruous with the modern state.

During the period from about AD 500 to 1200, the first ceramic traditions appeared along the modern California-Arizona border. Anasazi populations lived in the lower Virgin River basin in southern Nevada, with their largest settlements, including Lost City, along the Muddy River (Rafferty 1989). To the south, Patayán peoples dwelt on both sides of the Colorado River and as far west as Lake Cahuilla (the modern Salton Sea) (Waters 1982).

The presence of the Anasazi in southern Nevada and possibly in eastern California has been linked to the establishment of long-distance trade networks (Lyneis 1984). There were large turquoise mines in the Mojave desert at Halloran Springs (Warren 1984:422), which some early authors thought resulted from Anasazi occupation in the Mojave (Rodgers 1929; McKinney, Hafner, and Gothold 1971). More recently, Warren (1984:422) has argued that local peoples lived in permanent villages near the turquoise mines. The Virgin River Anasazi traded the turquoise from these mines into Arizona, where it reached as far south as the Hohokam village at Snaketown during the Gila Butte phase (Sigleo 1975; McGuire and Downum 1982). From AD 700 to 1100, salt was mined in the Lost City area and presumably traded into Arizona (Fowler and Madsen 1986:180–81). Prehistoric peoples on the west side of the Mojave desert in Antelope Valley lived in permanent villages and traded heavily with coastal California groups. These people lacked pottery and probably did not engage in agriculture (Hudson 1978; Hughes and Bennyhoff 1986).

Patayán ceramics and sites appeared in southern California and western Arizona at about AD 700. The center for this occupation appears to have been around Lake Cahuilla and along the lower Colorado River. There is limited evidence for trade and contact between these populations and the Hohokam of southern Arizona. Some of the small quantities of Pacific coast abalone shell found in Colonial (AD 700–1000) and Sedentary (AD 1000–1100) Hohokam sites may have passed through the Patayán, but only a handful of Hohokam sherds have been found in Patayán sites of this period and the shell could have reached the Hohokam through the same northern route as Nevada turquoise (McGuire and Howard 1987:123).

Major changes occur in the relations between the populations of the Mojave desert and western Arizona after AD 1200. Anasazi peoples abandoned southern Nevada in the late 1200s, and Anasazi pottery disappeared from the desert. The Patayán expanded their range and became involved in long-distance trade networks into both northern and southern Arizona.

From AD 1200 to 1450 Patayán ceramics spread over the Mojave desert. The villages in Antelope Valley thrived, but they had little pottery and seem to have been the eastern edge of a sphere of influence that originated on the western slopes of the Sierra Nevada (Warren 1984:426). Local populations established permanent villages along the upper Mojave River, and large quantities of Lower Colorado buff wares appear in these sites, suggesting that these peoples were passing California shell and perhaps turquoise to Patayán settlements. Patayán settlements extended as far north as the Providence and New York mountains (Warren 1984:426), but the major concentration of sites was still around Lake Cahuilla and along the Lower Colorado River (Waters 1982:288).

The Patayán tradition also spread eastward during this period. In southwestern Arizona, Patayán ceramics replaced Hohokam ceramics to the west of the modern Papago reservation and in the Gila Bend area (McGuire and Schiffer 1982:213–14); they also became far more common in Hohokam sites in the Phoenix Basin, and more Hohokam pottery occurred along the lower Colorado River (Waters 1982:290). The Patayán appear to have entered the Hohokam shell trade, bringing shell from the Gulf of California to Gila Bend for exchange into the Phoenix Basin (Huckell 1979).

The great freshwater Lake Cahuilla had been slowly drying up for several hundred years, and sometime between AD 1400 and 1500 it became too brackish to support life (Waters 1982). As the lake became spoiled, Patayán populations were forced eastward to the lower Colorado River. This population displacement sparked endemic warfare and strife between ethnically different Patayán populations, which continued into the 1800s.

GREAT BASIN–SOUTHWEST INTERACTIONS

The northern boundary of the Southwest is marked by no distinctive physiographic feature. On the Colorado Plateau, the growing season shortens and corn agriculture becomes more and more marginal, but the exact northern limit to corn agriculture varied over time with climatic fluctuations. Prehistoric cultures also pulsed within this region. An Anasazi artifact assemblage was found well into Utah from Basketmaker II times until the end of Pueblo III, when the northernmost extent of the Anasazi tradition receded to the Hopi Mesas. Beyond this northern bulge of the Anasazi lived the Fremont people, who had the pots, corn agriculture, and houses of the Southwest culture area.

The Fremont tradition dates from about AD 400 to 1300 and extended throughout Utah and as far north as Idaho (Madsen 1979). These people practiced corn horticulture, made gray ware pottery, lived in substantial pithouses with contiguous surface storage rooms, and developed a distinctive artistic expression in clay figurines and rock art. Marwitt (1986:161) describes Fremont culture as an oddity: in over ten thousand years of human occupation of the area, only during this nine-hundred-year period did agriculturalists appear in the Great Basin. The variation in material culture within the tradition is great, and some authors define more than one agricultural tradition in the region (Madsen and Lindsay 1977) though most retain the label Fremont for the entire region (Lohse 1980). Marwitt (1986) distinguishes five regional variants of the tradition, which he correlates with variations in environmental conditions. The Southwestern attributes associated with the culture—pottery, houses, and agriculture—declined in importance and in elaboration from south to north.

The relationship of the Fremont tradition to the Anasazi is problematic. Many scholars claim that Fremont represents a peripheral development of the Anasazi tradition that originated either with Basketmaker III or with the Anasazi's northern expansion at around AD 900 (Wormington 1955; Ambler 1966a, 1966b; Berry 1980). Marwitt (1986:161, 163) argues that Fremont is best seen as an indigenous development in the Great Basin, noting that the earliest Fremont sites predate Basketmaker III and appear in northern Utah. That the different Fremont traditions appear at different times suggests local developments. In marked contrast to east-west relations between southern California and the Anasazi, there is very little evidence for interaction between the Fremont and the Anasazi. Ceramics from neither area occur with any regularity in the other, and the Fremont do not appear to have provided the Anasazi with any minerals or food products. It is possible that the people of southern Utah adopted agriculture as a strategy appropriate to their particular situations and that such an adoption brought with it a suite of technological assemblages (i.e., ceramic technology) that caused these populations to appear "Anasazi-ized."

The Fremont tradition ends sometime between AD 1250 and 1350 (Marwitt 1986:171). Currently, most scholars feel that Fremont populations were replaced throughout the region by Numic speakers ancestral to the historic Shoshone. The

Shoshone of the Great Basin were hunter-gatherers who lacked agriculture and substantial structures. Fremont peoples were absorbed into Numic groups, migrated to the Plains to form the Dismal River complex, or moved south with the Anasazi.

Despite the apparent lack of regular exchange relations between the Fremont and Anasazi traditions, the broad course of Fremont prehistory parallels that of the northern Anasazi. The Fremont tradition is most widespread at the time of the Anasazi northward expansion between AD 800 and 900, and its greatest elaboration occurs in the AD 1100s to 1200s when Anasazi developments peak in Mesa Verde. The demise of the Fremont tradition corresponds in time with the abandonment of the Four Corners area by the Anasazi in the late thirteenth century. The lack of material indicators of relations between the two traditions suggests that these similarities may reflect environmental shifts more than changes in the interaction between the traditions.

MAKING SENSE OF FUZZY BOUNDARIES

In comparison with Mesoamerican–Southwestern interaction, interactions along the other margins of the Southwest do not appear to have been as pan-regional or permeating an influence on Southwestern prehistory. At various times, interaction with Mesoamerica provided a number of Southwestern populations with material goods, iconography, and perhaps religious cults that were incorporated into or used throughout large portions of the Southwest. In contrast, California, Great Basin, and Plains influence—in the form of iconography, rituals, political alliance, and material culture—is more restricted in scope (Spielmann 1983; McGuire and Schiffer 1982; Marwitt 1986).

One might conclude, then, that interaction with these regions is indeed peripheral to Southwestern prehistory writ large, though highly significant to the prehistory of subregions within the Southwest. It would be incorrect, however, to use the term "peripheral" in the Wallersteinian (see Wallerstein 1974) sense to describe the articulations between these populations. In world systems models, more politically advanced core populations economically dominate the peripheries. In none of these cases, however, is there hard prehistoric data indicating that Southwestern populations were dominated by peripheral populations either politically, economically, or socially.

Nowhere is the inappropriateness of the world systems model for understanding Southwestern social relations at this scale more apparent than in the interaction of Plains and Pueblo populations (but see Baugh 1982, 1984 for an opposing viewpoint). From AD 1100 to 1300, the period of small Eastern Pueblo and Plains farming villages, interaction was diffuse. No group had primacy over another in terms of population size or density, military might, or the desirability of goods. Beginning in the fourteenth century, relations changed as the Rio Grande became more densely populated and this population aggregated into large pueblos. By the fifteenth century, mobile bison hunters moved onto the southern Plains; interaction between the Southwest and Plains increased; and interdependence seems to have grown.

We do not have a clear understanding of how dependent either Plains or Pueblo populations were on this interaction. We do not know the degree to which one group could manipulate or affect the activities of the other. Spielmann (1991a) has argued that the relatively high density of protohistoric Plains hunter-gatherer populations suggests that they depended in part on Pueblo corn for their survival. What remains unanswered, however, is the nature of this dependence. Did each band have multiple trading ties, so that if one trade partner or one Pueblo were unable or unwilling to trade, others were available in their stead? Was the requirement for Puebloan corn an annual one? Though the Spanish chronicles mention yearly visits by Plains nomads, it is not clear if the same bands came to the Pueblos each year.

The Pueblos also depended to some degree on Plains supplies, though again the degree of that dependence is at present unknown. Faunal data from Gran Quivira Pueblo suggest that overhunting of local game led to a decrease in the supply of meat to the pueblo. This deficit may have been offset through trade for bison meat (Spielmann 1988). Though bison meat most likely was consumed primarily by eastern border pueblo populations, these groups traded bison hides to Pueblo populations in the Rio Grande valley and farther west. Through trade, this Plains product may have given the eastern border Pueblos access to items such as glazed pottery, cotton cloth, and turquoise, which were manufactured by other protohistoric Pueblo groups.

Militarily, the Plains nomads may have had the upper hand over Puebloan groups. Pecos Pueblo inhabitants told Coronado of an attack on several pueblos that he had seen in ruins on his trip from the Albuquerque area to Pecos. The Teyas, a nomadic Plains group, had besieged Pecos a number of years prior to the Spanish arrival (Winship 1896). This is one of only a few references to pre-seventeenth-century nomad hostilities, suggesting that overtly hostile interactions may not have been the norm in protohistoric Plains–Pueblo relations (Spielmann 1991b).

Politically, individual eastern border Pueblos may have used their relations with Plains nomads in their jockeying for power and access to goods within an increasingly populated Rio Grande world (Wilcox 1991b). Spanish chronicles document that various Pueblo and Plains groups in the sixteenth and seventeenth centuries were allied with one another in opposition to other such alliances (Hodge, Hammond, and Rey 1945; Hammond and Rey 1953:345; Schroeder 1984 and references therein).

What we propose, then, is that there was a dynamic balance of needs, goods, and power between protohistoric Plains hunter-gatherers and Puebloan farmers east of the Rio Grande. An economic division of labor existed, and the trade relations were predicated upon social ties such as the trade partnerships between individuals (see Ford 1972) and political alliances between particular Plains bands and particular pueblos.

Other researchers (Baugh 1982, 1984; and Wilcox 1981a, 1981b, 1984) argue that an interactive system extended beyond Plains hunter-gatherer/Pueblo horticultural alliances to Caddo and Wichita farming populations to the east and north of the Plains nomads. They suggest that these farmers also interacted directly with Puebloan farming populations, perhaps through ambassadors. Thus, they see the Plains–Southwest system as politically and economically integrated over the entire southern and portions of the central Plains.

We question whether the economic division of labor that typifies Plains–Southwest relations was ever this socially or politically coherent. Instead, we suggest that like the Puebloan farmers, the protohistoric farmers of Oklahoma and Kansas were engaging in mutualistic exchange with Plains nomads. We doubt, however, that Puebloan, Plains Caddoan, and Wichita farmers monitored and made decisions based upon one another's exchange activities. Most likely, Plains nomads had obtained the occasional Puebloan goods showing up in central Kansas (Wedel 1942, 1950) and western Oklahoma (Baugh 1982) villages.

Making similar sense of the relations on the northern and western borders of the Southwest will require a set of data as detailed as what we have for the eastern edge. At the present time such data do not exist, and much more research is needed in both these regions.

CONCLUSION

Our discussions of external connections of the Southwest have been built around two basic ideas. First, if we define the Southwest in terms of social relations between human groups, then the boundaries of the Southwest are fuzzy. The space that these social relations occupies changes over time, so that the area of the Southwest is historically created and dynamic. Even the distinction between internal and external becomes vague and changeable. Second, our analyses of Southwestern prehistory should be multiscaler. As we move our scale of analysis, we frame different sets of relations; as we change scale, the patterns that we see also change. We need to consider different theoretical models to reveal and understand the patterns that we find at different scales. We question the use of theories that dictate a priori what the nature of relations was or that specify a single scale of analysis.

If the Southwest was not a hard-bounded entity, then archaeological scholarship needs to range more widely. Throughout our discussions of external relations to the Southwest we have been able to write what we have because we are personally well versed in the appropriate archaeological data on both sides of the "borders." We have worked in the Southwest and in these "external" areas and have focused specifically on interrelationships in our research. Moreover, we interact extensively with colleagues in the "external" areas so that we are aware in general of data that pertain to the issue of interrelationships.

At the broadest scale we have found that the Southwest and Mesoamerica share many commonalities, but that the two regions were distinctive in the structure of relations. The Southwest was neither strictly the northernmost edge of Mesoamerica nor an isolated cultural climax separate from surrounding culture areas. The degree of sociopolitical complexity and community or polity size and of rank-size differentiation within polities was less in the Southwest than in Mesoamerica. Along both the interior of northern Durango and southern Chihuahua and the narrow coastal plain of Sinaloa, a pronounced geographical gap separates the southernmost Southwestern sites from the northernmost Mesoamerican sites.

In the northern Southwest we find that the processes that restructured the Pueblo world in the early fourteenth century were part and parcel of that world, springing from the social relations within and between Pueblo social groups and from the relations between these groups and the environment. The people of the late prehistoric Pueblo world drew on beliefs, symbols, and items from the south to create the katsina cult, but they adapted the cult to local conditions as the regional relations that structured their lives changed.

At the lowest scale of analysis, the boundaries of the Southwest had little or no meaning for the prehistoric populations that lived along them. Generally, the interactions across these boundaries were as (or more) important to the Southwestern populations involved in them as were their relations with other Southwestern peoples. The issue of what was inside and outside the Southwest is not a simple one. Clearly, the Southwest was never truly the Nuevo México that the sixteenth-century Spanish looked for. It was also never the clearly defined culture area that many modern archaeologists have assumed.

References

Abbott, David R.
  1985   Unbiased Estimates of Feature Frequencies with Computer Simulation. *American Archaeology* 5:3–11.
Accola, Richard M.
  1981   Mogollon Settlement Patterns in the Middle San Francisco River Drainage, West Central New Mexico. *The Kiva* 46(3):155–69.
Ackerly, Neal W.
  1982   Irrigation, Water Allocation Strategies, and the Hohokam Collapse. *The Kiva* 47:91–106.
Ackerly, Neal W., Jerry B. Howard, and Randall H. McGuire
  1985   La Ciudad Canals: A Study of Hohokam Irrigation Systems at the Community Level. *Anthropological Field Studies* 17. Tempe: Arizona State University.
Adair, J., K. W. Deuschle, and C. R. Barnett
  1988   *The People's Health: Anthropology and Medicine in a Navajo Community.* Albuquerque: University of New Mexico Press.
Adams, E. Charles
  1981   The View from the Hopi Mesas. In *The Protohistoric Period in the North American Southwest, A.D. 1450–1700,* D. R. Wilcox and W. B. Masse, eds., pp. 321–35. Anthropological Research Papers 24. Tempe: Arizona State University.
  1983   The Appearance, Evolution, and Meaning of the Katsina Cult to the Pre-hispanic Pueblo World of the Southwestern United States. Paper presented at the 11th International Congress of Anthropological and Ethnological Sciences, Vancouver.
  1989   The Case for Conflict during the Late Prehistoric and Protohistoric Periods in the Western Pueblo Area of the American Southwest. In *Cultures in Conflict: Current Archaeological Perspectives,* D. C. Tkaczuk and B. C. Vivian, eds., pp. 103–11. The Archaeological Association of the University of Calgary.
  1991   *The Origin and Development of the Pueblo Katsina Cult.* Tucson: University of Arizona Press.
Adams, E. Charles, and Jenny L. Adams
  n.d.   Thirteenth-Century Abandonment of the Four Corners: A Reevaluation. Ms., Arizona State Museum Library, University of Arizona, Tucson.
Adams, Robert McC.
  1956   Some Hypotheses on the Development of Early Civilizations. *American Antiquity* 21:227–32.
  1965   *The Land Behind Baghdad.* Chicago: University of Chicago Press.
  1978   *Strategies of Maximization, Stability, and Resilience in Mesopotamian Society, Settlement, and Agriculture.* Proceedings of the American Philosophical Society 1212:329–35.
Agenbroad, Larry D.
  1982   Geology and Lithic Resources of the Grasshopper Region. In *Multidisciplinary Research at Grasshopper Pueblo, Arizona,* W. A. Longacre, S. J. Holbrook, and M. W. Graves, eds., pp. 42–45. Anthropological Papers of the University of Arizona 45. Tucson: University of Arizona Press.
Agogino, George, and Frank C. Hibben
  1958   Central New Mexico Paleo-Indian Cultures. *American Antiquity* 28:422–25.
Ahlstrom, Richard Van Ness
  1985   The Interpretation of Archaeological Tree-Ring Dates. Ph.D. dissertation, Department of Anthropology, University of Arizona, Tucson.

Aikens, C. Melvin
   1966   *Virgin-Kayenta Cultural Relationships.* University of Utah Anthropological Papers 79. Salt
           Lake City.
Akins, Nancy J.
   1986   *A Biocultural Approach to Human Burials from Chaco Canyon, New Mexico.* National Park
           Service, Reports of the Chaco Center no. 9. Santa Fe.
Allen, Joseph W., and Charles H. McNutt
   1955   A Pit House Site near Santa Ana Pueblo, New Mexico. *American Antiquity* 20:241–55.
Allen, Wilma H., Charles F. Merbs, and Walter H. Birkby
   1985   Evidence for Prehistoric Scalping at Nuvakwewtaga (Chavez Pass) and Grasshopper Ruin,
           Arizona. In *Health and Disease in the Prehistoric Southwest,* C. F. Merbs and R. J. Miller,
           eds., pp. 23–42. Arizona State University Anthropological Research Papers 34. Tempe.
Allison, M. J.
   1984   Paleopathology in Peruvian and Chilean Populations. In *Paleopathology at the Origins
           of Agriculture,* M. N. Cohen and G. J. Armelagos, eds., pp. 515–30. New York: Aca-
           demic Press.
Altschul, Jeffrey
   1978   The Development of the Chacoan Interaction Sphere. *Journal of Anthropological Research*
           34(1):109–46.
Ambler, J. Richard
   1966a   Caldwell Village (NE Utah, Fremont Culture). University of Utah Anthropological Papers
           84. Salt Lake City.
   1966b   Caldwell Village and Fremont Prehistory. Ph.D. dissertation, University of Colorado,
           Boulder.
Ambler, J. Richard, Helen C. Fairley, and Phil R. Geib
   1983   Kayenta Anasazi Utilization of Canyon and Plateaus in the Navajo Mountain District.
           Paper presented at the 2nd Anasazi Symposium, Bloomfield, New Mexico.
Ambler, J. Richard, and Mark Q. Sutton
   1989   The Anasazi Abandonment of the San Juan Drainage and the Numic Expansion. *North
           American Archaeologist* 10:39–53.
Amsden, Charles A.
   1949   *Prehistoric Southwesterners from Basketmaker to Pueblo.* Los Angeles: Southwest Museum.
Antieu, John M.
   1981   *Hohokam Settlement at the Confluence: Excavations along the Palo Verde Pipeline.* NMA Re-
           search Paper 20. Flagstaff.
Anyon, Roger
   1984   Mogollon Settlement Patterns and Communal Architecture. M.A. thesis, Department of
           Anthropology, University of New Mexico, Albuquerque.
   1991   Protecting and Past, Protecting the Present: Cultural Resources and American Indians.
           In *Protecting the Past: Readings in Archaeological Resource Protection,* G. S. Smith and J. E.
           Ehrenhard, eds., pp. 215–22. Caldwell: The Telford Press.
Anyon, Roger, Susan M. Collins, and Kathryn H. Bennett (editors)
   1983   *Archaeological Investigations between Manuelito Canyon and Whitewater Arroyo, Northwest
           New Mexico.* Zuni Archaeology Program Report 185. Zuni.
Anyon, Roger, and Steven A. LeBlanc
   1980   The Architectural Evolution of Mogollon-Mimbres Ceremonial Structures. *The Kiva*
           45(4):209–25.
   1984   *The Galaz Ruin, A Prehistoric Mimbres Village in Southwestern New Mexico.* Albuquerque:
           Maxwell Museum of Anthropology and University of New Mexico Press.
Archaeology in Tucson
   1990   San Pedro River Prehistory. *Archaeology in Tucson* 4(1):1–3.
Armelagos, George J.
   1968   Aiken's Fremont Hypothesis and Use of Skeletal Material in Archaeological Interpreta-
           tion. *American Antiquity* 33:85–86.
Armelagos, George J., and J. R. Dewey
   1978   Evolutionary Response to Human Infectious Disease. In *Health and the Human Condition,*
           M. H. Logan and E. E. Hunt, eds., pp. 101–106. North Scituate, MA: Duxbury Press.

Armelagos, George J., D. S. Carlson, and Dennis P. Van Gerven
    1982   The Theoretical Foundations and Development of Skeletal Biology. In *A History of American Physical Anthropology,* pp. 305–28. New York: Academic Press.

Associated Press
    1991   Lead Poisoning Culprit in Omaha Tribe's Death. *Albuquerque Journal,* Friday, October 4:F1.

Atkinson, Ronald R.
    1989   The Evolution of Ethnicity among the Acholi of Uganda: The Precolonial Phase. *Ethnohistory* 36(1):19–43.

Austin, Ken
    1977   The Mountain Patayan People of West Central Arizona. Manuscript, Prescott National Forest, Prescott, AZ.

Bahti, Thomas N.
    1949   A Large-Gallina Pit House and Two Surface Structures. *El Palacio* 56(2):52–59.

Bailey, Robert C., Genevieve Head, Mark Jenike, Bruce Owen, Robert Rechtman, and Elzbieta Zechenter
    1989   Hunting and Gathering in Tropical Rain Forests: Is It Possible? *American Antiquity* 91:59–82.

Baker, B. J., and George J. Armelagos
    1988   The Origin and Antiquity of Syphilis: Paleopathological Diagnosis and Interpretation. *Current Anthropology* 29:703–20.

Baugh, Timothy G.
    1982   *Edwards (34BK2): Southern Plains Adaptations in the Protohistoric Period.* Studies in Oklahoma's Past 8. Norman: Oklahoma Archaeological Survey.
    1984   Southern Plains Societies and Eastern Frontier Pueblo Exchange during the Protohistoric Period. In *Collected Papers in Honor of Harry L. Hadlock,* N. L. Fox, ed., pp. 157–68. Papers of the Archaeological Society of New Mexico 9. Albuquerque.
    1986   Cultural History and Protohistoric Societies in the Southern Plains. Memoir 21, *Plains Anthropologist* 31(114:pt. 2).

Beal, John D.
    1987   *Foundations of the Rio Grande Classic: The Lower Chama River A.D. 1300–1500.* Santa Fe: Southwest Archaeological Consultants Research Series.

Beals, Ralph L.
    1932   *The Comparative Ethnology of Northern Mexico before 1750.* Ibero-Americana 2. Berkeley.
    1933   *The Acaxee.* Ibero-Americana 6. Berkeley.
    1943   *The Aboriginal Culture of the Cahita Indians.* Ibero-Americana 19. Berkeley.
    1944   Relations between Mesoamerica and the Southwest. In *El Norte de Mexico y el Sur de Estados Unidos,* pp. 245–52. Sociedad Mexicana de Antropologia, Mexico City.
    1954   Comment on Gatherers and Farmers in the Greater Southwest. *American Anthropologist* 56(4):551–53.

Beals, Ralph L., George W. Brainerd, and Watson Smith
    1945   *Archaeological Studies in Northeast Arizona.* University of California Publications in American Archaeology and Ethnology, vol. 44, no. 1. Berkeley and Los Angeles: University of California Press.

Bean, Lowell John
    1972   *Mukat's People: The Cahuilla Indians of Southern California.* Berkeley: University of California Press.

Bean, Lowell John, and Sylvia Brakke Vane
    1986   Cults and Their Transformations. In *Handbook of North American Indians.* Vol. 8, *California,* R. F. Heizer, ed., pp. 662–72. Washington, D.C.: Smithsonian Institution.

Beckwith, Frank
    1935   Ancient Indian Petroglyphs of Utah. *El Palacio* 38(6–8):33–39.

Bender, Barbara
    1985   Emergent Tribal Formations in the American Midcontinent. *American Antiquity* 50(1):52–62.

Bennett, John W.
    1946   The Interpretation of Pueblo Culture: A Question of Values. *Southwestern Journal of Anthropology* 2(4):361–74.

Bennett, Kenneth A.
    1966a   Appendix B: Analysis of Prehistoric Human Skeletal Remains from the Navajo Reser-
             voir District. In *Prehistory in the Navajo Reservoir District, Northwestern New Mexico*, F. W.
             Eddy, ed., pp. 523–46. Museum of New Mexico Papers in Anthropology 15, pt. 2. Santa
             Fe: Museum of New Mexico Press.
    1966b   Appendix III: Human Skeletal Remains. In *Archaeological Investigations in Lower Glen
             Canyon, Utah, 1959–1960*, P. V. Long, ed., pp. 73–74. Museum of Arizona Bulletin 42,
             Phoenix.
    1973   *The Indians of Point of Pines, Arizona. A Comparative Study of Their Physical Characteristics.*
             Anthropology Papers 23. Tucson: University of Arizona Press.
    1975   *Skeletal Remains from Mesa Verde National Park, Colorado.* National Park Service, Publica-
             tions in Archaeology 7F, Wetherill Mesa Study. Washington, D.C.
Bently, Mark T.
    1988   The Mimbres Butterfly Motif (The Rejuvenation of an Old Idea). *The Artifact* 26(1):39–80.
Benz, B. F.
    1986   Taxonomy and Evolution of Mexican Maize. Ph.D. dissertation, University of Wisconsin.
             Ann Arbor: University Microfilms.
Berman, Mary Jane
    1979   *Cultural Resources Overview, Socorro Area, New Mexico.* USDA Forest Service, Southwest-
             ern Regional Office, and USDI Bureau of Land Management, New Mexico State Office,
             Albuquerque and Santa Fe.
Bernor, R., S. Ponnech, and P. Miller
    1972   Human Skeletal Report: Pathologies and Anomalies for RB-MV 568, a Tsegi Phase Site
             near Kayenta, Arizona. Manuscript, Laboratory of Skeletal and Faunal Analysis, Univer-
             sity of California, Los Angeles.
Berry, Claudia F., and Michael S. Berry
    1986   Chronological and Conceptual Models of the Southwestern Archaic. In *Anthropology of the
             Desert West: Essays in Honor of Jesse D. Jennings*, C. Condie and D. Fowler, eds., pp. 253–
             57. University of Utah Anthropological Papers 110. Salt Lake City.
Berry, Claudia F., and William S. Marmaduke
    1982   *The Middle Gila Basin: An Archaeological and Historical Overview.* Flagstaff: Northland Re-
             search.
Berry, D. R.
    1983   Skeletal Remains from RB 568. In *Honoring the Dead: Anasazi Ceramics from the Rainbow
             Bridge Monument Valley Expedition*, H. K. Crotty, ed., pp. 64–69. Museum of Cultural
             History Monograph Series 22. Los Angeles.
    1985   Dental Paleopathology of Grasshopper Pueblo, Arizona. In *Health and Disease in the Pre-
             historic Southwest*, C. F. Merbs and R. J. Miller, eds., pp. 253–74. Arizona State University
             Anthropological Research Paper 34. Tempe.
Berry, Michael S.
    1980   Fremont Orgins: A Critique. In *Fremont Perspectives*, D. B. Madsen, ed., pp. 17–24, Utah
             Division of State History, Antiquities Section Selected Papers 7(16). Salt Lake City.
    1982   *Time, Space and Transition in Anasazi Prehistory.* Salt Lake City: University of Utah Press.
Bettinger, R. L.
    1989   *The Archaeology of Pinyon House, Two Eagles, and Crater Middens: Three Residential Sites
             in Owens Valley, Eastern California.* Anthropological Papers of the American Museum of
             Natural History 67. New York.
Biella, Jan V., and Richard C. Chapman
    1979   *Archaeological Investigations in Cochiti Reservoir, New Mexico.* Vol. 4, *Adaptive Change in the
             Northern Rio Grande Valley.* Albuquerque: University of New Mexico Press, Office of Con-
             tract Archaeology.
Binford, Lewis R.
    1968   Post-Pleistocene Adaptations. In *New Perspectives in Archaeology*, S. R. Binford and L. R.
             Binford, eds., pp. 313–42. Chicago: Aldine.
    1972   Mortuary Practices: Their Study and Their Potential. In *An Archaeological Perspective*, L. R.
             Binford, ed., pp. 208–51. New York: Academic Press.
    1980   Willow Smoke and Dog's Tails: Hunter-Gatherer Settlement Systems and Archaeological
             Site Formation. *American Antiquity* 45:1–17.

1982   The Archaeology of Place. *Journal of Anthropological Archaeology* 1:5–31.
Birkby, Walter H.
1982   Biosocial Interpretations from Cranial Nonmetric Traits of Grasshopper Pueblo Skeletal
        Remains. In *Multidisciplinary Research at Grasshopper Pueblo, Arizona,* W. A. Longacre, S. J.
        Holbrook, and M. Graves, eds., pp. 36–41. Anthropological Papers 40. Tucson: Univer-
        sity of Arizona Press.
Blackiston, A. Hooton
1908   Ruins of the Tenaja and Rio San Pedro. *Records of the Past* 7(6):282–90.
Blake, Michael, Steven A. LeBlanc, and Paul E. Minnis
1986   Changing Settlement and Population in the Mimbres Valley, SW New Mexico. *Journal of
        Field Archaeology* 13:439–64.
Blakely, R. L.
1977   Introduction: Changing Strategies for the Biological Anthropologist. In *Biocultural Adapta-
        tions in Prehistoric America,* R. L. Blakely, ed., pp. 1–9. Athens: University of Georgia Press.
Blanton, Richard E.
1975   The Cybertetic Analysis of Human Population Growth. *Memoirs of the Society for Ameri-
        can Archaeology* 30:116–26.
Blanton, Richard E., and Gary Feinman
1984   The Mesoamerican World System. *American Anthropologist* 86:673–82.
Blevins, Byron B., and Carol Joiner
1977   The Archaeological Survey of Tijeras Canyon. *Archaeological Report* 18, pp. 126–52. Albu-
        querque: USDA Forest Service, Southwestern Region.
Blitz, John H.
1988   Adoption of the Bow in Prehistoric North America. *North American Archaeologist* 9(2):123–
        46.
Bluhm, Elaine
1960   Mogollon Settlement Patterns in Pine Lawn Valley, New Mexico. *American Antiquity*
        25:539–46.
Blumenschein, Harriet
1958   Further Excavations and Surveys in the Taos Area. *El Palacio* 65:107–11.
Blumenthal, E. H., Jr.
1940   An Introduction to Gallina Archaeology. *New Mexico Anthropologist* 4(1):10–13.
Boulding, Kenneth E.
1962   *Conflict and Defence.* New York: Harper and Brothers.
Bourke, John G.
1884   *The Snake-Dance of the Moquis of Arizona.* London: Sampson Low, Marston, Searle, and
        Rivington.
Bowers, Janice E., and Steven P. McLaughlin
1980   Flora and Vegetation of the Rincon Mountains, Pima County, Arizona. *Desert Plants* 8:51–
        67.
Bradfield, W.
1931   *Cameron Creek: A Site in the Mimbres Area in Grant County, New Mexico.* Santa Fe: El Pala-
        cio and School of American Research Press.
Bradley, Bruce A., and Jim Kleidon
1989   *Annual Report of the 1988 Excavations at Sand Canyon Pueblo (5MT765).* Cortez: Crow
        Canyon Archaeological Center.
Brand, Donald D.
1943   Archaeological Relations between Northern Mexico and the Southwest. In *El Norte de
        Mexico y el Sur de los Estados Unidos,* pp. 199–203. Mexico City: Sociedad Mexicana de
        Antropologia.
Braniff, Beatriz
1974   Sequencias Arqueologicas en Guanajuato y las Cuenca de Mexico: Intento de Correla-
        cion. In *Teotihuacan: XI Mesa Redonda,* pp. 274–323. Mexico City: Sociedad Mexicana de
        Antropologia.
1988   The Mesoamerican Northern Frontier and the Gran Chichimeca. Paper presented at the
        Amerind Foundation New World Studies Seminar, Culture and Contact: Charles Di Peso's
        Gran Chichimeca. Dragoon, AZ.

Braun, David P.
    1990   Selection and Evolution in Nonhierarchial Organization. In *The Evolution of Political Systems: Sociopolitics in Small-Scale Sedentary Societies,* S. Upham, ed., pp. 21–61. School of American Research Advanced Seminar Series. Cambridge: Cambridge University Press.
    1991   Are There Cross-Cultural Regularities in Tribal Social Practices? In *Between Bands and States,* S. A. Gregg, ed., pp. 423–44. Occasional Paper 9. Center for Archaeological Investigations, Southern Illinois University, Carbondale.
Braun, David P., and Stephen Plog
    1982   Evolution of "Tribal" Social Networks: Theory and Prehistoric North American Evidence. *American Antiquity* 47(3):504–25.
Breitburg, Emanuel
    1988   Prehistoric New World Turkey Domestication: Origins, Developments, and Consequences. Ph.D. dissertation, Southern Illinois University, Carbondale.
Brew, John Otis
    1946   *Archaeology of Alkali Ridge, Southeastern Utah.* Papers of the Peabody Museum of American Archaeology and Ethnology, Harvard University, vol. 21. Cambridge.
British Museum Library
    n.d.   *Sonoran and Chihuahuan Acequia Maps.* British Museum Library Manuscript no. 17662, Folio E. Copies on file, Southwest Documentary Relations, Arizona State Museum, University of Arizona, Tucson.
Brock, S. L., and C. B. Ruff
    1988   Diachronic Patterns of Change in Structural Properties of the Femur in the Prehistoric American Southwest. *American Journal of Physical Anthropology* 75:113–27.
Brody, J. J.
    1977   *Mimbres Painted Pottery.* Albuquerque: School of American Research and University of New Mexico Press.
    1991   *Anasazi and Pueblo Painting.* Albuquerque: School of American Research and University of New Mexico Press.
Brooks, Richard Howard
    1971   Lithic Traditions in Northwestern Mexico, Paleo-Indian to Chalchihuites. Ph.D. dissertation, University of Colorado, Boulder.
Brown, Gary
    1990   Old Wood and Early Navajos: A Chronometric Analysis of the Dinetah Phase. Paper presented at the 5th Annual Navajo Conference, Shiprock, NM, October 18.
Bruder, J. Simon
    1991   A Look at Archaeological-Ethnobiological Collaboration in Hohokam Studies. *The Kiva* 56:193–206.
Brugge, David
    1983   Navajo Prehistory and History to 1850. In *Handbook of North American Indians.* Vol. 10, *Southwest,* A. Ortiz, ed., pp. 489–501. Washington, D.C.: Smithsonian Institution Press.
Bryan, Kirk
    1929   Flood-water Farming. *The Geographical Review* 19:444–57.
Buikstra, James E.
    1977   Biocultural Dimensions of Archaeological Study: A Regional Perspective. In *Biocultural Adaptation in Prehistoric America,* R. L. Blakely, ed., pp. 67–84. Athens: University of Georgia Press.
    1984   The Lower Illinois River Region: A Prehistoric Context for the Study of Ancient Diet and Health. In *Paleopathology at the Origins of Agriculture,* M. N. Cohen and G. J. Armelagos, eds., pp. 215–34. New York: Academic Press.
Buikstra, James E., J. Bullington, D. K. Charles, D. C. Cook, S. R. Frankenberg, L. W. Konigsberg, J. B. Lambert, and L. Xue
    1987   Diet, Demography, and the Development of Horticulture. In *Emergent Horticultural Economies of the Eastern Woodlands,* W. F. Keegan, ed., pp. 67–86. Center for Archaeological Investigations, Occasional Paper 7. Carbondale: Southern Illinois University.
Bullard, William R.
    1962   *The Cerro Colorado Site and Pithouse Architecture in the Southwestern United States prior to A.D. 900.* Papers of the Peabody Museum of Archaeology and Ethnology 44(2).

Burger, Richard L.
    1988   Unity and Heterogeneity within the Chavin Horizon. In *Peruvian Prehistory,* R. W. Keatinge, ed., pp. 99–144. Cambridge: Cambridge University Press.

Burns, Barney T.
    1983   Simulated Anasazi Storage Behavior Using Crop Yields Reconstructed from Tree Rings: A.D. 652–1968. Ph.D. dissertation, University of Arizona, Tucson.

Cable, John S., and David E. Doyel
    1985   Hohokam Land-Use Patterns along the Terraces of the Lower Salt River Valley: The Central Phoenix Project. In *Proceedings of the 1985 Hohokam Symposium,* A. E. Dittert and D. E. Dove, eds., pp. 263–310. Arizona Archaeological Society Occasional Paper 2. Phoenix.
    1987   Pioneer Period Village Structure and Settlement Pattern in the Phoenix Basin. In *The Hohokam Village: Site Structure and Organization,* D. E. Doyel, ed., pp. 21–71. Glenwood Springs: American Association for the Advancement of Science.

Cable, John S., K. Hoffman, David E. Doyel, and F. Rits (editors)
    1985   *City of Phoenix, Archaeology of the Original Townsite: Block 24-east.* Soil Systems Publications in Archaeology 8. Phoenix.

Cameron, Catherine M.
    1984   A Regional View of Chipped Stone Raw Material Use in Chaco Canyon. In *Recent Research on Chaco Prehistory,* W. J. Judge and J. D. Schelberg, eds., pp. 137–52. Albuquerque: Division of Cultural Research, National Park Service.
    1990   Pit Structure Abandonment in the Four Corners Region of the American Southwest: Late Basketmaker III and Pueblo I. *Journal of Field Archaeology* 17(1):27–37.

Canouts, Veletta (assembler)
    1975   *An Archaeological Survey of the Orme Reservoir.* Arizona State Museum Archaeological Series 92. Tucson.

Carlson, Roy L.
    1963   *Basketmaker III Sites near Durango, Colorado.* University of Colorado Studies, Series in Anthropology 8. Boulder.
    1970   *White Mountain Redware: A Pottery Tradition of East-Central Arizona and Western New Mexico.* Anthropological Paper 4, no. 19. Tucson: University of Arizona.
    1982   The Polychrome Complexes. In *Southwestern Ceramics: A Comparative Review,* A. H. Schroeder, ed., pp. 201–34. The Arizona Archaeologist 15, Arizona Archaeological Society, Phoenix.

Cartledge, Thomas R.
    1976   Prehistory in Vosberg Valley, Central Arizona. *The Kiva* 42:95–104.

Casti, John L.
    1986   On System Complexity: Identification, Measurement, and Management. In *Complexity, Language, and Life: Mathematical Approaches,* J. L. Casti and A. Karlqvist, eds. Biomathematics 16:146–73. Berlin: Springer-Verlag.

Castleton, Kenneth B., and David B. Madsen
    1981   The Distribution of Rock Art Elements and Styles in Utah. *Journal of California and Great Basin Anthropology* 3(2):163–75.

Cater, John D., and Mark L. Chenault
    1988   Kiva Use Reinterpreted. *Southwestern Lore* 54(3):19–32.

Chapman, Richard C.
    1985   Architecture and Use of Site Space. In *Class II Cultural Resource Survey, Upper Gila Water Supply Study, Central Arizona Project,* R. C. Chapman, C. W. Gossett, and W. J. Gossett, eds., pp. 347–58. Albuquerque: Deuel and Associates, Inc.

Chapman, Richard C., and Jan V. Biella
    1977   *Archaeological Investigations in Cochiti Reservoir, New Mexico. Excavation and Analysis, 1975 Season.* Albuquerque: Office of Contract Archaeology, University of New Mexico.

Chase, James E.
    1976   Appendix: Deviance in the Gallina: A Report on a Small Series of Gallina Human Skeleton Remains. In *Archaeological Excavations in the Llaves Area, Santa Fe National Forest, New Mexico, 1972–1974,* by N. W. Dick, pp. 66–106. Archaeological Report 13. Albuquerque: USDA Forest Service, Southwestern Region.

Cherry, John F., and Colin Renfrew
   1986   Epilogue and Prospects. In *Peer Polity Interaction and Socio-Political Change*, C. Renfrew
           and J. F. Cherry, eds., pp. 149–58. Cambridge: Cambridge University Press.
Christaller, W.
   1966   *Central Places in Southern Germany*, transl. by C. W. Baskin. Englewood Cliffs, NJ:
           Prentice-Hall.
Claessen, Henri J. M., and Peter Skalnik
   1978   The Early State: Theories and Hypotheses. In *The Early State*, H. J. M. Claessen and
           P. Skalnik, eds., pp. 3–29. The Hague: Mouton.
Clark, Ira G.
   1987   *Water in New Mexico: A History of Its Management and Use*. Albuquerque: University of
           New Mexico Press.
Clarke, David L.
   1978   *Analytical Archaeology* (rev. ed.). New York: Columbia University Press.
Cohen, Mark N.
   1977   *The Food Crisis in Prehistory: Overpopulation and the Origins of Agriculture*. New Haven:
           Yale University Press.
Cohen, Mark N., and George J. Armelagos
   1984   *Paleopathology at the Origins of Agriculture*. New York: Academic Press.
Cole, Sally J.
   1984   Analysis of a San Juan (Basketmaker) Style Painted Mask in Grand Gulch, Utah. *South-
           western Lore* 50(1):1–6.
   1985   Additional Information on Basketmaker Mask or Face Representations in Rock Art of
           Southeastern Utah. *Southwestern Lore* 51(1):14–18.
   1989   Iconography and Symbolism in Basketmaker Rock Art. In *Rock Art of the Western Canyons*,
           J. S. Day, P. D. Friedman, and M. J. Tate, eds., p. 85. Colorado Archaeological Society
           Memoir 3.
   1990   *Legacy on Stone: Rock Art of the Colorado Plateau and Four Corners Region*. Boulder: Johnson.
Colton, Harold S.
   1936   The Rise and Fall of the Prehistoric Population of Northern Arizona. *Science* 84:337–43.
   1939a   *An Archaeological Survey of Northwestern Arizona Including the Description of Fifteen New
           Pottery Types*. Museum of Northern Arizona Bulletin 16. Flagstaff.
   1939b   *Prehistoric Culture Units and Their Relationships in Northern Arizona*. Museum of Northern
           Arizona Bulletin 17. Flagstaff.
   1946   *The Sinagua: A Summary of the Archaeology of the Region of Flagstaff*. Arizona Museum of
           Northern Arizona Bulletin 22. Flagstaff.
   1960   *Black Sand: Prehistory in Northern Arizona*. Albuquerque: University of New Mexico Press.
Cordell, Linda S.
   1977   The 1976 Excavation of Tijeras Pueblo, Cibola National Forest, New Mexico. *Archaeologi-
           cal Report* 18:1–43. USDA Forest Service, Southwestern Region.
   1979   *Middle Rio Grande Valley, New Mexico*. Cultural Resources Overview Service, Southwest-
           ern Region.
   1980   The Setting. In *Tijeras Canyon: Analyses of the Past*, L. S. Cordell, ed., pp. 1–11. Albu-
           querque: Maxwell Museum of Anthropology and University of New Mexico Press.
   1984   *Prehistory of the Southwest*. New York: Academic Press.
   1989   Evaluating Population Models of Ethnic Diversity. Paper presented at the 1st Joint
           Archaeological Conference. Baltimore.
Cordell, Linda S., and George J. Gumerman
   1989   Cultural Interaction in the Prehistoric Southwest. In *Dynamics of Southwest Prehistory*,
           L. S. Cordell and G. J. Gumerman, eds., pp. 1–17. A School of American Research Ad-
           vanced Seminar Book. Washington, D.C.: Smithsonian Institution Press.
Cordell, Linda S., and Fred Plog
   1979   Escaping the Confines of Normative Thought: A Reevaluation of Puebloan Prehistory.
           American Antiquity 44:405–29.
Corruccini, Robert S.
   1974   The Biological Relationships of Some Prehistoric and Historic Pueblo Populations. *Ameri-
           can Journal of Physical Anthropology* 37:373–88.

Cosgrove, H. S., and C. B. Cosgrove
  1932   *The Swarts Ruin: A Typical Mimbres Site in Southwestern New Mexico.* Peabody Museum of
          American Archaeology and Ethnology, Harvard University, Cambridge.
Creamer, Winifred, and Jonathan Haas
  1991   Political Integration in the Protohistoric Rio Grande Valley: Chieftaincy among Semi-
          Sedentary Horticulturalists. Paper presented at the 47th International Congress of Ameri-
          canists, New Orleans, July 8.
Creel, Darrell
  1989   A Primary Cremation at the NAN Ranch Ruin, with Comparative Data on Other Crema-
          tions in the Mimbres Area, New Mexico. *Journal of Field Archaeology* 16:309–29.
Crown, Patricia L.
  1983   An X-Ray Fluorescence Analysis of Hohokam Ceramics. In *Hohokam Archaeology along the
          Salt-Gila Aqueduct, Central Arizona Project.* Vol. 8, *Material Culture,* L. S. Teague and P. L.
          Crown, eds. Arizona State Museum Archaeological Series 150. Tucson: University of Ari-
          zona.
  1984   Ceramic Vessel Exchange in Southern Arizona. In *Hohokam Archaeology along the Salt-
          Gila Aqueduct, Central Arizona Project.* Vol. 9, *Synthesis and Conclusions,* L. S. Teague and
          P. L. Crown, eds. pp. 251–304. Arizona State Museum Archaeological Series 150. Tucson:
          University of Arizona.
  1985   Intrusive Ceramics and the Identification of Hohokam Exchange Networks. In *Proceedings
          of the 1983 Hohokam Symposium,* A. E. Dittert, Jr., and D. E. Dove, eds., pp. 439–58. Ari-
          zona Archaeological Society Occasional Paper 2. Phoenix: Arizona Archaeological Society.
  1987a   Classic Period Hohokam Settlement and Land Use in the Casa Grande Ruins Area. *Jour-
          nal of Field Archaeology* 14:147–62.
  1987b   The Hohokam: Current Views of Prehistory and the Regional System. Paper presented at
          the Advanced Seminar, Cultural Complexity in the Arid Southwest: The Hohokam and
          Chacoan Regional Systems. School of American Research, Santa Fe, October.
  1989   The Recycled Site: Evaluating the Construction Sequence and Population of Pot Creek
          Pueblo, Northern New Mexico. Manuscript, Department of Anthropology, Southern
          Methodist University, Dallas.
  1990   The Hohokam of the American Southwest. *Journal of World Prehistory* 4:223–55.
  1991   The Role of Exchange and Interaction in Salt-Gila Basin Hohokam Prehistory. In *Explor-
          ing the Hohokam: Prehistoric Desert Dwellers of the Southwest,* G. J. Gumerman, ed. Albu-
          querque: University of New Mexico Press.
Crown, Patricia L., and Ronald L. Bishop
  1987   The Manufacture of the Salado Polychromes. *Pottery Southwest* 14(4):1–4.
Crown, Patricia L., and W. James Judge (editors)
  1991a   *Chaco & Hohokam: Prehistoric Regional Systems in the American Southwest.* Santa Fe: School
          of American Research Press.
  1991b   Introduction. In *Chaco and Hohokam: Prehistoric Regional Systems in the American Southwest,*
          P. L. Crown and W. J. Judge, eds., pp. 1–10. Santa Fe: School of American Research Press.
Crown, Patricia L., and Timothy A. Kohler
  1990   Community Dynamics, Site Structure and Aggregation in the Northern Rio Grande. Paper
          presented at the 2nd Southwest Symposium, Albuquerque, January.
Crown, Patricia L., Janet D. Orcutt, and Timothy A. Kohler
  1990   Pueblo Cultures in Transition: The Northern Rio Grande. Paper presented at the Crow
          Canyon Archaeological Center Conference, Pueblo Cultures in Transition. Cortez, CO.
Crown, Patricia L., Larry A. Schwalbe, and J. Ronald London
  1985   An X-Ray Fluorescence Analysis of Material Variability in Las Colinas Ceramics. In *Ex-
          cavations at Las Colinas, Phoenix, Arizona.* Vol. 4, *Material Culture,* D. A. Gregory and
          C. Heathington, eds., pp. 29–68. Arizona State Museum Archaeological Series 162. Uni-
          versity of Arizona, Tucson.
Crutchfield, James P., J. Doyne Farmer, Norman H. Packard, and Robert S. Shaw
  1986   Chaos. *Scientific American* 255(6):46–57.
Cummings, B.
  1953   *First Inhabitants of Arizona and the Southwest.* Tucson: Cummings Publication Council.

Cushing, Frank Hamilton
    1892   The Hemenway Southwestern Archaeological Expedition. Manuscript, Peabody Museum,
            Harvard University.
Cutler, Hugh C., and Leonard W. Blake
    1976   Corn from Snaketown. In *The Hohokam: Desert Farmers and Craftsmen,* by E. W. Haury,
            pp. 365–66. Tucson: University of Arizona Press.
Cutler, Hugh C., and T. W. Whitaker
    1961   History and Distribution of the Cultivated Cucurbits in the Americas. *American Antiquity*
            26:469–85.
Dallas, Herb
    1977   Tower Line-of-Sight Determination in the Hovenweep Area. Paper prepared for the Hoven-
            weep Archeology Project.
Danson, Edward Bridge
    1957   *An Archaeological Survey of West Central New Mexico and East Central Arizona.* Papers of the
            Peabody Museum of American Archaeology and Ethnology, Harvard University, vol. 44,
            no. 1.
Danson, Edward B., and Roberts M. Wallace
    1956   A Petrographic Study of Gila Polychrome. *American Antiquity* 22:180–83.
Dean, Jeffrey S.
    1969   *Chronological Analysis of Tsegi Phase Sites in Northeastern Arizona.* Papers of the Labora-
            tory of Tree-Ring Research 3. Tucson: University of Arizona Press.
    1970   Aspects of Tsegi Phase Social Organization: A Trial Reconstruction. In *Reconstructing Pre-
            historic Pueblo Societies,* W. Longacre, ed., pp. 140–74. Albuquerque: University of New
            Mexico Press.
    1984   Environmental Aspects of Modeling Human Activity-Locating Behavior. In *Theory and
            Model Building: Refining Survey Strategies for Locating Prehistoric Heritage Resources. Trial
            Formulations for Southwestern Forests,* L. S. Cordell and D. F. Green, eds., pp. 8–20. Cul-
            tural Resources Management Report 5. Albuquerque: USDA Forest Service, Southwestern
            Region.
    1987   Review: "Southwest U.S.: The Archaic of Southern Arizona," by E. B. Sayles (Anthropologi-
            cal Papers of the University of Arizona, No. 42, 1983), "Cultural and Environmental His-
            tory of Cienega Valley, Southeastern Arizona," by Frank W. Eddy and Maurice E. Cooley
            (Anthropological Papers of the University of Arizona. No. 43, 1983), and "The Geoarchae-
            ology of Whitewater Draw, Arizona," by Michael R. Waters (Anthropological Papers of
            the University of Arizona, No. 45, 1986). *Quarterly Review of Archaeology* 8(4):10–14.
    1988a   Dendrochronology and Paleoenvironmental Reconstruction on the Colorado Plateaus. In
            The Anasazi in a Changing Environment, G. J. Gumerman, ed., pp. 119–67. Cambridge:
            Cambridge University Press.
    1988b   A Model of Anasazi Behavioral Adaptation. In *The Anasazi in a Changing Environment,*
            G. J. Gumerman, ed., pp. 25–44. Cambridge: Cambridge University Press.
    1988c   The View from the North: An Anasazi Perspective on the Mogollon. *The Kiva* 53:197–99.
    1991   Thoughts on Hohokam Chronology. In *Exploring the Hohokam: Prehistoric Desert Peoples
            of the American Southwest,* G. J. Gumerman, ed., pp. 61–149. Albuquerque: University of
            New Mexico Press.
Dean, Jeffrey S., Robert C. Euler, George J. Gumerman, Fred Plog, Richard H. Hevly, and Thor N. V.
    Karlstrom
    1985   Human Behavior, Demography, and Paleoenvironment on the Colorado Plateaus. *Ameri-
            can Antiquity* 50:537–54.
Dean, Jeffrey S., Alexander J. Lindsay, and William Robinson
    1978   Prehistoric Settlement in Long House Valley, Northeastern Arizona. In *Investigation of
            the Southwestern Anthropological Research Group: The Proceedings of the 1976 Conference,*
            R. Euler and G. Gumerman, eds., pp. 25–44. Flagstaff: Museum of Northern Arizona.
Dean, Jeffrey S., and John Ravesloot
    1988   The Chronology of Cultural Interaction in the Gran Chichimeca. Paper presented at
            the Advanced Seminar, "A Charles Di Peso Retrospective," Amerind Foundation, Dra-
            goon, AZ.
    1993   The Chronology of Cultural Interaction in the Gran Chichimeca. In *Culture and Contact:*

Charles C. Di Peso's Gran Chichimeca, A. Woosley and J. Ravesloot, eds. Albuquerque: University of New Mexico Press. In press.

Dean, Jeffrey S., and William J. Robinson
1977   *Dendroclimatic Variability in the American Southwest, A.D. 680–1970.* Laboratory of Tree-Ring Research, University of Arizona, Tucson.

DeBloois, Evan I.
1975   *The Elk Ridge Archeological Project: A Test of Random Sampling in Archeological Surveying.* Archeological Report No. 2. USDA Forest Service, Intermountain Region, Ogden.

DeBoer, Warren R.
1984   The Last Pottery Show: System and Sense in Ceramic Studies. In *The Many Dimensions of Pottery: Ceramics in Archaeology and Anthropology,* S. E. Vander Leeum, ed., pp. 529–68. Amsterdam: University of Amsterdam Press.

Debowski, Sharon, A. George, Richard Goddard, and D. Mullon
1976   *An Archaeological Survey of the Buttes Reservoir.* Arizona State Museum Archaeological Series 93. Tucson: University of Arizona.

Decker, D. S.
1988   Origin(s), Evolution, and Systematics of *Cucurbito pepo* (Cucurbitaceae). *Economic Botany* 42:4–15.

Decker, Kenneth
1986   Isotopic and Chemical Reconstruction of Diet and Its Biological and Social Dimensions at Grasshopper Pueblo. Paper presented at the annual meeting of the Society for American Archaeology, New Orleans.

Deloria, Vine
1989   A Simple Question of Humanity: The Moral Dimensions of the Reburial Issue. *NARF Legal Review* 14:1–12.

Denbow, J. R.
1984   Prehistoric Herders and Foragers of the Kalahari: The Evidence for 1500 Years of Interaction. In *Past and Present in Hunter-Gatherer Studies,* C. Schrire, ed., pp. 175–93. Orlando: Academic Press.

DeNiro, M. J.
1987   Stable Isotopy and Archaeology. *American Scientist* 75:182–91.

DePratter,
1985   Coosa: A Chiefdom in the Sixteenth-Century Southeastern United States. *American Antiquity* 50:723–37.

Dering, J. P.
1979   *Pollen and Plant Macrofossil Vegetation Recovered from Hinds Cave, Val Verde County, Texas.* College Station: Texas A & M University.

Dibble, David S.
1968   *Bonfire Shelter: A Stratified Bison Kill Site, Val Verde County, Texas.* Texas Memorial Museum Miscellaneous Papers 1.

Dick, Herbert W.
1954   The Bat Cave Pod Corn Complex: A Note on Its Distribution and Archaeological Significance. *El Palacio* 61:138–44.
1965   *Bat Cave.* School of American Research Monograph 27. Santa Fe.

Dickson, D. Bruce, Jr.
1979   *Prehistoric Pueblo Settlement Patterns: The Arroyo Hondo, New Mexico, Site Survey.* Arroyo Hondo Archaeological Series, vol. 2. Santa Fe: School of American Research Press.

Di Peso, Charles C.
1953   *The Sobaipuri Indians of the Upper San Pedro Valley, Southeastern Arizona.* Amerind Foundation Publications 6. Dragoon, AZ.
1958   *The Reeve Ruin of Southeastern Arizona.* The Amerind Foundation, no. 8. Dragoon, AZ.
1968   Casas Grandes: A Fallen Trade Center of the Gran Chichimeca. *Masterkey* 42(1):20–47.
1974a   *Casa Grandes: A Fallen Trade Center of the Gran Chichimeca.* Vols. 1–3. Amerind Foundation Publication 8. Dragoon, AZ.
1974b   *Casas Grandes: Preceramic-Viejo Periods.* Flagstaff: Northland Press.
1976   Polychrome in the Casas Grandes Region. *The Kiva* 42:57–64.
1979   Prehistory: Southern Periphery. In *Handbook of North American Indians.* Vol. 9, *Southwest,*

A. Ortiz, ed., pp. 152–61. Washington, D.C.: Smithsonian Institution.

1983   The Northern Sector of the Mesoamerican World System. In *Forgotten Places and Things,*
A. E. Ward, ed., pp. 11–22. Albuquerque: Center for Archaeological Studies.

Dittert, Alfred E.

1959   Culture Change in the Cebolleta Mesa Region, Central Western New Mexico. Ph.D. dissertation, University of Arizona. Ann Arbor: University Microfilms.

Dodge, William A., E. L. Pearson, and T. J. Ferguson

1977   Archaeological Clearance Investigations, State Highway Right-of-Way Fenceline Project, Zuni Indian Reservation, McKinley County, New Mexico. Manuscript, Zuni Archaeology Program, Zuni.

Doebly, J. F.

1984   "Seeds" of Wild Grasses: A Major Food of Southwestern Indians. *Economic Botany* 38:52–64.

Doelle, William H.

1985   *Excavations at the Valencia Site. A Preclassic Hohokam Village in the Southern Tucson Basin.* Institute for American Research Anthropological Papers 3. Tucson.

1990   Thousand Year Old Census: Tucson in A.D. 990. *Archaeology in Tucson* 4(2):1–5.

Doelle, William H., Allen Dart, and Henry Wallace

1985   *The Southern Tucson Basin: An Intensive Survey along the Santa Cruz River.* Technical Report 85–3. Tucson: Institute for American Research.

Doelle, William H., Frederick Huntington, and Henry Wallace

1987   Rincon Phase Reorganization in the Tucson Basin. In *The Hohokam Village: Site Structure and Organization,* D. Doyel, ed., pp. 71–96. Glenwood Springs: Southwestern and Rocky Mountain Division of the American Association for the Advancement of Science.

Doelle, William H., and Henry Wallace

1988   The Transition to History in Pimeria Alta. Paper presented at the Southwest Symposium, Tempe.

1990   The Transition to History in Pimeria Alta. In *Perspectives on Southwestern Prehistory,* P. E. Minnis and C. Redman, eds., pp. 239–57. Boulder: Westview Press.

1991   The Changing Role in the Tucson Basin in the Hohokam Regional System. In *Exploring the Hohokam: Prehistoric Desert Peoples of the Southwest,* G. J. Gumerman, ed., pp. 279–346. Albuquerque: University of New Mexico Press.

Donaldson, M. L.

1984   Botanical Remains from Sheep Camp and Ashislepah Shelters. In *Archaic Prehistory and Paleoenvironments in the San Juan Basin, New Mexico: the Cahcoa Shelters Project,* A. H. Simmons, ed., pp. 167–85. University of Kansas Museum of Anthropology, Project Report Series 53. Lawrence.

Downton, W. J. S.

1975   The Occurrence of C4 Photosynthesis among Plants. *Photosynthetica* 9:96–105.

Downum, Christian E., and Alan P. Sullivan

1990   Settlement Patterns. In *The Wupatki Archaeological Inventory Survey Project: Final Report,* compiled by B. A. Anderson. Southwest Cultural Resources Center Professional Paper 35. Santa Fe: National Park Service.

Doyel, David E.

1976   Classic Period Hohokam in the Gila River Basin, Arizona. *The Kiva* 42:27–37.

1977   Classic Period Hohokam in the Escalante Ruin Group. Ph.D. dissertation, Department of Anthropology, University of Arizona, Tucson.

1980   Hohokam Social Organization and the Sedentary to Classic Transition. In *Current Issues in Hohokam Prehistory,* D. E. Doyel and F. Plog, eds., pp. 23–40. Anthropological Research Papers 23. Tempe: Arizona State University.

1981   *Late Hohokam Prehistory in Southern Arizona.* Contributions to Archaeology 2. Scottsdale: Gila Press.

1987a   *The Hohokam Village: Site Structure and Organization.* D. E. Doyel, ed. Glenwood Springs: American Association for the Advancement of Science.

1987b   The Role of Commerce in Hohokam Society. Paper presented at the advanced seminar, Cultural Complexity in the Arid Southwest: The Hohokam and Chacoan Regional Systems. School of American Research, Santa Fe.

1989   Prehistoric Inter-Regional Ceramic Exchange in the Phoenix Basin. Paper presented at the 54th Annual Meeting of the Society for American Archaeology, Atlanta.

1991   Hohokam Cultural Evolution in the Phoenix Basin. In *Exploring the Hohokam: Prehistoric Desert Peoples of the American Southwest*, G. J. Gumerman, ed., pp. 231–78. Albuquerque: University of New Mexico Press.

Doyel, David E., and Mark D. Elson (editors)

1985   *Hohokam Settlement and Economic Systems in the Central New River Drainage.* Arizona Soil Systems Publications in Archaeology 4. Phoenix.

Dozier, Edward P.

1954   *The Hopi-Tewa of Arizona.* University of California Publications in American Archaeology and Ethnology No. 44:259–376.

1970   *The Pueblo Indians of North America.* New York: Holt, Rinehart and Winston.

Drennan, Robert D.

1984   Long-Distant Transport Costs in Pre-Hispanic Mesoamerica. *American Anthropologist* 86:105–12.

Driver, Harold E., and William C. Massey

1957   Comparative Studies of North American Indians. *Transactions of the American Philosophical Society* 47(2):165–456.

Dutton, Bertha

1963   *Sun Father's Way: The Kiva Murals of Kuaua.* Albuquerque: University of New Mexico Press.

Dye, David H., and Cheryl Anne Cox (editors)

1990   *Towns and Temples along to Mississippi.* Tuscaloosa: University of Alabama Press.

Dryson, Stephen L.

1985   *The Creation of the Roman Frontier.* Princeton: Princeton University Press.

Earle, Timothy K.

1980   A Model of Subsistence Change. In *Modeling Change in Prehistoric Subsistence Economies,* T. K. Earle and A. Christenson, eds., pp. 1–29. New York: Academic Press.

Earle, Timothy K., and Robert W. Pruecel

1987   Processual Archaeology and the Radical Critique. *Current Anthropology* 28:501–38.

Earls, A.

1987   *An Archaeological Assessment of Las Huertas, Socorro.* Papers of the Maxwell Museum 3. Albuquerque.

Ebert, James I., and Robert K. Hitchcock

1973   Spatial Inference and the Archaeology of Complex Societies. Paper prepared for the Mathematics in Social Sciences Board Conference on Formal Methods for the Analysis of Regional Social Structure, Santa Fe.

Eddy, Frank W.

1958   A Sequence of Cultural and Alluvial Deposits in the Cienega Creek Basin Southeastern Arizona. M.A. thesis, University of Arizona, Tucson.

1966   *Prehistory of the Navajo Reservoir District, Northwestern New Mexico.* Museum of New Mexico Papers in Anthropology 15. Santa Fe.

1977   *Archaeological Investigations at Chimney Rock Mesa: 1970–1972.* Memoirs of the Colorado Archaeological Society 1. Boulder.

Eddy, Frank W., and M. E. Cooley

1983   *Cultural and Environmental History of Cienega Valley, Southeastern Arizona.* Anthropological Papers of the University of Arizona 43. Tucson.

Eddy, Frank W., Allen E. Kane, and Paul R. Nickens

1983   *Southwest Colorado Prehistoric Context: Archaeological Background and Research Directions.* Denver: State Historical Society of Colorado.

Edwards, G., and D. Walker

1983   *C3, C4: Mechanisms, and Cellular and Environmental Regulation of Photosynthesis.* Berkeley and Los Angeles: University of California Press.

Effland, Richard Wayne, Jr.

1979   A Study of Prehistoric Spatial Behavior: Long House Valley, Northeastern Arizona. Ph.D. dissertation, Arizona State University. Ann Arbor: University Microfilms International.

Eggan, Fred

1950   *Social Organization of the Western Pueblos.* Chicago: University of Chicago Press.

1966 *The American Indian: Perspectives for the Study of Social Change.* Chicago: Aldine.
1980 Shoshoni Kinship Structures and Their Significance for Anthropological Theory. *Journal of the Steward Anthropological Society* 11:165–93.

Eidenbach, Peter L.
1982 Along the "Dotted Line": A Reexamination of the Rio Salado. In *Mogollon Archaeology: Proceedings of the 1980 Mogollon Conference,* P. H. Beckett, ed., pp. 11–16. Ramona, CA: Acoma Books.

Eighmy, Jeffrey L. and Randall H. McGuire
1988 *Archaeomagnetic Dates and the Hohokam Phase Sequence.* Technical Series 3. Fort Collins: Colorado State University Archaeometric Lab.
1989 Dating the Hohokam Phase Sequence: An Analysis of Archaeomagnetic Dates. *Journal of Field Archaeology* 16:15–31.

Ellis, Florence Hawley
1951 Patterns of Aggression and War Cult in Southwestern Pueblos. *Southwestern Journal of Anthropology* 7:177–201.
1974 Anthropological Data Pertaining to Taos Land Claim. In *American Indian Ethnohistory,* vol. 1, *Indians of the Southwest,* D. A. Horr, ed., pp. 29–150. New York: Garland Publishing.

El-Najjar, M. Y.
1979 Human Treponematosis and Tuberculosis: Evidence from the New World. *American Journal of Physical Anthropology* 51:599–618.

El-Najjar, M. Y., B. Lozoff, and D. Ryan
1975 The Paleoepidemiology of Porotic Hyperostosis in the American Southwest: A Biological and Ecological Considerations. *American Journal of Roentaenology, Radium and Thermal Nuclear Medicine* 125:918–24.

El-Najjar, M. Y., and T. M. J. Mulinski
1980 Mummies and Mummification Practices in the Southwestern and Southern United States. In *Mummies, Disease and Ancient Cultures,* A. Cockburn and E. Cockburn, eds., pp. 103–17. New York: Cambridge University Press.

El-Najjar, M. Y., and A. Robinson
1976 Spongy Bones in Prehistoric America. *Science* 193:141–43.

El-Najjar, M. Y., D. J. Ryan, C. G. Turner, and B. Lozoff
1976 The Etiology of Porotic Hyperstosis among the Prehistoric and Historic Anasazi Indians of the Southwestern United States. *American Journal of Physical Anthropology* 44:477–88.

Engelbrecht, William
1985 New York Iroquois Political Development. In *Cultures in Contact,* W. W. Fitzhugh, ed., pp. 163–83. Washington, D.C.: Smithsonian Institution Press.

Euler, Robert C.
1981 Havasupai-Cohonina Relationships in Grand Canyon. In *Collected Papers in Honor of Erik Kellerman Reed,* A. H. Schroeder, ed., pp. 167–76. Archaeological Society of New Mexico Anthropological Papers 6.
1988 Demography and Cultural Dynamics on the Colorado Plateaus. In *The Anasazi in a Changing Environment,* G. Gumerman, ed., pp. 192–229. Cambridge: Cambridge University Press.

Euler, Robert C., George J. Gumerman, Thor N. V. Karlstrom, Jeffrey S. Dean, and Richard H. Hevly
1979 The Colorado Plateaus: Cultural Dynamics and Paleoenvironment. *Science* 205:1089–1101.

Eveleth, P. B., and J. M. Tanner
1976 *Worldwide Variation in Human Growth.* International Biological Programme 8. Cambridge: Cambridge University Press.

Ezell, Paul H., and Alan P. Olson
1955 An Artifact of Human Bone from Eastern Arizona. *Plateau* 27(3):8–11.

Fagan, Brian M.
1988 *In the Beginning: An Introduction to Archaeology.* 6th ed. Glenview, IL.: Scott, Foresman, and Company.

Fairley, Helen C.
1989 Culture History. In *Man, Models and Management: An Overview of the Archaeology of the Arizona Strip and the Management of Its Cultural Resources,* J. H. Altschul and H. C. Fairley, eds., pp. 85–152. Tucson: Statistical Research.

Farmer, Malcolm F.
  1957   A Suggested Typology of Defensive Systems of the Southwest. *Southwestern Journal of Anthropology* 13:249–66.
Fay, Patricia, and Pamela Klein
  1988   A Reexamination of the Leroux Wash Skeletal Material for Evidence of Human Modification. Manuscript, Museum of Northern Arizona Library, Flagstaff.
Fenneman, N. M.
  1931   *Physiography of the Western United States.* New York: McGraw-Hill Book Company.
Ferguson, C.
  1980   Analysis of Human Skeletal Remains. In *Tijeras Canyon, Analyses of the Past,* L. S. Cordell, ed., pp. 121–48. Albuquerque: University of New Mexico Press.
Ferguson, R. Brian (editor)
  1984   *Warfare, Culture, and Environment.* New York: Academic Press.
Ferguson, T. J., and E. Richard Hart
  1985   *A Zuni Atlas.* Norman: University of Oklahoma Press.
Fetterman, Jerry, and Linda Honeycutt
  1990   *In the Fremont Anasazi Transition Zone: Excavations in Verdure Canyon.* Yellow Jacket: Woods Canyon Archaeological Consultants.
Fetterman, Jerry, Linda Honeycutt, and Kristin Kuckelman
  1988   *Salvage Excavations of 425A12209, A Pueblo I Habitation Site in Cottonwood Canyon, Manti-Lasal National Forest, Southeastern Utah.* Yellow Jacket: Woods Canyon Archaeological Consultants.
Fewkes, Jesse Walter
  1900   Tusayan Migration Traditions. In *Nineteenth Annual Report of the Bureau of American Ethnology,* pt. 2, J. W. Powell, ed. Washington, D.C.: U.S. Government Printing Office.
  1912   *Antiquities of the Upper Verde River and Walnut Creek Valleys, Arizona.* 28th Annual Report of the Bureau of American Ethnology for the Years 1906–1907, pp. 181–220. Washington, D.C.: Smithsonian Institution.
  1923   *Designs on Prehistoric Pottery from the Mimbres Valley, New Mexico.* Smithsonian Miscellaneous Collections 74(6). Washington, D.C.
  1926   *An Archaeological Collection from Young's Canyon, near Flagstaff, Arizona.* Smithsonian Miscellaneous Collection 77(10). Washington, D.C.
Fields, R. C., and J. S. Girard
  1983   *Investigations at Site 32 (41EP325), Keystone Dam Project.* Reports of Investigations 21. Austin: Prewitt and Associates, Inc.
Fink, T. M., and C. F. Merbs
  1991   Paleonutrition and Paleopathology of the Salt River Hohokam: A Search for Correlates. *The Kiva* 56(3):293–317.
Fish, Paul R.
  1989   The Hohokam: 1,000 Years of Prehistory in the Sonoran Desert. In *Dynamics of Southwest Prehistory,* L. S. Cordell and G. J. Gumerman, eds., pp. 19–63. A School of American Research Advanced Seminar Book. Washington, D.C.: Smithsonian Institution Press.
Fish, Paul R., and Suzanne K. Fish
  1977   *Verde Valley Archaeology: Review and Prospective.* Research Paper 8. Flagstaff: Museum of Northern Arizona.
  1989   Hohokam Warfare from a Regional Perspective. In *Cultures in Conflict: Current Archaeological Perspectives,* D. C. Tkaczuk and B. C. Vivian, eds., pp. 112–28. Proceedings of the Twentieth Chacmool Conference, Department of Archaeology, University of Calgary.
  1991   Hohokam Political and Social Organization. In *Exploring the Hohokam: Prehistoric Desert Peoples of the American Southwest,* G. Gumerman, ed., pp. 151–76. Albuquerque: University of New Mexico Press.
Fish, Paul R., Suzanne K. Fish, A. Long, and C. Miksicek
  1986   Early Corn Remains from Tumamoc Hill, Southern Arizona. *American Antiquity* 51:563–72.
Fish, Suzanne K., and Paul R. Fish
  1990   An Archaeological Assessment of Ecosystems in the Tucson Basin of Southern Arizona. In *The Ecosystem Approach in Anthropology: From Concept to Practice,* E. Moran, ed., pp. 159–88. Ann Arbor: University of Michigan Press.

Fish, Suzanne K., Paul R. Fish, and Christian Downum
    1984   Hohokam Terraces and Agricultural Production in the Tucson Basin. In *Prehistoric Agri-cultural Strategies in the Southwest,* S. K. Fish and P. R. Fish, eds., pp. 55–72. Arizona State University Anthropological Research Papers 33. Tempe.
Fish, Suzanne K., Paul R. Fish, and John Madsen
    1989   Differentiation and Integration in a Tucson Basin Classic Period Hohokam Community. In *Socio-Political Structure of Prehistoric Southwestern Societies,* S. Upham, K. Lightfoot, and R. Jewett, eds., pp. 237–67. Boulder: Westview Press.
    1990   Analyzing Prehistoric Agriculture: A Hohokam Example. In *The Archaeology of Regions: The Case for Full-Coverage Survey,* S. K. Fish and S. Kowalewski, eds., pp. 189–218. Wash-ington, D.C.: Smithsonian Institution Press.
Fish, Suzanne K., Paul R. Fish, Charles Miksicek, and John Madsen
    1985   Prehistoric Agave Cultivation in Southern Arizona. *Desert Plants* 7:102–16.
Fish, Suzanne K., and Gary P. Nabhan
    1991   Desert as Context: The Hohokam Environment. In *Exploring the Prehistoric Desert Peoples of the American Southwest,* G. Gumerman, ed., pp. 29–60. Albuquerque: University of New Mexico Press.
Fitting, James E.
    1973   An Early Mogollon Community: A Preliminary Report on the Winn Canyon Site. *The Arti-fact,* vols. 1 and 2.
Flannery, Kent V.
    1968   The Olmecs and the Valley of Oaxaca: A Model for Inter-regional Interaction in Forma-tive Times. In *Dumbarton Oaks Conference on the Olmec,* E. P. Benson, ed., pp. 79–110. Washington, D.C.: Dumbarton Oaks.
    1972a   The Cultural Evolution of Civilizations. *Annual Review of Ecology and Systematics* 3:399–426.
    1972b   The Origins of the Village as a Settlement Type in Mesoamerica and the Near East: A Com-parative Approach. In *Man, Settlement and Urbanism,* P. J. Ucko, R. Tringham, and G. W. Dimbleby, eds., pp. 22–53. Cambridge: Gerald Duckworth.
    1973   The Origins of Agriculture. *Annual Review of Anthropology* 2:271–309.
    1976   The Early Mesoamerican Village. New York: Academic Press.
Flinn, Lynn, Christy G. Turner II, and Alan Brew
    1976   Additional Evidence for Cannibalism in the Southwest: The Case of LA 4528. *American Antiquity* 41:308–18.
Florance, Charles A.
    1985   Recent Work in the Chupicuaro Region. In *The Archaeology of West and Northwest Meso-america,* M. S. Foster and P. C. Weigand, eds., pp. 9–46. Boulder: Westview Press.
Fontana, Bernard L., J. Cameron Greenleaf, and Donnely D. Cassidy
    1959   A Fortified Arizona Mountain. *The Kiva* 25(2):41–63.
Ford, Richard I.
    1968   Jemez Cave and Its Place in an Early Horticultural Settlement Pattern. Paper presented at the 33rd annual meeting of the Society for American Archaeology. Santa Fe.
    1972   Barter, Gift or Violence: An Analysis of Tewa Inter-Tribal Exchange. In *Social Exchange and Interaction,* E. Wilmsen, ed., pp. 21–45. Anthropological Papers of the Museum of Anthropology 51. Ann Arbor: University of Michigan.
    1981   Gardening and Farming before A.D. 1000: Patterns of Prehistoric Cultivation North of Mexico. *Journal of Ethnobiology* 1:6–27.
    1984   Ecological Consequences of Early Agriculture in the Southwest. In *Papers on the Archae-ology of Black Mesa Arizona,* vol. 2, S. Plog and S. Powell, eds., pp. 127–38. Carbondale and Edwardsville: Southern Illinois Press.
    1985   Patterns of Food Production in Prehistoric North America. In *Prehistoric Food Production in North America,* R. I. Ford, ed., pp. 341–64. Anthropological Papers of the Museum of Anthropology 75. Ann Arbor: University of Michigan.
Ford, Richard I., Albert H. Schroeder, and Stewart L. Peckham
    1972   Three Perspectives on Puebloan Prehistory. In *New Perspectives on the Pueblos,* A. Ortiz, ed., pp. 19–39. Albuquerque: University of New Mexico Press.

Foreman, Grant (editor)
1941 A Pathfinder in the Southwest. The Itinerary of Lieutenant A. W. Whipple during His Explorations for a Railway Route from Fort Smith to Los Angeles in the Years 1853 & 1854. Norman: University of Oklahoma Press.

Foster, Michael S.
1982 The Loma San Gabriel–Mogollon Continuum. In Mogollon Archaeology: Proceedings of the 1980 Mogollon Conference, P. H. Beckett and K. Silverbird, eds., pp. 251–61. Ramona, CA: Acoma Books.
1986 The Mesoamerican Connection: A View from the South. In Ripples in the Chichimec Sea: New Considerations of Southwestern-Mesoamerican Interactions, F. J. Mathien and R. H. McGuire, eds., pp. 55–69. Carbondale: Southern Illinois University Press.

Fowler, Andrew P.
1980 An Archaeological Clearance Investigation, Acque Chaining and Reseeding Project, Zuni Indian Reservation, McKinley County, New Mexico. ZAP-020-78S. Zuni Archaeology Program. Pueblo of Zuni.

Fowler, Andrew P., John R. Stein, and Roger Anyon
1987 An Archaeological Reconnaissance of West-Central New Mexico: The Anasazi Monuments Project. Report submitted to the Office of Cultural Affairs, Historic Preservation Division. Santa Fe.

Fowler, Don D., and David B. Madsen
1986 Prehistory of the Southeastern Area. In Handbook of North American Indians. Vol. 11, Great Basin, W. L. D'Azevedo, ed., pp. 173–82. Washington, D.C.: Smithsonian Institution Press.

Franklin, Hayward H., and W. Bruce Masse
1976 The San Pedro Salado: A Case of Prehistoric Migration. The Kiva 42:47–56.

Fredlund, Glen
1984 Palynological Analysis of Sediments from Sheep Camp and Ashislepah Shelters. In Archaic Prehistory and Paleo-Environments in the San Juan Basin New Mexico: The Chaco Shelters Project, A. Simmons, ed., pp. 186–211. University of Kansas Museum of Anthropology, Project Report Series 53.

Freeman, C. E.
1972 Pollen Study of Some Alluvial Deposits in Dona Ana County, Southern New Mexico. Texas Journal of Science 24:203–20.

Friederici, G.
1907 Scalping in America. Annual Report of the Smithsonian Institution for 1906, pp. 423–30. Washington, D.C.

Frisbe, Theodore R.
1967 The Excavation and Interpretation of the Artificial Leg Basketmaker III-Pueblo I Sites near Corrales, New Mexico. M.A. thesis, Department of Anthropology, University of New Mexico.
1982 The Anasazi-Mogollon Frontier? Perspectives from the Albuquerque Area, or Brown vs. Gray: a Paste Case from the Albuquerque Region. In Mogollon Archaeology: Proceedings of the 1980 Mogollon Conference, P. H. Beckett, ed., pp. 17–25. Ramona, CA: Acoma Books.

Frison, George
1978 Prehistoric Hunters of the High Plains. New York: Academic Press.

Fritz, John M.
1978 Paleopsychology Today: Ideational Systems and Human Adaptation in Prehistory. In Social Archaeology beyond Subsistence and Dating, C. L. Redman, M. J. Berman, E. V. Curtin, W. T. Langhorne, Jr., N. M. Versaggi, and J. C. Wanser, eds., pp. 37–60. New York: Academic Press.

Fry, Gary F.
1976 Analysis of Prehistoric Coprolites from Utah. University of Utah Anthropological Papers 97. Salt Lake City.

Fuller, J. E.
1987 Paleoflood Hydrology of the Alluvial Salt River, Tempe, Arizona. M.A. thesis, Department of Geosciences, University of Arizona, Tucson.

Fuller, Steven L.
1984 An Archaeological Survey of the Aneth Road Corridor, Ute Mountain Reservation, Montezuma County, Colorado. Cortez: CASA.

1987   *Cultural Resource Inventories for the Dolores Project: The Dove Creek Canal Distribution System and Dawson Draw Reservoir.* Four Corners Archaeological Project Report 7. Report prepared for Cultural Resource Program, Bureau of Reclamation, Upper Colorado Region, Salt Lake City. Contract No. 4-CS-40-01650, Delivery Order 23.

1988   *Archaeological Investigations in the Bodo Canyon Area, La Plata County, Colorado.* UMTRA Archaeological Report 25. Cortez: CASA.

Galinat, W. C.
1985   Domestication and Diffusion of Maize. In *Prehistoric Food Production in North America,* R. Ford, ed. Museum of Anthropology Papers 75. University of Michigan, Ann Arbor.
1988   The Origin of Maiz de Ocho. *American Anthropologist* 90:682.

Gasser, Robert E., and S. J. Kwiatkowski
1991   Regional Signatures of Hohokam Plant Use. *The Kiva* 56:207–26.

Geib, Phil R.
1990   A Basketmaker Wooden Tool Cache from Lower Glen Canyon. *The Kiva* 55:265–78.

Geib, Phil R., and Peter W. Bungart
1989   Implications of Early Bow Use in Glen Canyon. *Utah Archaeology* 1989:32–47.

Gell-Mann, Murray
1992   Complexity and Complex Adaptive Systems. In *The Evolution of Human Languages,* J. Hawkins and M. Gell-Mann, eds., pp. 3–18. Proceedings of the Santa Fe Institute Studies in the Sciences of Complexity, vol. 11. Redwood City: Addison Wesley.

Gerald, Rex E.
1976   A Conceptual Framework for Evaluating Salado and Salado-Related Material in the El Paso Area. *The Kiva* 42:65–70.
1990   Report on a U.T. El Paso Mini-Grant to Investigate Prehistoric Fortifications in a Primitive State in the Casas Grandes Area of Chihuahua. *The Artifact* 28(3):59–64.

Gillespie, William B.
1985   Holocene Climate and Environment of Chaco Canyon. In *Environment and Subsistence of Chaco Canyon, New Mexico,* F. J. Mathien, ed., pp. 13–37. Publications in Archaeology 18E, Chaco Canyon Studies. Albuquerque: National Park Service, U.S. Department of the Interior.

Gilman, Patricia A.
1987   Architecture as Artifact: Pit Structures and Pueblos in the American Southwest. *American Antiquity* 52:538–64.

Gladwin, Harold S.
1945   *The Chaco Branch, Excavations at White Mound in the Red Mesa Valley.* Medallion Papers No. 33. Globe: Gila Pueblo.
1957   *A History of the Ancient Southwest.* Portland: Bond, Wheelright Co.

Gladwin, Harold S., and Winifred Gladwin
1935   *The Eastern Range of the Red-on-Buff Culture.* Medallion Papers 14. Globe: Gila Pueblo.

Gladwin, Harold S., Emil W. Haury, Edwin B. Sayles, and Nora Gladwin
1937   *Excavations at Snaketown, Material Culture.* Medallion Papers 25. Globe: Gila Pueblo.

Gladwin, Winifred, and Harold S. Gladwin
1930   *Some Southwestern Pottery Types, Series I.* Medallion Papers 16. Globe: Gila Pueblo.
1935   *The Eastern Range of Red-on-Buff Culture.* Medallion Papers 16. Globe: Gila Pueblo.

Glassow, Michael A.
1980   *Prehistoric Agricultural Development in the Northern Southwest: A Study in Changing Patterns of Land Use.* Ballena Press Anthropological Papers 16. Socorro.

Gledhill, John
1978   Formative Development in the North American Southwest. *British Archaeological Reports* 47:241–84.

Gleick, James
1987   *Chaos: Making a New Science.* New York: Penguin.

Goddard, P. E.
1913   *Indians of the Southwest.* American Museum of Natural History, Handbook Series 2. New York.

Goodman, Alan H., L. H. Allen, G. P. Hernandez, A. Amador, L. V. Arriola, A. Chavez, and G. H. Pelto
1987   Prevalence and Age at Development of Enamel Hypoplasias in Mexican Children. *American Journal of Physical Anthropology* 72:7–19.

Goodman, Alan H., and George J. Armelagos
    1985a   The Chronological Distribution of Enamel Hypoplasias in Human Permanent Incisor and Canine Teeth. *Archives of Oral Biology* 30:503–7.
    1985b   Factors Affecting the Distribution of Enamel Hypoplasias within the Human Permanent Dentition. *American Journal of Physical Anthropology* 68:479–93.
    1989   Infant and Childhood Morbidity and Mortality Risks in Archaeological Populations. *World Archaeology* 21:225–43.
Goodman, Alan H., George J. Armelagos, and J. C. Rose
    1984   The Chronological Distribution of Enamel Hypoplasias from Prehistoric Dickson Mounds Populations. *American Journal of Physical Anthropology* 65:259–66.
Goodman, Alan H., J. Lallo, George J. Armelagos, and J. C. Rose
    1984   Health Changes at Dickson Mounds, Illinois (AD 950–1300). In *Paleopathology at the Origins of Agriculture,* M. N. Cohen and G. J. Armelagos, eds., pp. 271–306. New York: Academic Press.
Goodman, Alan H., G. H. Pelto, and L. A. Allen
    1988   Socioeconomic and Nutritional Status Correlates of Enamel Developmental Defect in Mild-to-Moderately Malnourished Mexican Children. Abstract. *American Journal of Physical Anthropology* 75:215.
Goodman, Alan H., R. B. Thomas, Alan C. Swedlund, and George J. Armelagos
    1988   Biocultural Perspectives on Stress in Prehistoric, Historical, and Contemporary Population Research. *Yearbook of Physical Anthropology* 31:169–202.
Goodwin, Grenville
    1942   *The Social Organization of the Western Apache.* Tucson: University of Arizona Press.
Gordon, J. E., J. B. Wyon, and W. Ascoll
    1967   The Second Year Death Rate in Less Developed Countries. *American Journal of Medical Sciences* 245:121–44.
Gordon, Theodore J., and David Greenspan
    1988   Chaos and Fractals: New Tools for Technological and Social Forecasting. *Technological Forecasting and Social Change* 34:1–25.
Gould, Stephen J.
    1987   *An Urchin in the Storm: Essays about Books and Ideas.* New York: W. W. Norton.
    1991   *Bully for Brontosaurus: Reflections in Natural History.* New York: W. W. Norton.
Grady, Mark A.
    1976   Aboriginal Agrarian Adaptation to the Sonoran Desert: A Regional Synthesis and Research Design. Ph.D. dissertation, University of Arizona, Tucson.
Graham, M., and A. Roberts
    1986   Residentially Constrained Mobility: A Preliminary Investigation of Variability in Settlement Organization. *Haliksa'i UNM Contributions to Anthropology* 5:104–15.
Grant, Campbell
    1979   The Occurrence of the Atlatl in Rock Art. *AIRA* 5:1–21.
Graves, Michael W.
    1982   Anomalous Tree-Ring Dates and the Sequence of Room Construction at Canyon Creek Ruin, East-Central Arizona. *The Kiva* 47:107–31.
    1983   Growth and Aggregation at Canyon Creek Ruin: Implications for Evolutionary Change in East-Central Arizona. *American Antiquity* 48:290–315.
Graves, Michael W., Sally J. Holbrook, and William A. Longacre
    1982   Aggregation and Abandonment at Grasshopper Pueblo: Evolutionary Trends in the Late Prehistory of East-Central Arizona. In *Multidisciplinary Studies at Grasshopper Pueblo,* W. A. Longacre, S. J. Holbrook, and M. W. Graves, eds., pp. 110–22. Anthropological Papers of the University of Arizona 40. Tucson.
Graves, Michael W., William Longacre, and Sally Holbrook
    1982   Aggregation and Abandonment at Grasshopper Pueblo, Arizona. *Journal of Field Archaeology* 9:193–206.
Graybill, Donald A.
    1989   The Reconstruction of Prehistoric Salt River Streamflow. In *The 1982–1984 Excavations at Las Colinas: Environment and Subsistence,* D. A. Graybill, D. A. Gregory, F. L. Nials, S. K. Fish, R. E. Gasser, C. H. Miksicek, and C. R. Szuter, eds., pp. 25–38. Archaeological Series 162, vol. 5. Tucson: Cultural Resource Management Division, Arizona State Museum.

Graybill, Donald, and J. Jefferson Reid
    1982   A Cluster Analysis of Chipped Stone Tools. In *Cholla Project Archaeology Introduction and Specialized Studies,* J. Jefferson Reid, ed., pp. 47–50. Arizona State Museum Archaeological Series 161. Tucson: University of Arizona.
Grebinger, Paul
    1976   Salado-Perspectives from the Middle Santa Cruz Valley. *The Kiva* 42:39–46.
Green, E. L.
    1963   *Valdez Phase Occupation near Taos, New Mexico.* Fort Burgwin Research Center Paper 10. Dallas: Southern Methodist University.
Green, Roger C.
    1962   The Hormigas Site of the Largo-Gallina Phase. *El Palacio* 69(3):142–57.
    1964   Tarricito Community. *El Palacio* 71(2):27–40.
Greenleaf, J. Cameron
    1975   The Fortified Hill Site near Gila Bend, Arizona. *The Kiva* 40:213–82.
Gregory, David A.
    1979   The Tonto-Roosevelt Area. In *Archaeological Survey of the Cholla-Saguaro Transmission Line Corridor,* assembled by L. S. Teague and L. L. Mayro, pp. 175–226. Arizona State Museum Archaeological Series 135. Tucson: University of Arizona.
    1982   The Morphology of Platform Mounds and the Structure of Classic Period Hohokam Sites. Paper presented at the 47th annual meeting of the Society for American Archaeology. Minneapolis.
    1987   The Morphology of Platform Mounds and Structure of Classic Period Hohokam Sites. In *The Hohokam Village,* D. E. Doyel, ed., pp. 183–210. Glenwood Springs: American Association for the Advancement of Science.
    1991   Form and Variation in Hohokam Settlement Patterns. In *Chaco & Hohokam: Prehistoric Regional Systems in the American Southwest,* P. L. Crown and W. J. Judge, eds., pp. 159–94. Santa Fe: School of American Research Press.
Gregory, David A., and Fred L. Nials
    1985   Observations Concerning the Distribution of Classic Period Platform Mounds. In *Proceedings of the 1983 Hohokam Conference,* A. E. Dittert, Jr., and D. E. Doyel, eds., pp. 373–88. Occasional Paper 2, Phoenix Chapter, Arizona Archaeological Society, Phoenix.
Guernsey, Samuel J.
    1931   *Explorations in Northeastern Arizona. Report of the Archaeological Fieldwork of 1920–1923.* Papers of the Peabody Museum of American Archaeology and Ethnology 12(1). Cambridge: Harvard University.
Guernsey, Samuel J., and Alfred V. Kidder
    1921   Basket-Maker Caves of Northeastern Arizona. *Papers of the Peabody Museum of American Archaeology and Ethnology* 8(2). Cambridge: Harvard University.
Gumerman, George J.
    1984   *A View from Black Mesa: The Changing Face of Archaeology.* Tucson: University of Arizona Press.
    1988   *The Archaeology of the Hopi Buttes District, Arizona.* Southern Illinois University at Carbondale, Center for Archaeological Investigations Research Paper. No. 49. Southern Illinois University, Carbondale.
Gumerman, George J. (editor)
    1988   *The Anasazi in a Changing Environment.* Cambridge: The School of American Research and Cambridge University Press.
    1991   *Exploring the Hohokam: Prehistoric Desert Dwellers of the Southwest.* Albuquerque: University of New Mexico Press.
Gumerman, George J., and Jeffrey S. Dean
    1989   Prehistoric Cooperation and Competition in the Western Anasazi Area. In *Dynamics of Southwestern Prehistory,* L. Cordell and G. J. Gumerman, eds., pp. 99–148. A School of American Research Advanced Seminar Book. Washington, D.C.: Smithsonian Institution Press.

Gumerman, George J., and Carol S. Weed
  1976   The Question of Salado in the Agua Fria and New River Drainages of Central Arizona.
           The Kiva 42:105–12.
Gunnerson, Dolores A.
  1956   The Southern Athabascans: Their Arrival in the Southwest. *El Palacio* 63:346–65.
Haas, Jonathan
  1986   The Evolution of Kayenta Anasazi. In *Tse Yaa Kin: Houses Beneath the Rock*. Exploration.
           Santa Fe: School of American Research.
  1989   The Evolution of the Kayenta Regional System. In *The Sociopolitical Structure of Prehistoric
           Southwestern Societies*, S. Upham, K. G. Lightfoot, and R. A. Jewett, eds., pp. 491–508.
           Boulder: Westview Press.
  1990   Warfare and the Evolution of Tribal Polities in the Prehistoric Southwest. In *The Anthro-
           pology of War*, J. Haas, ed., pp. 171–89. Cambridge: Cambridge University Press.
Haas, Jonathan, and Winifred Creamer
  1985   Warfare and Tribalization in the Prehistoric Southwest: Report on the First Season's
           Work—1984. Report submitted to the Harry Frank Guggenheim Foundation, New York.
           Santa Fe: School of American Research.
  1993   *Stress and Warfare among the Kayenta Anasazi of the 13th Century A.D.* Fieldiana: Anthro-
           pology, vol. 88.
Haas, Jonathan, Edmund Ladd, Jerrold E. Levy, Randall H. McGuire, and Norman Yoffee
  n.d.   Historical Processes in the Prehistoric Southwest. In *Understanding Complexity in the Pre-
           historic Southwest*. Santa Fe Institute Studies in the Sciences of Complexity. In press.
Habicht-Mauche, Judith A., and Winifred Creamer
  1989   Analysis of Room Use and Residence Units at Arroyo Hondo. Paper presented at the 54th
           annual meeting of the Society for American Archaeology, April. Atlanta.
Hall, Edward Twitchell, Jr.
  1944   Early Stockaded Settlements in the Governador, New Mexico. *Columbia Studies in Archae-*
Hall, S. A.
  1985   Quaternary Pollen Analysis and Vegetational History of the Southwest. In *Pollen Records
           of Late Quaternary North American Sediments*, V. M. Bryant and R. G. Holloway, eds., 95–
           123. Dallas: American Association of Stratigraphic Palynologists Foundation.
Halseth, Odd S.
  1936   Letter to J. G. Buchanan. Odd Halseth Collection, 1936. Pueblo Grande Museum Ar-
           chives, Phoenix.
Hammond, George P., and Agapito Rey
  1953   *Don Juan de Patayán, Colonizer of New Mexico*. Coronado Cuarto Centennial Publication,
           vols. 5 and 6. Albuquerque: University of New Mexico Press.
  1966   *The Rediscovery of New Mexico, 1580–1594*. Albuquerque: University of New Mexico Press.
Hammond, Norman
  1974   The Distribution of Late Classic Maya Major Ceremonial Centers in the Central Area. In
           Mesoamerican Archaeology: New Approaches, N. Hammond, ed., pp. 313–34. Austin: Uni-
           versity of Texas Press.
Hantman, Jeffrey L.
  1983   Stylistic Distributions and Social Networks in the Prehistoric Plateau Southwest. Ph.D.
           dissertation, Department of Anthropology, Arizona State University. Ann Arbor: Univer-
           sity Microfilms.
  1984   Regional Organization of the Northern Mogollon. *American Archeology* 4:171–80.
Harary, Frank
  1959   Status and Contrastatus. *Sociometry* 22:23–43.
Hard, Robert J.
  1985   Ecological Relationships Affecting the Rise of Farming Economies: A Test from the Ameri-
           can Southwest. Ph.D. dissertation, University of New Mexico.
  1990   Agricultural Dependence in the Mountain Mogollon. In *Perspectives on Southwestern Pre-
           history*, P. E. Minnis and C. L. Redman, eds., pp. 135–49. Boulder: Westview Press.

Hard, Robert J., and R. P. Mauldin
  1989   Indicators of Agricultural Dependence in the Southwestern U.S. Paper presented at the
          symposium, The Organization of Land and Space Use, Technology and Activities in Past
          ad Present Societies. November, University of New Mexico.
Hargrave, Lyndon
  1933   Pueblo II House of the San Francisco Mountains, Arizona. *Museum of Northern Arizona
          Bulletin* 4:15–73.
  1938   Results of a Study of the Cohonina Branch of the Patayan Culture in 1938. *Museum Notes*
          11(6). Flagstaff.
Hartman, Dana
  1975   Preliminary Assessment of Mass Burials in the Southwest. *American Journal of Physical
          Anthropology* 42(2):305–6.
Hassan, Fekri A.
  1981   *Demographic Archaeology.* New York: Academic Press.
Hassig, Ross
  1988   Structure and Growth of the Aztec Empire. Paper presented at the annual meetings of the
          Society for American Archaeology. Phoenix.
Haury, Emil W.
  1934   *The Canyon Creek Ruin and the Cliff Dwellings of the Sierra Ancha.* Medallion Papers 20.
          Globe: Gila Pueblo.
  1936   *The Mogollon Culture of Southwestern New Mexico.* Medallion Papers 20, Globe: Gila Pueblo.
  1937   A Pre-Spanish Rubber Ball from Arizona. *American Antiquity* 2:282–88.
  1943   Mexico and the Southwestern United States. In *El Norte de Mexico y el Sur de los Estados
          Unidos,* pp. 203–205. Sociedad Mexicana de Antropologia, Mexico City.
  1945a   *The Excavation of Los Muertos and Neighboring Ruins in the Salt River Valley, Southern Ari-
          zona.* Papers of the Peabody Museum of American Archaeology and Ethnology 24(1).
          Cambridge: Harvard University.
  1945b   The Problem of Contacts between the Southwestern United States and Mexico. *Southwest-
          ern Journal of Anthropology* 1:55–74.
  1950   A Sequence of Great Kivas in Forestdale Valley, Arizona. In *For the Dean,* E. K. Reed and
          D. S. King, eds., pp. 29–39. Hohokam Museums Association, Tucson, and Southwestern
          Monuments Association, Santa Fe.
  1957   An Alluvial Site on the San Carlos Indian Reservation. *American Antiquity* 23:2–27.
  1958   Evidence at Point of Pines for a Prehistoric Migration from Northern Arizona. In *Migra-
          tions in the New World Culture History,* R. H. Thompson, ed. University of Arizona Bulletin
          29(2), Social Science Bulletin 27. Tucson: University of Arizona Press.
  1962a   The Greater American Southwest. In *Courses toward Urban Life,* R. Braidwood and
          G. Willey, eds., pp. 106–31. Viking Fund Publications in Anthropology 32.
  1962b   HH 39: Recollections of a Dramatic Moment in Southwestern Archaeology. *Tree-Ring Bul-
          letin* 24:11–14.
  1976a   *The Hohokam: Desert Farmers and Craftsmen.* Tucson: University of Arizona Press.
  1976b   Salado: The View from Point of Pines. *The Kiva* 42:81–84.
  1983   Concluding Remarks. In *The Cochise Cultural Sequence in Southeastern Arizona,* E. B. Sayles,
          ed., pp. 158–66. Anthropological Papers of the University of Arizona 42. Tucson.
  1985   *Mogollon Culture in the Forestdale Valley, East-Central Arizona.* Tucson: University of Ari-
          zona Press.
Haviland, William A.
  1970   Tikal, Guatemala, and Mesoamerican Urbanism. *World Archaeology* 2:186–97.
Hawley, Florence
  1937   Pueblo Social Organization as a Lead to Pueblo Prehistory. *American Anthropologist*
          39:504–22.
Hayden, Julian D.
  1957   *Excavations, 1940, at University Indian Ruin, Tucson, Arizona.* Southwestern Monuments
          Association, Technical Series 5. Globe: Gila Pueblo.
Hayes, Alden C.
  1964   *The Archaeological Survey of Wetherill Mesa, Mesa Verde National Park-Colorado.* Archeo-
          logical Research Series 7A. Washington, D.C.: National Park Service.

1981   A Survey of Chaco Canyon Archeology. In *Archeological Surveys of Chaco Canyon,* A. C. Hayes, D. M. Brugge, and W. J. Judge, eds., pp. 1–68. Publications in Archeology 18A, Chaco Canyon Studies. Washington, D.C.: National Park Service.

Hays, Kelley A.
1989   Katsina Depictions on Homol'ovi Ceramics: Toward a Fourteenth Century Pueblo Iconography. *The Kiva* 54(3).

Headland, T. N.
1987   The Wild Yam Question: How Well Could Independent Hunter-Gatherers Live in a Tropical Rain Forest Ecosystem? *Human Ecology* 15:463–87.

Headland, T. N., and L. A. Reid
1989   Hunter-Gatherers and Their Neighbors from Prehistory to the Present. *Current Anthropology* 30:43–66.

Hegmon, Michelle
1986   Information Exchange and Integration on Black Mesa, Arizona, A.D. 931 to 1150. In *Spatial Organization and Exchange,* S. Plog, ed., pp. 256–81. Carbondale: Southern Illinois Press.
1987   To Share and Share Alike: Food Sharing and Agricultural Risk. Paper presented at the 86th annual meeting of the American Anthropological Association. Chicago.
1989   Risk Reduction and Variation in Agricultural Economies: A Computer Simulation of Hopi Agriculture. *Research in Economic Anthropology* 11:89–121.
1990   Style as a Social Strategy: Dimensions of Ceramic Stylistic Variation in the Ninth Century Northern Southwest. Ph.D. dissertation, Department of Anthropology, University of Michigan, Ann Arbor.
1991   The Risks of Sharing and Sharing as Risk Reduction: Inter-Household Food Sharing in Egalitarian Societies. In *Between Bands and States: Sedentism, Subsistence, and Interaction in Small Scale Societies,* S. A. Gregg, ed., pp. 309–30. Southern Illinois University at Carbondale Center for Archaeological Investigations Research Series 2.

Helms, Mary W.
1979   *Ancient Panama: Chiefs in Search of Power.* Austin: University of Texas Press.

Herold, Laurance C.
1965   *Trincheras and Physical Environment along the Rio Gavilan, Chihuahua, Mexico.* Publications in Geography, Technical Paper No. 65-1. Department of Geography, University of Denver.

Hevly, Richard H.
1983   High-Altitude Biotic Resources, Paleoenvironments, and Demographic Patterns: Southern Colorado Plateaus, A.D. 500–1400. In *High Altitude Adaptations in the Southwest,* J. Winter, ed., pp. 22–40. Cultural Resources Management Report 2. Albuquerque: USDA Forest Service.
1988   Prehistoric Vegetation and Paleoclimates on the Colorado Plateaus. In *The Anasazi in a Changing Environment,* G. Gumerman, ed., pp. 92–118. Cambridge: Cambridge University Press.

Hewett, Edgar Lee
1906   *Antiquities of the Jemez Plateau, New Mexico.* Bureau of American Ethnology Bulletin 32. Washington, D.C.: Smithsonian Institution.

Hibben, Frank
1948   The Gallina Architectural Forms. *American Antiquity* 14:32–36.
1975   *Kiva Art of the Anasazi at Pottery Mound.* Las Vegas: KC Publications.

Hickerson, Harold
1962   *The Southwestern Chippewa, An Ethnohistorical Study.* American Anthropological Association Memoir 92.

Hill, James N., and W. Nicholas Trierweiler
1986   Prehistoric Response to Food Stress on the Pajarito Plateau, New Mexico. Technical report and results of the Pajarito Archaeological Research Project, 1977–1985. Final report to the National Science Foundation for Grant #BNS-78-08118.

Hinkes, M. J.
1983   Skeletal Evidence of Stress in Subadults: Trying to Come of Age at Grasshopper Pueblo. Ph.D. dissertation, Department of Anthropology, University of Arizona, Tucson.

Hitchens, Christopher
1988   *Prepared for the Worst.* New York: Hill and Wang.

Hodder, Ian, and Clive Orton
   1976   *Spatial Analysis in Archaeology.* Cambridge: Cambridge University Press.
Hodge, F. W., G. P. Hammond, and Agapito Rey
   1945   *Fray Alonso de Benavides' Revised Memorial of 1634.* Albuquerque: University of New Mexico Press.
Hodge, Hiram C.
   1877   *Arizona as It Is: Or, The Coming Country.* New York: Hurd and Houghton.
Hogan, Patrick
   1985   Foragers to Farmers: The Adoption of Agriculture in Northwestern New Mexico. Paper presented at the 50th annual meeting of the Society for American Archaeology. Denver.
   1989   Dinetah: A Reevaluation of Pre-Revolt Navajo Occupation in Northwest New Mexico. *Journal of Anthropological Research* 45:53–66.
Holbrook, Sally J., and James C. Mackey
   1976   Prehistoric Environmental Change in Northern New Mexico: Evidence from a Gallina Phase Archaeological Site. *The Kiva* 41:309–17.
Holden, W. C.
   1929   Some Explorations and Excavations in Northwest Texas. *Bulletin of the Texas Archaeological and Paleontological Society* 1:23–35.
   1930   The Canadian Valley Expedition of March, 1930. *Bulletin of the Texas Archaeological and Paleontological Society* 2:21–32.
   1931   Texas Tech Archaeological Expedition, Summer 1930. *Bulletin of the Texas Archaeological and Paleontological Society* 3:43–52.
   1932   Recent Archaeological Discoveries in the Texas Panhandle. *Southwestern Social Science Quarterly* 13:289–93.
   1933   Excavations at Saddleback Ruin. *Bulletin of the Texas Archaeological and Paleontological Society* 5:39–52.
Holmer, Richard N.
   1985   Common Projectile Points of the Intermountain West. In *Anthropology of the Desert West: Essays in Honor of Jesse D. Jennings,* C. J. Condie and D. D. Fowler, eds., pp. 89–116. University of Utah Anthropological Papers 110. Salt Lake City.
Holmes, William H.
   1878   Report of the Ancient Ruins of Southwestern Colorado, Examined during the Summers of 1875 and 1876. In *Tenth Annual Report of the United States Geology and Geography Survey,* F. V. Hayden, ed., pp. 381–408. Washington, D.C.: U.S. Government Printing Office.
Honea, Kenneth
   1973   The Technology of Eastern Pueblo Pottery on the Llano Estacado. *Plains Anthropologist* 18(59):73–88.
Honeycutt, Linda, and Jerry Fetterman
   1985   *The Alkali Ridge Cultural Resource Survey and Vandalism Study, Southeastern Utah.* Report prepared for the Bureau of Land Management, San Juan Resource Area, Moab District. Contract No YA-551-RFP3-440023. Yellow Jacket, CO: Woods Canyon Archaeological Consultants.
Hooton, Ernest A.
   1930   *The Indians of Pecos Pueblo: A Study of Their Skeletal Remains.* Paper of the Southwestern Expedition 4. New Haven: Yale University Press.
Hough, Walter
   1903   Archaeological Field Work in Northeastern Arizona. The Museum-Gates Expedition of 1901. In *Report of the United States National Museum for 1901,* pp. 279–358. Washington, D.C.
   1914   *Culture of the Ancient Pueblos of the Upper Gila.* Smithsonian Institution Bulletin 87, Washington, D.C.
Howard, Jerry B.
   1991   System Reconstruction: The Evolution of an Irrigation System. In *The Operation and Evolution of an Irrigation System: The East Papago Canal Study,* J. B. Howard and G. Huckleberry, eds., pp. 5.1–5.33. Publications in Archaeology 18. Phoenix: Soil Systems, Inc.
Hrdlicka, A.
   1908   Physiological and Medical Observations among the Indians of the Southwestern United States and Northern Mexico. *Bureau of American Ethnology Bulletin* 37:103–12.

1935 The Pueblos, with Comparative Data on the Bulk of the Tribes of the Southwest and Northern Mexico. *American Journal of Physical Anthropology* 20:235–460.

Huckell, Bruce B.
1979 *The Coronet Real Project: Archaeological Investigations on the Luke Range, Southwestern Arizona.* Arizona State Museum Archaeological Series 129. Tucson.
1984 *The Archaic Occupation of the Rosemont Area, Northern Santa Rita Mountains, Southeastern Arizona.* Cultural Resource Management Division, Arizona State Museum, Archaeological Series 147, vol. 1. Tucson.
1987 Agriculture and Late Archaic Settlements in the River Valleys of Southeastern Arizona. Paper presented at the 1987 Hohokam Conference, Arizona State University, Tempe.
1988 Late Archaic Archaeology of the Tucson Basin: A Status Report. In *Recent Research on Tucson Basin Prehistory: Proceedings of the Second Tucson Basin Conference,* W. Doelle and P. Fish, eds., pp. 57–80. Institute for American Research Anthropological Papers 10.
1990 Late Preceramic Farmers-Foragers in Southeastern Arizona: A Cultural and Ecological Consideration of the Spread of Agriculture into the Arid Southwestern United States. Ph.D. dissertation, Department of Arid Lands Resource Sciences, University of Arizona, Tucson.

Huckell, Bruce B., and L. Huckell
1984 *Excavations at Milagro, A Late Archaic Site in the Eastern Tucson Basin.* Tucson: Arizona State Museum.
1985 New Light on the Late Archaic of the Southern Southwest. Paper presented at the 50th annual meeting of the Society for American Archaeology. Denver.
1988 Crops Come to the Desert: Late Preceramic Agriculture in Southeastern Arizona. Paper presented at the 53rd annual meeting of the Society for American Archaeology. Phoenix.

Hudson, Charles, Marvin Smith, David Hally, Richard Polhemus, and Chester DePratter
1985 Coosa: A Chiefdom in the Sixteenth-Century Southeastern United States. *American Antiquity* 50:723–37.

Hudson, Luanne B.
1978 A Quantitative Analysis of Prehistoric Exchange in the Southwestern United States. Ph.D. dissertation, Department of Anthropology, University of California, Los Angeles.

Hughes, Richard E., and James A. Bennyhoff
1986 Early Trade. In *Handbook of North American Indians.* Vol. 11, *Great Basin,* W. L. D'Azevedo, ed., pp. 238–55. Washington, D.C.: Smithsonian Institution Press.

Hummert, J.
1981 The Human Osteological Collection of the Colorado State Historical Society. Manuscript, Colorado State Historical Society, Denver.

Hunter-Anderson, Rosalind D.
1979 Explaining Residential Aggregation in the Northern Rio Grande: A Competition Reduction Model. In *Archaeological Investigations in Cochiti Reservoir, New Mexico.* Vol. 4, *Adaptive Change in the Northern Rio Grande Valley,* J. V. Biella and R. C. Chapman, eds., pp. 56–67. Office of Contract Archaeology, University of New Mexico, Albuquerque.
1986 *Prehistoric Adaptation in the American Southwest.* Cambridge: Cambridge University Press.

Hurst, Winston, Mark Bond, and Sloan E. Emery Schwindt
1985 Piedra Black-on-White, White Mesa Variety: Formal Description of a Western Mesa Verde Anasazi Pueblo White Ware Type. *Pottery Southwest* 12(3):1–7.

Hurst, Winston B., and Christy G. Turner II
1990 Rediscovering the "Great Discovery": Wetherill's First Cave 7 and Its Implications Regarding Basketmaker Violence. Paper presented at the Anasazi Basketmaker Symposium, Wetherill-Grand Gulch Research Project, Blanding, Utah, May 26–28.

Hutterer, Karl L.
1991 Losing Track of the Tribes: Evolutionary Sequences in Southeast Asia. In *Profiles in Cultural Evolution,* A. T. Rambo and K. Gillogy, eds., pp. 219–46. Anthropological Papers of the Museum of Anthropology 85. Ann Arbor: University of Michigan.

Iltis, H. H.
1983 From Teosinte to Maize: The Catastrophic Sexual Transmutation. *Science* 222:886–94.

Irwin-Williams, Cynthia
1973 *The Oshara Tradition: Origins of the Anasazi Culture.* Eastern New Mexico University Contributions in Anthropology 5. Portales.

1979   Post-Pleistocene Archeology, 7000–2000 B.C. In *Handbook of North American Indians.* Vol. 9, *Southwest*, A. Ortiz, ed., pp. 31–42. Washington, D.C.: Smithsonian Institution.

1981   Alternative Forms of Prehistoric Pueblo Organization: Dispersed, Aggregated and Nucleated Systems. Paper presented at the 46th annual meeting of the Society for American Archaeology. San Diego.

Irwin-Williams, Cynthia (editor)

1967   Picosa: The Elementary Southwestern Culture. *American Antiquity* 32(4):441–57.

1972   The Structure of Chacoan Society in the Northern Southwest: Investigations at the Salmon Site–1972. *Eastern New Mexico University Contributions in Anthropology* 4(3). Portales.

Isbell, William H.

1978   Environmental Perturbations and the Origin of the Andean State. In *Social Archaeology: Beyond Subsistence and Dating,* C. L. Redman, M. J. Berman, E. V. Curtin, W. T. Langhorne, Jr., N. M. Versaggi, and J. C. Wanser, eds., pp. 303–13. New York: Academic Press.

James, Harry C.

1974   *Pages from Hopi History.* Tucson: University of Arizona Press.

Jeançon, J. A.

1912   Ruins at Pesedeuinge. *Records of the Past* 11:28–37.

1922   *Archaeological Research in the Northeastern San Juan Basin of Colorado during the Summer of 1921.* Denver: State History Society of Colorado and the University of Denver.

1923   *Excavations in the Chama Valley, New Mexico.* Bureau of American Ethnology Bulletin 81. Washington, D.C.

Jelinek, Arthur J.

1961   Mimbres Warfare. *The Kiva* 27(2):28–30.

1967   *A Prehistoric Sequence in the Middle Pecos Valley, New Mexico.* University of Michigan Museum of Anthropology, Anthropological Paper 31. Ann Arbor.

Jenkins, L.

1991   Tribal Initiatives in Research: A New Partnership between Science and Native Peoples. Paper presented at the 90th annual meeting of the American Anthropological Association. Chicago.

Jennings, Jesse D.

1956   The American Southwest: A Problem in Cultural Isolation. *Memoirs of the Society for American Archaeology* 11:59–127.

1964   The Desert West. In *Prehistoric Man in the New World,* J. D. Jennings and E. Norbeck, eds., pp. 149–74. Chicago: University of Chicago Press.

1978   *Prehistory of Utah and the Eastern Great Basin.* University of Utah Anthropological Papers 98. Salt Lake City.

Jett, Stephen C.

1964   Pueblo Indian Migration: An Evaluation of the Possible Physical and Cultural Determinants. *American Antiquity* 29:281–300.

Jewett, Robert A.

1989   Distance, Integration, and Complexity: The Spatial Organization of Pan-Regional Settlement Clusters in the American Southwest. In *The Sociopolitical Structure of Prehistoric Southwestern Societies,* S. Upham, K. G. Lightfoot, and R. A. Jewett, eds., pp. 363–88. Boulder: Westview Press.

Jiménez Betts, Peter

1989   *Informe de Trabajos Efectuados Dentro del Proyecto La Quemada 1987–1988.* Report to the Instituto Nacional de Antropologia e Historia, Mexico City.

Johannessen, C. L.

1982   Domestication Process of Maize Continues in Guatemala. *Economic Botany* 36:84–99.

Johansson, S. Ryan, and S. H. Preston

1978   Tribal Demography: The Hopi and Navajo Populations as Seen through Manuscripts from the 1900 U.S. Census. *Social Science History* 3:1–33.

Johnson, Alfred E.

1964   Archaeological Excavations in Hohokam Sites in Southern Arizona. *American Antiquity* 30:145–61.

1965   The Development of Western Pueblo Culture. Ph.D. dissertation, University of Arizona. Ann Arbor: University Microfilms.

Johnson, Allen W., and Timothy Earle
    1987   *The Evolution of Human Societies: From Foraging Group to Agrarian State.* Stanford: Stanford
            University Press.
Johnson, Gregory A.
    1973   *Local Exchange and Early State Development in Southwestern Iran.* Anthropology Papers
            No. 51, Museum of Anthropology, University of Michigan, Ann Arbor.
    1982   Organizational Structure and Scalar Stress. In *Theory and Explanation in Archaeology:
            The Southampton Conference,* C. Renfrew, M. J. Rowlands, and B. Abbott Segraves, eds.,
            pp. 389–421. New York: Academic Press.
    1983   Decision-Making Organization and Pastoral Nomad Camp Size. *Human Ecology*
            11(2):175–99.
    1989   Dynamics of Southwestern Prehistory: Far Outside—Looking In. In *Dynamics of Southwest
            Prehistory,* L. S. Cordell and G. J. Gumerman, eds., pp. 371–89. A School of American
            Research Advanced Seminar Book. Washington, D.C.: Smithsonian Institution Press.
Johnson, R. L.
    1967   Chronic Otitis Media in School Age Navajo Indians. *Laryngoscope* 77:1990–95.
Jones, C. A.
    1985   *C4 Grasses and Cereals: Growth Development and Stress Response.* New York: John Wiley &
            Sons.
Jones, Oakan L.
    1966   *Pueblo Warriors.* Norman: University of Oklahoma Press.
Jorde, L. B.
    1977   Precipitation Cycles and Cultural Buffering in the Prehistoric Southwest. In *For Theory
            Building in Archaeology,* L. R. Binford, ed., pp. 385–96. New York: Academic Press.
Jorgensen, Joseph G.
    1974   *Comparative Studies by Harold Driver and Essays in His Honor.* New Haven: HRAF Press.
    1980   *Western Indians: Comparative Environment, Languages, and Culture of 172 Western American
            Indian Tribes.* San Francisco: W. H. Freeman.
    1987   Political Society in Aboriginal Western North America. In *Themes in Ethnology and Cul-
            ture History: Essays in Honor of David F. Aberle,* L. Donald, ed., pp. 175–226. The Folklore
            Institute, Meerut, India: Archana Publications.
Judd, Neil M.
    1952   A Pueblo III Warclub from Southeastern Utah. *The Masterkey* 26(2):60–63.
    1954   *The Material Culture of Pueblo Bonito.* Smithsonian Miscellaneous Collections 124. Wash-
            ington, D.C.
    1959   *Pueblo del Arroyo, Chaco Canyon, New Mexico.* Smithsonian Miscellaneous Collections
            138(1). Washington, D.C.
    1964   *The Architecture of Pueblo Bonito.* Smithsonian Miscellaneous Collections 147(1). Washing-
            ton, D.C.
Judge, W. James
    1979   The Development of a Complex Cultural Ecosystem in the Chaco Basin, New Mexico. In
            Proceedings of the First Conference on Scientific Research in the National Parks, R. Linn, ed.,
            pp. 901–905. National Park Service Transactions and Proceedings Series 5.
    1982   The Paleo-Indian and Basketmaker Periods: An Overview and Some Research Problems.
            In *The San Juan Tomorrow: Planning for the Conservation of Cultural Resources in the San
            Juan Basin,* F. Plog and W. Wait, eds., pp. 5–58. Santa Fe: National Park Service.
    1989   Chaco Canyon-San Juan Basin. In *Dynamics of Southwest Prehistory,* L. S. Cordell and G. J.
            Gumerman, eds., pp. 209–61. A School of American Research Advanced Seminar Book.
            Washington, D.C.: Smithsonian Institution Press.
Judge, W. James, W. B. Gillespie, S. H. Lekson, and H. W. Toll
    1981   Tenth Century Developments in Chaco Canyon. In *Collected Papers in Honor of Erik
            Kellerman Reed,* A. H. Schroeder, ed., pp. 65–98. Archaeological Society of New Mexico
            Anthropological Papers 6.
Judge, W. James, and John D. Schelberg (editors)
    1984   *Recent Research on Chaco Prehistory.* Reports of the Chaco Center 8. Albuquerque: Divi-
            sion of Cultural Resources, National Park Service.

Kane, Allen E.
  1989   Did the Sheep Look Up? Sociopolitical Complexity in Ninth Century Dolores Society. In *The Sociopolitical Structure of Prehistoric Southwestern Societies,* S. Upham, K. G. Lightfoot, and R. A. Jewett, eds., pp. 307–62. Boulder: Westview Press.
Kaplan, L.
  1981   What Is the Origin of the Common Bean? *Economic Botany* 35:40–54.
Katzer, Keith
  1987   A Geomorphic Evaluation of the Agricultural Potential of Cerros de Trincheras. *Journal of the Arizona-Nevada Academy of Science* 21:5.
Keegan, William F., and Brian M. Butler
  1987   The Microeconomic Logic of Horticultural Intensification in the Eastern Woodlands. In *Emergent Horticultural Economies of the Eastern Woodlands,* W. F. Keegan, ed., pp. 109–28. Center for Archaeological Investigations Occasional Paper 7.1. Carbondale: Southern Illinois University.
Kelley, J. Charles
  1952   Factors Involved in the Abandonment of Certain Peripheral Southwestern Settlements. *American Anthropologist* 54:356–87.
  1966   Mesoamerica and the Southwestern United States. In *Archaeological Frontiers and External Connections,* G. F. Ekholm and G. R. Willey, eds., pp. 95–110. *Handbook of Middle American Indians,* vol. 4. Austin: University of Texas Press.
  1976   Alta Vista: Outpost of Mesoamerican Empire on the Tropic of Cancer. In *Las Fronteras de Mesoamerica: XIV Mesa Redonda,* pp. 21–40. Sociedad Mexicana de Antropologia, Mexico City.
  1980   Discussion of Papers by Plog, Doyel, and Riley. In *Current Issues in Hohokam Prehistory: Proceedings of a Symposium,* D. E. Doyel and F. Plog, eds., pp. 49–66. Anthropological Papers 23. Tempe: Arizona State University.
  1985   The Chronology of the Chalchihuites Culture. In *The Archaeology of West and Northwest Mesoamerica,* M. S. Foster and P. C. Weigand, eds., pp. 269–88. Boulder: Westview Press.
  1986a   *Jumano and Patarabueye, Relations at La Junta de los Rios.* Anthropological Papers 77, Museum of Anthropology, University of Michigan, Ann Arbor.
  1986b   The Mobile Merchants of Molino. In *Ripples in the Chichimec Sea: New Considerations of Southwestern-Mesoamerican Interactions,* F. J. Mathien and R. H. McGuire, eds., pp. 97–124. Carbondale: Southern Illinois University Press.
Kelley, J. Charles, and Ellen Abbot Kelley
  1975   An Alternative Hypothesis for the Explanation of Anasazi Culture History. In *Papers in Honor of Florence Hawley Ellis,* T. R. Frisbie, ed., pp. 178–223. Papers of the Archaeological Society of New Mexico 2. Santa Fe.
Kelley, Jane Holden
  1984   *The Archaeology of the Sierra Blanca Region of Southeastern New Mexico.* University of Michigan Museum of Anthropology Anthropological Paper 74. Ann Arbor.
Kelly, Isabel T.
  1943   West Mexico and the Hohokam. In *El Norte de Mexico y el Sur de Estados Unidos: Tercera Reunion de Mesa Redonda Sobre Problemas Antropologicos de Mexico y Centro America,* pp. 206–22. Sociedad Mexicana de Antropologia, Mexico City.
Kennard, Edward A.
  n.d.   Genealogies of Third Mesa. Manuscript, Laboratory of Anthropology. Santa Fe.
Keusch, G. T., and M. J. Farthing
  1986   Nutrition and Infection. *Annual Reviews in Nutrition* 6:131–54.
Kidder, Alfred V.
  1924   *An Introduction to the Study of Southwestern Archaeology, with a Preliminary Account of the Excavations at Pecos.* Papers of the Phillips Academy Southwestern Expedition 1. New Haven: Yale University Press.
Kidder, Alfred V., and Samuel J. Guernsey
  1919   *Archaeological Exploration in Northeastern Arizona.* Bureau of American Ethnology Bulletin 65. Washington, D.C.
Kincaid, Chris (editor)
  1983   *Chaco Roads Project, Phase I: A Reappraisal of Prehistoric Roads in the San Juan Basin.* USDI

Bureau of Land Management, New Mexico State Office and Albuquerque District Office, Santa Fe and Albuquerque.

King, F. B.
1987   Prehistoric Maize in Eastern North America: An Evolutionary Evaluation. Ph.D. dissertation, University of Illinois. Ann Arbor: University Microfilms.

Kintigh, Keith W.
1985   *Settlement, Subsistence, and Society in Late Zuni Prehistory.* Anthropological Papers of the University of Arizona 44. Tucson: University of Arizona Press.
1988   Protohistoric Transitions in the Western Pueblo Area. Paper presented in the invited session, "Prehistoric to Historic Transitions," the Southwestern Symposium, January. Tempe.
1990a   Chaco Communal Architecture and Cibolan Aggregation. Paper presented at the invited session, "Aggregation in the Southwest." 2nd Southwest Symposium, January. Albuquerque.
1990b   Villages and Towns: The Organization of Prehistoric Cibolan Settlements. Paper presented at the 2nd Southwest Symposium, January. Albuquerque.

Kirchhoff, Paul
1943   Mesoamerica: Sus Limites Geographicas, Composition Ethnica y Caracteres Culturales. *Acta Americana* 1:92–107.
1954   Gatherers and Farmers in the Greater Southwest: A Problem in Classification. *American Anthropologist* 56(4):529–50.

Kirkby, A. V.
1973   *The Use of Land and Water Resources in the Past and Present Valley of Oaxaca, Mexico.* Memoirs of the Museum of Anthropology, University of Michigan 5. Ann Arbor.

Kluckhohn, Clyde, and Paul Reiter (editors)
1939   *Preliminary Report on the 1937 Excavations: Bc 50–51, Chaco Canyon, New Mexico.* University of New Mexico Bulletin 345, Anthropological Series 3(2). Albuquerque.

Knudson, S. J.
1985   *Culture in Retrospect: An Introduction to Archaeology.* Prospect Heights, IL: Waveland Press.

Kohl, Philip
1987   The Use and Abuse of World Systems Theory. *Advances in Archaeological Method and Theory* 11:1–35.

Kohler, Timothy A.
1989   Introduction. In *Bandelier Archaeological Excavation Project: Research Design and Summer 1988 Sampling,* pp. 1–12. Department of Anthropology, Washington State University, Pullman.

Kohler, Timothy A., Janet D. Orcutt, Kenneth L. Petersen, and Eric Blinman
1986   Anasazi Spreadsheets: The Cost of Doing Agricultural Business in Prehistoric Dolores. In *Dolores Archaeological Program: Final Synthetic Report,* D. A. Breternitz, C. K. Robinson, and G. T. Gross, comps., pp. 525–38. Denver: Bureau of Reclamation, Engineering and Research Center.

Kroeber, Alfred L.
1925   *Handbook of the Indians of California.* Bureau of American Ethnology Bulletin No. 78. Washington, D.C.: Smithsonian Institution.
1939   *Cultural and Natural Areas of North America.* University of California Publications in American Archaeology and Ethnology 38. Berkeley.

Kuckelman, Kristin A., and James N. Morris (compilers)
1988   *Archaeological Investigations on South Canal.* Vol. 2, Four Corners Archaeological Project, Report 11. Cortez: CASA.

Kunitz, Stephen J.
1970   Disease and Death among the Anasazi. *El Palacio* 76:17–22.

Kunitz, Stephen J., and Robert C. Euler
1972   *Aspects of Southwestern Paleoepidemiology.* Prescott College Anthropological Reports 2. Prescott: Prescott College Press.

Lancaster, J. W.
1983   An Analysis of Manos and Metates from the Mimbres Valley, New Mexico. M.A. thesis, University of New Mexico, Albuquerque.

Lang, Richard W.
1980   Archaeological Investigations at a Pueblo Agricultural Site, and Archaic and Puebloan Encampments on the Rio Ojo Caliente, Rio Arriba County, New Mexico. Santa Fe: School of American Research Press.
Lange, Richard
1989   A Survey of Homolovi State Park. The Kiva 54:195–216.
Lambert, Marjorie
1954   Paa-Ko. School of American Research Monographs 19. Santa Fe: School of American Research Press.
Larsen, C. S.
1984   Health and Disease in Prehistoric Georgia: The Transition to Agriculture. In Paleopathology at the Origins of Agriculture, M. N. Cohen and G. J. Armelagos, eds., pp. 367–92. New York: Academic Press.
Larson, Daniel O., and Joel Michaelsen
1990   Impacts of Climatic Variability and Population Growth on Virgin Branch Anasazi Cultural Developments. American Antiquity 55:227–49.
LeBlanc, Steven A.
1982   The Advent of Pottery in the Southwest. In Southwestern Ceramics: A Comparative Review, A. Schroeder, ed., pp. 107–28. The Arizona Archaeologist 15.
1983   Mimbres People. New York: Thames & Hudson.
1986   Aspects of Southwestern Prehistory: A.D. 900–1400. In Ripples in the Chichimec Sea, F. J. Mathien and R. H. McGuire, eds., pp. 105–34. Carbondale: Southern Illinois University Press.
1989a   Cibola: Shifting Cultural Boundaries. In Dynamics of Southwest Prehistory, L. S. Cordell and G. J. Gumerman, eds., pp. 337–69. A School of American Research Advanced Seminar Book. Washington, D.C.: Smithsonian Institution Press.
1989b   Cultural Dynamics in the Southern Mogollon Area. In Dynamics of Southwest Prehistory, L. S. Cordell and G. J. Gumerman, eds., pp. 179–207. A School of American Research Advanced Seminar Book. Washington, D.C.: Smithsonian Institution Press.
LeBlanc, Steven, and Ben Nelson
1976   The Salado in Southwestern New Mexico. The Kiva 42:71–80.
LeBlanc, Steven A., and Michael E. Whalen
1980   An Archaeological Synthesis of South-Central and Southwestern New Mexico. Office of Contract Archaeology, University of New Mexico, Albuquerque.
Lee, Richard Borshay
1979   The Kung San. New York: Cambridge University Press.
Lekson, Stephen H.
1984   Great Pueblo Architecture of Chaco Canyon. USDI National Park Service Publications in Archeology 188.
1986   Mesa Verde-like Ceramics near Truth-or-Consequences, New Mexico. Pottery Southwest 13(4):1–3.
1988   Sociopolitical Complexity at Chaco Canyon, New Mexico. Ph.D. dissertation, University of New Mexico. Ann Arbor: University Microfilms International.
1989   Analysis and Statement of Significance on the Mimbres Culture in Southwestern Prehistory. Mesilla Park, NM: Human Systems Research Inc.
1991   Settlement Patterns and the Chaco Region. In Chaco & Hohokam: Prehistoric Regional Systems in the American Southwest, P. L. Crown and W. J. Judge, eds., pp. 31–56. Santa Fe: School of American Research Press.
Lekson, Stephen H., Thomas C. Windes, John R. Stein, and W. James Judge
1988   The Chaco Canyon Community. Scientific American 259(1):100–109.
Leonard, Robert D., M. Gould, J. Garucci, and P. H. McCartney
1985   Arizona D:11:449. In Excavations on Black Mesa, 1983: A Descriptive Report, A. L. Christenson and W. J. Parry, eds., pp. 125–54. Center for Archaeological Investigations, Research Paper 46. Carbondale: Southern Illinois University.
Leonard, R. D., and G. T. Jones
1987   Elements of an Inclusive Evolutionary Model for Archaeology. Journal of Anthropological Archaeology 6:199–219.

Lévi-Strauss, Claude
1969   *The Elementary Structures of Kinship*. Boston: Beacon Press.
Levy, Jerrold E.
1989   Ethnographic Analogs: Strategies for the Reconstruction of Archaeological Cultures. Paper presented at the advanced seminar "The Organization and Evolution of Prehistoric Southwestern Society." Santa Fe: School of American Research.
1990   The Demographic Consequences of Social Stratification in an "Egalitarian" Society. Paper presented at the annual meeting of the American Anthropological Association. New Orleans.
Lightfoot, Kent G.
1979   Food Redistribution among Prehistoric Pueblo Groups. *The Kiva* 44(4):319–40.
1984   *Prehistoric Political Dynamics: A Case Study from the American Southwest*. DeKalb: Northern Illinois University Press.
Lightfoot, Kent G., and Roberta Jewett
1984   Late Prehistoric Ceramics Distributions in East Central Arizona: An Examination of Cibola, White Mountain and Salado Wares. In *Regional Analysis of Prehistoric Ceramic Variation: Contemporary Studies of the Cibola Whitewares*, A. P. Sullivan and J. L. Hantman, eds., pp. 36–73. Arizona State University Anthropological Research Papers 31. Tempe.
Lightfoot, Kent, and Fred Plog
1984   Intensification along the North Side of the Mogollon Rim. In *Prehistoric Agricultural Strategies in the Southwest*, S. K. Fish and P. R. Fish, eds., pp. 179–96. Anthropological Research Paper 33. Tempe: Arizona State University.
Lindsay, Alexander J., Jr.
1961   The Beaver Creek Agricultural Community on the San Juan River, Utah. *American Antiquity* 27:174–87.
1987   Anasazi Population Movements to Southeastern Arizona. *American Archeology* 6:190–99.
1969   The Tsegi Phase of the Kayenta Cultural Tradition in Northeastern Arizona. Ph.D. dissertation, Department of Anthropology, University of Arizona, Tucson.
Lindsay, Alexander J., J. Richard Ambler, Mary Anne Stein, and Philip M. Hobler
1968   *Survey and Excavations North and East of Navajo Mountain, Utah. 1959–1962*. Flagstaff: Museum of Northern Arizona Bulletin 45.
Lindsay, Alexander, J., Jr., and Calvin H. Jennings
1968   *Salado Red Ware Conference, Ninth Ceramic Seminar*. Museum of Northern Arizona Ceramic Series 4. Flagstaff.
Linton, Ralph
1944   Nomad Raids and Fortified Pueblos. *American Antiquity* 10(1):28–32.
Lintz, Christopher
1991   Texas Panhandle–Pueblo Interactions from the Thirteenth through the Sixteenth Century. In *Farmers, Hunters, and Colonists: Interaction between the Southwest and Southern Plains*, K. A. Spielmann, ed., pp. 89–106. Tucson: University of Arizona Press.
Lipe, William D.
1970   Anasazi Communities in the Red Rock Plateau, Southeastern Utah. In *Reconstructing Prehistoric Pueblo Societies*, W. A. Longacre, ed., pp. 84–139. Albuquerque: University of New Mexico Press.
Lister, Robert H.
1965   *Contributions to Mesa Verde Archaeology: II, Site 875, Mesa Verde National Park, Colorado*. University of Colorado Studies, Series in Anthropology 11. Boulder.
1978   Mesoamerican Influences at Chaco Canyon, New Mexico. In *Across the Chichimec Sea: Papers in Honor of J. Charles Kelley*, C. L. Riley and B. C. Hedrick, eds., pp. 233–41. Carbondale: Southern Illinois University.
Lister, Robert H., Florence C. Lister, and J. Richard Ambler
1960   *The Coombs Site, Part II*. Anthropological Papers of the University of Utah No. 41(2). Salt Lake City.
Lockett, H. Clairbourne, and Lyndon L. Hargrave
1953   *Woodchuck Cave: A Basketmaker II Site in Tsegi Canyon, Arizona*. Museum of Northern Arizona Bulletin 26. Flagstaff.

Loeb, E. M.
    1932   *The Western Kuksu Cult.* University of California Publications in American Archaeology
            and Ethnology No. 33(1). Berkeley.
Loendorf, Lawrence L.
    1990   A Dated Rock Art Panel of Shield Bearing Warriors in South Central Montana. *Plains
            Anthropologist* 35:45–54.
Lohse, Ernest S.
    1980   Fremont Settlement Pattern and Architectural Variation. In *Fremont Perspectives,* D. B.
            Madsen, ed., pp. 41–54. Utah Division of State History, Antiquities Section Selected
            Papers 7(16). Salt Lake City.
London, M., and K. Tobler
    1979   Pindi Site—Paleopathology Abstract. Manuscript, Maxwell Museum of Anthropology,
            University of New Mexico.
Long, A., Richard I. Ford, D. J. Donahue, A. T. Jull, T. W. Linick, and Ted Zabel
    1986   Tandem Accelerator Dating of Archaeological Cultigens. Paper delivered at the 51st an-
            nual meeting of the Society for American Archaeology. New Orleans.
Longacre, William A.
    1964   A Synthesis of Upper Little Colorado Prehistory, Eastern Arizona. In Chapters in the Pre-
            history of Arizona II. *Fieldiana: Anthropology* 55:201–15.
    1966   Changing Patterns of Social Integration: A Prehistoric Example from the American South-
            west. *American Anthropologist* 68(1):94–102.
    1970   A Historical Review. In *Reconstructing Prehistoric Pueblo Societies,* W. A. Longacre, ed.,
            pp. 1–10. A School of American Research Book. Albuquerque: University of New Mexico
            Press.
Losch, A.
    1954   *The Economics of Location,* transl. by H. Stolpher. New Haven: Yale University Press.
    1980   Change or Stability? Hydraulics, Hunter-Gatherers and Population in Temperate Aus-
            tralia. *World Archaeology* 11:245–64.
Lowe, C. H., and D. E. Brown
    1980   Biotic Communities of the American Southwest. *Desert Plants* 2(1):7–131.
Lowell, Julie
    1986   The Structure and Function of the Prehistoric Household in the Pueblo Southwest: A Case
            Study for Turkey Creek Pueblo. Ph.D. dissertation, University of Arizona. Ann Arbor:
            University Microfilms.
    1988   The Social Use of Space at Turkey Creek Pueblo: An Architectural Analysis. *The Kiva*
            53(2):85–100.
Luebben, Ralph A., Jonathan G. Andelson, and Laurance C. Herrold
    1986   Elvino Whetten Pueblo and Its Relationship to Terraces and Nearby Small Structures,
            Chihuahua, Mexico. *The Kiva* 51:165–88.
Luebben, Ralph A., and Paul R. Nickens
    1982   A Mass Interment in an Early Pueblo III Kiva in Southwestern Colorado. *Journal of Inter-
            mountain Archaeology* 1:66–79.
Lyneis, Margaret M.
    1982   Prehistory in the Southern Great Basin. In *Man and Environment in the Great Basin,* D. B.
            Madsen and J. F. O'Connell, eds., pp. 172–85. SAA Papers 2. Society for American
            Archaeology, Washington, D.C.
    1984   The Western Anasazi Frontier: Cultural Processes along a Prehistoric Boundary. In *Ex-
            ploring the Limit: Frontiers and Boundaries in Prehistory,* S. P. DeAtley and F. J. Findlow,
            eds. pp. 81–92. Oxford: British Archaeological Reports, International Series 223.
Marby, J. B.
    1990   *A Late Archaic Occupation at AZ AA:12:105 (ASM).* Center for Desert Archaeology Techni-
            cal Report No. 90-6. Tucson.
Mackey, James C., and Roger C. Green
    1979   Largo-Gallina Towers: An Explanation. *American Antiquity* 44:145–54.
Mackey, James C., and Sally J. Holbrook
    1978   Environmental Reconstruction and the Abandonment of the Largo-Gallina Area, New
            Mexico. *Journal of Field Archaeology* 5:29–49.

MacNeish, Richard S.
1991   *Preliminary Investigations for the Archaic in the Region of Las Cruces, New Mexico.* Andover, MA: Andover Foundation for Archaeological Research.
MacNeish, Richard S., and P. H. Beckett
1987   *The Archaic Tradition of South-Central New Mexico and Chihuahua, Mexico.* COAS Monograph No. 7, COAS Bookstore, Las Cruces, NM.
Madsen, David B.
1979   The Fremont and the Sevier: Defining Prehistoric Agriculturalists North of the Anasazi. *American Antiquity* 44(4):711–22.
1986   Great Basin Nuts: A Short Treatise on the Distribution, Productivity, and Prehistoric Use of Pinyon. In *Anthropology of the Desert West: Essays in Honor of Jessee D. Jennings,* C. J. Condie and D. D. Fowler, eds., pp. 21–42. University of Utah Anthropological Papers 110. Salt Lake City.
Madsen, David B., and La Mar W. Lindsay
1977   *Backhoe Village.* Utah Division of State History, Antiquities Section Selected Papers 4(2). Salt Lake City.
Mangelsdorf, Paul C.
1950   The Mystery of Corn. *Scientific American* 183:20–29.
1974   *Corn: Its Origin, Evolution, and Improvement.* Cambridge: The Belknap Press of Harvard University Press.
Mangelsdorf, Paul C., and C. E. Smith
1949   New Archaeological Evidence on Evolution in Maize. *Harvard Botanical Museum Leaflets* 13:213–47.
Marquardt, William, and Carole L. Crumley
1987   Theoretical Issues in the Analysis of Spatial Patterning. In *Regional Dynamics: Burgundian Landscapes in Historical Perspective,* C. L. Crumley and W. H. Marquardt, eds., pp. 1–18. Orlando: Academic Press.
Marshall, Michael P.
n.d.   A Review of Culture History in the Zuni Region. Manuscript, Zuni Archaeology Program, Zuni.
Marshall, Michael P., John R. Stein, Richard W. Loose, and Judith E. Novotny
1979   *Anasazi Communities of the San Juan Basin.* Public Service Company of New Mexico and New Mexico Historic Preservation Bureau, Albuquerque and Santa Fe.
Marshall, Michael P., and Henry J. Walt
1984   *Rio Abajo, Prehistory of a Rio Grande Province.* New Mexico Historic Preservation Program, Historic Preservation Division, Santa Fe.
Martin, Debra L., George J. Armelagos, and K. A. Henderson
1989   The Persistence of Nutritional Stress in Northeastern African (Sudanese Nubian) Populations. In *Famine in Africa.* Vol. 1, *Microperspectives,* R. Huss-Ashmore and S. Katz, eds., pp. 185–209. London: Gordon and Breach.
Martin, Debra L., Alan H. Goodman, George J. Armelagos, and Ann L. Magennis
1991   *Black Mesa Anasazi Health: Reconstructing Life from Patterns of Death and Disease.* Southern Illinois University at Carbondale, Center for Archaeological Investigations, Occasional Paper 14.
Martin, Paul S.
1929   The 1928 Archaeological Expedition of the State Historical Society of Colorado. *The Colorado Magazine* 6(1):1–35.
Martin, Paul S., and Fred Plog
1973   *The Archaeology of Arizona: A Study of the Southwest Region.* Garden City, NY: Natural History Press.
Martin, Paul S., and John B. Rinaldo
1950   Sites of the Reserve Phase, Pine Lawn Valley, New Mexico. *Fieldiana: Anthropology* 38(3).
1960   Table Rock Pueblo, Arizona. *Fieldiana: Anthropology* 51(2).
Martin, Paul S., John B. Rinaldo, and E. Bluhm
1954   Caves of the Reserve Area. *Fieldiana: Anthropology* 42.
Martin, Paul S., J. B. Rinaldo, E. Bluhm, H. Cutler, and R. Grange, Jr.
1952   Mogollon Cultural Continuity and Change. *Fieldiana: Anthropology* 40.

Martin, Paul S., and Elizabeth Willis
    1940   *Anasazi Painted Pottery in Field Museum of Natural History.* Anthropology, Memoirs, Field
            Museum of Natural History 5.
Marwitt, John P.
    1986   Fremont Cultures. In *Handbook of North American Indians.* Vol. 11, *Great Basin,* W. L.
            D'Azevedo, ed., pp. 161–72. Washington, D.C.: Smithsonian Institution.
Masayesva, V.
    1991   Research and Indian People: A Time to Examine the Real Human Issues. Paper presented
            at the 90th annual meeting of the American Anthropological Association. Chicago.
Masse, W. Bruce
    1980   *Excavations at Gu Achi: A Reappraisal of Hohokam Settlement and Subsistence in the Ari-
            zona Papagueria.* Western Archaeological Center Publications in Anthropology 12. Tucson:
            National Park Service.
    1981   Prehistoric Irrigation Systems in the Salt River Valley, Arizona. *Science* 214:408–15.
    1991   The Quest for Subsistence Sufficiency and Civilization in the Sonoran Desert. In *Chaco
            & Hohokam: Cultural Complexity in the Arid Southwest,* P. L. Crown and W. J. Judge, eds.,
            pp. 195–223. Santa Fe: School of American Research Press.
Mathien, Frances Joan, and Randall H. McGuire (editors)
    1986   *Ripples in the Chichimec Sea: New Considerations of Mesoamerican-Southwestern Interactions.*
            Carbondale: Southern Illinois University Press.
Matson, R. G., and Brian Chisholm
    1986   Basketmaker II Subsistence: Carbon Isotopes and Other Dietary Indicators from Cedar
            Mesa, Utah. Paper presented at the 3rd Anasazi Symposium, October.
    1991   Basketmaker II Subsistence: Carbon Isotopes and Other Dietary Indicators from Cedar
            Mesa, Utah. *American Antiquity* 56:444–59.
Matson, R. G., William D. Lipe, and William R. Haase IV
    1988   Adaptational Continuities and Occupation Discontinuities: The Cedar Mesa Anasazi.
            Journal of Field Archaeology 15:245–64.
Matthews, W., J. L. Wortman, and J. S. Billings
    1893   Human Bones of the Hemenway Collection in the United States Medical Museum. *Mem-
            oirs of the National Academy of Sciences* 7:141–286.
Mauldin, R. P.
    1983   An Inquiry into the Past: Basketmaker II Settlement on Northeastern Black Mesa, Ari-
            zona. M.A. thesis, University of Texas, Austin.
Mayro, Linda L., Stephanie M. Whittlesey, and J. Jefferson Reid
    1976   Observations on the Salado Presence at Grasshopper Pueblo. *The Kiva* 42:85–94.
McDonald, James A.
    1976   *An Archeological Assessment of Canyon de Chelly National Monument.* Western Archeologi-
            cal Center Publications in Anthropology 5. Tucson: National Park Service.
McGimsey, Charles R., III
    1980   *Mariana Mesa: Seven Prehistoric Settlements in West-Central New Mexico.* Papers of the Pea-
            body Museum of Archeology and Ethnology 72. Cambridge: Harvard University.
McGregor, John C.
    1943   Burial of an Early American Magician. *Proceedings of the American Philosophical Society*
            86(2):270–98.
    1965   *Southwestern Archaeology.* Urbana: University of Illinois Press.
McGuire, Randall H.
    1980   The Mesoamerican Connection in the Southwest. *The Kiva* 46:3–38.
    1983   Breaking Down Cultural Complexity: Inequality and Heterogeneity. *Advances in Archaeo-
            logical Method and Theory* 6:91–142.
    1986   Economies and Modes of Production in the Prehistoric Southwestern Periphery. In *Ripples
            in the Chichimec Sea: New Considerations of Southwestern-Mesoamerican Interactions,* F. J.
            Mathien and R. H. McGuire, eds., pp. 243–69. Carbondale: Southern Illinois Univer-
            sity Press.
    1989   The Greater Southwest as a Periphery of Mesoamerica. In *Centre and Periphery,* T. C.
            Champion, ed., pp. 40–66. London: Allen and Unwin.
    1991   On the Outside Looking In: The Concept of Periphery in Hohokam Archaeology. In *Ex-*

ploring the Hohokam: Prehistoric Desert Dwellers of the Southwest, G. J. Gumerman, ed., pp. 347–82. Albuquerque: University of New Mexico Press.

1992   A Marxist Archaeology. Orlando: Academic Press.

n.d.   Death, Society and Ideology in the Hohokam Community of La Ciudad, A.D. 800 to 1100. Boulder: Westview Press. In press.

McGuire, Randall H., and Christian E. Downum

1982   A Preliminary Consideration of Desert-Mountain Trade Relations. In Mogollon Archaeology: Proceedings of the 1980 Mogollon Conference, P. H. Beckett and K. Silverbird, eds., pp. 111–22, Ramona: Acoma Books.

McGuire, Randall H., and Ann Valdo Howard

1987   The Structure and Organization of Hohokam Shell Exchange. The Kiva 52(2):113–46.

McGuire, Randall H., and Michael B. Schiffer

1982   Hohokam and Patayan: The Archaeology of Southwestern Arizona. New York: Academic Press.

1983   A Theory of Architectural Design. Journal of Anthropological Archaeology 2(3):277–303.

McGuire, Randall H., and Maria Elisa Villalpando

1989   Prehistory and the Making of History in Sonora. In Columbian Consequences I: Archaeological and Historical Perspectives on the Spanish Borderlands West, D. H. Thomas, ed., pp. 159–77. Washington: Smithsonian Institution Press.

McKenna, Peter J.

1984   The Architecture and Material Culture of 29SJ1360. Reports of the Chaco Center 7. Albuquerque: Division of Cultural Research, National Park Service.

McKinlay, J. B., and D. McKinlay

1974   A Case for Refocusing Upstream: The Political Economy of Illness. In Applying Behavioral Science to Cardiovascular Risk, pp. 7–17. Washington, D.C.: American Heart Association.

McKinney, A., D. Hafner, and J. Gothold

1971   A Report on the China Ranch Area. Pacific Coast Archaeological Society Quarterly 4(3):39–56.

Mera, H. P.

1935   Ceramic Clues to the Prehistory of North Central New Mexico. Laboratory of Anthropology Technical Series, Bulletin 8. Santa Fe.

1938   Some Aspects of the Largo Cultural Phase, Northern New Mexico. American Antiquity 3:236–43.

1940   Population Changes in the Rio Grande Glaze-Paint Area. Laboratory of Anthropology Technical Series, Bulletin 9. Santa Fe.

Merbs, Charles F.

1989   Patterns of Health and Sickness in the Precontact Southwest. In Columbian Consequences. Vol. I, Archaeological and Historical Perspectives on the Spanish Borderlands West, D. H. Thomas, ed., pp. 41–55. Washington, D.C.: Smithsonian Institution Press.

Merbs, Charles F., and Robert C. Euler

1985   Atlanto-Occipital Fusion and Spondylolisthesis in an Anasazi Skeleton from Bright Angel Ruin, Grand Canyon National Park, Arizona. American Journal of Physical Anthropology 67:381–91.

Michaelson, David R.

1988   A Data Gathering Report for Four Prehistoric Sites in the Kaibab. Manuscript, Museum of Northern Arizona Library, Flagstaff.

Miles, J. S.

1975   Orthopedic Problems of the Wetherill Mesa Populations. National Park Service, Publications in Archaeology 7G, Wetherill Mesa Studies. Washington, D.C.

Miller, R. J.

1981   Chavez Pass and Biological Relationships in Prehistoric Central Arizona. Ph.D. dissertation, Department of Anthropology, Arizona State University, Tempe.

Miller, William C., and David Breternitz

1958a   1957 Navajo Canyon Survey: Preliminary Report. Plateau 30:72–74.

1985b   1958 Navajo Canyon Survey: Preliminary Report. Plateau 31:3–7.

Milton, K.

1984   Protein and Carbohydrate Resources of the Maku Indians of Northwestern Amazonia. American Anthropologist 86:7–27.

Mindeleff, Cosmos
    1900   Localization of Tusayan Clans. *Nineteenth Annual Report of the Bureau of American Ethnology*, pt. 2, pp. 635–53. Washington, D.C.: Smithsonian Institution.

Mindeleff, Victor
    1891   A Study of Pueblo Architecture: Tusayan and Cibola. *Eighth Annual Report of the Bureau of Ethnology*, pp. 3–228.

Minnis, Paul E.
    1985a   Domesticating People and Plants in the Greater Southwest. In *Prehistoric Food Production in North America*, R. I. Ford, ed., pp. 309–40. Museum of Anthropology, University of Michigan Anthropological Papers 75. Ann Arbor.
    1985b   *Social Adaptation to Food Stress: A Prehistoric Southwestern Example.* Chicago: University of Chicago Press.
    1989a   The Casas Grandes Polity in the International Four Corners. In *The Sociopolitical Structure of Prehistoric Southwestern Societies*, S. Upham, K. G. Lightfoot, and R. A. Jewitt, eds., pp. 269–305. Boulder: Westview Press.
    1989b   Prehistoric Diet in the Northern Southwest: Macroplant Remains from Four Corners Feces. *American Antiquity* 54:543–63.

Moore, J. A.
    1980   The Effects of Information Networks in Hunter-Gatherer Societies. In *Hunter-Gatherer Foraging Strategies: Ethnographic and Archeological Analyses*, B. Winterhalder and E. Smith, eds., pp. 194–217. Chicago: University of Chicago Press.

Morales, E., J. Lembcke, and G. G. Graham
    1988   Nutritional Value for Young Children of Grain Amaranth and Maize-Amaranth Mixtures: Effect of Processing. *Journal of Nutrition* 118:78–85.

Morgan, Lewis Henry
    1881   *Houses and House-Life of the American Aborigines.* Contributions to North American Ethnology 4. Washington. (University of Chicago Press, Chicago, 1965).

Morris, Ann Axtell
    1933   *Digging in the Southwest.* Garden City, NY: Doubleday and Doran.

Morris, D. H.
    1990   Changes in Groundstone Following the Introduction of Maize into the American Southwest. *Journal of Anthropological Research* 46:177–94.

Morris, Earl H.
    1919   Preliminary Accounts of the Antiquities of the Region between the Mancos and La Plata Rivers in Southwestern Colorado. *33rd Annual Report of the Bureau of American Ethnology*, pp. 157–206. Washington, D.C.
    1924   *Burials in the Aztec Ruin. The Aztec Ruin Annex.* Anthropological Papers of the American Museum of Natural History 26(3, 4).
    1939   *Archaeological Studies in the La Plata District; Southwestern Colorado and Northwestern New Mexico.* Carnegie Institution of Washington Publication No. 519. Washington, D.C.

Morris, Earl H., and Robert F. Burgh
    1941   *Anasazi Basketry. Basket Maker II Through Pueblo III.* Carnegie Institution Publication No. 533. Washington, D.C.

Morris, Elizabeth Ann
    1959   Basketmaker Caves in the Prayer Rock District, North-Eastern Arizona. Ph.D. dissertation, Department of Anthropology, University of Arizona, Tucson.
    1980   *Basketmaker Caves in the Prayer Rock District, Northeastern Arizona.* Anthropological Papers of the University of Arizona 35. Tucson: University of Arizona Press.

Morris, S. Conway
    1989   Burgess Shales Faunas and the Cambrian Explosion. *Science* 246:339–45.

Morse, Dan F., and Phyllis A. Morse
    1983   *Archaeology of the Central Mississippi Valley.* New York: Academic Press.

Murdock, George Peter
    1949   *Social Structure.* The Free Press: New York.

Nabhan, Gary
    1983   Papago Fields: Arid Lands Ethnobotany and Agricultural Ecology. Ph.D. dissertation, Office of Arid Lands Studies, University of Arizona, Tucson. Ann Arbor: University Microfilms.

Nass, G. Gisella, and Nicholas F. Bellantoni
    1982   A Prehistoric Multiple Burial from Monument Valley Evidencing Trauma and Possible
            Cannibalism. *The Kiva* 47:257–71.
Naylor, Thomas
    1983   Review of Riley: The Frontier People. *The Kiva* 49:119–21.
Neely, James A., and Alan P. Olson
    1977   *Archaeological Reconnaissance of Monument Valley in Northeastern Arizona.* MNA Research
            Paper 3. Museum of Northern Arizona, Flagstaff.
Neily, Robert B.
    1983   The Prehistoric Community on the Colorado Plateau: An Approach to the Study of Change
            and Survival in the Northern San Juan Area of the American Southwest. Ph.D. disserta-
            tion, Department of Anthropology, Southern Illinois University, Carbondale. Ann Arbor:
            University Microfilms International.
Neitzel, Jill
    1984   The Regional Organization of the Hohokam in the American Southwest: A Stylistic Analy-
            sis of Red-on-Buff Pottery. Ph.D. dissertation, Department of Anthropology, Arizona State
            University, Tempe.
    1991   Hohokam Material Culture and Behavior: The Dimensions of Organizational Change. In
            Exploring the Hohokam Prehistoric Desert Peoples of the American Southwest, G. J. Gumer-
            man, ed., pp. 177–230. Albuquerque: University of New Mexico Press.
Nelson, Ben A.
    1990   Observaciones Acerca de la Presencia Tolteca en La Quemada, Zacatecas. In *Mesoamerica
            y Norte de Mexico Siglo IX–XII,* vol. 2, coordinated by Frerica Sodi Miranda, pp. 521–40.
            Museo Nacional de Antropologia, Instituto National de Antropologia e Historia, Mexico
            City. In press.
    1993   Outposts of Mesoamerican Empire and Residential Patterning at La Quemada, Zacatecas.
            In *Culture and Contact: Charles C. Di Peso's Gran Chichimeca.* Albuquerque: University of
            New Mexico Press.
Nelson, Ben A., and Linda S. Cordell
    1982   Dynamics of the Anasazi Adaption. In *Anasazi and Navajo Land Use in the McKinley Mine
            Area near Gallup, New Mexico,* C. G. Allen and B. A. Nelson, eds., pp. 867–93. Office of
            Contract Archaeology, University of New Mexico, Albuquerque.
Nelson, Ben A., and Steven A. LeBlanc
    1986   *Short-term Sedentism in the American Southwest: The Mimbres Valley Salado.* Albuquerque:
            University of New Mexico Press.
Nelson, Richard S.
    1981   The Role of the Pochteca System in Hohokam Exchange. Ph.D. dissertation, Department
            of Anthropology, New York University.
    1986   Pochtecas and Prestige: Mesoamerican Artifacts in Hohokam Sites. In *Ripples in the Chi-
            chimec Sea, New Consideration of Southwestern-Mesoamerican Interactions,* F. J. Mathien and
            R. H. McGuire, eds., pp. 154–82. Carbondale: Southern Illinois University Press.
Netting, Robert McC.
    1990   Population, Permanent Agriculture, and Polities: Unpacking the Evolutionary Portman-
            teau. In *The Evolution of Political Systems: Sociopolitics in Small-Scale Sedentary Societies,*
            S. Upham, ed., pp. 21–61. School of American Research Advanced Seminar Series. Cam-
            bridge University Press, Cambridge.
Nials, Fred L., David A. Gregory, and Donald A. Graybill
    1989   Salt River Streamflow and Hohokam Irrigation Systems. In *The 1982–1984 Excavations at
            Las Colinas: Environment and Subsistence,* D. A. Graybill, D. A. Gregory, F. L. Nials, S. K.
            Fish, R. E. Gasser, C. H. Miksicek, and C. R. Szuter, eds., pp. 59–76. Archaeological
            Series 162(5). Tucson: Cultural Resource Management Division, Arizona State Museum.
Nicholas, Linda M.
    1981   Irrigation and Sociopolitical Development in the Salt River Valley, Arizona: An Exami-
            nation of Three Prehistoric Canal Systems. M.A. thesis, Department of Anthropology,
            Arizona State University, Tempe.
Nicholas, Linda M., and Jill Neitzel
    1983a   Canal Irrigation and Sociopolitical Organization in the Lower Salt River Valley: A Dis-
            chronic Analysis. In *Prehistoric Agricultural Strategies in the Southwest,* S. K. Fish and P. R.

Fish, eds., pp. 161–78. Anthropological Research Papers 33. Tempe: Arizona State University.

1983b   An Examination of Three Prehistoric Canal Systems in the Lower Salt River Valley, Arizona. Manuscript, Department of Anthropology, Arizona State University, Tempe.

Nicholas, Linda M., and Gary M. Feinman

1989   A Regional Perspective on Hohokam Irrigation in the Lower Salt River Valley, Arizona. In *The Sociopolitical Structure of Prehistoric Southwestern Societies*, S. Upham, K. G. Lightfoot, and R. Jewett, eds., pp. 199–236. Boulder: Westview Press.

Nichols, Deborah L.

1987   Risk and Agricultural Intensification during the Formative Period in the Northern Basin of Mexico. *American Anthropologist* 89:596–615.

Nichols, Deborah L., and F. E. Smiley

1985   An Overview of Northern Black Mesa. In *Excavations on Black Mesa, 1983, A Descriptive Report*, A. L. Christenson and W. J. Perry, eds., pp. 47–82. Center for Archaeological Investigations Research Paper 46. Carbondale: Southern Illinois University.

Nickens, Paul R.

1975a   Osteological Analysis of Five Human Burials from Mesa Verde National Park, Colorado. *Southwestern Lore* 41:13–26.

1975b   Prehistoric Cannibalism in the Mancos Canyon, Southwestern Colorado. *The Kiva* 40:283–93.

Nusbaum, Jesse L.

1922   *A Basket-Maker Cave in Kane County, Utah*. New York: Museum of the American Indian, Heye Foundation.

O'Brien, M. J., and T. D. Holland

1990   Variation, Selection, and the Archaeological Record. In *Archaeological Method and Theory*, vol. 2, M. B. Schiffer, ed., pp. 31–79. Tucson: University of Arizona Press.

O'Laughlin, T. C.

1980   *The Keystone Dam Site and Other Archaic and Formative Sites in Northwest El Paso, Texas*. Publications in Anthropology 8. El Paso Centennial Museum.

O'Leary, B. L., and J. V. Biella

1987   Archaeological Investigations at the Taylor Ranch Site. In *Secrets of a City: Papers on Albuquerque Area Archaeology*, A. V. Poore and J. Montgomery, eds., pp. 192–208. The Archaeological Society of New Mexico 13. Albuquerque.

Olsen, John W.

1980   A Zooarchaeological Analysis of Vertabrate Faunal Remains from Grasshopper Pueblo, Arizona. Ph.D. dissertation, University of California, Berkeley.

1990   *Vertebrate Faunal Remains from Grasshopper Pueblo, Arizona*. Museum of Anthropology Paper 83. Ann Arbor: University of Michigan.

Olson, Alan P.

1966   A Mass Secondary Burial from Northern Arizona. *American Antiquity* 31:822–26.

Orcutt, Janet D.

1981   Changing Settlement Locations on the Pajarito Plateau, New Mexico. Ph.D. dissertation, University of California, Los Angeles. Ann Arbor: University Microfilms International.

1991   Environment Variability and Settlement Changes on the Pajarito Plateau, New Mexico. *American Antiquity* 56:315–32.

Orcutt, Janet D., Eric Blinman, and Timothy A. Kohler

1990   Explanations of Population Aggregation in the Mesa Verde Region prior to A.D. 900. In *Perspectives on the Prehistoric Southwest*, P. E. Minnis and C. Redman, eds., pp. 196–212. Boulder: Westview Press.

Ortiz, Alfonso

1962   *The Tewa World*. Chicago: University of Chicago Press.

Ortner, D. J., and W. G. J. Putschar

1981   *Identification of Pathological Conditions in Human Skeletal Remains*. Washington, D.C.: Smithsonian Institution Press.

O'Shea, J.

1981   Coping with Scarcity: Exchange and Social Storage. In *Economic Archaeology*, Sheridan and Bailey, eds., pp. 167–85. Archaeological Reports International Series 96.

O'Shea, J., and M. Zvelebil
    1984   Oleneostrovski Mogilnik: Reconstructing the Social and Economic Organization of Pre-
            historic Foragers in Northern Russia. *Journal of Anthropological Archaeology* 3:1–40.
Oswalt, Wendell H., with the assistance of Gloria and Leonn Saterthwaite
    1976   *An Anthropological Analysis of Food-Getting Technology.* New York: Wiley-Interscience.
Otterbein, Keith E.
    1985   *The Evolution of War.* 2nd ed. New Haven: HRAF Press.
Page, Gordon B.
    1940   Hopi Land Patterns. *Plateau* 13:29–36.
Page, Robert G., Jr.
    1970   Primitive Warfare in the Prescott Area. *The Arizona Archaeologist* 5:47–56.
Pailes, Richard
    1980   The Upper Rio Sonora Valley in Prehistoric Trade. *Transactions of the Illinois Academy of
            Science* 72(4):20–39.
Palerm, Angel, and Eric R. Wolf
    1957   Ecological Potential and Cultural Development in Mesoamerica. In *Studies in Human
            Ecology*, pp. 1–37. Anthropological Society of Washington, D.C.
Palkovich, Ann M.
    1980   *Pueblo Population and Society: The Arroyo Hondo Skeletal and Mortuary Remains.* Arroyo
            Hondo Archaeological Series, vol. 3. Santa Fe: School of American Research Press.
    1984a   Disease and Mortality Patterns in the Burial Rooms of Pueblo Bonito: Preliminary Con-
            siderations. In *Recent Research on Chaco Prehistory*, W. J. Judge and J. D. Schelberg, eds.,
            pp. 103–13. Report of the Chaco Center 8. Albuquerque: Division of Cultural Research.
    1984b   Agriculture, Marginal Environments, and Nutritional Stress in the Prehistoric Southwest.
            In *Paleopathology at the Origins of Agriculture*, M. N. Cohen and G. J. Armelagos, eds.,
            pp. 425–61. New York: Academic Press.
    1987   Endemic Disease Patterns in Paleopathology: Porotic Hyperostosis. *American Journal of
            Physical Anthropology* 74:527–37.
Parkington, J.
    1987   On Stable Isotopes and Dietary Reconstruction. *Current Anthropology* 28:91–93.
Parsons, Elsie Clews
    1924   *The Scalp Ceremonial of the Zuni.* Memoirs of the American Anthropological Association
            No. 31.
Partridge, J., and V. Baker
    1987   Paleoflood Hydrology of the Salt River, Arizona. *Earth Surface and Landforms* 12:109–25.
Patterson, Thomas C.
    1986   The Last Sixty Years: Toward a Social History of Americanist Archaeology in the United
            States. *American Anthropologist* 88(1):7–26.
Peckham, Stewart
    1957   Three Pithouse Sites near Albuquerque, New Mexico. In *Highway Salvage Archaeology*,
            vol. 3, S. Peckham, ed. Santa Fe: Museum of New Mexico.
    1965   *Prehistoric Weapons in the Southwest.* Santa Fe: Museum of New Mexico Press.
    1981   The Palisade Ruin (LA 3505): A Coalition Period Pueblo near Abiquiu Dam, New Mexico.
            In *Collected Papers in Honor of Erik Kellerman Reed*, A. H. Schroeder, ed., pp. 113–47.
            Papers of the Archaeological Society of New Mexico 6. Albuquerque.
Pendleton, L.
    1952   The Gallina Phase of Northern New Mexico. In *Indian Tribes of Aboriginal America*, S. Tax,
            ed., pp. 145–52. Chicago: University of Chicago Press.
Pepper, George H.
    1909   The Exploration of a Burial-Room in Pueblo Bonito, New Mexico. In *Putnam Anniversary
            Volume*, F. Boas, ed., pp. 196–252. Cedar Rapids, IA.
    1920   *Pueblo Bonito.* Anthropological Papers of the American Museum of Natural History 27.
            New York.
Petersen, Kenneth L.
    1988   *Climate and the Dolores River Anasazi.* University of Utah Anthropological Papers 113. Salt
            Lake City: University of Utah Press.

Peterson, John A.
   1988a   Change or Continuity? Pithouse to Pueblo Transition along the Middle San Francisco
            River, West Central New Mexico. Paper presented at the Society for American Archae-
            ology annual meeting. Phoenix.
   1988b   Settlement and Subsistence Patterns in the Reserve Phase and Mountain Mogollon: A Test
            Case in Devil's Park, New Mexico. The Kiva 53(2):113–29.
Phillips, David A., Jr.
   1989   Prehistory of Chihuahua and Sonora, Mexico. Journal of World Prehistory 3(4):373–401.
Pinkley, Jean M.
   1965   The Pueblos and the Turkey: Who Domesticated Whom? In Contributions of the Wetherill
            Mesa Archaeological Project, assembled by D. Osborne, pp. 70–72. Memoirs of the Society
            for American Archaeology 19.
Pippin, Lonnie C.
   1979   The Prehistory and Paleoecology of Guadalupe Ruin, Sandoval County, New Mexico.
            Ph.D. dissertation, Washington State University. Ann Arbor: University Microfilms.
   1987   Prehistory and Paleoecology of Guadalupe Ruin, New Mexico. University of Utah Anthropo-
            logical Papers 107. Salt Lake City.
Plog, Fred
   1974   The Study of Prehistoric Change. New York: Academic Press.
   1978   The Keresan Bridge: An Ecological and Archaeological Account. In Social Archaeology:
            Beyond Subsistence and Dating, C. L. Redman, M. J. Berman, E. V. Curtin, W. T. Lang-
            horne, Jr., N. M. Versaggi, and J. C. Wanser, eds., pp. 349–79. New York: Academic Press.
   1979   Prehistory: Western Anasazi. In Handbook of North American Indians. Vol. 9, The South-
            west, A. Ortiz, ed., pp. 108–30. Washington, D.C.: Smithsonian Institution.
   1983a   Human Responses to Environmental Variation: The Anasazi Case. Paper presented at the
            2nd Anasazi Conference. Farmington.
   1983b   Political and Economic Alliances on the Colorado Plateaus, A.D. 400–1450. In Advances
            in World Archaeology, vol. 2, F. Wendorf and A. E. Close, eds., pp. 289–330. New York:
            Academic Press.
   1984   Exchange, Tribes, and Alliances: The Northern Southwest. American Archaeology 4:217–
            23.
   1989   The Sinagua and Their Relations. In Dynamics of Southwest Prehistory, L. S. Cordell and
            G. J. Gumerman, eds., pp. 263–91. A School of American Research Advanced Seminar
            Book. Washington, D.C.: Smithsonian Institution.
Plog, Fred, George J. Gumerman, Robert C. Euler, Jeffrey S. Dean, Richard H. Hevly, and Thor N. V.
      Karlstrom
   1988   Anasazi Adaptive Strategies: The Model, Predictions, and Results. In The Anasazi in a
            Changing Environment, G. J. Gumerman, ed., pp. 230–76. Cambridge: Cambridge Uni-
            versity Press.
Plog, Fred, Stedman Upham, and Phillip C. Weigand
   1982   A Perspective on Mogollon-Mesoamerican Interaction. In Mogollon Archaeology: Proceed-
            ings of the 1980 Conference, P. H. Beckett, ed., pp. 227–38. Ramona: Acoma Books.
Plog, Stephen
   1980a   Hohokam Exchange, Subsistence and Interaction: Some Comments. In Current Issues in
            Hohokam Prehistory, Proceedings of a Symposium, D. Doyel and F. Plog, eds., pp. 106–12.
            Arizona State University Anthropological Research Papers 23. Tempe.
   1980b   Village Autonomy in the American Southwest: An Evaluation of the Evidence. In Models
            and Methods in Regional Exchange, R. E. Fry, ed., pp. 135–46. SAA Papers 1.
   1986a   Patterns of Demographic Growth and Decline. In Spatial Organization and Exchange,
            S. Plog, ed., pp. 224–55. Carbondale: Southern Illinois University Press.
   1986b   Understanding Culture Change in the Northern Southwest. In Spatial Organization and
            Exchange, S. Plog, ed., pp. 310–36. Carbondale: Southern Illinois University Press.
   1987   Agriculture, Sedentism, and Environment in the Evolution of Political Systems. Paper
            presented at the School of American Research Advanced Seminar, Santa Fe.
   1990a   Agriculture, Sedentism, and Environment in the Evolution of Political Systems. In The
            Evolution of Political Systems: Sociopolitics in Small-Scale Sedentary Societies, S. Upham, ed.,
            pp. 177–99, pt. 2. Cambridge: Cambridge University Press.

1990b   Sociopolitical Implications of Southwestern Stylistic Variation. In *The Use of Style in Archaeology*, M. Conkey and C. Hastorf, eds., pp. 61–77. Cambridge: Cambridge University Press.

Plog, Stephen, and Jeffrey L. Hantman

1990   Chronology Construction and the Study of Prehistoric Culture Change. Manuscript, Department of Anthropology, University of Virginia.

Powell, Shirley

1983   *Mobility and Adaptation: The Anasazi of Black Mesa Arizona.* Carbondale: Southern Illinois University Press.

Powers, Robert P.

1988   *Final Archaeological Research Design for a Sample Inventory Survey of Bandelier National Monument.* Branch of Cultural Research, National Park Service. Santa Fe.

Powers, Robert P., William B. Gillespie, and Stephen H. Lekson

1983   *The Outlier Survey: A Regional View of Settlement in the San Juan Basin.* Reports of the Chaco Center 3. Albuquerque: Division of Cultural Research, National Park Service.

Preucel, Robert Washington

1987   Settlement Succession on the Parjarito Plateau, New Mexico. *The Kiva* 53:3–33.

1988   Seasonal Agricultural Circulation and Residential Mobility: A Prehistoric Example from the Parjarito Plateau, New Mexico. Ph.D. dissertation, Department of Anthropology, University of California, Los Angeles.

1991   The Philosophy of Archaeology. In *Processual and Postprocessual Archaeologies: Multiple Ways of Knowing the Past,* R. W. Preucel, ed., pp. 17–29. Occasional Paper 10. Southern Illinois University, Carbondale.

Price, T. D. (editor)

1989   *The Chemistry of Prehistoric Human Bone.* Cambridge: University of Cambridge Press.

Price, T. D., and J. A. Brown (editors)

1985   *Prehistoric Hunter-Gatherers: The Emergence of Cultural Complexity.* New York: Academic Press.

Prudden, T. Mitchell

1896   A Summer among the Cliff-Dwellers. *Harper's Magazine* 556:545–61.

1897   An Elder Brother to the Cliff-Dwellers. *Harper's Magazine* 95(565):56–62.

Pryor, F. L.

1986   The Adoption of Agriculture: Some Theoretical and Empirical Evidence. *American Anthropologist* 88:879–97.

Rafferty, Kevin

1989   Virgin Anasazi Sociopolitical Organization, A.D. 1 to 1150. In *The Sociopolitical Structure of Prehistoric Southwestern Societies,* S. Upham, K. G. Lightfoot, and R. A. Jewett, eds., pp. 557–82. Boulder: Westview Press.

Raghavendra, A. S., and V. S. Das

1978   The Occurrence of C4-Photosynthesis: A Supplementary List of /C4 Plants Reported during Late 1974–Mid 1977. *Photosynthetica* 12:200–208.

Rathje, William

1971   The Origin and Development of Lowland Classic Maya Civilization. *American Antiquity* 36:275–85.

Ravesloot, John, and Patricia Spoerl

1989   The Role of Warfare in the Development of Status Hierarchies at Casas Grandes, Chihuahua, Mexico. In *Cultures in Conflict: Current Archaeological Perspectives,* D. C. Tkaczuk and B. C. Vivian, eds., pp. 130–37. Proceedings of the 20th Chacmool Conference, Department of Archaeology, University of Calgary.

Reagan, Albert B.

1931   The Pictographs of Ashley and Dry Fork Valleys in Northeastern Utah. *Transactions of the Kansas Academy of Science* 34:168–216.

1933   Anciently Inhabited Caves of the Vernal (Utah) District with Some Additional Notes on Nine Mile Canyon, Northeast Utah. *Transactions of the Kansas Academy of Science* 36:41–67.

Redding, R. W.

1988   A General Explanation of Subsistence Change: From Hunting and Gathering to Food Production. *Journal of Anthropological Archaeology* 7:56–97.

Reed, Erik K.
  1946   The Distinctive Features and Distribution of the San Juan Anasazi Culture. *Southwestern Journal of Anthropology* 2:295–305.
  1948a   *Fractional Burials, Trophy Skulls, and Cannibalism.* Anthropological Notes 79. National Park Service Region 3, Santa Fe.
  1948b   The Western Pueblo Archaeological Complex. *El Palacio* 55(1):9–15.
  1950   East-Central Arizona Archaeology in Relation to the Western Pueblos. *Southwestern Journal of Anthropology* 6:120–38.
  1953   Appendix III: Human Skeletal Remains from Te'ewi. In *Salvage Archaeology in the Chama Valley, New Mexico,* F. Wendorf, ed., pp. 104–18. Monographs of the School of American Research 17. Santa Fe.
  1955   Painted Pottery and Zuni History. *Southwestern Journal of Anthropology* 11:178–93.
  1956   Types of Village-Plan Layouts in the Southwest. In *Prehistoric Settlement Patterns in the New World,* G. R. Willey, ed., pp. 11–17. Viking Fund Publications in Anthropology 23.
  1964   The Greater Southwest. In *Prehistoric Men in the New World,* J. D. Jennings and E. Norbeck, eds., pp. 175–91. Chicago: University of Chicago Press.
  1965   Human Skeletal Material from Site 34, Mesa Verde National Park. *El Palacio* (Autumn):31–45.
Reed, Lori Stephens
  1990   X-ray Diffraction Analysis of Glaze-Painted Ceramics from the Northern Rio Grande Region, New Mexico: Implications of Glazeware Production and Exchange. In *Economy and Polity in Late Rio Grande Prehistory,* S. Upham and B. D. Staley, eds., pp. 90–149. Occasional Papers of the University Museum 16. Las Cruces: New Mexico State University.
Reid, J. Jefferson
  1989   A Grasshopper Perspective on the Mogollon of the Arizona Mountains. In *Dynamics of Southwestern Prehistory,* L. S. Cordell and G. J. Gumerman, eds., pp. 65–97. A School of American Research Advanced Seminar Book. Washington, D.C.: Smithsonian Institution Press.
Reid, J. Jefferson, and Donald Graybill
  1984   Paleoclimate and Human Behavior in the Grasshopper Region, Arizona. Paper presented at the annual meeting of the Society for American Archaeology. Portland.
Reid, J. Jefferson, H. David Tuggle, and Barbra J. Klie
  1982   The Q Ranch Sites. In *Cholla Project Archaeology.* Vol. 3, The Q Ranch Region, J. Jefferson Reid, ed., pp. 33–104. Archaeological Series, 161. Cultural Resource Management Division, Arizona State Museum, University of Arizona, Tucson.
Reid, J. Jefferson, and Stephanie Whittlesey
  1982   Households at Grasshopper Pueblo. *American Behavioral Scientist* 25:687–703.
  1990   The Complicated and the Complex: Observations on the Archaeological Record of Large Pueblos. In *Perspectives on Southwest Prehistory,* P. Minnis and C. Redman, eds., pp. 184–95. Boulder: Westview Press.
Reinhard, K. J.
  1988   Cultural Ecology of Prehistoric Parasitism on the Colorado Plateau as Evidenced by Coprology. *American Journal of Physical Anthropology* 77:355–66.
  1990   Archaeoarasitology in North America. *American Journal of Physical Anthropology* 82:145–63.
Reinhard, K. J., J. R. Ambler, and M. McGuffie
  1985   Diet and Parasitism at Dust Devil Cave. *American Antiquity* 50:819–24.
Reinhard, K. J., and Richard H. Hevly
  1991   Dietary and Parasitological Analysis of Coprolites Recovered from Mummy 5, Ventana Cave, Arizona. *The Kiva* 56(3):319–25.
Reinhart, Theodore R.
  1967   Late Archaic Cultures of the Middle Rio Grande Valley, New Mexico: A Study in the Process of Culture Change. Ph.D. dissertation, University of New Mexico. Ann Arbor: University Microfilms.
Remley, Al
  1989   Comparison of Architecture between Forts, Lookouts, and Distribution Centers in the Kaibab Forest. Manuscript, Museum of Northern Arizona Library, Flagstaff.

Renfrew, Colin
    1977   Alternative Models for Exchange and Spatial Distribution. In *Exchange Systems in Prehis-tory,* R. K. Earle and J. E. Erickson, eds., pp. 71–90. New York: Academic Press.
    1986   Introduction: Peer Polity Interaction and Socio-political Change. In *Peer Polity Interaction and Socio-political Change,* C. Renfrew and J. F. Cherry, eds., pp. 1–18. Cambridge: Cambridge University Press.
Reyman, Jonathan E.
    1978   Pochteca Burials at Anasazi Sites? In *Across the Chichimec Sea: Papers in Honor of J. Charles Kelley,* C. L. Riley and B. C. Hedrick, eds., pp. 242–59. Carbondale: Southern Illinois University Press.
Reynolds, William E.
    1980   An Analytical Overview of the Mogollon Tradition. In *Studies in the Prehistory of the Forest-dale Region,* Arizona, C. R. Stafford and G. E. Rice, eds., pp. 9–40. Anthropological Field Studies 1. Office of Cultural Resource Management, Department of Anthropology, Arizona State University, Tempe.
    1981   The Ethnoarchaeology of Pueblo Architecture. Ph.D. dissertation, Department of Anthropology, University of Washington, Seattle. Ann Arbor: University Microfilms International.
    1986   Working Hypothesis for the Study of Hohokam Community Complexes. Paper presented at the spring meeting of the Arizona Archaeological Council, Phoenix.
    1987   *A Spatial Analysis of the Hohokam Community of La Ciudad.* OCRM Anthropological Field Studies 16. Department of Anthropology, Arizona State University, Tempe.
Rice, Glen E.
    1986   Working Hypotheses for the Study of Hohokam Community Complexes. Paper presented at the Spring 1986 meeting of the Arizona Archaeological Council, Phoenix.
Rice, Glen, Jeffrey Hantman, and Rachael Most (editors)
    1982   *The Ash Creek Archaeological Project: Preliminary Field Report.* Office of Cultural Resource Management Report 56. Department of Anthropology, Arizona State University, Tempe.
Riley, Carroll L.
    1987   *The Frontier People: The Greater Southwest in the Protohistoric Period.* Albuquerque: University of New Mexico Press.
Riley, Carol L., and Basil C. Hedrick (editors)
    1978   *Across the Chichimec Sea: Papers in Honor of J. Charles Kelley.* Carbondale: Southern Illinois University Press.
Rindos, David
    1984   *The Origins of Agriculture: An Evolutionary Perspective.* New York: Academic Press.
Roberts, Frank H. H., Jr.
    1930   *Early Pueblo Ruins in the Piedra District, Southwestern Colorado.* Bureau of American Ethnology Bulletin 96. Washington, D.C.
    1931   *The Ruins at Kiatuthlanna, Eastern Arizona.* Bureau of American Ethnology Bulletin 100. Washington, D.C.
    1932   *Village of the Great Kivas on the Zuni Reservation, New Mexico.* Bureau of American Ethnology Bulletin 111. Washington, D.C.
    1939   *Archaeological Remains in the Whitewater District, Eastern Arizona. Part I: House Types.* Bureau of American Ethnology Bulletin 121. Washington, D.C.
    1940   *Archaeological Remains in the Whitewater District, Eastern Arizona. Part II: Artifacts and Burials.* Bureau of American Ethnology Bulletin 126. Washington, D.C.
Rocek, Thomas R., and John D. Speth
    1986   *The Henderson Site Burials: Glimpses of a Late Prehistoric Population in the Pecos Valley.* Museum of Anthropology Technical Report 18. Ann Arbor: University of Michigan.
Rodgers, Malcom J.
    1929   *Report on an Archaeological Reconnaissance in the Mojave Sink Region.* San Diego Museum of Man Papers 1, San Diego.
Roff, Daniel T.
    1986   The Demographic and Cultural Consequences of Old World Diseases in the Greater Southwest, 1519–1660. Ph.D. dissertation, University of Oklahoma, Norman.

Rohn, Arthur H.
1971   *Mug House, Mesa Verde National Park, Colorado.* National Park Service Archaeological Research Series No. 7-D. Washington, D.C.
1975   A Stockaded Basketmaker III Village at Yellow Jacket, Colorado. *The Kiva* 40:113–19.
1977   *Cultural Change and Continuity on Chapin Mesa.* Lawrence: The Regents Press of Kansas.
1989   Northern San Juan Prehistory. In *Dynamics of Southwestern Prehistory,* L. S. Cordell and G. J. Gumerman, eds., pp. 149–78. A School of American Research Advanced Seminar Book. Washington, D.C.: Smithsonian Institution Press.

Roney, John
1990   Pueblo III Communities in the San Juan Basin, Rio Puerco, and Acoma Areas. Paper presented at the conference "Pueblo Cultures in Transition, A.D. 1150–1350, in the American Southwest." Crow Canyon Center, Cortez, CO. March 28–April 1.

Rose, J. C., B. A. Burnett, M. S. Nassaney, and M. W. Blaeuer
1984   Paleopathology and the Origins of Maize Agriculture in the Lower Mississippi Valley and Caddoan Culture Areas. In *Paleopathology at the Origins of Agriculture,* M. N. Cohen and G. J. Armelagos, eds., pp. 393–424. New York: Academic Press.

Rose, Martin R., Jeffrey S. Dean, and William J. Robinson
1981   *The Past Climate of Arroyo Hondo, New Mexico, Reconstructed from Tree Rings.* Arroyo Hondo Archaeological Series, vol. 4. Santa Fe: School of American Research Press.

Rose, Martin R., William J. Robinson, and Jeffrey S. Dean
1982   *Dendroclimatic Reconstruction for the Southeastern Colorado Plateau.* Final Report to Division of Chaco Research, National Park Service, Albuquerque. Laboratory of Tree-Ring Research, The University of Arizona, Tucson.

Roseberry, William
1989   *Anthropologies and Histories.* New Brunswick, NJ: Rutgers University Press.

Roth, B.
1989   Changing Perceptions of the Late Archaic: An Example of the Tucson Basin. Paper presented at the 54th annual meeting of the Society for American Archaeology.

Rowlands, M. J.
1973   Defense: A Factor in the Organization of Settlements. In *Territoriality and Proxemics: Archaeological and Ethnographic Evidence for the Use and Organization of Space,* R. Tringham, ed., pp. 1–16. Andover, MA: Warner Modular Publications.

Ruff, C. B.
1981   A Reassessment of Demographic Estimates for Pecos Pueblo. *American Journal of Physical Anthropology* 54:147–51.

Ruppé, Reynold J.
1953   The Acoma Culture Province: An Archaeological Concept. Ph.D. dissertation, Department of Anthropology, Harvard University.

Russell, Frank
1908   *The Pima Indians.* Annual Report of the Bureau of American Ethnology for the Years 1904–1905. Vol. 26, pp. 3–389. Washington, D.C. Reprint 1975. Tucson: University of Arizona Press.

Ryan, D. J.
1977   The Paleopathology and Paleoepidemiology of the Kayenta Anasazi Indians of Northeastern Arizona. Ph.D. dissertation, Department of Anthropology, Arizona State University, Phoenix.

Ryan, Richard
1988   National Register Nomination for Prescott Culture Fortified Sites of the Prescott National Forest. Manuscript, Prescott National Forest, Prescott.

Sahlins, Marshall D.
1972   *Stone Age Economics.* Chicago: Aldine.
1985   *Islands of History.* Chicago: University of Chicago Press.

Sahlins, Marshall David, and Elman R. Service (editors)
1960   *Evolution and Culture.* Ann Arbor: University of Michigan Press.

Saitta, Dean
1988   Marxism, Prehistory, and Primitive Communism. *Rethinking Marxism* 1(4):145–68.

Saitta, Dean J., and Arthur S. Keene
    1990   Politics and Surplus Flow in Prehistoric Communal Societies. In *The Evolution of Political Systems: Sociopolitics in Small Scale Sedentary Societies,* S. Upham, ed., pp. 225–46. Cambridge: Cambridge University Press.
Sanders, William T., Jeffrey R. Parsons, and Robert S. Santley
    1979   *The Basin of Mexico: Ecological Processes in the Evolution of a Civilization.* New York: Academic Press.
Sauer, Carol O., and Donald D. Brand
    1930   Pueblo Sites in Southeastern Arizona. *University of California Publications in Geography* 3(7):415–58.
    1931   Prehistoric Settlements of Sonora with Special Reference to Cerros de Trincheras. *University of California Publications in Geography* 5(3):67–148.
Saul, Marilyn B.
    1981   Appendix B: Disposal of the Dead at Las Colinas Ruins. In *The 1968 Excavations at Mound 8, Las Colinas Ruins Group, Phoenix, Arizona,* L. C. Hammack and A. P. Sullivan, eds., pp. 257–68. Arizona State Museum Archaeological Series 154. University of Arizona, Tucson.
Sawyer, P. H.
    1982   *Kings and Vikings.* London: Methuen.
Sayles, Edward B.
    1945   *The San Simeon Branch.* Medallion Papers 34. Globe: Gila Pueblo.
    1983   *The Cochise Cultural Sequence in Southeastern Arizona.* Anthropological Papers of the University of Arizona 42. Tucson.
Sayles, Edward B., and E. Antevs
    1941   *The Cochise Culture.* Medallion Papers 29. Globe: Gila Pueblo.
Schaafsma, Polly
    1971   *The Rock Art of Utah.* Papers of the Peabody Museum of Archaeology and Ethnology 65. Cambridge: Harvard University.
    1980   *Indian Rock Art of the Southwest.* School of American Research, Santa Fe, and University of New Mexico Press, Albuquerque.
Schaafsma, Polly, and Curtis F. Schaafsma
    1974   Evidence for the Origins of the Pueblo Katchina Cult as Suggested by Southwestern Rock Art. *American Antiquity* 39:535–45.
Schaffer, William M.
    1986   Chaos in Ecological Systems: The Coals That Newcastle Forgot. *Trends in Ecological Systems* 1:63.
Schamschula, R. G., M. H. Cooper, M. C. Wright, H. M. Agus, and P. S. Hun
    1980   Oral Health of Adolescent and Adult Australian Aborigines. *Community Dentition and Oral Epidemiology* 8:3790–94.
Schelberg, John D.
    1982   Economic and Social Development as an Adaptation to a Marginal Environment in Chaco Canyon, New Mexico. Ph.D. dissertation, Northwestern University. Ann Arbor: University Microfilms.
Schiffer, Michael B.
    1972   Cultural Laws and the Reconstruction of Past Lifeways. *The Kiva* 37:148–57.
    1975   Archaeology as Behavioral Science. *American Anthropologist* 77(4):836–48.
    1976   *Behavioral Archaeology.* New York: Academic Press.
Schlanger, Sarah
    1988   Patterns of Population Movement and Long-Term Population Growth in Southwestern Colorado. *American Antiquity* 53:773–93.
Schlanger, Sarah H., and Richard H. Wilshusen
    1990   Local Abandonments and Regional Conditions in the North American Southwest. Paper presented at the 55th annual meeting of the Society for American Archaeology. Las Vegas.
Schmidt, Erich F.
    1928   Time-Relations of Prehistoric Pottery in Southern Arizona. *Anthropological Papers of the American Museum of Natural History* 30:245–302.

Schneider, Jane
    1975   Peacocks and Penguins: The Political Economy of European Cloth and Colours. *American Ethnologist* 5:413–47.
    1977   Was There a Pre-Capitalist World-System? *Peasant Studies* 6:20–29.
Schoeninger, M. J.
    1989   Reconstructing Prehistoric Human Diet. In *The Chemistry of Prehistoric Bone,* T. D. Price, ed., pp. 38–67. New York: Cambridge University Press.
    1990   Carbon Isotope Evidence for Diet. Paper presented at the 2nd Southwest Symposium. Albuquerque.
Schoenwetter, James, and Alfred E. Dittert
    1968   An Ecological Interpretation of Anasazi Settlement Patterns. In *Anthropological Archaeology in the Americas,* B. J. Meggars, ed., pp. 41–66. Washington, D.C.: Anthropological Society of Washington.
Schorsch, Russell L.
    1962   A Basket Maker III Pit House near Albuquerque. *El Palacio* 69(2):114–18.
Schroeder, Albert H.
    1947   Did the Sinagua of the Verde Valley Settle in the Salt River Valley? *Southwestern Journal of Anthropology* 3(3):230–46.
    1952   The Bearing of Ceramics on Developments in the Hohokam Classic Period. *Southwestern Journal of Anthropology* 8:320–35.
    1981   How Far Can a Pochteca Leap without Leaving Foot Prints? In *Collected Papers in Honor of Erik Kellerman Reed,* A. H. Schroeder, ed., pp. 43–64. Papers of the Archaeological Society of New Mexico 6. Albuquerque.
    1984   The Protohistoric and Pitfalls of Archaeological Interpretation. In *Collected Papers in Honor of Harry L. Hadlock,* N. L. Fox, ed., pp. 133–39. Papers of the Archaeological Society of New Mexico 9.
Schulman, Albert
    1950   Pre-Columbian Towers in the Southwest. *American Antiquity* 15:288–97.
Schwartz, Douglas W.
    1981   Foreword. In *The Past Climate of Arroyo Hondo, New Mexico, Reconstructed from Tree Rings,* M. R. Rose, J. S. Dean, and W. J. Robinson, eds., pp. ix–xv. Arroyo Hondo Archaeological Series, vol. 4. Santa Fe: School of American Research Press.
    1986   Foreword. In *Food, Diet, and Population at Prehistoric Arroyo Hondo Pueblo, New Mexico,* by W. Wetterstrom, pp. xiii–xxi. Arroyo Hondo Archaeological Series, vol. 6. Santa Fe: School of American Research Press.
    1989   *On the Edge of Splendor: Exploring Grand Canyon's Human Past.* Santa Fe: School of American Research Press.
Schwartz, Douglas W., Richard C. Chapman, and Jane Kepp
    1980   *Archaeology of the Grand Canyon: Unkar Delta.* Grand Canyon Archaeological Series, vol. 2. Santa Fe: School of American Research Press.
Scott, L. J.
    1979   Dietary Inference from Hoy House Coprolites. *The Kiva* 44:257–81.
Scrimshaw, N. S.
    1991   Iron Deficiency. *Scientific American* (October):46–52.
Seaman, T. J.
    1976   Excavation on LA 11843: An Early Stockaded Settlement of the Gallina Phase. Laboratory of Anthropology Note 111g. Santa Fe.
Sebastian, Lynne
    1991   Sociopolitical Complexity and the Chaco System. In *Chaco and Hohokam: Prehistoric Regional Systems in the American Southwest,* P. L. Crown and W. J. Judge, eds., pp. 109–34. Santa Fe: School of American Research Press.
Semé, Michelle
    1984   The Effects of Agricultural Fields on Faunal Assemblage Variation. In *Papers on the Archaeology of Black Mesa, Arizona,* vol. 2, S. Plog and S. Powell, eds., pp. 139–57. Carbondale: Southern Illinois University Press.
Service, Elman R.
    1962   *Primitive Social Organization, an Evolutionary Perspective.* New York: Random House.

1971   *Cultural Evolutionism Theory in Practice.* New York: Holt, Rinehart and Winston.
Seymour, Deni J.
    1988   An Alternative View of Sedentary Period Hohokam Shell Ornament Production. *American Antiquity* 53(4):812–28.
Shackley, M. S.
    1990   Early Hunter-Gatherer Procurement Ranges and Mobility in the American Southwest. Paper presented at the annual meeting of the Society for American Archaeology. Las Vegas.
Shafer, J. J., M. Marek, and K. J. Reinhard
    1989   A Mimbres Burial with Associated Colon Remains from the NAN Ranch Ruin, New Mexico. *Journal of Field Archaeology* 16: 17–30.
Shanks, Michael, and Christopher Tilley
    1987   *Re-constructing Archaeology. Theory and Practice.* Cambridge: Cambridge University Press.
Sharrock, Floyd W., David Dibble, and Keith M. Anderson
    1961   The Creeping Dune Irrigation Site in Glen Canyon, Utah. *American Antiquity* 27:188–202.
Shelford, V. E.
    1963   *The Ecology of North America.* Urbana: University of Illinois Press.
Shepard, Anna O.
    1942   *Rio Grande Glaze Paint Ware: A Study Illustrating the Place of Ceramic Technological Analysis in Archaeological Research.* Contributions to American Anthropology and History 39.
Shutler, Richard, Jr.
    1961   *Lost City, Pueblo Grande de Nevada.* Nevada State Museum Anthropological Papers 5. Carson City.
Sigleo, A. C.
    1975   Turquoise Mine and Artifact Correlation for Snaketown Site, Arizona. *Science* 189:459–60.
Sillen, A., J. C. Sealy, and N. J. van der Merwe
    1989   Chemistry and Paleodietary Research: No More Easy Answers. *American Antiquity* 54:504–12.
Simmons, Alan H.
    1986   New Evidence for the Early Use of Cultigens in the American Southwest. *American Antiquity* 51:73–88.
Simon, Alan H.
    1965   The Architecture of Complexity. *General Systems* 10:63–76.
Slatter, Edwin Darnell
    1979   Drought and Demographic Change in the Prehistoric Southwest United States: A Preliminary Quantitative Assessment. Ph.D. dissertation, Department of Anthropology, University of California, Los Angeles. Ann Arbor: University Microfilms International.
Sleeter, Richard Stanley
    1987   Cultural Interaction of the Prehistoric Gallina: A Study of Settlement Patterns in North-Central New Mexico. M.A. thesis, Department of Anthropology, New Mexico State University, Las Cruces.
Smiley, Francis E.
    1985   The Chronometrics of Early Agricultural Sites in Northeastern Arizona: Approaches to the Interpretation of Radiocarbon Dates. Ph.D. dissertation, University of Michigan. Ann Arbor: University Microfilms.
Smiley, Francis E., William J. Parry, and George J. Gumerman
    1986   Early Agriculture in the Black Mesa/Marsh Pass Region of Arizona: New Chronometric Data and Recent Excavations at Three Fir Shelter. Paper presented at the 51st annual meeting of the Society for American Archaeology. New Orleans.
Smiley, Francis E., and William J. Parry
    1990   Early, Intensive, and Rapid: Rethinking the Agricultural Transition in the Northern Southwest. Paper presented at the 55th annual meeting of the Society for American Archaeology. Las Vegas.
Smith, Bruce D.
    1986   The Archaeology of the Southeastern United States: From Dalton to de Soto, 10,500 b.p.–500 b.p. In *Advances in World Archaeology,* vol. 5, F. Wendorf and A. E. Close, eds., pp. 1–92. New York: Academic Press.

Smith, Carol A.
    1976   Regional Economic Systems: Linking Geographical Models and Socioeconomic Problems.
              In *Regional Analysis*. Vol. 1, *Economic Systems,* C. A. Smith, ed., pp. 3–69. New York: Aca-
              demic Press.
Smith, Michael E., and Cynthia M. Heath-Smith
    1980   Waves of Influence in Postclassic Mesoamerica: A Critique of the Mixteca Puebla Con-
              cept. *Anthropology* 4(2):15–50.
Smith, Watson
    1952   *Excavations in Big Hawk Valley, Wupatki National Monument, Arizona.* Museum of North-
              ern Arizona Bulletin 24. Flagstaff.
    1971   *Painted Ceramics of the Western Mound at Awatovi.* Papers of the Peabody Museum of
              Archaeology and Ethnology 38. Cambridge: Harvard University.
Snow, David H.
    1981   Protohistoric Rio Grande Pueblo Economics: A Review of Trends. In *The Protohistoric
              Period in the North American Southwest,* AD *1450–1700,* D. R. Wilcox and W. B. Masse, eds.,
              pp. 354–77. Anthropological Research Paper 24. Tempe: Arizona State University.
    1984   Prologue to Rio Grande Protohistory. In *Collected Papers in Honor of Harry L. Hadlock,*
              N. L. Fox, ed., pp. 125–32. Papers of the Archaeological Society of New Mexico 9.
Sofaer, A., M. P. Marshall, and R. M. Sinclair
    1989   The Great North Road. In *World Archaeoastronomy,* A. F. Aveni, ed., pp. 365–76. Cam-
              bridge: Cambridge University Press.
Sokolov, R.
    1986   The Good Seed. *Natural History* (April):102.
Speth, John D.
    1983   *Bison Kills and Bone Counts: Decision Making by Ancient Hunters.* Chicago: University of
              Chicago Press.
    1988   Do We Need Concepts Like "Mogollon," "Anasazi," and "Hohokam" Today? A Cultural
              Anthropological Perspective. *The Kiva* 53:201–4.
    1989   Early Hominid Hunting and Scavenging: The Role of Meat as an Energy Source. *Journal
              of Human Evolution* 18:329–43.
Speth, John D., and W. J. Parry
    1980   *Late Prehistoric Bison Procurement in Southeastern New Mexico: The 1978 Season at the Garn-
              sey Site (LS-18399).* Museum of Anthropology Technical Report 12. Ann Arbor: University
              of Michigan.
Speth, John D., and Katherine A. Spielmann
    1983   Energy Source, Protein Metabolism and Hunter-Gatherer Subsistence Strategies. *Journal
              of Anthropological Archaeology* 2:1–31.
Spicer, Edward H.
    1962   *Cycles of Conquest.* Tucson: University of Arizona Press.
Spielmann, Katherine A.
    1982   Inter-Societal Food Acquisition among Egalitarian Societies: An Ecological Study of
              Plains/Pueblo Interaction in the American Southwest. Ph.D. dissertation, Department of
              Anthropology, University of Michigan, Ann Arbor.
    1983   Late Prehistoric Exchange between the Southwest and Southern Plains. *Plains Anthropolo-
              gist* 28:246–72.
    1986   Interdependence among Egalitarian Societies. *Journal of Anthropological Archaeology*
              5:279–312.
    1988   Changing Faunal Procurement Strategies at Gran Quivira Pueblo, New Mexico. Paper
              presented at the 53rd annual meeting of the Society for American Archaeology. Phoenix.
    1989   Colonist, Hunters, and Farmers: Plains-Pueblo Interactions in the Seventeenth Century.
              In *Columbian Consequences*, vol. 1, D. H. Thomas, ed., pp. 101–14. Washington, D.C.:
              Smithsonian Institution Press.
    1991a   Coercion or Cooperation? Plains-Pueblo Interaction in the Protohistoric Period. In
              Farmers, Hunters and Colonists, Interaction between the Southwest and the Southern Plains,
              K. A. Spielmann, ed., pp. 36–50. Tucson: University of Arizona Press.
    1991b   *Interdependence in the Prehistoric Southwest.* New York: Garland Press.

Spielmann, Katherine A. (editor)
1991   *Farmers, Hunters, and Colonists: Interaction between the Southwest and the Southern Plains.* Tucson: University of Arizona Press.
Spielman, Katherine A., M. J. Schoeninger, and K. Moore
1990   Plains-Pueblo Interdependence and Human Diet at Pecos Pueblo, New Mexico. *American Antiquity* 55:745–65.
Spoerl, Patricia M.
1984   Prehistoric Fortifications in Central Arizona. In *Prehistoric Cultural Development in Central Arizona: Archaeology of the Upper New River Region,* P. M. Spoerl and G. J. Gumerman, eds., pp. 261–78. Southern Illinois University at Carbondale Center for Archaeological Investigations Occasional Paper 5. Carbondale.
Spoerl, Patricia M., and George J. Gumerman
1984   *Prehistoric Cultural Development in Central Arizona: Archaeology of the Upper New River Region.* Center for Archaeological Investigations Occasional Paper 15. Carbondale: Southern Illinois University.
Stacy, V. K. Pheriba
1974   Cerros de Trincheras in the Arizona Papagueria. Ph.D. dissertation, Department of Anthropology, University of Arizona, Tucson.
Stafford, C. Russell, and Glen E. Rice (editors)
1980   *Studies in the Prehistory of the Foresdale Region.* Arizona Anthropological Field Studies Number 1. Office of Cultural Resource Management, Department of Anthropology, Arizona State University, Tempe.
Stark, Barbara L.
1986   Perspectives on the Peripheries of Mesoamerica. In *Ripples in the Chichimec Sea,* F. J. Mathien and R. H. McGuire, eds., pp. 270–90. Carbondale: Southern Illinois University Press.
Steen, Charlie R.
1962   Excavations at the Upper Ruin, Tonto National Monument. In *Archaeological Studies at Tonto National Monument,* L. Caywood Technical Series 2. Globe: Southwestern Monuments Association.
1966   *Excavations at Tse-Ta'a, Canyon de Chelly National Monument, Arizona.* Archaeological Research Series 9, National Park Service, Washington, D.C.
Stein, John R., and Peter J. McKenna
1988   *An Archeological Reconnaissance of a Late Bonito Phase Occupation near Aztec Ruins National Monument, New Mexico.* Santa Fe: Division of Anthropology, Branch of Cultural Resources Management, Southwest Cultural Resources Center, National Park Service.
Steward, Julian H.
1937   Ecological Aspects of Southwestern Society. *Anthropos* 32:87–104.
1938   *Basin-Plateau Aboriginal Sociopolitical Groups.* Bureau of Ethnology Bulletin 120. Washington, D.C.
1941   *Archeological Reconnaissance of Southern Utah.* Anthropological Paper 18. Bureau of American Ethnology Bulletin 128. Washington, D.C.: Smithsonian Institution.
1955   *Theory of Culture Change.* Urbana: University of Illinois Press.
Stewart, G. R.
1940   Conservation in Pueblo Agriculture: Present Day Flood Water Irrigation. *Scientific Monthly* 51:329–40.
Stewart, Yvonne G.
1980   *An Archeological Overview of Petrified Forest National Park.* USDI National Park Service, Western Archeological Center, Publications in Anthropology 10.
Stiger, M. A.
1975   Anasazi Diet: The Coprolite Evidence. M.A. thesis, Department of Anthropology, University of Colorado, Boulder.
1979   Mesa Verde Subsistence Patterns from Basketmaker to Pueblo II. *The Kiva* 44:133–44.
Stodder, A. W.
1987   The Physical Anthropology and Mortuary Practice of the Dolores Anasazi: An Early Pueblo Population in Local and Regional Perspective. In *Dolores Archaeological Program Support-*

ing Studies: Settlement and Environment, K. L. Peterson and J. D. Orcutt, eds., pp. 339–504. U.S. Bureau of Reclamation Engineering and Research Center, Denver.

1988   The Status of Bioarchaeological Research in the American Southwest. Paper presented at the 53rd annual meeting of the Society for American Archaeology. Phoenix.

1989a   Bioarchaeological Research in the Basin and Range Region. In *Human Adaptations and Cultural Change in the Greater Southwest*, A. H. Simons, A. L. W. Stodder, D. D. Dykeman, and P. A. Hicks, eds., pp. 167–90. Arkansas Archaeological Survey Research Series 32, Fayetteville, Arkansas.

1989b   The Physical Anthropology and Mortuary Practice of the Dolores Anasazi: An Early Pueblo Population in Local and Regional Perspective. In *Dolores Archaeological Program Supporting Studies: Settlement and Environment*, K. L. Peterson and J. D. Orcutt, eds., pp. 339–504. Denver: U.S. Bureau of Reclamation Engineering and Research Center.

1990   Paleoepidemiology of Eastern and Western Pueblo Communities in Protohistoric New Mexico. Ph.D. dissertation, Department of Anthropology, University of Colorado, Boulder.

Stodder, A. W., and D. L. Martin
1989   Native Health and Disease in the American Southwest before and after Spanish Contact. Paper presented at the Smithsonian Institution Symposium, Disease and Demography in the Americas, Changing Patterns before and after 1492.

1991   Native Health and Disease in the American Southwest before and after Spanish Contact. In *Disease and Demography in the Americas, Changing Patterns before and after 1492*. Washington, D.C.: Smithsonian Institution Press.

Strong, William Duncan
1927   An Analysis of Southwestern Society. *American Anthropologist* 29:1–61.

Stuart, David E., and Robin E. Farwell
1983   Out of Phase: Late Pithouse Occupations in the Highlands of New Mexico. In *High Altitude Adaptations in the Southwest*, J. C. Winter, ed., pp. 115–58. Cultural Resources Management Report 2, U.S.D.A. Forest Service, Southwestern Region, Albuquerque.

Stuart, David E., and Rory P. Gauthier
1981   *Prehistoric New Mexico: Background for Survey*. New Mexico Historic Preservation Bureau, Santa Fe.

1984   *Prehistoric New Mexico: Background for Survey*. Albuquerque: New Mexico Archaeological Council.

Stuiver, M., and P. J. Reimer
1986   A Computer Program for Radiocarbon Age Calibration. *Radiocarbon* 28:1022–30.

Sullivan, Alan P.
1987   Artifact Scatters, Adaptive Diversity, and Southwestern Abandonments: The Upham Hypothesis Reconsidered. *Journal of Anthropological Research* 43:345–60.

Sutphen, J. L.
1985   Growth as a Measure of Nutritional Stress. *Journal of Pediatric Gastoenterology and Nutrition* 4:169–81.

Swanton, John R.
1928   Social Organization and Social Usages of the Indians of the Creek Confederacy. *Forty-second Annual Report of the Bureau of American Ethnology*, pp. 25–472. Washington, D.C.

Swedlund, Alan C.
1965   Human Skeletal Material from the Yellow Jacket Canyon Area, Southwestern Colorado. M.A. thesis, Department of Anthropology, University of Colorado, Boulder.

Szuter, Christine R.
1991   Hunting by Hohokam Desert Farmers. *The Kiva* 56:277–92.

Tainter, Joseph A.
1982   Symbolism, Interaction, and Cultural Boundaries: The Anasazi-Mogollon Transition Zone in West-Central New Mexico. In *Mogollon Archaeology: Proceedings of the 1980 Mogollon Conference*, P. H. Beckett, ed., pp. 3–9. Ramona: Acoma Books.

1984   Perspectives on the Northern Mogollon Boundary Phenomenon. In *Recent Research in Mogollon Prehistory*, S. Upham, F. Plog, D. G. Batcho, and B. E. Kauffman, eds., pp. 45–58. New Mexico State University Museum Occasional Paper 10.

1985   Perspectives on the Abandonment of the Northern Tularosa Basin. In *Views of the Jornada*

Mogollon: Proceedings of the Second Jornada Mogollon Archaeology Conference, C. M. Beck, ed., pp. 143–47. Eastern New Mexico University Contributions in Anthropology 12.

1988   *The Collapse of Complex Societies.* Cambridge: Cambridge University Press.

1991   Review of "Archeological Surveys of Chaco Canyon," edited by Alden C. Hayes, David M. Brugge, and W. James Judge. *The Kiva* 56:183–86.

Tainter, Joseph A., and David "A" Gillio

1980   *Cultural Resources Overview, Mt. Taylor Area, New Mexico.* Albuquerque and Santa Fe: USDA Forest Service, Southwestern Regional Office and USDI Bureau of Land Management, New Mexico State Office.

Tainter, Joseph A., and Frances Levine

1987   *Cultural Resources Overview, Central New Mexico.* Albuquerque and Santa Fe: USDA Forest Service, Southwestern Regional Office and USDI Bureau of Land Management, New Mexico State Office.

Taylor, Walter W.

1954   Southwestern Archaeology, Its History and Theory. *American Anthropologist* 56:561–75.

Teague, Lynne S.

1984   Settlement and Population. In *Hohokam Archaeology along the Salt-Gila Aqueduct,* vol. 9. L. Teague and P. Crown, eds., pp. 141–85. Arizona State Museum of Archaeology Series 150. Tucson.

1989   The Postclassic and the Fate of the Hohokam. In *Syntheses and Conclusions,* L. S. Teague and W. L. Deaver, eds., pp. 145–67. *The 1982–1984 Excavations at Las Colinas,* vol. 6. Archaeological Series 162. Tucson: Arizona State Museum, University of Arizona.

Terrell, John

1990   Storytelling and Prehistory. In *Archaeological Method and Theory,* M. B. Schiffer, ed., pp. 1–29. Tucson: University of Arizona Press.

Textor, Robert B.

1967   *A Cross-Cultural Summary.* New Haven: HRAF Press.

Thomas, David Hurst

1989   *Archaeology.* Fort Worth: Holt, Rinehart, and Winston.

Titche, L. L., S. W. Coulthard, R. D. Wachter, A. C. Thies, and L. L. Harris

1981   Prevalence of Mastoid Infection in Prehistoric Arizona Indians. *American Journal of Physical Anthropology* 56:269–73.

Titiev, Mischa

n.d.   Census Notes from Old Oraibi. Manuscript, Peabody Museum of Archaeology and Ethnology, Harvard University, Cambridge.

Toll, H. Wolcott

1984   Trends in Ceramic Import and Distribution in Chaco Canyon. In *Recent Research on Chaco Prehistory,* W. J. Judge and J. D. Schelberg, eds., pp. 115–35. Reports of the Chaco Center 8. Division of Cultural Research, National Park Service, Albuquerque.

1985   Pottery, Production, Public Architecture and the Chaco Anasazi System. Ph.D. dissertation, Department of Anthropology, University of Colorado. Ann Arbor: University Microfilms.

Toll, H. Wolcott, M. S. Toll, M. L. Newren, and W. B. Gillespie

1985   Experimental Corn Plots in Chaco Canyon: The Life and Hard Times of *Zea mays L.* In *Environment and Subsistence of Chaco Canyon, New Mexico,* F. J. Mathien, ed., pp. 79–143. Publications in Archeology 18E, National Park Service, Albuquerque.

Tooker, Elisabeth

1978   The League of the Iroquois: Its History, Politics and Ritual. In *Handbook of North American Indians.* Vol. 15, *Northeast,* B. E. Trigger, ed., pp. 418–41. Washington, D.C.: Smithsonian Institution.

Trager, G. L.

1967   The Tanoan Settlement of the Rio Grande Area: A Possible Chronology. In *Studies in Southwestern Ethnolinguistics,* D. H. Hymes and W. E. Bittle, eds., pp. 123–36. The Hague: Mouton.

Trigger, Bruce G

1984   Archaeology at the Crossroads: What's New? *Annual Review of Anthropology* 13:275–300. Palo Alto.

1989   *A History of Archaeological Thought.* Cambridge: Cambridge University Press.
1991   Distinguished Lecture in Archeology: Constraint and Freedom. *American Anthropologist* 93:551–69.
Tuan, Y., C. E. Everard, J. G. Widdison and I. Bennett
1973   *The Climate of New Mexico.* Santa Fe: State Planning Office.
Tuggle, H. David, J. Jefferson Reid, and Robert C. Cole
1984   Fourteenth Century Mogollon Agriculture in the Grasshopper Region of Arizona. In *Prehistoric Agricultural Strategies in the Southwest,* S. Fish and P. Fish, eds., pp. 101–10. Anthropological Research Papers 33. Tempe: Arizona State University.
Turner, Christy G., II
1983   Taphonomic Reconstructions of Human Violence and Cannibalism Based on Mass Burials in the American Southwest. In *Carnivores, Human Scavengers and Predators: A Question of Bone Technology,* G. M. LeMoine and A. S. MacEachem, eds., pp. 219–40. Proceedings of the Fifteenth Annual Conference, Archaeological Association of the University of Calgary, Alberta.
1989   Teec Nos Pos: More Possible Cannibalism in Northeastern Arizona. *The Kiva* 54:147–52.
Turner, Christy G., II and Nancy T. Morris
1970   A Massacre at Hopi. *American Antiquity* 35:320–31.
Turner, Christy G., II, and Jacqueline A. Turner
1990   Perimorten Damage to Human Skeletal Remains from Wupatki National Monument, Northern Arizona. *The Kiva* 55:187–212.
Turney, Omar A.
1924   *The Lady of the Stone Hoe.* Phoenix: Arizona Republican Print Shop.
Turney-High, Harry Holbert
1949   *Primitive War: Its Practice and Concepts.* Columbia: University of South Carolina Press.
Underhill, Ruth M.
1939   *Social Organization of the Papago Indians.* New York: Columbia University Press.
United States Bureau of the Census
1990   Enumerators' Schedules, Microfilm Series T623 (Arizona reels).
United States Government
1901   United States Census Record. Washington, D.C.: U.S. Government Printing Office. Map copies on file, University of Arizona Library Map Room, Tucson.
Upham, Steadman
1980   Political Continuity and Change in the Plateau Southwest. Ph.D. dissertation, Department of Anthropology, Arizona State University.
1982   *Polities and Power: An Economic and Political History of the Western Pueblo.* New York: Academic Press.
1984   Adaptive Diversity and Southwestern Abandonment. *Journal of Anthropological Research* 40:235–56.
1987   The Tyranny of Ethnographic Analogy. In *Coasts, Deserts and Plains: Papers in Honor of Reynold J. Ruppé,* S. Gaines and G. A. Clark, eds., pp. 265–76. Arizona State University, Anthropological Research Paper 38.
1988   Archaeological Visibility and the Underclass of Southwestern Prehistory. *American Antiquity* 53:245–61.
Upham, Steadman, Kent G. Lightfoot, and Gary M. Feinman
1981   Explaining Socially Determined Ceramic Distributions in the Prehistoric Plateau Southwest. *American Antiquity* 46:822–33.
Upham, Steadman, Kent G. Lightfoot, and Roberta A. Jewett (editors)
1989   *The Sociopolitical Structure of Prehistoric Southwestern Societies.* Boulder: Westview Press.
Upham, Steadman, Richard S. MacNeish, W. C. Galinat, and C. M. Stevenson
1987   Evidence Concerning the Origin of Maiz de Ocho. *American Anthropologist* 89:410–19.
Upham, Steadman, and Fred Plog
1986   The Interpretation of Prehistoric Political Complexity in the Central and Northern Southwest: Toward a Mending of the Models. *Journal of Field Archaeology* 13(2):223–38.
Upham, Steadman, and Lori Stevens Reed
1989   Regional Systems in the Central and Northern Southwest: Demography, Economy, and Sociopolitics Preceding Contact. In *Columbian Consequences: Archaeological and Historical*

Perspectives on the Spanish Borderlands West, D. H. Thomas, ed., pp. 57–76, vol. 1. Washington, D.C.: Smithsonian Institution Press.

Upham, Steadman, and Paul F. Reed
1989   Inferring the Structure of Anasazi Warfare. In *Cultures in Conflict: Current Archaeological Perspectives,* D. C. Tkaczuk and B. C. Vivian, eds., pp. 153–62. Proceedings of the Twentieth Chacmool Conference, Department of Archaeology, University of Calgary.

Upham, Steadman, and Glen Rice
1980   Up the Canal Without a Pattern: Modeling Hohokam Interaction and Exchange. In *Current Issues in Hohokam Prehistory,* D. Doyel and F. Plog, eds., pp. 78–105. Anthropological Research Paper 23. Tempe: Arizona State University.

Van Blerkom, L. M.
1985   The Evolution of Human Infectious Disease in the Eastern and Western Hemispheres. Ph.D. dissertation, Department of Anthropology, University of Colorado, Boulder.

van der Merwe, N.
1982   Carbon Isotopes, Photosynthesis, and Archaeology. *American Scientist* 70:596–606.

Varien, Mark, Michael Adler, Bruce Bradley, William P. Lipe, and Sandy Thompson
1990   Northern San Juan. Paper presented at "Pueblo Cultures in Transition: A.D. 1150–1350 in the American Southwest." Crow Canyon Center, Cortez, CO. March 28–April 1.

Vayda, Andrew P.
1967   Pomo Trade Feasts. In *Tribal and Peasant Economies,* G. Dalton, ed., pp. 494–500. New York: Natural History Press.
1989   Explaining Why Marings Fought. *Journal of Archaeological Research* 45(2):159–77.

Vencl, Sl.
1984   War and Warfare in Archaeology. *Journal of Anthropological Archaeology* 3:116–32.

Vita-Finzi, C., and E. S. Higgs
1970   Prehistoric Economy in the Mt. Carmel Area of Palestine: Site Catchment Analysis. *Proceedings of the Prehistoric Society* 36:1–37.

Vivian, Gordon
1964   *Excavations at a Seventeenth-Century Jumano Pueblo: Gran Quivira.* Archaeological Research Series 8, National Park Service, Washington, D.C.

Vivian, R. Gwinn
1974   Conservation and Diversion: Water-Control Systems in the Anasazi Southwest. In *Irrigation's Impact on Society,* T. Downing and McG. Gibson, eds., pp. 95–112. Anthropological Papers of the University of Arizona 25, Tucson.
1990   *The Chacoan Prehistory of the San Juan Basin, New Mexico.* Orlando: Academic Press.
1991   Chacoan Subsistence. In *Chaco & Hohokam: Prehistoric Regional Systems in the American Southwest,* P. L. Crown and W. J. Judge, eds., pp. 57–75. Santa Fe: School of American Research Press.

Vivian, R. Gwinn, and Nancy W. Clendenen
1965   The Denison Site: Four Pit Houses near Isleta, New Mexico. *El Palacio* 72(2):5–26.

Wade, William D.
1970   Skeletal Remains of a Prehistoric Population for the Puerco Valley, Eastern Arizona. M.A. thesis, Department of Anthropology, University of Colorado, Boulder.

Wade, William D., and George J. Armelagos
1966   Anthropometric Data and Observations upon Human Skeletal Material. In *Contributions to Mesa Verde Archaeology III,* R. H. Lister, ed., pp. 64–91. University of Colorado Studies, Series in Anthropology 12, Boulder.

Wagner, Gail, T. Smart, Richard I. Ford, and H. Trigg
1984   Ethnobotanical Recovery, 1982: Summary of Analysis and Frequency Tables. In *Excavations on Black Mesa, 1982: A Descriptive Report,* Nichols and Smiley, eds., pp. 611–32. Center for Archaeological Investigations Research Paper 39. Southern Illinois University, Carbondale.

Walker, P. L.
1985   Anemia among Prehistoric Indians of the American Southwest. In *Health and Disease in the Prehistoric Southwest,* C. F. Merbs and R. J. Miller, eds., pp. 139–63. Anthropological Research Papers 34. Tempe: Arizona State University.

Wallace, Henry D., and D. Craig
    1988   A Reconsideration of the Tucson Basin Hohokam Chronology. In *Recent Research on Tucson Basin Prehistory: Proceedings of the Second Tucson Basin Conference,* W. H. Doelle and P. R. Fish, eds., pp. 53–70. Institute for American Research Anthropology Papers 10. Tucson.
Wallace, Roberts M.
    1954   Petrographic Analysis of Pottery from University Indian Ruins. Appendix F in *Excavations, 1940, at University Indian Ruin,* J. Hayden, ed. Southwestern Monuments Association Technical Series 5(1957).
Wallerstein, Immanuel
    1974   *The Modern World-System I.* New York: Academic Press.
    1980   *The Modern World-System II.* New York: Academic Press.
Walt, Henry J.
    1985   The Function of Stockade Structures. In *The Excavation of the Cortez CO2 Pipeline Project Sites, 1982–1983,* M. P. Marshall, ed., pp. 165–70. Albuquerque: Office of Contract Archaeology, University of New Mexico.
Walthall, John A.
    1980   *Prehistoric Indians of the Southeast, Archaeology of Alabama and the Middle South.* Tuscaloosa: University of Alabama Press.
Warren, Helene
    1970   Notes on Manufacture and Trade of Rio Grande Glazes. *The Artifact* 8(4):1–7.
    1979   The Glaze Paint Wares of the Upper Middle Rio Grande. In *Adaptive Change in the Northern Rio Grande Valley,* J. V. Biella and R. C. Chapman, eds., pp. 187–216. Archaeological Investigations in Cochiti Reservoir, New Mexico, vol. 4. Albuquerque: Office of Contract Archaeology, Department of Anthropology, University of New Mexico.
    1980   Prehistoric Pottery of Tijeras Canyon. In *Tijeras Canyon: Analyses of the Past,* L. S. Cordell, ed., pp. 149–68. The Maxwell Museum of Anthropology and the University of New Mexico Press, Albuquerque.
Warren, Claude N.
    1984   The Desert Region. In *California Archaeology,* M. J. Moratto, pp. 339–431. New York: Academic Press.
Wasley, William W.
    1960a   A Hohokam Platform Mound at the Gatlin Site, Gila Bend, Arizona. *American Antiquity* 26:244–62.
    1960b   Salvage Archaeology on Highway 66 in Eastern Arizona. *American Antiquity* 26:30–42.
    1960c   Hospital-Turnkey Site Excavations. Manuscript, Arizona State Museum, University of Arizona, Tucson.
    1966   Classic Period Hohokam. Paper presented at the 31st annual meeting of the Society for American Archaeology. Reno.
Water Resources Institute
    1953   Map of Irrigated Lands and Source of Water Areas of Similar Consumptive Use Factors in New Mexico. Las Cruces: New Mexico State University.
Waters, Frank
    1963   *Book of the Hopi.* New York: Ballantine Books.
Waters, Michael R.
    1982   The Lowland Patayan Ceramic Tradition. In *Hohokam and Patayan Prehistoric Southwestern Arizona,* R. H. McGuire and M. B. Schiffer, eds., pp. 275–97. New York: Academic Press.
    1986   *The Geoarchaeology of Whitewater Draw, Arizona.* Anthropological Papers of the University of Arizona 45. Tucson: University of Arizona Press.
    1987   Holocene Alluvial Geology and Geoarchaeology of AZ BB: 13:14 and the San Xavier Reach of the Santa Cruz. In *The Archaeology of the San Xavier Bridge Site (AZ BB:13:14), Tucson Basin, Southern Arizona,* J. C. Ravesloot, ed., pp. 39–60. Archaeological Series No. 171. Cultural Resource Management Division, Arizona State Museum. Tucson: University of Arizona.
    1988   The Impact of Fluvial Processes and Landscape Evolution on Archaeological Sites and Settlement Patterns along the San Xavier Reach of the Santa Cruz River, Arizona. *Geoarchaeology* 3:205–19.
    1989   The Influence of Late Quaternary Landscape Processes on Hohokam Settlement Patterning in Southern Arizona. In *Hohokam Archaeology along Phase B of the Tucson Aqueduct,*

Central Arizona Project. Volume 1, *Syntheses and Interpretations,* part 1, J. S. Czaplicki and J. C. Ravesloot, eds., pp. 79–130. Archaeological Series 178. Cultural Resource Management Division, Arizona State Museum. Tucson: University of Arizona.

Watson, Patty Jo, Steven A. LeBlanc, and Charles Redman
  1980 Aspects of Zuni Prehistory: Preliminary Report on Excavation and Survey in the El Morro Valley of New Mexico. *Journal of Field Archaeology* 7:201–18.

Weaver, Donald E., Jr.
  1972 A Cultural-Ecological Model for the Classic Hohokam Period in the Lower Salt River Valley. *The Kiva* 38(1):43–52.
  1976 Salado Influences in the Lower Salt River Valley. *The Kiva* 42(1):17–26.

Wedel, Waldo R.
  1942 *Archaeological Remains in Central Kansas and Their Possible Bearing on the Location of Quivira.* Smithsonian Miscellaneous Collections 101. Washington, D.C.
  1950 Notes on Plains-Southwestern Contacts in Light of Archaeology. In *For the Dean: Essays in Anthropology in Honor of Byron Cummings,* E. K. Reed and D. S. King, eds., pp. 99–116. Tucson: Hohokam Museums Association.

Weigand, Phil C.
  1968 The Mines and Mining Techniques of the Chalchihuites Culture. *American Antiquity* 33:45–61.
  1978 The Prehistory of the State of Zacatecas: An Interpretation. In *Anuario de Historia Zacatecana,* C. E. Sanchez, ed., pp. 1–39. Universidad Autonoma de Zacatecas, Zacatecas, Mexico. (Reprinted in two parts in *Anthropology* 2(1):67–87, 1978, and *Anthropology* 2(2):103–117, 1978).
  1982 Mining and Mineral Trade in Prehispanic Zacatecas. In *Mining and Mineral Techniques in Ancient Mesoamerica,* P. C. Weigand and G. Gwynne, eds., pp. 87–134. Special issue of *Anthropology,* vol. 6.
  1988 Ancient Rare Resource Procurement in Northwestern Mesoamerica and the Southwest U.S.A. Paper presented at the Amerind Foundation New World Studies Seminar "Culture and Contact: Charles Di Peso's Gran Chichimeca." Dragoon, AZ.

Weigand, Phil C., George Harbottle, and E. V. Sayre
  1977 Turquoise Sources and Source Analysis: Mesoamerica and the Southwestern U.S.A. In *Exchange Systems in Prehistory,* T. K. Earle and J. E. Ericson, eds., pp. 15–34. New York: Academic Press.

Wendorf, Fred
  1953 *Salvage Archaeology in the Chama Valley, New Mexico.* Monographs of the School of American Research No. 17. Santa Fe.
  1956 Some Distributions of Settlement Patterns in the Pueblo Southwest. In *Prehistoric Settlement Patterns in the New World,* G. R. Willey, ed., pp. 18–25. Viking Fund Publications in Anthropology 23.

Wendorf, Fred, and Erik K. Reed
  1955 An Alternative Reconstruction of Northern Rio Grande Prehistory. *El Palacio* 62:131–73.

Werbner, R. P.
  1977 Introduction. In *Regional Cults,* R. P. Werbner, ed., pp. ix–xxvii. London: Academic Press.

Wetterstrom, W.
  1986 *Food, Diet, and Population at Prehistoric Arroyo Hondo Pueblo, New Mexico.* Arroyo Hondo Archaeological Series vol. 6. Santa Fe: School of American Research Press.

Whalen, Michael
  1981 Cultural-Ecological Aspects of the Pithouse-to-Pueblo Transition in a Portion of the Southwest. *American Antiquity* 46(1):75–92.

Wheat, Joe Ben
  1955 *Mogollon Culture Prior to A.D. 1000.* Memoirs of the Society for American Archaeology 10.

White, Leslie A.
  1959 *The Development of Civilization to the Fall of Rome.* McGraw-Hill Book Company.

White, Tim D.
  1991 Archeological Case Study: Anasazi Remains from Cottonwood Canyon. In *Human Osteology,* P. A. Felkens, ed., pp. 393–406. New York: Academic Press.

Whitecotten, Joseph W., and Richard A. Pailes
  1986 New World Precolumbian World Systems. In *Ripples in the Chichimec Sea: New Consider-*

ations of Southwestern-Mesoamerican Interactions, F. J. Mathien and R. H. McGuire, eds., pp. 183–204. Carbondale: Southern Illinois University Press.

Whiteley, Peter M.

1986   Unpacking Hopi "Clans" II: Further Questions about Hopi Descent Groups. *Journal of Anthropological Research* 42:69–79.

Whittlesey, Stephanie M., and J. Jefferson Reid

1982   Cholla Project Settlement Summary. In *Cholla Project Archaeology: Introduction and Special Studies,* J. Jefferson Reid, ed., pp. 205–16. Arizona State Museum Archaeological Series 161(1).

Wiessner, Pauline W.

1977   Hxaro: A Regional System of Reciprocity for Reducing Risk among the !Kung San. Ph.D. dissertation, Department of Anthropology, University of Michigan, Ann Arbor.

Wiessner, Polly

1982   Risk, Reciprocity and Social Influences on !Kung San Economics. In *Politics and History in Band Societies,* E. Leacock and R. Lee, eds., pp. 61–84. Cambridge: Cambridge University Press.

1983   Style and Social Information in Kalahari San Projectile Points. *American Antiquity* 48:253–76.

Wilcox, David R.

1979a   The Warfare Implications of Dry-Laid Masonry Walls on Tumamoc Hiss. *The Kiva* 45:15–38.

1979b   The Hohokam Regional System. In *An Archaeological Test of Sites in the Gila Butte-Santan Region,* G. Rice et al., eds., pp. 77–116. Arizona State University Anthropological Research Paper 18. Tempe.

1980   The Current Status of the Hohokam Concept. In *Current Issues in Hohokam Prehistory,* D. E. Doyel and F. Plog, eds. Anthropological Research Papers 23. Tempe: Arizona State University.

1981a   Changing Perspectives in the Protohistoric Pueblos, A.D. 1450–1700. In *The Protohistoric Periods in the North American Southwest, A.D. 1450–1700,* D. R. Wilcox and W. B. Masse, eds., pp. 378–409. Research Paper 24. Tempe: Arizona State University.

1981b   The Entry of Athapaskan Speakers into the American Southwest: The Problem Today. In *The Protohistoric Period in the North American Southwest, A.D. 1450–1700,* D. R. Wilcox and W. B. Masse, eds., pp. 213–56. Anthropological Research Papers 24. Tempe: Arizona State University.

1984   Multi-Ethnic Division of Labor in the Protohistoric Southwest. In *Collected Papers in Honor of Harry L. Hadlock,* N. L. Fox, ed., pp. 141–56. Papers of the New Mexico Archaeological Society 9. Albuquerque.

1985   Preliminary Report on New Data on Hohokam Ballcourts. In *Proceedings of the 1983 Hohokam Symposium,* part 2, A. E. Dittert, Jr., and D. E. Dove, eds., pp. 641–54. Occasional Papers No. 2, Phoenix Chapter, Arizona Archaeological Society.

1986a   Excavations of Three Sites on Bottomless Pits Mesa, Flagstaff, Arizona. Manuscript, Interim Report, Coconino National Forest, Flagstaff.

1986b   A Historical Analysis of the Problem of Southwestern-Mesoamerican Connections. In *Ripples in the Chichimec Sea: New Considerations of Southwestern-Mesoamerican Interactions,* F. J. Mathien and R. H. McGuire, eds., pp. 9–45. Carbondale: Southern Illinois University Press.

1986c   The Tepiman Connection: A Model of Mesoamerican-Southwestern Interaction. In *Ripples in the Chichimec Sea: New Considerations of Southwestern-Mesoamerican Interactions,* F. J. Mathien and R. H. McGuire, eds., pp. 135–54. Carbondale: Southern Illinois University Press.

1987   *Frank Midvale's Investigation of the Site of La Ciudad.* Arizona State University Anthropological Field Study 19. Tempe.

1988a   A Processual Model of Charles C. Di Peso's Babocomari Site and Related Systems. Manuscript, Museum of Northern Arizona Library, Flagstaff.

1988b   The Regional Context of the Brady Wash and Picacho Area Sites. In *Hohokam Settlement along the Slopes of the Picacho Mountains, Synthesis and Conclusions, Tucson Aqueduct Project,* R. Ciolek-Torrello and D. R. Wilcox, eds., pp. 244–67. MNA Research Papers 35(6). Flagstaff.

1989 Hohokam Warfare. In *Cultures in Conflict: Current Archaeological Perspectives,* D. C. Tkaczuk and B. C. Vivian, pp. 163–72. Proceedings of the 20th Chacmool Conference, Department of Archaeology, University of Calgary.

1991a The Changing Structure of Macroregional Organization in the North American Southwest: A New World Perspective. Manuscript, Museum of Northern Arizona, Flagstaff.

1991b Changing Contexts of Pueblo Adaptations, A.D. 1250–1600. In *Farmers, Hunters, and Colonists, Interaction Between the Southwest and the Southern Plains,* K. A. Spielmann, ed., pp. 128–54. Tucson: University of Arizona Press.

1991c Hohokam Social Complexity. In *Chaco & Hohokam: Prehistoric Regional Systems in the American Southwest,* P. L. Crown and W. J. Judge, eds., pp. 253–76. Santa Fe: School of American Research Press.

1991d The Mesoamerican Ballgame in the American Southwest. In *The Mesoamerican Ballgame,* V. L. Scarborough and D. R. Wilcox, eds., pp. 101–28. Tucson: University of Arizona Press.

Wilcox, David R., R. R. McGuire, and C. Sternberg
1981 *Snaketown Revisited.* Arizona State Museum Archaeological Series 155. Tucson: Arizona State University.

Wilcox, David R., and Lynette O. Shenk
1977 *The Architecture of the Casa Grande and Its Interpretation.* Arizona State Museum Archaeology Series 115. Tucson: University of Arizona.

Wilcox, David R., and Charles Sternberg
1983 *Hohokam Ballcourts and Their Interpretation.* Arizona State Museum Archaeological Series 160. Tucson: University of Arizona.

Willey, Gordon R.
1953 *Prehistoric Settlement Patterns in the Viru Valley, Peru.* Bulletin of the Bureau of American Ethnology, 155. Washington, D.C.

1966 *An Introduction to American Archaeology I.* Englewood Cliffs: Prentice-Hall.

1991 Horizontal Integration and Regional Diversity: An Alternating Process in the Rise of Civilizations. *American Antiquity* 56(2):197–215.

Williams, J. L., and P. E. McAllister
1979 *New Mexico in Maps.* Albuquerque: University of New Mexico Press.

Williams, N. M., and E. S. Hunn
1982 *Resource Managers: North American and Australian Hunter-Gatherers.* Washington, D.C.: American Association for the Advancement of Science.

Wills, W. H.
1988a *Early Prehistoric Agriculture in the American Southwest.* Santa Fe: School of American Research Press.

1988b Early Agriculture and Sedentism in the American Southwest: Evidence and Interpretations. *Journal of World Prehistory* 2:445–88.

1989 Patterns of Prehistoric Food Production in West-Central New Mexico. *Journal of Anthropological Research* 45:116–37.

1990 Cultivating Ideas: The Changing Intellectual History of the Introduction of Agriculture in the American Southwest. In *Perspectives on Southwestern Prehistory,* P. E. Minnis and C. L. Redman, eds., pp. 319–31. Boulder: Westview Press.

Wills, W. H., and Thomas C. Windes
1989 Evidence for Population Aggregation and Dispersal during the Basketmaker III Period in Chaco Canyon, New Mexico. *American Antiquity* 54:347–69.

Wilshusen, Richard H.
1986 The Relationship between Abandonment Mode and Ritual Use in Pueblo I Anasazi Protokivas. *Journal of Field Archaeology* 13:245–54.

Windes, Thomas
1984 A New Look at Population in Chaco Canyon. In *Recent Research on Chaco Prehistory,* W. J. Judge and J. D. Schelberg, eds., pp. 75–84. Reports of the Chaco Center 8. Albuquerque: National Park Service.

Winship, George P.
1896 *The Coronado Expedition, 1540–1542.* Bureau of American Ethnology Annual Report 14, pt. 1.

Winter, Joseph C.
    1981   Anasazi Agriculture at Hovenweep II: The Development and Use of Towers. *Contract Abstracts and CRM Archeology* 2(2):28–36.
Wiseman, Regge N.
    1976   *An Archaeological Impact Statement and Mitigation Proposal for New Mexico.* Laboratory of Anthropology Notes 125.
    1982   *The Tsaya Project: Archaeological Excavations near Lake Valley, San Juan County, New Mexico.* Laboratory of Anthropology Note No. 308. Museum of New Mexico, Santa Fe.
Wissler, Clark
    1917   *The American Indian.* New York: Oxford University Press.
    1938   *The American Indian.* 3rd ed. New York: Oxford University Press.
Wobst, H. M.
    1949   *Human Behavior and the Principle of Least Effort.* Cambridge: Harvard University Press.
    1977   Stylistic Behavior and Information Exchange. In *Papers for the Director: Research Essays in Honor of James B. Griffin,* C. E. Cleland, ed., pp. 317–42. Anthropological Papers 61. Ann Arbor: Museum of Anthropology, University of Michigan.
Wolf, Eric
    1982   *Europe and the People without History.* Berkeley: University of California Press.
Wood, Jon Scott
    1978   *An Archaeological Survey of the Battle Flat Watershed Experiment Chaparral Conversion Project, Crown King Ranger District, Prescott National Forest.* Archaeological Report No. 24. U.S.D.A., Forest Service, Albuquerque.
    1986   Veil of Tiers: Tonto Basin in the 14th Century. Paper presented at Pecos Conference. Payson, AZ.
Woodbury, Richard B.
    1959   A Reconsideration of Pueblo Warfare in the Southwestern United States. *33rd Congreso Internacional de Americanistas, San Jose de Costa Rica del 20 al 27 de Julio de 1958,* vol. 2, pp. 124–33.
    1965   *Prehistoric Agriculture at Point of Pines, Arizona.* Memoirs of the Society for American Archaeology 17.
Woodbury, Richard B., and Ezra B. W. Zubrow
    1979   Agricultural Beginnings, 1000 B.C.–A.D. 500. In *Handbook of North American Indians.* Vol. 9, *Southwest.* A. Ortiz, ed., pp. 43–60. Washington, D.C.: Smithsonian Institution.
Woosley, Anne I.
    1980   Agricultural Diversity in the Prehistoric Southwest. *The Kiva* 45:317–36.
Wormington, H. Marie
    1947   *Prehistoric Indians of the Southwest.* Denver: Denver Museum of Natural History.
    1955   *A Reappraisal of the Fremont Culture with a Summary of the Archaeology of the Northern Periphery.* Proceedings of the Denver Museum of Natural History 1. Denver.
Yoffee, Norman, and George Cowgill
    1987   *The Collapse of Ancient States and Civilizations.* Tucson: University of Arizona Press.
Yohe, Robert M., Mark Q. Sutton, and Daniel F. McCarthy
    1986   A "Battle Scene" Petroglyph Panel in the Coso Range, California. *Journal of California and Great Basin Anthropology* 8:133–37.
Zipf, G. K.
    1949   *Human Behavior and the Principle of Least Effort.* Cambridge: Harvard University Press.

Index

Abandonment, 23, 25–26; aggregation and, 162; definition of, 136–37; general model of, 137–42, 162–63; of Grasshopper region, 159, 161–62; Hohokam, in Tucson Basin, 151, 153; regional, 142–43; reoccupation following, 143–45; warfare and, 236–37; in Western Anasazi area, 23, 148–50

Acholi, as example of alliance, 184–86, 188–89, 200, 201, 203, 210

Acoma area. *See* Cebolleta Mesa

Acoma Pueblo, 84

Adaptation, 10

Agave, 123, 151, 157

Aggregation, 8–9, 26; abandonment and, 162; causes of, 109, 110–11, 131–33; consequences of, 109–10; in Eastern Anasazi area, 113–18; in Grasshopper region, 158, 159; Hohokam, 118–24, 131–32; in Mimbres area, 20–21, 125–28; in Mogollon/Western Pueblo area, 128–30, 132–33; in southeastern Arizona, 125; in Tonto Basin, 124–25; warfare and, 234, 235–36

Agricultural technology, Late Archaic, 39. *See also* Irrigation

Akins, Nancy, 102

Alkali Ridge, 204

Alliance system: Chaco, 205–7; definition of, 192; Jeddito, 199, 208; preceramic, 201; Rio Grande, 208–9; Salado, 199–200, 208; Salt-Gila Hohokam, 193–96; Tucson Basin Hohokam, 196–97. *See also* Regional systems

Alta Vista site, 245, 247, 248

Amaranths, 37, 45, 91, 98

Anasazi: no longer useful concept, 179; Numic speakers and, 144, 214; standardization of architecture, 19–20; transition zone with Mogollon, 173–79

Anasazi, Eastern: aggregation, 113–18. *See also* Rio Grande, northern

Anasazi, Western: abandonment, 23, 148–50; agricultural settlements, 146, 149; environment, 145–46, 147, 148; regional variation in organization, 28; relation with Fremont, 261, 262. *See also* Kayenta Anasazi; Virgin Anasazi

Antelope House, 103

Anyon, Roger, 126

Archaic period, 201, 257. *See also* Late Archaic period

Architecture: Anasazi, 19–20; indicative of warfare, 216–23; pithouse-to-pueblo transition, 201–4. *See also* Ballcourts; Kivas; Platform mounds

Arroyo Hondo Pueblo, 68, 91, 104–5, 112, 116

Athapaskans, 83, 84, 214, 258–59

Atkinson, Ronald, 184–85

Awatovi site, 253

Aztec Ruin, 112, 224, 226, 228

Babocomari Village, 125

Ballcourts, 20, 120, 193–95, 196

Basketmaker II: Black Mesa, 43–45, 46; Cedar Mesa, 45–46; evidence of violence in, 213, 226–27; health, 97–99; trophy heads, 228

Basketmaker III, 113, 175, 176–77

Bat Cave, 46, 47

Battle Cave, 227

Bc51 site, 228

Beans, 19; Basketmaker, 98; Late Archaic, 35, 36, 47

Beeweed, 98

Benson 5:16 site, 40

Betatakin site, 112, 133, 143

Black Mesa: Basketmaker II, 42–45, 46; climatic variability, 147; health, 99; population, 147; site organization, 28

Bow and arrow, 18, 19

Brady site, 154

California-Southwest interaction, 259–60

Cambrian "explosion," 10, 27

Cameron Creek site, 89

Cannibalism, 213, 229

Canyon Creek Pueblo, 160

Canyon de Chelly, 100

Casa Blanca site, 232

Casa Grande site, 120, 155; location, 154, 232; settlement cluster, 231, 232; village plan, 121

Casas Grandes site: evidence for head-hunting at, 229; hierarchy at, 163; location, 245; population, 82, 83; as regional center, 246, 249; trade in parrots, 255; trophy skulls from, 227

Cashion site, 122, 231

Caves 1–2, Kin Biko, 43

Cebolleta Mesa: population, 66–67, 80, 174, 176

Cedar Mesa, 45–46, 58–59

Ceramic: change, post-1300, 252; evidence of Chaco influence, 205–6; exchange, 193, 196–97, 202; production, 116, 117; symbols, 252–53

Ceramic styles: Dogoszhi, 205; Kana-a, 20, 202; Lino, 20, 202, White Mound, 20

Ceramic types: Alma Plain, 175; El Paso Polychrome, 252; Forestdale Smudged, 175; Gila Polychrome, 198, 199, 252; Jeddito Black-on-yellow, 255; Jeddito Polychrome, 144; Jemez Black-on-white, 208; Kana-a Black-on-white, 175; Kiatuthlanna Black-on-white, 175; Lino Fugitive Red, 175; Lino Gray, 175; Matsaki Polychrome, 252; Piedra Black-on-white, 231; Ramos Polychrome, 144, 252; St. Johns Polychrome, 116; San Francisco Red, 175; Sikyatki Polychrome, 144, 252; Tanque Verde Red-on-brown, 197; White Mound Black-on-white, 175

Ceramic wares: biscuit, 116, 208, 209; brown, 246, 258; Casas Grandes polychromes, 125, 255; Chacoan red, 207; Jeddito Yellow, 199, 208; Mogollon brown, 174, 175; paddle-and-anvil, 258; red, 175, 176; red-on-brown, 196–97; red-on-buff, 193; Rio Grande Glaze, 116, 208, 209; Salado polychromes, 123, 125, 144, 153, 155, 197, 198–99, 200; San Juan Red, 202;

White Mountain Red, 116, 125, 254

Cerbat culture, 16, 82

Cerro de Trincheras site, 245

Chaco Canyon: aggregation in, 113; ceramic style, 205–6; decline of, 22; environment, 117, 170; great kivas, 128, 129; health, 102, 104; Hosta Butte phase, 166; human sacrifice in, 214; influence in surrounding areas, 117–18, 175–76; location, 245; Mesoamerican connections, 249; population, 65; ranking in, 166, 171–72; regional system, 21, 28, 170–73, 205–7; as religious center, 180, 206; revisionist interpretations of, 180–81; roads, 28, 171; southern periphery of system, 173, 175–76, 179

Chalchihuites, 245, 247, 250

Chama Valley, 213

Chaos theory, 167, 178

Charleston site, 40

Charnal House Tower, 227

Chaves Pass, 105, 227

Chenopods, 37, 45, 91

Chimney Rock Pueblo, 223

Chisholm, Brian, 37–38, 45–46

Chodistaas site, 157, 159, 225

Chupícuaro, 246

Cibecue Creek Pueblo, 159

Cíbola, 22, 23, 239

Cienega Creek site, 47–48

Citadel Ruin, 220

Classic period: Hohokam, 120–22, 123, 124, 125, 151–57; Rio Grande, 115–16

Cline Terrace site, 232

Coalition period, 115

Colonial period, 119–20, 122, 124

Colorado Plateau(s): environment, 54–56, 118; Late Archaic period, 42–46; population, 74

Complexity, 5, 16: definition of, 14–15, 166–67; key periods of change in, 17–26

Coombs Site, 225

Copper bells, 21, 24, 194

Core-periphery model, 189–90, 191, 194

Corn. See Maize

Cortaro Fan site, 41

Cotton, 123

Cross-cultural regularities, 3–6

Culiacán, 239, 245

Cultural evolution, 3–4. See also Complexity

Culture: archaeological definition of, 183–84, 186; formation of new, 184, 185

D:11:449 (SIU) site, 43, 44

D:11:2045 (SIU) site, 44

D:11:3133 (SIU) site, 43, 44

Developmental period, 115
Donaldson site, 40

Eaton site, 48
Elites: exchange between, 194–95, 199. *See also* Ranking
Escalante site, 121, 123
Ethnography, use in archaeology of, 25
Exchange: ceramic, 193, 197, 202; elite, 194–95, 199; Hohokam, 123, 196–97; with Plains nomads, 257–58, 259; of prestige goods, 21, 249, 250–51; ritual and, 203–4, 205

Fairbank site, 40
Fortified Hill site, 222
Forts, 124, 219–21
Fremont tradition, 261–62

Galaz Ruin, 126–27, 228
Galisteo Basin, 259
Galisteo Pueblo, 116
Gallina area, 216, 217
Garnsey site, 245, 258
Genizaro settlements, 222
Gila Pueblo, 225
Gourd, bottle, 35
Grand Canyon area, 62–63
Gran Quivira Pueblo, 105, 166, 245, 259, 263
Grasshopper Pueblo, 130, 157; aggregation at, 129, 130; evidence of scalping at, 227; health, 103–4; location, 232; social organization, 159, 160
Grasshopper region: abandonment of, 159, 161–62; aggregation in, 158, 159; settlement clusters in, 157–58
Grasshopper Spring site, 157, 159, 225
Great Basin–Southwest interaction, 261–62
Green Mask site, 229
Grewe site, 120
Guadalupe Ruin, 177, 226
Guardian Pueblo, 223
Guard villages, 222–23

Haas, Jonathan, 111
Halloran Springs, 245, 259
Hano village, 222
Hawikku site, 96, 105, 106
Head-hunting, 229, 230
Hill, James N., 110
Hill-slope retreats, 221–222
Hinkson Site, 129–30

Hohokam: abandonments, 26, 151, 153; aggregation, 118–24, 131–32, 155; ball-courts, 20, 120, 193–95, 196; decline, 22, 73; effects of flooding upon, 122–23; environment, 57; exchange, 123, 196–97; health, 103; irrigation, 120, 122–23, 142, 153, 155; Mesoamerican interaction, 20, 21, 194–95; Mogollon relationships, 18; no-man's lands, 231–32; platform mounds, 20, 154, 155, 196; population, 70–73, 121–22; Salt-Gila regional system, 21, 193–96; subsistence, 123; Tucson Basin regional system, 150–57, 196–97; warfare, 197
Homol'ovi II site, 255
Hopi, 83, 84, 143
Hopi Buttes, 28, 146, 148, 149
Hopi Mesas, 147, 150
Horse Camp Mill Pueblo, 225
Hovenweep area, 217
Howiri site, 116
Human sacrifice, 213–14, 229

Indian Peak site, 220
Indian rice grass, 45
Iron deficiency anemia, 92, 99, 102
Irrigation: gravity, 141; Phoenix Basin Hohokam, 120, 122–23, 142; Tucson Basin Hohokam, 153, 155

Jackrabbit Ruin, 232
Jeddito alliance, 199, 208
Jemez Cave, 43
Johannessen, Sissell, 36
Johnson, Gregory, 132
Jones Ranch Road sites, 225

Katsina cult, 150, 253, 254–55, 256, 265
Kayenta Anasazi: health, 102–3; migration south, 253; palisades, 219; population, 60–61. *See also* Anasazi, Western; Black Mesa
Keresan speakers, 83
Keystone Dam site, 42
Kiatuthlanna site, 129, 168, 229
Kiet Siel site, 112, 133, 143
Kintigh, Keith, 126–27
Kiowa, 258
Kivas: great, 128, 129, 254; increased integration and, 203
Kohler, Timothy, 111
Kuaua Pueblo, 225
Kuykendall site, 125

LA 18901 site, 43
La Ciudad site, 227
La Quemada site, 245, 247, 248, 249
Las Colinas site, 120, 227, 232
Las Cremaciones site, 231
Late Archaic, 33; architecture, 34, 40, 42, 48; burials, 41–42; cultigens, 35–36, 40, 41, 42, 43–44, 45–46, 47, 50; diet, 37–39; food production, 39, 50–52; grinding tools, 39; mobility patterns, 48–49; radiocarbon dates, 41, 43, 47; rockshelter use, 44. *See also* Basketmaker II
Leafwater Ruin, 221, 225
LeBlanc, Steven, 126
Linton, Ralph, 214–16
Little Colorado area, 63–64, 79, 81, 147
Long House and Klethla valleys, 147, 148, 149, 226, 231
Los Hornos site, 228
Los Muertos site, 120, 121, 163, 232
Los Ojitos site, 40, 41
Lost City, 245, 259

Maize, 17; Basketmaker, 98; Late Archaic period, 35–36, 40, 41, 42, 43–44, 45, 47, 50; productivity, 50
Marana community, 151; abandonment, 153; agave cultivation at, 123; aggregation, 131; location, 154, 232; map, 152
Martinez Hill site, 232
Matson, R. G., 37–38, 45–46
McClellan site, 154
Mesa Grande site, 120, 163, 232
Mesa Verde: aggregation, 113–14; health, 100–102
Mesoamerica-Southwest interaction, 19, 24, 240, 242, 244, 262; artifacts indicating, 246, 255; ceramic similarities, 246; direct intervention models of, 245–46, 249, 252; exchange of prestige goods, 21, 249, 250–51; role of regional centers in, 246–47, 248, 250; spread of farming, 246
Milagro site, 40–41
Mimbreños Blanco site, 213
Mimbres area: aggregation, 20–21, 125–28; hilltop sites, 221–22; population, 67–68, 126–27
Minnis, Paul E., 89
Mobility, and environmental variation, 85
Modularity, 168
Mogollon area: aggregation, 128–30, 132–33; environment, 56; great kivas. 128; Late Archaic, 46–49; northern transition zone with Anasazi, 173–79; population, 69–70, 79. *See also* Mimbres area

Mogollon culture: loss of distinctiveness after AD 1000, 22; no longer useful concept, 179; relation to Hohokam, 18; in southeastern Arizona, 125
Mogollon Village, 228
Moiety system, 254
Morris, Earl, 224

NA 7519 site, 142–43
NAN Ranch Ruin, 89
Navajo Mountain area, 147, 148
Neskahai Village, 219
No-man's lands, 230–32
Nuevo Culiacán, 239, 240
Numic speakers: Anasazi and, 144, 214; population, 82, 83; replaced Fremont, 261–62

Olberg site, 231
Old Fort site, 226
Otowi site, 116, 208

P:14:197 (ASM) site, 159, 225
P:16:9 (ASM) site, 129
Pa'ako site, 105, 112
Pai, 83, 84
Paiute. *See* Numic speakers
Pajarito Archaeological Project, 110, 233
Pajarito Plateau, 233–34
Palisade Ruin, 221, 225
Palisades, 218–19, 222
Palo Parado site, 125
Pantano site, 40
Parrots, 194, 252, 255
Patayán, 229, 259, 260
Patterning: in Chaco system, 173–79; strong vs. weak, 168–70
Pecos Pueblo, 84; diet, 105; health, 106; interaction with Plains nomads, 259, 263; location, 245
Peer polity interaction, 242
Pesedeuinge site, 213, 225
Phoenix Basin. *See* Salt-Gila region
Picuris Pueblo, 245, 259
Piedra River area, 218
Pimans, 84, 123
Pinedale Pueblo, 158
Piñon nuts, 45
Pioneer period, 119, 121, 122
Pithouse-to-pueblo transition, 201–4
Plains-Southwest interaction, 257–59, 262–64
Platform mounds, 20, 154, 155, 196
Pochteca, 241, 245–46
Point of Pines Pueblo, 105, 158, 225, 253

Population: Cebolleta Mesa, 66–67; Chaco
 Canyon, 65; Grand Canyon, 62–63;
 Hohokam, 70–73; as independent variable,
 76–78; Kayenta area, 60–61; Little
 Colorado, 63–64; Mimbres, 67–68;
 Mogollon area, 69–70; reconstructing,
 57–58, 112; Rio Grande area, 68–69; San
 Juan Basin, 65–66; southwestern
 Colorado–southeastern Utah, 58–59;
 Southwest trends in, 73–85; stress and,
 95–96; Virgin area, 61–62
Poseuinge site, 116
Poshuinge site, 116
Poshu site, 223
Pot Creek Pueblo, 112, 116
Pottery Mound, 213
Prescott area, 213
Preucel, Robert, 233–34
Prickly pear, 98
Prudden unit, 203
Pueblo I, 99–100, 113–14
Pueblo II, 99–100, 114, 204–5
Pueblo III: abandonments, 207; conflict,
 215–16; health, 100–105; Mesa Verde, 114
Pueblo IV, 105–6, 231
Pueblo Bonito: evidence of violence at, 226;
 health, 87, 102, 105; human sacrifice at,
 214
Pueblo Colorado, 116
Pueblo Grande, 120, 231; irrigation at, 93;
 location, 232; settlement plan, 121; skull
 burial at, 228; specialized production at,
 123
Pueblo Pintado, 222
Pueblo Shé, 116
Puerco site, 103–4
Puye site, 208
Pyrite mirrors, 194

Querechos, 144
Quetzalcoatl, 253

Ranking: aggregation and, 132; at Chaco
 Canyon, 166, 171–72
Reed, Eric, 225–26
Reed, Lori S., 189, 208
Reeve Ruin, 125
Regional integration, 167–68
Regional systems, 189–91; Salt-Gila
 Hohokam, 193–96; Tucson Basin
 Hohokam, 196–97
Riana site, 221, 225
Rickets, 103
Ridge Ruin, 224

Ringo site, 125
Rio Grande, northern: aggregation, 115–17,
 118; Albuquerque area, 174–75, 176–77;
 environment, 117, 118; late alliances,
 208–9; population, 68–69, 80, 81, 116,
 118
Rock art, evidence of warfare in, 229–30
Rohn, Arthur, 217–19
Rye Creek Ruin, 124, 232

Sacaton site, 231
Salado, 23–24; alliance system, 199–200, 208;
 cult, 200; definition, 197–98; Tonto Basin,
 124–25
Salmon Ruin, 104
Salt-Gila region, 21, 120, 122–23, 142,
 193–96
San Cristobal site, 87, 96, 105, 106, 116
San Juan Basin: population, 65–66, 75, 76, 79,
 80, 81; strong and weak patterning in,
 178–79. See also Chaco Canyon
San Pascual site, 221
Sapawe site, 116
Scale of analysis, importance of, 5–6, 243–44
Scalping, 227–28
Scribe S site, 129, 130
Second Canyon Ruin, 125
Sedentary period, 119–20, 122
Sedentism: in absence of food production, 35;
 Basketmaker, 17; disease and, 92–93; Late
 Archaic period, 17
Sheep Camp Shelter, 43
Shell, 123, 196
Sinagua/Cohonina area, 219–21
Site 103, Taos area, 228
Site 616, Mariana Mesa, 226
Snaketown: abandonment, 231; location, 232;
 settlement plan, 120; size, 119; popula-
 tion, 122; turquoise, 259
Social stratification, and aggregation, 132
Sonoran desert: environment, 56–57; Late
 Archaic in, 40–42
Southwest: abandonment models, 137–42,
 162–63; agricultural peoples, distribution
 of, 139, 140, 156; bioarchaeology, 88–89,
 96; complexity, 5, 14–16; cultigens,
 90–91; cultural trends, 4–5; as culture
 area, 240–41; definition of, 13–14; environment, 54, 256; game animals, 91;
 health, 86, 92–93, 97–108; interaction
 with California, 259–60; interaction with
 Great Basin, 261–62; interaction with
 Plains, 257–59, 262–64; languages,
 187–88; Mesoamerica and, 19, 244–56;
 plants, 37–38, 90; population trends,

73–85; regional centers, 246, 248; settlement mobility, 85; settlement spacing, 191; site size, 166; synthesizing vs. diversifying traditions in, 12
Squash: Basketmaker, 98; Late Archaic, 35, 36, 43, 46, 47
Stodder, A. W., 101
Stress, 90; aggregation and, 133, 170; health and, 91–92; indicators of, 93–95; population growth and, 95–96; scalar, 132; subsistence, 53, 89
SU site, 47
Swarts Ruin, 228

TA 18 site, 226
Taos Pueblo, 245, 259
Technology: complexity and change in, 30; Late Archaic, 18, 39. *See also* Irrigation
Te'ewi site, 225–26
Teotihuacán, 20, 245, 250, 251
Tewa, 143
Three Fir Shelter, 42, 43, 44
Tijeras Pueblo, 105, 106, 112
Togetzoge, 232
Tohono O'odham (Papagos), 84, 123
Toltecs, 249
Tonto Basin, 124–25
Tornillo Rockshelter, 41, 42
Towers, 217–18
Trade. *See* Exchange
Treponematosis, 105, 106
Tres Alamos site, 125
Tribalization, 205
Trincheras sites, 221–22
Tsankowi site, 208
Tshirigi site, 116, 208
Tsiping site, 221
Tuberculosis, 102, 105–6
Tucson Basin region, 150–57, 193–97, 221
Tula, 21, 22, 245, 249
Tularosa Cave, 47
Tumamoc Hill site, 41, 221
Tundustusa site, 129
Turkey Creek Pueblo, 103–4, 129
Turkey Pen cave, 45–46
Turkeys, 18, 19, 92–93, 219
Turquoise, 249, 259
Tuzigoot site, 87

Tyounyi site, 116, 208
Tzin Kletzin site, 222

Uinta Basin, 230
University Indian Ruin, 154
Upham, Steadman, 189, 208
Utes, 84

Valencia site, 41
Van Liere site, 231
Ventana Cave, 103
Village of the Great Kivas, 129
Virgin Anasazi, 61–62, 259

Wade, William, 102–3
Warfare, 211–12; abandonment and, 236–37; aggregation and, 234, 235–36; architectural evidence of, 216–23; artifactual evidence of, 223–24; burned sites as evidence of, 224–25; early data and models of, 212–16; Hohokam, 124; no-man's lands as evidence of, 230–32; rock art evidence for, 229–30; skeletal evidence for, 225–29; in southern Arizona, 197; tribal, 234–35
Western Pueblo: origins, 254; in Zuni area, 175–76, 177–78
Wet Leggett Pueblo, 47
White Dog Cave, 43, 44
Wilcox, David, 199, 221
Wills, W. H., 201
Winn Canyon site, 48
Woodchuck Cave, 229
World systems theory, 241, 243, 250, 262
Wupatki site, 220, 228

Yapashi site, 208
Yellow Jacket site, 168, 226
Yumans, 82, 83, 84

Zape site, 245
Zuni area: Chaco influence in, 175–76; development of Western Pueblo in, 177–78; population, 83, 84
Zuni Pueblo, 143

SCHOOL OF AMERICAN RESEARCH ADVANCED SEMINAR SERIES

SCHOOL OF AMERICAN RESEARCH ADVANCED SEMINAR SERIES

Published by University of New Mexico Press

Reconstructing Prehistoric Pueblo
Societies
WILLIAM A. LONGACRE, ed.

New Perspectives on the Pueblos
ALFONSO ORTIZ, ed.

Structure and Process in Latin America
A. STRICKON & S. M. GREENFIELD, eds.

The Classic Maya Collapse
T. PATRICK CULBERT, ed.

Methods and Theories of Anthropological
Genetics
M. H. CRAWFORD & P. L. WORKMAN, eds.

Sixteenth-Century Mexico: The Work of
Sahagun
MUNRO S. EDMONSON, ed.

Ancient Civilization and Trade
J. A. SABLOFF & C. C. LAMBERG-KARLOVSKY, eds.

Photography in Archaeological Research
ELMER HARP, JR., ed.

Meaning in Anthropology
K. H. BASSO & H. A. SELBY, eds.

The Valley of Mexico: Studies in
Pre-Hispanic Ecology and Society
ERIC R. WOLF, ed.

Demographic Anthropology: Quantitative
Approaches
EZRA B. W. ZUBROW, ed.

The Origins of Maya Civilization
RICHARD E. W. ADAMS, ed.

Explanation of Prehistoric Change
JAMES N. HILL, ed.

Explorations in Ethnoarchaeology
RICHARD A. GOULD, ed.

Entrepreneurs in Cultural Context
SIDNEY M. GREENFIELD, A. STRICKON,
& R. T. AUBEY, eds.

The Dying Community
ART GALLAHER, JR., & H. PADFIELD, eds.

Southwestern Indian Ritual Drama
CHARLOTTE J. FRISBIE, ed.

Lowland Maya Settlement Patterns
WENDY ASHMORE, ed.

Simulations in Archaeology
JEREMY A. SABLOFF, ed.

Chan Chan: Andean Desert City
M. E. MOSELEY & K. C. DAY, eds.

Shipwreck Anthropology
RICHARD A. GOULD, ed.

Elites: Ethnographic Issues
GEORGE E. MARCUS, ed.

The Archaeology of Lower Central
America
F. W. LANGE & D. Z. STONE, eds.

Late Lowland Maya Civilization: Classic to
Postclassic
J. A. SABLOFF & E. W. ANDREWS V, eds.

Published by University of California Press

Writing Culture: The Poetics and Politics
of Ethnography
J. CLIFFORD & G. E. MARCUS, eds.

The papers in this volume result from the advanced seminar "The Organization and Evolution of Prehistoric Southwestern Society," held at the School of American Research in Santa Fe, New Mexico, in September 1989.

Participants in the advanced seminar *(clockwise from top right):*

Steadman Upham

Jeffrey S. Dean

Murray Gell-Mann

W. H. Wills

David R. Wilcox

Fred Plog

George J. Gumerman

Debra L. Martin

Paul R. Fish

Jerrold E. Levy

Robert McC. Adams

Randall H. McGuire

Inset:

Linda S. Cordell